Ctrl Alt Delete

Tom Baldwin

Ctrl
Alt
Delete

/ How Politics and
the Media Crashed
Our Democracy

Hurst & Company, London

First published in the United Kingdom in 2018 by
C. Hurst & Co. (Publishers) Ltd.,
41 Great Russell Street, London, WC1B 3PL
© Tom Baldwin, 2018
All rights reserved.

The right of Tom Baldwin to be identified as the author of
this publication is asserted by him in accordance with the
Copyright, Designs and Patents Act, 1988.

A Cataloguing-in-Publication data record for this book
is available from the British Library.

ISBN: 9781787380066

This book is printed using paper from registered sustainable
and managed sources.

www.hurstpublishers.com

Printed and bound in Great Britain by Bell & Bain Ltd, Glasgow

To Rebecca, Frankie and Arthur
And in loving memory of my parents, Robin and Sylvia Baldwin

Contents

Acknowledgements

There are people without whom this book would certainly not exist. Rebecca Nicolson, my wife, who has been a constant source of wise counsel, encouragement and tolerance. Marc Stears has provided a stream of ideas, energy and ad hoc political theory tutorials, even from the other side of the world. Georgina Capel, my agent, is a hugely positive and generous force of nature. Emma Craigie has given me brilliantly precise suggestions, as well as occasional reminders of the need for a degree of political balance. Emily Spence and Mathew Baldwin, my sister and brother, have watched my back and told me where I am going wrong in the way that only older siblings can—especially now that our much-missed parents have gone.

Many other friends have kindly read chapters and offered much-valued advice. They include Spencer Livermore, Aurea Carpenter, Rachel Sylvester, Alastair Campbell, Douglas Alexander, Patrick Wintour, Matthew McGregor, Andrew Cooper, Rachel Kinnock, Robert Peston and Roger Alton. I am also very grateful to Michael Dwyer, Jon de Peyer, Alison Alexanian and the whole team at Hurst Publishers for the patient and professional way they have published this book.

Although readers may notice I am critical of both the media and politics, I know both are filled with good people and I am far more appreciative than I might seem for the opportunities they have given me.

Most of all, I want to say thank you to my fantastic family—Rebecca, Frankie and Arthur—for all the love and laughter they have given me. I would be utterly lost and even grumpier than usual without them.

Introduction

Imagine being a weather forecaster and getting it wrong. Not just a bit wrong—like predicting it will be a sunny day and finding yourself caught in showers—but wrong, wrong, wrong. So badly wrong, so catastrophically wrong, that people get stuck in snow blizzards and families freeze to death in their cars.

That is how much of the media and politics have felt after getting it wrong over and over again these last few years. When Jeremy Corbyn first ran for the Labour leadership, no one—including him—really thought he would win, let alone almost become Prime Minister. And, although the polls were close in the referendum on membership of the European Union, few people in either the Remain or Leave campaigns sincerely believed Britain would vote for Brexit. As for Donald Trump, who had initially acted as a joke candidate and was treated as such, he got himself elected president just 24 hours after some esteemed analysts estimated his chance of victory was between 1 and 2 per cent.[1]

I was one of those who had pretended for so long that I knew What's Going On, I had come to believe that I did. For the best part of twenty years I hustled around Westminster and Washington, my mobile phone hot against my ear, while I sought out scraps of information and intermittent access to power so that I could pass on my elite knowledge to readers of the *Sunday Telegraph* or *The Times*. Later, I slipped across the small patch of ground that is meant to separate the media from politics and, for a while, I got to offer little bits of access or information too.

But being part of Labour's General Election campaign in 2015, which we lost by an unexpectedly wide margin, is one way to learn some humility. It certainly gave me time to reflect as, in the months that followed, evidence began to pile up that none of us who had played this game of elite knowledge could really claim to know very much about what was going on at all. Corbyn, Brexit, Trump, then Corbyn again: few saw them coming, I certainly didn't.

The sense of disorientation in the media and political mainstream was deeper than merely the shock of unexpected events, it shook the pillars of conventional wisdom. The values that seemed to be succeeding—protectionism, old-style socialism, nationalism, illiberalism—were precisely those we had confidently consigned to the past. Sure, the Iraq War, the rise of China and the global financial crisis, had caused some wobbles. But it was not until those most stable democracies of Britain and America started to vote in strange, compass-spinning ways, that confidence about what the future would look like came crashing down.

When I started writing this book, I was no longer cocksure about knowing what was going on. Instead, I wanted to use my conflicted perspective, derived from my time in the media and politics, to discover what had gone wrong with both over the past three decades. In short, I have sought to find out why the worlds I once understood, no longer understood the world.

It is a story that begins in the final years of the last century when everyone had more reason to be optimistic than perhaps at any time in history: Communism had collapsed across Eastern Europe, Apartheid was crumbling into dust in South Africa, nationalism was in retreat.

We were not wrong, back then, to be so excited. The big change coming down the tracks was about how information was produced, distributed and consumed. We were at the start of a new information age, a revolution powered by data and driven by technology, that over the next few years promised to break down old borders and overcome ancient prejudice, make people richer, create citizens who were contented because they were connected. For progressively-minded journalists and politicians it seemed like a pretty good bet that, because free information was the currency that a free press traded in free market democracies, the future belonged to people like us.

It was a forecast, an assumption, that turned out to be horribly wrong. At the time of writing, a malevolent Twitter-troll is in the White House as Leader of the Free World, a journalist who made his name inventing stories about Brussels banning prawn cocktail crisps is Britain's Foreign Secretary, while an authoritarian nationalist leader of Russia sprays toxin over Western democracy. And, oh yes, the BBC's first female political editor needs a bodyguard to protect her from assault when she attends Labour Party events.

We had expected sunshine, but we have found ourselves in a hurricane. And what I have learnt in writing this book is that the hurricane did not just happen, we helped make it: we sowed the wind and reaped a whirlwind; and the blow-hard, abusive relationship that media and politics had with this new information age must take some of the blame for causing democracy to crash.

The title of this book, *Ctrl Alt Delete*, will be familiar to anyone who experienced Microsoft Windows crashing in the 1990s. Ctrl+Alt+Del was the 'three-fingered salute' we used to restart our computers when they froze, as they often did, and that dread blue message appeared saying 'any unsaved data will be lost'. The engineer who came up with Ctrl Alt Del, David Bradley, described his thinking: 'We had brand new hardware, brand new software, it would hang up all the time. ... The only solution you had was to turn the power off, wait a few seconds, and turn the power back on again. I said, "I'm writing all this code for the keyboards and we can just shortcut it."'[2] Bill Gates was less effusive, saying it all been 'a mistake' to adopt it for Windows and, if he had his time again, he would have given us all just 'a single button'.[3]

I'm glad he didn't because there is something very human about the three-fingered salute. The buttons that must be pressed simultaneously are at the opposite ends of the keyboard to prevent people hitting them accidently when spilling a cup of tea. And, somehow, each of those key strokes have come to dictate the rhythm of this story. In the pages that follow, I will describe an epic battle for control of information at the turn of this century fought by an insurgent media against politicians and their advisers. I will show how this was followed by the ground-trembling rise of an alternative in the form of resurgent populism after the financial crisis of 2008 that culminated with Brexit, Trump and, albeit slightly differently, Corbyn too. And now it seems democracy faces a great crisis, even the prospect of people pressing a single-button 'delete' on it all together—because media and politics, as well as the titanic technology firms that have been created, have failed so miserably to meet the challenges of this tumultuous new age of information.

But Ctrl Alt Del was designed to be a solution to a problem. It was the best route for desperate people whose systems had crashed, enabling them to perform a 'soft re-boot', when the only other way to fix the system was the 'hard reboot' of kicking the power supply out altogether. And the final pages of this book set out some ideas for how we can save and restore for democracy, rather than react simply out of frustration and anger.

There are, I have discovered, some pitfalls involved in tackling this rapidly moving subject. I am not a technology expert and, at times, I risk sounding as phobic about the power of the internet as other members of my confused and frightened generation. But, in truth, I am in awe of it. I don't think I could have written this book without access to this extraordinary repository of human knowledge that is—and must remain—the greatest open library in history.

I also suspect that some people from my old life will regard me with suspicion as a shop-soiled member of a media, political and economic elite who has been part of the problem over the past quarter of a century. Indeed, I fear every chapter is filled with voices a bit similar to my own. And, while I am hugely grateful to everyone who consented to interviews, I recognise too many are men of a certain age and class, as well as a fair few who seem to have studied the same subject at the same university at the same time as me. In part, this is a merely reflection of the flawed and elitist era about which I have written. But, when I look across at the similarly white, male and privileged populists from both left and right who spend so much energy attacking elites, I am less inclined to believe they are more qualified to proffer their solutions—or even that they have any.

Finally, as the last sentence may have indicated, I have written this from an unashamedly progressively left-of-centre, small 'l' liberal perspective. I am ashamed of Brexit. I am disgusted by Trump. And, for all his many qualities, I do not think Corbyn is the right leader for either my party or my country. I have tried to be fair, if not impartial, but in trying to be honest about what has gone wrong—including my own multiple failings—I have to be honest about where I am coming from, who I am and why I think what I do.

Anyhow, here it is.

Part One

The Battle for Control

1

How the Media Challenged for Control

'Like it's nineteen-eighty-nine'

There was once a time, between the fall of The Wall in Berlin and the Twin Towers in New York, when it felt like our species had arrived at the best era it had ever known. Or, at least, the best party ever thrown.

Big Money was whispering love into the soft ears of Social Justice and nobody seemed to mind too much. The forces of reaction were not on the list and sulking at home. The rest of our shrinking planet was queuing up outside and waiting to be let in.

This party, a dozen years of what might be called 'peak optimism', really began in Berlin on the night of 9 November 1989. Armed guards watched helplessly as tens of thousands of people from the East forced their way towards the ecstatic embrace of the West. Young and old climbed atop the wall that had divided them. Some danced and kissed people they had never met; a few decorated it with flowers and notes for those who had died seeking freedom before; still more attacked it with chisels and hammers.

The energy and joy were so intense partly because none of this had been expected or planned. Only months before almost no journalist, scholar or politician predicted the imminent collapse of Communist rule across Eastern Europe.[1] This was a surprise party which had the grown-ups worried. Even as the Soviet Empire began to wobble, British

Prime Minister Margaret Thatcher was telling Moscow that this was all happening too fast and she wanted the old borders—even the wall itself—to remain.[2]

As people suddenly surged across the old frontiers, so too did information—and lots of it. Millions of once-secret files, the whole towering archived bureaucracy of totalitarianism, were flung open as free speech and a free press released decades of pent-up creativity to burst spectacularly across Eastern Europe. That year also saw the launch of Sky News in Britain, pumping out information twenty-four hours a day, seven days a week. Even Britain's antiquated Parliament allowed television to broadcast its proceedings for the first time.

And, at a research centre in Geneva, in March 1989, Tim Berners-Lee found a way to connect hypertext with the internet to create, as he put it, 'ta-da!—the World Wide Web'. If the immediate reaction from his boss was less than effusive, scrawling the words 'vague but exciting' on the proposal,[3] such technology would soon be heralded as an engine of progress—breaking down borders, connecting people and opening minds.

Change was coming, politics was global, and progress seemed inevitable. Nelson Mandela was released from prison in South Africa in February 1990 and, in November, just a year after the Berlin Wall came down, Thatcher was gone too.

She had set her face against closer European integration and, just as she feared German re-unification, she did not want a 'super-state exercising a new dominance from Brussels' or forcing a sovereign British state to abolish frontier controls.[4] Pro-European Tories brutally ousted her from Downing Street, replaced her with John Major and triggered decades of trauma for the Conservative Party.

For every action, there is a reaction. This one did not begin in Parliament, at the ballot box or on the streets. Its most vivid expression was to be found in the system that existed for gathering and distributing information: the media.

Even at the outset of this decade of soaring optimism, sparks were beginning to fly, smoke was coming from the system and signals flashed red on our still analogue dashboard, warning that the new information age might not, after all, help dissolve borders, spread truth and nurture tolerance.

It was also in 1989 that *The Sun* smeared the dead and dying football fans caught in the Hillsborough disaster, Chinese students protesting against the Communist regime were massacred in Tiananmen Square, and—unnoticed amid all these great global events—a young British journalist arrived in Brussels, hoping to make his name. That name, as it has been so often since, was Boris Johnson.

Blowing Up Brussels

His last job had ended with him being sacked by *The Times* for making up a quote from his own godfather, so, initially at least, the new Brussels Correspondent for the *Daily Telegraph* approached this latest opportunity with uncharacteristic caution. Most of the reports Johnson filed in his first few months were not markedly different from the dry, factual coverage the European Union usually received in British broadsheets.

But the fall of the Berlin Wall a few months later would have reminded him how steel and concrete can symbolise power and change in politics. The fall of Thatcher the following year also affected him deeply: according to his wife's—playfully disputed—account, she found him sobbing in the street as if 'someone had shot nanny'.[5] And, perhaps, the confluence of these seismic events triggered something in his head as he strode around the headquarters of the European Commission each working day.

Whatever the case, the Berlaymont building appears to have heated his imagination, and he began writing a series of spurious exclusives about what was being plotted inside. Johnson announced that Brussels was banning pink sausages, ploughman's lunches and prawn cocktail flavour crisps, not to mention imposing undersized condoms on the British penis and recruiting sniffer teams to ensure all 'Euro-manure smells the same.'

But he really hit his stride in May 1991. Beneath a front-page headline declaring 'Euro headquarters to be blown up', *Daily Telegraph* readers were told the Commission had decided that demolition by powerful explosives was the only way it could deal with tons of deadly asbestos that had been discovered in the Berlaymont walls.

'Sappers will lay explosive charges at key points so that the structure can implode and subside gently,' wrote Johnson, 'British sources suggested wryly that detonation could be declared a European holiday.'[6]

Anyone looking for a new symbol of a vast, remote and apparently undemocratic state bureaucracy could do a lot worse than the

Berlaymont. Its starfish-shaped arms stretch out across three hectares of land where a convent once stood. Outside, a line of blue and gold European Union flags hang deferentially from gleaming poles: one for each of the member states bound by the directives crafted by thousands of unseen officials inside.

And Johnson's story was based on a tiny kernel—a shard—of truth: the Commission had discovered large quantities of asbestos and was considering how it could possibly get rid of it given the building's foundations were entwined with a series of road and rail tunnels. But no one who knew the faintest thing about the issue would have advocated demolition.

Thirty years later, the building still stands—all thirteen floors of it—across the Schuman roundabout and the Rue de la Loi. A £500 million renovation funded by the Belgian taxpayer carefully removed all traces of the asbestos without destroying the city's infrastructure—or poisoning the lungs of anyone who lived nearby.

Geoff Meade, the venerable former Europe editor for the Press Association in Brussels, remembers being woken by a phone call from his news desk in London on the night Johnson filed his Berlaymont story. They had just got the *Telegraph*'s first edition front page announcing the demolition plan and they wanted him to write a version too.

'Is this story by Boris Johnson?', Meade asked wearily. 'Yes', came the reply. He went back to bed. 'There are some you follow up on the night and some you don't,' he explains. 'Boris was definitely in the latter category.'

When the two met the next day, Meade said: 'Boris, you are infinitely cleverer than me but let me ask you this, what is the one thing you think someone might not do with a building filled with asbestos?' Johnson looked perplexed. 'Blow it up,' said Meade, making a fluttering motion with his hands to indicate the way asbestos dust would then fall, like fine rain, over the Belgian capital. 'Ah,' replied the future Foreign Secretary, clutching his head as if in pain to indicate he had never thought of that. 'Good point, good point.'[7]

It did not stop other newspapers copying Johnson's story. One even asked the Commission's press office if it would sponsor a readers' competition so that a lucky winner could win the chance to push the plunger and detonate the explosives.

Johnson himself wrote a follow up claiming Berlaymont was going to be replaced by a new headquarters three times higher than the Eiffel

Tower. This time, his exclusive was based on an unsolicited architectural drawing sent to the Commission.

# # #

Although he did not succeed in blowing up Brussels, Johnson's journalism was more than just harmless fun. A front-page story in spring 1992, headlined 'Delors plans to rule Europe'[8] claimed, on flimsy evidence, that proposals were being drawn up by the then Commission president to centralise more power in Brussels after the Maastricht Treaty was agreed.

Johnson's own account of this, written more than decade later as part of his collected works, is worth quoting at length because he claims it altered the course of history: 'My boast, and I make it in the confidence that no one gives a monkey's, is that I probably did contribute to the Danish rejection of Maastricht. ... I wasn't sure that my chums in the EC commission would be thrilled. But the splash was the splash—the main article on the front page—and I happily consented. That story went down big. It may not have caused the dropping of marmalade over the breakfast tables of England, but it was huge in Denmark. With less than a month until their referendum, and with mounting paranoia about the erosion of Danish independence, the story was seized on by the 'No' campaign. They photocopied it a thousandfold. They marched the streets of Copenhagen with my story fixed to their banners. And on 2 June, a spectacularly sunny day, they joyously rejected the treaty and derailed the project. Jacques Delors was not the only victim of the disaster; the aftershocks were felt across Europe, and above all in Britain.'[9]

Those aftershocks arguably included a continent-wide loss of confidence in the European project, the humiliating departure of the UK from an early European effort to synchronise fluctuations in currency rates, the derailment of John Major's government and the election of Tony Blair. But still, as Johnson says, a 'splash was a splash'.

Others working in Brussels at the time recognise that the traditionally inside-page stories coming out of Europe had changed with German reunification and the advent of the Single Market. According to Jonathan Faull, who later had the unhappy task of taking charge of the Commission's communications, 'the EU became more interesting' because the integration agenda being pursued by Delors created rows about the standardisation of everyday items that readers could taste and smell—such as the ingredients of chocolate, crisps and milk.

Johnson, like the populist politician he would later become, already knew how to arouse people's emotions and stimulate their senses. Unvarnished facts could not compete. 'We would put out a rebuttal to some of his stuff on the website and no one would listen,' says Faull. 'If we really kicked up a fuss, we might get a correction on page 96 or something.'[10]

Peter Guilford, who was a competitor at *The Times* before going to work for the Commission himself, is clear about the effect Johnson had on Brussels. 'I think Boris was a prime proponent of what people now call "fake news". He would pick up on one tiny thing and then blow it up out of all proportion to serve the agenda of *The Telegraph*,' he says.

Charles Grant, who arrived in Brussels at the same time to work for *The Economist*, is among those who doubt whether Johnson—whose father is a former Commission official himself—was really as Euro-sceptic as he made out. 'We all thought it was just about getting himself on the front page, about advancing his career more than anything else. But he invented a series of Brussels-bashing tropes—the UK has no influence, it's all run by France and Germany—that helped turn a lot of people against the EU.'[11]

This conflicted nature possibly explains why Johnson became such a frenzied figure when it came to filing his reports. A biographer describes Johnson having to work himself up into his 'four o'clock rant' by shouting at yucca plants, scarring his hands with broken biros and screaming abuse at anyone who disturbed him.[12]

Johnson did not invent Euro-scepticism and nor was he the first to write 'Brussels to ban bendy bananas' stories in British newspapers, which were already stock-in-trade for the likes of *The Sun* and *The Daily Mail*. But, Guilford says, 'He was the first to do this on a broadsheet—he made it respectable—and he did it so well that everyone started following him. We all got sucked into it.'

Guilford could sense the effect Johnson's stardom was having on politics back in Britain. 'These ministers would come out and all they wanted was to get in *The Telegraph*. I remember John Gummer [then agriculture minister] was so desperate he waited an hour for Boris to turn up before starting a press conference at the end of a summit.'[13]

Johnson himself relished his influence. '[I] was sort of chucking these rocks over the garden wall and I listened to this amazing crash from the greenhouse next door over in England as everything I wrote from Brussels was having this amazing, explosive effect on the Tory party—and it really gave me this, I suppose, rather weird sense of power,' he told the BBC years later.[14]

The consequences of Johnson's five factually-challenged years in Brussels would not be fully realised until a quarter of a century later when he led the Leave Campaign in Britain's EU referendum. Martin Fletcher, a former Foreign Editor at *The Times* who was also a Brussels correspondent in the 1990s, says: 'The referendum was not lost in a few weeks in 2016 but in the twenty-five years that preceded it. During that time the British public never heard anything positive about the EU or its achievements and Britain's role in it. All they got was this cartoon caricature of Brussels which, frankly, Boris largely invented.'[15]

Johnson had become a star in Brussels and he was brought home to add spice to the *Telegraph*'s domestic political commentary. The man who had the tricky task of succeeding him in *The Telegraph*'s Brussels bureau, Chris Lockwood, is more generous to Johnson than most of his contemporaries: 'I don't think Boris made stuff up, it was more a case of exaggerating and simplifying facts that were out there already in one form or another.' But Lockwood also suggests the 1990s was a time when facts mattered less than they had before. 'Foreign news used to be something that could kill you,' he said. 'European integration is a serious subject but not quite as serious as Soviet missiles being aimed at your capital.'[16]

Dittoheads

The Cold War was over, Democracy had won and America was feeling a swelling surge of self-confidence about a future where its technology could help drive freedom ever further forward.

Laser-guided and computer-operated smart bombs drove Saddam Hussein's invading Iraqi forces out of Kuwait in the Gulf War of 1991 to enforce the rule of international law. Those were the days when an American-led invasion of the Middle East could complete its ground operations within 100 hours. And each of those hours was carried live on CNN with satellite pictures beamed to the remotest corners of the world.

The number of countries defined as electoral democracies by Freedom House increased dramatically from 69 in 1990 to 120 by the end of the decade.[17] And now that those awkward ideological battles were over, countries that were already democracies were turning to young progressive leaders, hard-headed but tender-hearted, who were ready to embrace the future.

First and foremost among them was Bill Clinton, who won the White House in 1992 to the soundtrack of Fleetwood Mac. 'Don't stop, thinking about tomorrow,' went the song, 'Yesterday's gone, yesterday's gone.'

Starbucks coffee shops began sprouting up across America, while McDonalds opened in Moscow. Clinton heralded the North American Free Trade Agreement with Mexico and Canada by comparing the flow of goods, people, ideas and information to an unstoppable force of nature. 'A new global economy of constant innovation and instant communication is cutting through our world like a new river,' he said, 'providing both power and disruption to the people and nations who live along its course.'[18]

Clinton himself appeared much more stoppable. The mid-term elections of 1994 saw the Democrats lose control of the House of Representatives for the first time in forty years, Newt Gingrich became Speaker and his sharply conservative 'Contract with America' set the agenda.

The fightback against Clinton's New Democrats, however, had not immediately been led by politicians like Gingrich so much as a new form of insurgent journalist who kicked against liberal orthodoxy, shook people loose from a shared set of facts and, in some cases, made up some new ones.

In this respect, Rush Limbaugh probably has more in common with Boris Johnson than probably either would like to admit. One of them went to Eton, studied Classics at Oxford and, at the time of writing is Secretary of State for Foreign and Commonwealth Affairs in the British Government. The other dropped out of Southeast Missouri State University after a year and now spends his spare time watching American football from his sofa in Florida.

But both 'Boris' and 'Rush' became lucrative brands instantly recognisable by their first names alone. Both used humour to deflect criticism as they merged politics and journalism with light entertainment. And both staged their populist revolt using old technology that was going through its own changes in these early days of the information revolution.

While Johnson used the frumpy, broadsheet pages of the *Daily Telegraph*; Limbaugh used radio. In the 1980s, the bulk of American radio stations were facing a bleak future. They were broadcasting on the century-old system of AM transmissions, or Medium Wave as it's known in Britain, from where listeners were steadily migrating over to FM where the sound quality was so much better for music. These stations were saved by a decision of Ronald Reagan's Federal Communications Commission in 1987 to scrap the Fairness Doctrine that required broadcasters to present controversial issues in an honest and balanced fashion. Conservatives claimed, with some justification, that this post-war regulation had been used by liberals to curtail their freedom of speech.

And it was free speech, of a kind, that soon began to swamp AM transmissions where highly partisan, cheap-to-produce and lucrative Talk Radio shows swiftly proliferated. In 1980, there were just 100 talk radio shows but in little more than a quarter of a century this figure had ballooned to 1,700.[19]

Talk Radio stars range from Michael Savage and Laura Ingraham to Glenn Beck and Sean Hannity, but Limbaugh was—and still is—the one that stands out from all the rest. Within months of the Fairness Doctrine being abolished, Limbaugh had taken to airwaves with his syndicated three-hour, five-days-a-week show and he has never really stopped since.

By 1992, he was reaching 20 million people a week on 660 stations and had Clinton in his sights. His shows followed a simple dramatic structure, painting his audience as victims of liberals, socialists and 'feminazis'. He declared the day before Clinton's 1992 inauguration the 'last day of freedom for most Americans.' His biographer, Zev Chafets, put it like this: 'Clinton was the 60s, long hair, jeans, JFK and McGovern, an FM kind of guy. Limbaugh, despite being five years younger than Clinton, was an older American, a product of the Eisenhower years, strictly AM.'[20] Limbaugh used his radio show to campaign relentlessly against Clinton, and in particular the health care reforms that he did so much to help defeat in 1994.

Mary Matalin, the Republican strategist, watched Limbaugh lead her party back to power in Congress at the end of that year. She said: 'I would go to political meetings all over the country and hear conservatives speaking the way her speaks and saying the things he says. ... Along with Gingrich he is one of the two most important conservatives in the country. Newt had come up with a plan but Rush had sold it in every district.'[21]

At the height of his power, he was credited with inspiring a whole generation of 'movement conservatives' called 'Rush Babies'. Republicans were so grateful for what he did for them in 1994 that they made him an honorary member of Congress and awarded him a 'Majority Maker' medal.

# # #

Ratings have fallen somewhat since those heady days. Limbaugh's audience is ageing and some advertisers have grown weary of his capacity for nastiness. These include calling a 12-year-old Chelsea Clinton 'the White House dog', a law student campaigning for campus contraception a 'prostitute', and suggesting that the actor Michael J. Fox was feigning his symptoms of Parkinson's Disease to garner support for stem cell research funding.

Still, every weekday lunchtime Limbaugh holds forth from the walled compound at Palm Beach, Florida, he calls, with characteristic grandiloquence, 'Southern Command'. Listening to him is an audience of around 14 million, more than that of the CBS and NBC evening news combined. He has written a best-selling children's book series in which a teacher called Rush Revere travels through time on his talking horse, Liberty, to chat with notables from American history. He does speaking tours where he is feted like a rock star. His global earnings in 2017 were $84 million, which according to *Forbes* magazine puts him ahead of Lionel Messi and only just behind Cristiano Ronaldo, the two most talented footballers of their generation.

For all the controversies that make so many liberals loathe him so much (and rage when such earning power gets mentioned) his genuine talent as a broadcaster—the little inflections in his voice, the timing—still make him attractive company for many millions of Americans.

Most remarkably of all, Limbaugh has done this while being profoundly deaf. At one stage he lost his hearing altogether but carried on broadcasting regardless and even now, after surgery, it is severely impaired. This explains the strangely intimate feel of his shows in which for much of the time he is in a dialogue with himself—sometimes reasonable, often repetitive and boastful, increasingly cajoling, sarcastic and funny. The temperature of his language rises slowly through almost imperceptibly until it boils over into a full rant.

Limbaugh describes his style in this way: 'I don't deny I'm an entertainer; this is showbiz. But I also don't deny that I am deadly serious about the things I care about. And I definitely want certain things, ideas, to triumph, and others to lose, big time.'[22] Although he takes calls from listeners during his shows, they are little more than props. As he puts it, the primary purpose of callers is not to provide a forum 'but to make me look good.'[23] Ultimately this is about what comes out of his mouth, not what goes into his ears—he is a talker, not a listener—and his fans relish being called 'Dittoheads'.

Limbaugh will often pick on some fragment of news and build fortifications so filled with bombast they are highly resistant to fact checkers or rebuttal. He has asserted that the corpse of a dead aide was found in Hillary Clinton's apartment (it wasn't), that Barack Obama was planning to make circumcision compulsory (he wasn't) and the 'presence of gorillas calls into question the concept of evolution'.

But of all Limbaugh's battles over the past thirty years, perhaps the one with the most lasting consequence in terms of its influence on a governing party was his crusade against people he calls 'envirowackos'. His consistent position has been that climate change is a hoax perpetrated by so-called 'watermelons'—green on the outside, red on the inside—whose real targets are capitalism and the American way of life.

In 1994, Fairness and Accuracy in Reporting (FAIR) issued a lengthy report on Limbaugh. In one instance, he had claimed: 'Do you know we have more acreage of forest land in the US today than we did at the time the Constitution was written?' FAIR noted: 'In what are now the 50 US states, there were 850 million acres of forest land in the late 1700s vs. only 730 million acres today.'[24] Limbaugh hit back, citing figures showing the acreage of forests had increased since 1952. But that, as almost everyone else pointed out, to little avail, had nothing to do with Limbaugh's original false claim about America in 1787.

Many years later, in the summer of 2017, Limbaugh dismissed the media's warnings about the looming Hurricane Irma saying it was being hyped up to 'advance this climate change agenda' and boost the sales of bottled water for local businesses.[25] Within a few days, as he was forced to evacuate his Palm Beach home, he complained he was the victim of gloating environmentalists. 'They want to be right, and so they're milking this,' he said. 'They're milking it for all they can get out of it.'[26] Facts, even when they are flying in his face and at hurricane-speed into his home, really don't matter much to Rush Limbaugh.

Heretic Republicans who disputed a tenet of Limbaugh faith as set out in his '35 Undeniable Truths' were often brought to heel and sometimes, at the zenith of his power, even dragged on the show to deliver an on-air apology to 'El Rushbo'.[27] By May 2014, PolitiFact could count just 'eight out of 278, or about 3 per cent' of Republican members of Congress who 'accept the prevailing scientific conclusion that global warming is both real and man-made.'

He now has a president who is a 'dittohead' on climate change too. Limbaugh is pretty confident about his role in history, saying: 'I normally don't pat myself on the back, but today global warming is an issue that has the concern of 30 per cent of the American people, and years ago it was over 50 per cent. That's because somebody spoke up, day-in and day-out and said, "this is a hoax, this is BS." That somebody was me.'[28]

Charlie Sykes, one of the other conservative Talk Radio hosts who prospered after the abolition of the Fairness Doctrine, is among those who have felt a pang of regret at what they created. 'I was very excited back in the 1990s to realise that we were part of creating an alternative media,' he said. 'I was not perhaps aware that it was going to also then, at some point, morph into an alternative reality silo. And when you try to point out, OK this is not true, this is a lie, and then you cite *The Washington Post* or *The New York Times*, their response is, "ah that's the mainstream media." So we've done such a good job of discrediting them, that there's almost no, there's no place to go to be able to fact check.'[29]

'Utter contempt'

When Rush Limbaugh went to the White House Correspondents' Association Dinner in May 1993, he would have already known he was in enemy territory. And, that night, Bill Clinton had him in his sights as he used the platform of the presidency to mock him and even brand him as a racist. The rest of the audience laughed, Limbaugh did not—and never forgot.[30]

These annual events are like a combination of a High School prom and the Oscars. Political journalists dress up for the night in black tie and big dresses alongside a smattering of Hollywood stars and White House staffers, desperate to impress their editors or each other with the quality of their table's guests. The President of the United States, the star guest on the top table, is usually obliged to make a televised speech filled with insider jokes about his relationship with the media that must exclude and baffle the average voter.

Some journalists argued that this annual Spring event painted a ter-rible picture for the rest of America of an out-of-touch media elite determined to celebrate itself and congratulate each other while cosying up to its sources. Tom Brokaw, the former NBC anchor, compared it to saying to voters, 'we're Versailles, the rest of you eat cake.'[31]

But most of the White House press corps regarded the dinner as an entirely logical extension of a world view in which they are some of the most important, talented and amusing people in America. They mattered, and of course the President should make a speech to them. It was the mindset that underpinned Mark Halperin's 'The Note', which began appearing on the ABC News website from 2002. Packed with jargon incomprehensible to most people, he referred to the 'Gang of 500' political insiders, pollsters, strategists, campaign consultants and journalists who influence the daily narrative from Washington. And the self-referential elitism of these self-appointed guardians of truth was the equivalent of a boxer's glass jaw, just waiting for someone to come and shatter it.

Indeed, over the previous thirty years a few more of those bemoaning the end of their golden era might have been better off unpursing their lips long enough to ask whether they were part of the problem. One of those who did was the *Atlantic* journalist, James Fallows, who examined the dissonance between the media and the people in his 1996 book, *Breaking the News*.[32] He told the story of how two star names from TV journalism—Peter Jennings, of ABC and Mike Wallace of CBS—had appeared on a late night show to discuss a moral dilemma. They were presented with a hypothetical example where they had inside access to make a film with enemy soldiers. But what would they do if these troops were about to ambush American servicemen? Jennings initially said he would try to send a warning. But Wallace insisted that they would just roll the tape and cover the killing. 'You don't have a higher duty,' Wallace told him. 'No. No. You're a reporter!' An embarrassed Jennings surrendered to Wallace's superior understanding of journalistic ethics. He even apologised. A few minutes later on the same show, George M. Connell, a Marine colonel in full uniform was asked how he felt about the morality of these journalists who would stand and watch their countrymen die so they could do their duty as reporters. Fallows describes the colonel's response: 'Jaw muscles flexing in anger, with stress on each word, Connell looks at the TV stars and said, "I feel utter … contempt."'[33]

# # #

Fallows was not only warning that the media's habits of mind made the profession look odd, aloof or immoral when viewed from the outside, he felt even then that they were at risk of corroding faith in democracy. As he put it: 'The media were making citizens and voters even more fatalistic and jaded about public affairs than they would otherwise be—even more willing to assume that all public figures were fools and crooks, even less willing to be involved in public affairs, and unfortunately for the media even less interested in following news at all.'[34]

If a politician visited a school, it would often be covered by a political journalist seeking to interpret motives rather than describe the event. A reporter might, for instance, explain that the politician was showing concern for education because he or she were concerned to boost numbers among young parents, 'soccer moms' or whoever. The assumption was that the real motives were camouflaged by stated motives and that the substance of what a politician was saying was less important that what the journalist was telling you about the clever strategy behind it. Even impartial coverage routinely implies that a politician is faking concern on the issue of the day, with academic experiments showing 'strategic coverage' of an event elicits more cynical interpretations by readers and viewers.[35]

Such an analysis is borne out by academic studies conducted later. One found that 71 per cent of stories on American network news were primarily concerned with the 'horse race' rather than the issues in the 2000 presidential election. Another showed that the number of stories deemed 'negative' had risen steadily in each presidential contest from 25 per cent in 1980 to 60 per cent in 2000.[36] The Harvard study suggested the public was beginning to lose in interest in the news, only for their attention to be shocked back by an ever-greater voltage of scandal and a higher dose of negativity.

It is, of course, possible to over-state the problem. Newspapers like *The New York Times* or *The Washington Post* have maintained extraordinarily high standards of accuracy and objectivity. And, if the brittleness of the Washington media elite's coverage of politics was at least partly to blame for the alienation felt by many voters, then so too was the daily dose of Rush Limbaugh. But there was a reason that the phrase 'post-truth' was coined as early as 1992 when Steve Tesich wrote in *The Nation* that a public traumatised by Vietnam, Watergate and a never-ending diet of negativity was starting to turn away from the horrors of the real truth and collude in its suppression.

He said: 'We are rapidly becoming prototypes of a people that totalitarian monsters could only drool about in their dreams. All the dictators up to now have had to work hard at suppressing the truth. We, by our actions, are saying that this is no longer necessary, that we have acquired a spiritual mechanism that can denude truth of any significance. In a very fundamental way we, as a free people, have freely decided that we want to live in some post-truth world.'[37]

'Beyond belief'

'We don't want another three of the bastards out there', said the prime minister.

It was July 1993 and John Major's Conservative government lurched from crisis to crisis. The bloom of his surprise election win the year before had withered in the heat of renewed Euroscepticism and political chaos. But Major had just secured a crucial vote of confidence in the Commons, and sought to capitalise on the moment by recording an interview with ITN's political editor, Michael Brunson. Afterwards, they had a private conversation in which the prime minister complained about the problems he was having with three of his Eurosceptic cabinet members—widely considered to be Peter Lilley, Michael Portillo and John Redwood. When Brunson asked why he didn't just sack them, Major replied that he did not want 'bastards' out there causing more trouble.

The BBC, which had provided the equipment for the interview on a pooled basis, had kept the tape running. His remarks were picked up by their cameras and subsequently leaked to *The Observer*. In those days, hearing the prime minister refer to his Cabinet colleagues as 'bastards' was a big story and *The Sun* was among the papers that subsequently opened a special premium rate phone line for readers to listen to him.

This story is worth telling again now is because it shows how old, deferential conventions regulating the relationship between journalists and politicians had been tossed aside. Just as Boris Johnson in Brussels had ripped up the rule book on writing about Europe, journalists in Westminster were growing in power and self-regard; they were challenging for control of the agenda.

This is how Brunson described it in his memoirs: 'Over the years, I have had countless conversations with all kinds of people after the formality of an interview had been completed. On all those occasions, a formal "thank you" from me and the relaxation of the crew as they no longer operated their equipment, was the clear signal to the interviewee that what was being said "on the record" had come to an end. According to the usual convention anything that was said subsequently was to be regarded as either "off the record" or, with politicians, as being on Lobby terms—for use as background information, but not for quotation or attribution. On this occasion, technology, and some questionable behaviour by the BBC, had betrayed us.'[38]

The 'Lobby terms' referred to by Brunson were rules drawn up in Queen Victoria's reign used by political correspondents in Westminster to conceal or protect the identity of their sources.[39] Journalists in the Lobby were distinguished from those in the Press Gallery, who covered debates in the chamber of the House of Commons, by dint of their special access to a hallway outside where they could speak privately to MPs. The Lobby was often described as operating like a Gentleman's Club because of its quasi-masonic customs and secret briefings from the Government. But this fusty establishment curtain between the people and the powerful was fraying in the final years of the twentieth century. For all the old deference and petty regulations—no running in the corridors, jackets and ties to be worn at all times—it was even possible to smell the decay. Visitors to newspapers offices in Parliament, which then as now were found at the top of 102 brown-carpeted stairs, were greeted by a gents toilet that regularly leaked a pool of urine or some other unspecified fluid into the hallway outside. Next to the toilet was a bar where the names of those journalists elected to be Press Gallery or Lobby officials were painted in gold on wooden boards like those found in minor private schools listing ex-pupils who had died in the First World War. If you got past that, through a pair of swing doors, lay what was grimly known as the 'Burma Road', a corridor of a dozen-or-so overcrowded, badly ventilated and sometimes mouse-infested offices where most of the work was done.

By the early 1990s, there was tension between journalists caricatured as 'Old Lobby' and those labelled 'New Lobby'. The distinction was often overdone but it served a purpose in marking a transition in this profession. The former group was caricatured as a group of older, often over-fed and occasionally pompous men who generally disapproved of the under-shaved laddish antics and football banter of slightly younger men (they were, and are, mostly men) who formed the New Lobby.[40] This latter group were less deferential but dodgier. Off-the-record quotes were sometimes manipulated, sources played off against each other, and stories that could not quite be stood up laid off to another newspaper. They did not mind getting close to people in politics—sometimes very close—but the purpose was less about discovering the truth than finding a story in the right territory that would get readers talking.

There are endless examples from this period to illustrate the kind of journalism being written in the period, but let's take just one: in February 1997, just a few months before the General Election, *The Sunday Telegraph* had a front-page story which was one of those exclusives that were so prized at the time for their capacity to cause controversy.

The headline was, 'Labour's first privatisation: we will sell off the Tote.'[41] The newspaper suggested the £400 million sale of the Tote, a government-run betting company, was 'being considered as a way of freeing extra money for Labour's spending projects.' It quoted a 'senior Labour insider' as saying the old-fashioned view that a state-run gambling firm should still be a 'priority for the nation's finances' really was 'beyond belief'.

The report was widely followed up in other newspapers over the few next days with members of Labour's Treasury team apparently confirming the idea was being actively discussed while other shadow ministers, including Jack Straw who had direct responsibility for it, issued strong denials. Robin Cook, a keen race-goer and notionally in charge of developing the election manifesto, even declared: 'There will be no proposal by Labour to sell the Tote. I can authoritatively pull down the curtain on this story.' But, within months of Labour entering government, that curtain was up again as ministers ordered a full review of the Tote's 272 betting shops which, after more in-fighting, eventually concluded in May 1999 that privatisation would become the official policy.[42]

On the face of it, this was a decent enough story reflecting some high-level discussions of an issue that had split the Shadow Cabinet. There were not, however, any shadow Cabinet discussions before this story appeared. It had not even occurred to Labour policy-makers before they read it in the newspaper. And, the first time the idea was mentioned to anyone in the party, was the night before it was published when a journalist phoned a Treasury aide who eventually agreed 'not to deny it', possibly because he was a bit drunk at the time.

I know all this because, if you haven't guessed already, I wrote it.

CTRL ALT DELETE

How news breaks

The story about the Tote's privatisation was a product of the regular Tuesday morning meeting of the *Sunday Telegraph's* editorial team where, on the fourteenth floor of Canary Wharf's glass-and-steel skyscraper, all of us were required to suggest at least two original ideas each week. The fear of going in empty-handed to face the newspaper's formidable editor, Dominic Lawson, was often the agent of creativity.

In this instance, I knew that the Conservatives had just ducked the privatisation for fear of offending the Tote's chairman, Woodrow Wyatt, himself a powerful figure in the media. And, in the absence of anything else to say, I suggested Labour was now looking at the sell-off and hoped everyone would forget about it by the end of the week. Unfortunately, Lawson was seized with the counter-intuitive quality of the story and I was under pressure to stand it up.

And, as so often was the case, Charlie Whelan, the free-wheeling press secretary to Shadow Chancellor Gordon Brown, was my best chance. He was habitually in a pub called the Red Lion across the road from Parliament on Friday nights. When I found him there, he first asked me to find out how much the Tote was worth, then decreed he had decided 'not to deny it'. In the article, Whelan is described as a 'senior' source because, well, no one ever quoted a junior one, did they? Quite a lot of what appeared in the febrile Sunday market was reverse-engineered in this way, beginning with the kind of headline we would like and working back from there. This one met a minimal test of veracity in that a real source was confirming it—or, at least, not denying it. Whelan says he texted Brown that night to get his permission to stand up the story.[43] Maybe Labour would have got around to proposing the privatisation of the Tote anyway—maybe not. I tell this story not because I am proud of it but because I know how this bit of news was put together. There is an old adage attributed to Otto von Bismarck that 'Laws are like sausages: it's better not to see them being made.' The same is sometimes true of news stories.

A year earlier I had arrived at *The Sunday Telegraph*, a little dazzled after several years working for local and regional newspapers, where I had spent night after night covering the proceedings not only of council committees, but sub-committees too. I soon discovered that writing about politics for a national newspaper required a very different set of skills. As in the US, the focus was becoming less about the substance than the game of politics to the point where journalists became active participants in it. A dull secret document was always judged more newsworthy than an interesting one that had been published so 'Memos to Be Leaked'—known as MTBLs—were commissioned from pliant contacts. There always had to be a person to blame and shame, and a drama always became a crisis, even when there was no real drama.

Often, the most news-worthy aspect of politicians was not what they were doing or saying but how we judged they fitted into different factions and the who-hates-who storyline that elevated some into becoming into national figures. Looking back at the stories I wrote in the 1990s, it's striking how many of them were about communications strategy, brand or the advisers who had most contact with the press. I had exclusives about how Peter Mandelson had been given a chauffeur-driven limousine by a nightclub owner for the 1997 election campaign, how the 'three most important women in Blair's life' (one wife, two aides) were fighting 'like rats in a sack', and details of the clever advertising campaigns being run by Steve Hilton for the Tories. In the new information age, the people who controlled information seemed more important—more glamorous—than the politicians themselves. A particular obsession for me was the identity and motives of political donors. One of my better stories was about how Bernie Ecclestone had given £1 million to the Labour Party and then secured concessions for Formula 1 that allowed it to keep tobacco sponsorship.[44] But underpinning most of this coverage was the implication that politicians—and people in politics—were in it for themselves or trying to manipulate voters.

Even as sections of the press seemed intent on undermining respect for politics, there was a tumescent self-regard among political journalists at the time that was generally not justified by the quality of our product. This is how Andrew Marr, who was political editor of the BBC, described the scene: 'There is a strong sense that the power to set the agenda and initiate the terms of national debate has passed from ministers to journalists. Trevor Kavanagh, political editor of *The Sun*, was first called the most powerful man in British politics by the former Tory Chancellor Kenneth Clarke with whom he has a longstanding disagreement over the euro. It is an exaggeration, but a telling one. In the Commons today the Lobby reporters are generally polite and, on the surface, respectful to the MPs they mingle with. But many feel themselves to be greater, or at least more immediately powerful, than the back-benchers desperate for publicity; and even many ministers.'[45]

That quotation was from a book Marr wrote, called *My Trade*. But part of the problem was that journalism was no longer a 'trade' for some people but an attractive career for the kind of person who might otherwise have wanted to run the country.

The puffed-up egotism of this powerful new breed of journalist cannot be understated. Years later, when I was working in politics, I would bring various members of what was known as the commentariat in for an off-the-record chat and cup of tea on the sofa with Ed Miliband, then Leader of the Labour Party. The idea was they would ask him some questions to help frame their next piece and he would get the chance to set out the thinking behind his next speech. But quite often these meetings would turn out to be based on a complete misunderstanding, with the journalists telling Miliband about their latest book or their own vision for Britain and the world. I remember one leaving early for another meeting with the parting line, 'I hope you found that useful'.

Nor was commentary confined to the comment section, with many stories suffused with political judgments. We believed that our opinion mattered. I was one of those who strutted around Westminster in my big suit and fat mobile phone. We were only dimly aware of how ridiculous we all were.

All too often we were writing to impress each other or our sources, rather than inform our readers. It was a sealed game of elite knowledge, networks and access that must have deeply alienating to people outside—even other journalists without a House of Commons pass. I lost count of the number of times colleagues would describe stories they knew to be misleading as 'a bit of fun' or 'causing mischief' simply for the impact it would have within Westminster. Sometimes it was, genuinely, fun. Occasionally it served a purpose of pricking the pomposity of the old Establishment. But all too often it was self-serving rubbish.

The worst perpetrators would point out that they were an 'equal opportunity offender'—someone inclined to distort the news about any politician or party. Personally, I had more respect for people who did so because of genuine political bias than such borderline sociopaths who postured as impartial. At least the former group were interested enough in the issues to have an opinion.

Perhaps I am over-stating how tawdry the process had become. There were lots of good people and excellent journalists who covered politics at this time, including a few I count as life-long friends. Patrick Wintour of *The Guardian* and Robert Peston, then of the *Financial Times*, showed it was possible to break big stories without distorting them. Philip Webster and Roland Watson at *The Times* were always calmer and fairer than I ever managed to be. There were plenty of others like this, too, but the overall package of pessimism and cynicism which spewed out of an entitled Lobby was enough to fill the widest of eyes with jaundice. One study often referred to by Robin Cook, the former Labour Foreign Secretary, compared the ratio of positive to negative stories in the British press. In 1974 that ratio was 1:3. But by 2001, in the same two weeks of the year, the gap had widened to 1:18. 'It is hard to nurture trust in the parliamentary process when the public are unremittingly fed a news agenda that demonstrates failure,' said Cook.[46]

The likes of Jeremy Paxman on BBC 2's *Newsnight* and John Humphrys on Radio 4's *Today Programme* were setting a new bar for aggression that most of their rivals aspired to meet. Although both denied that they approached every interview with a politician with the attitude of 'why is this bastard lying to me', they exuded a general air of doubt towards their subjects which meant answers were rarely taken at face value. Sometimes Paxman himself seemed to be growing weary of treading the wheel of hyperbole. 'Sometimes you want to sit there and say, "Not much has happened today, I'd go to bed if I were you."' he said.[47]

In 1993, Martyn Lewis, the BBC newsreader, was derided by many of his colleagues when he called for more good news—or 'nice shocks' as he put it—on TV bulletins. 'Judgments on the relative value of news stories have,' he lamented, 'come to be based on the extent to which things go wrong.'[48] He later proved his point, and prefigured a whole generation of viral videos, by publishing two best-selling books: *Dogs in the News* and *Cats in the News*.

Golden eras, dark ages

In recent years, the shocks of Brexit and the election of Donald Trump have caused an awful lot to be written about 'fake news', as if the blame for these electoral shocks lay entirely with Facebook or Russian trolls. But the success of Boris Johnson and Rush Limbaugh, as well as the way political journalism was evolving, shows the challenge to a common set of shared facts began long before Mark Zuckerberg had left high school and Vladimir Putin entered the Kremlin.

And, if the phrase 'fake news' means anything, then it has existed for a very long time. One recent account detected it in the disinformation war between Mark Antony and Octavium in 44 BC when the latter 'proved the shrewder propagandist, using short, sharp slogans written upon coins in the style of archaic tweets.'[49]

Many still yearn for a lost golden age of journalism. Some of this is a function of a profession attuned to an easy phrase and habitually inclined to indulge itself about how things used to be better in the old days. But for most of the twentieth century much of Europe lived under totalitarian dictatorships in which the act of free speech cost people their freedom or sometimes their lives. Today's sanctimonious columns complaining about declining newspaper standards conveniently gloss over how the 'yellow press' circulation battle in the late nineteenth and early early twentieth centuries between Randolph Hearst and Joseph Pulitzer (yes, he of the Pulitzer prize) helped provoke the Spanish–American war over Cuba and maybe the assassination of President William McKinley. Similarly, any account of political bias in the media must recognise how Lord Beaverbrook or Viscount Rothermere in Britain used their newspapers to get their noble titles and their preferred governments.

And yet, when you scrape away all the nostalgic cant, it is still possible to argue that a golden age did—sort of—exist in different forms in the 1950s, 1960s and 1970s.

This was a time when Walter Cronkite, the face of the *CBS Evening News* for more than two decades until 1981, was declared by pollsters to be 'the most trusted man in America'. Cronkite is often said to have been the first TV news presenter to be described as an 'anchorman', a word that conveys not only a reassuring sense of weight and authority but also the way he connected much of America to a seabed of hard fact. He would end each evening bulletin with the words, 'and that's the way it is'—and, for a nightly audience of up to 30 million people watching at home, that really was how it was.

News was a communal experience, shared across class, ethnicity and political affiliation. When Cronkite ventured into opinion, saying the Vietnam War could not be won, it was the product of impeccably impartial analysis rather than grandstanding bluster.[50] As President Obama later said at Cronkite's memorial service, his journalism was still about 'what happened today?' rather than 'who won today?'

In Britain, the 'golden age' was when *The Times* provided a public service as a paper of record and the editor of the best-selling *Daily Mirror* saw himself pursuing an Enlightenment project to educate the working classes in post-War Britain. *The Sunday Times* under Harold Evans unmasked Kim Philby as a Soviet spy and revealed how Thalidomide was causing babies to be born with terrible physical disabilities. And in America, *The Washington Post*'s Carl Bernstein and Bob Woodward exposed the Watergate scandal in the 1970s, a story so massive that it has donated its suffix to every subsequent scandal and inspired a whole generation of investigative journalists to be sceptical of anyone and everyone in power.

For many, the blame for what went wrong falls squarely on the shoulders of one man and someone I would later work for myself: Rupert Murdoch.

This is how Hugh Cudlipp described the moment when the circulation of his worthy, left-of-centre *Daily Mirror* first slipped behind Murdoch's breezy populist and, by then, Thatcher-loving *Sun* in 1978: 'It was the dawn of the Dark Ages of tabloid journalism, the decades, still with us, when the proprietors and editors—not all, but most—decided that playing a continuing role in public enlightenment was no longer any business of the popular press. Information about foreign affairs was relegated to a three-inch yapping editorial insulting foreigners. It was the age when investigative journalism in the public interest shed its integrity and became intrusive journalism for the prurient, when nothing, however personal, was any longer secret or sacred and the basic human right to privacy was banished in the interest of publishing profit—when bingo became a new journalistic art form—when the daily nipple-count and the sleazy stories about bonking bimbos achieved a dominant influence in the circulation charts.'[51]

Harold Evans believes the rot really set in when Murdoch was allowed to purchase *The Times* and *The Sunday Times* in 1981 after making a secret deal with Margaret Thatcher to avoid scrutiny from the mergers watchdog.[52] He wrote: 'All the wretches in the subsequent hacking sagas—the predators in the red-tops, the scavengers and sleaze merchants, the blackmailers and bribers, the liars, the bullies, the cowed politicians and the bent coppers—were but the detritus of a collapse of integrity in British journalism and political life.'[53]

And Cronkite, long since retired and saddened by what had become of his profession, suggested the way Americans get their news had changed forever when Murdoch launched Fox News in 1996. 'It was quite clear', he wrote, 'when they founded the Fox Network that they intended it to be a conservative organisation—beyond conservative—a far right wing organisation.'[54]

# # #

There are endless stories about Murdoch as a media mogul and ruthless businessman, but it was his ownership of *The Sun* in Britain, then later Fox News in the US, that defined his challenge to the liberal establishment and is seen as having brought that golden era to such a messy end.

As far back as the 1960s, Murdoch relaunched *The Sun* and *The News of the World* as sensationalist, aggressive red top tabloids with a streak of defiant, pomposity-pricking populism that came straight from the Australian-born proprietor himself.

The Sun, much as it is portrayed in James Graham's play *Ink*, was all about refusing to defer to liberal elites, kowtow to the Royals or listen to the 'experts'. If people didn't like its offering of sex, sport and TV, they didn't have to buy the paper. If members of the Establishment didn't like the way it went about covering them, well, they probably had something to hide.

By 1989, Murdoch was celebrating the twentieth anniversary of his purchase of the newspaper. *The Sun* wrote an editorial to mark its place in history, its role in politics—and to serve warning about the future. This said:

> The Establishment does not like the Sun. Never has.
>
> There is a growing band of people in positions of influence and privilege who want OUR newspaper to suit THEIR private convenience.
>
> They wish to conceal from readers' eyes anything that they find annoying or embarrassing.
>
> LIVING LIES AND HYPOCRISY ON HIGH CAN HAVE NO PLACE IN OUR SOCIETY. IT IS THE STRUGGLE OF ALL THOSE CONCERNED FOR FREEDOM IN BRITAIN.

There was more to it than scrappy populism. That same year, it delivered what two of its own reporters would later call a 'classic smear' on the innocent victims of what later turned out to be police incompetence and an establishment cover-up.[55] On 19 April 1989, the newspaper splashed its front page with two words, 'THE TRUTH'. Beneath that headline was a set of grotesque lies about the behaviour of Liverpool football fans in the Hillsborough stadium disaster, which had killed 96 four days earlier. *The Sun* claimed supporters had picked pockets of victims, 'urinated on the brave cops', and beaten up a policeman giving the kiss of life.

Far from standing up for ordinary people, *The Sun*'s editor had overruled the objections of its own reporters and chosen to believe sources, including a Tory MP and police chiefs, because both football hooligans and 'Scousers' had been a favourite target for the press. *The Sun* is still boycotted across Merseyside as a result.

This newspaper was often stained with prejudice. It was the paper which greeted news that Benjamin Zephaniah was going to teach at the University of Cambridge with a picture of the dreadlocked black poet and the headline: 'Would you let this man near your daughter?' When it was accused of hounding TV presenter Russell Harty on his deathbed, *The Sun* was similarly concerned about the fate of its readers' children. 'The truth is that he died from a sexually transmitted disease. The press didn't give it to him. He caught it from his own choice. And by paying young rent boys he broke the law,' it said. 'What if it had been YOUR son Harty had bedded?'

The Sun's 'pollution of British political life', prompted the playwright Dennis Potter to name the tumour in his pancreas that killed him, 'Rupert'.[56] But much of the resentment towards Murdoch on the Left has been rooted not in his standards but in his support for the Conservatives. It was *The Sun*'s editor, Larry Lamb, who first used Shakespeare's 'winter of discontent' to describe the wave of strikes that propelled the Tories into power in 1979. And, according to its critics, *The Sun*'s bias was instrumental in keeping them there for the next eighteen years. Murdoch's ruthless defeat of the once formidable print unions—again with Thatcher's support—behind the razor wire and police lines at Wapping in 1986 prompted the Labour Party to ban his newspapers from press conferences and to promise to break up media empires. *The Sun* relentlessly attacked Labour's leader, Neil Kinnock, in ways that now seem dated but were shocking at the time. 'IF KINNOCK WINS TODAY WILL THE LAST PERSON TO LEAVE BRITAIN PLEASE TURN OUT THE LIGHTS,' declared its front page on the day of the General Election in 1992 along with a picture of the Labour leader's head inside a light bulb. Afterwards, the paper declared: 'IT'S THE SUN WOT WON IT.'

Murdoch later said that he had given a 'bollocking' to the paper's then editor, Kelvin MacKenzie, for that last headline because it was 'tasteless and wrong...we don't have that sort of power'.[57] Like any populist, Murdoch's claim was that his tabloid newspapers were giving voice to ordinary people, not telling them what to think or how to vote. In private, MacKenzie is said to have described those ordinary people as 'the bloke you see in the pub—a right old fascist, wants to send the wogs back, buy his poxy council house, he's afraid of the unions, afraid of the Russians, hates the queers and weirdos and drug-dealers.'[58] But, as Steve Dunleavy, another one of Murdoch's editors, put it: 'Rupe doesn't dictate public tastes, you know. He has lots of bosses out there, millions of them. The public tells him what they want to read and Rupe gives it to them.'[59]

And, in fairness, *The Sun* does change with its readership. When it was lagging behind an increasingly liberal public on issues like race and sexual orientation, it eventually caught up. If Murdoch thought progressive politicians would win, he was willing to swallow his own 'small-c' conservative instincts to protect his business interests and relationship with his readers. And he backed Bob Hawke as a Labour prime minister in Australia, as well as Ed Koch as the Democratic mayor of New York, long before he had ever heard of Tony Blair, a politician to whom he later became so close that he would make him godfather to one of his children.

In China, he was so keen to appease the Communist regime, he is said to have stopped HarperCollins—which he also owned—from publishing Chris Patten's critical book on the handover of Hong Kong,[60] praised the annexation of Tibet in an interview where he criticised the Dalai Lama as 'a very political old monk shuffling around in Gucci shoes,'[61] and blocked the BBC World Service from broadcasting on his Star satellite to Asia.[62]

The 1990s was the decade in which stories of 'sleaze' began to wash over Westminster like some toxic tide spreading disease into democracy itself. Sexual and financial scandal in British politics were nothing new, but now MPs were a favourite target for a media that sometimes seemed intent on proving that elected representatives were some of the worst people in the world. In 1992, David Mellor was forced to resign from the Cabinet after his telephone conversations with his lover, Antonia de Sancha, were secretly recorded and sold to Murdoch's *News of the World* along with lurid claims about how he liked to have toe-sucking sex while wearing a replica Chelsea kit—which it later emerged were completely made up.

By this time Murdoch had begun to expand into broadcasting. He had taken US citizenship in order to buy what became the Fox Network and launched Sky TV in the UK with a characteristic swipe at the elitist liberals he thought dominated British broadcasting. As ever, he promised to give the people more of what they want: 'For fifty years British television has operated on the assumption that people could not be trusted to watch what they wanted to watch, so that it had to be controlled by like-minded people who knew what was good for us. ... My own view is that anybody who, within the law of the land, provides a service which the public wants at a price it can afford is providing a public service.'[63]

# # #

In 1996, when Murdoch was preparing to launch Fox News, he adopted 'Fair and Balanced' as a slogan designed to rebuke—or infuriate—the liberal mainstream media. Fox News was a revolt against the idea that information should be handed out once a day like spoonfuls of cod liver oil to a docile public. Instead, it was ready to give the American public the news equivalent of a continuous supersized diet of hormone-packed red meat.

Murdoch appointed Roger Ailes, a close friend of Limbaugh's, to be the channel's chief executive. He was a magnetic, corpulent, paranoid and often terrifyingly determined man. As a small boy growing up in working class Ohio he was diagnosed with life-threatening haemophilia and later he would sometimes sit through business meetings in extreme pain with 'his shoes filling up with blood from a cut.'[64] Later he was exposed as a serial sexual predator. Throughout his two decades in charge of Fox, he aggressively pursued not only a clear ideological project but also the channel's female presenters.

Ailes was clear from the outset that his mission was to redefine TV news for a whole generation of conservative American viewers and voters. From its first broadcast on 7 October 1996, Fox News sought to speak for the 'flyover states'—the rest of America sandwiched between the coastal elites. It set out to be the antithesis of the 'liberal media bias' represented by the big networks and the established cable news channel CNN.

'We will be the insurgents,' Murdoch declared in February that year, adding that there was 'a growing disconnect between television news and its audience, an increasing gap between those that deliver the news and those that receive it.'[65]

Another cable news channel, MSNBC, also launched in 1996. Although it would later find its own shrill liberal voice, it was not particularly partisan at the outset. MSNBC, a joint venture between NBC and Microsoft, was intended to combine enduring elite news values with the software corporation's modernity. The idea was to meld TV and the internet so that viewers would browse the web on their TVs. The slogan, repeated in endless promos was the tech-friendly, 'It's Time to Get Connected'. Sets for MSNBC shows were modelled on a chic Manhattan loft apartment like you might see on *Friends*, or an espresso bar in downtown Seattle.[66] But that outward-looking digitally-connected America did not exist for most of its citizens in 1996. And Fox News, despite starting at a considerable disadvantage in the number of American homes it could reach, began to thrash MSNBC in cable TV ratings. Within six years of its launch, it had also overtaken CNN to take first place—a position it has more or less maintained ever since.

Fox News had a formula: talking heads rather than expensive foreign news; endless controversy and hyperbole; and, as one admiring commentary put it at the time, the aim of driving 'the liberal establishment mad by calling the whole thing "fair and balanced"'.[67] Often it played tag-team with new websites like The Drudge Report to give a megaphone to the internet's scandalous, conspiracy-tinted allegations about Clinton's affairs. The liberal establishment was predictably furious. Ted Turner, the founder of CNN compared Murdoch to 'the late Fuhrer'.[68] Bill Clinton described Fox News as 'a right-wing, bullying propaganda machine.'[69] And, according to the Pew Research Centre that conducts vast polls every year, there was a sharp rise in the political polarisation of American voters, with the trend most pronounced among viewers of Murdoch's cable news channel.[70] Some academic studies attribute this specifically to the launch of Fox News and MSNBC in 1996.[71]

Progressives sometimes suggest that Murdoch's advance against liberal media in Britain and America—the success of *The Sun* and Fox News— was achieved by brainwashing people too stupid to realise they were being fed lies. This argument is undermined somewhat by polling evidence showing how US voters were beginning to turn against the mainstream American media before Fox News came along to shake it all up. Gallup found that 'trust and confidence in the mass media to report the news fully, accurately and fairly' fell from more than 70 per cent after in the 1970s to barely 50 per cent in the mid-1990s. The decline was particularly severe among conservatives.[72] In the build-up to launching Fox, Ailes commissioned his own polling showing, in his words, that 'somewhere between 56 and 82 per cent of American people think news is biased, negative and boring.' He added: 'So let's take 60 per cent as the number—it looks like a marketing niche to me.'[73]

The idea that there was a boiling cauldron of angry voters out there who were not being served by conventional media is a justification that would also be used by the hyper-partisan sites that rallied around Donald Trump—or, on the left in Britain, Jeremy Corbyn—a quarter of a century later. But there were reasons in the 1990s, as there are now, for people to feel angry and alienated by a global economy. And, however painful it may be to admit it, populist insurgents in the media have often been better at speaking for 'the people' on both sides of the Atlantic than any progressive journalist, politician or party.

In this sense, the success of *The Sun* and Fox News, like that of Boris Johnson and Rush Limbaugh, was as much a reaction to the golden era as the cause of its demise. After all, there had always been something patronising in Cudlipp's eat-your-greens paternalism, a brittleness in Cronkite's 'that's the way it is', and also a degree of posturing—or outright pomposity—in a media that took itself so seriously.

But none of this was happening in isolation from the new information age taking shape. Driving change was the technology that enabled an extraordinary expansion of both print and broadcast. And, for all Murdoch's influence on politics and standards in journalism, his biggest impact may have been in the way he moved so ruthlessly to exploit this technology.

Size matters

It is easy to forget now how newspapers, the so-called 'dead tree' or 'legacy' press, were seen in the 1990s as lucrative money-making machines. And it was Murdoch who made this decrepit industry profitable again and triggered the last great expansion of print.

After his destruction of the print unions at Wapping in the mid-1980s, there had been a great flowering of diversity and competition in the British newspaper industry. The routine spelling mistakes, the noise, and the smeary black and white print of the old hot metal industry were replaced with a clinical word-processed quality, colour on every page. Newspapers were experiencing a surge in profits, size and sales. There were more sections with more pages. There were more titles with new launches ranging from the highbrow *Independent* to the freesheet *Metro*. There was more hyperbole, more sections, just more of everything.

The British press had always been uniquely competitive largely because a relatively-high level of literacy and fast railway connections meant a dozen or more national titles could be sustained in London.[74] The new injection of profits and sales after Wapping had made this competition cut-throat and, too often, that meant cutting corners too. The cost of getting the story late was greater than that for getting it wrong. The job of journalists was to write stories that sold newspapers. And the only real constraint was to work within the law or, as was later shown in the phone hacking trials, crossing beyond its boundaries.

In the UK, 1989 was once again a pivotal year as Murdoch launched Sky News, Britain's first 24-hours-a-day, seven-days-a-week dedicated news channel. It was never going to be like *The Sun* or Fox News, with Murdoch making it clear to staff at the outset their job was to compete with the BBC in the UK's regulated and impartial broadcast tradition. But, even with high standards and good intentions, it still challenged and changed politics over the years to come in ways no one really predicted at the time.

Adam Boulton, who was political editor of Sky News for the next quarter of a century, says: 'What we did was increase the level of scrutiny and the level of analysis of politics. Before we came along the news was someone from the BBC telling viewers what he thought it was impor- tant—there was an inhibition on commentary—we let journalists specu- late and say why it mattered. We were painting a picture as we went along, rather than just presenting one to people.'[75]

Although the audience for Sky News was initially tiny—significantly less than 1 per cent of the viewing public—it included every newsroom and newspaper office. For journalists watching detailed and endless cov- erage of events on TV, it meant that much of what they were paid to report on was no longer news: almost everyone in their profession had seen it already. Sky News's launch was followed by BBC Radio's 24-hour news and sports station 5 Live in 1994, the BBC's 24-hour news TV channel in 1997, and ITV News for a few years in the 2000s. This vast expansion in broadcast news meant the pressure on journalists in the press was to write something different and, often, this would be something much more tendentious, hyperbolic or riddled with the writer's own opinions.

This effect was exacerbated by the introduction of televised parliamentary proceedings, which also began in 1989. Opponents of the measure had argued it would lead to more grandstanding by MPs and an emphasis on soundbites rather than considered debate. But the real consequence was unexpected: within a few years coverage of Parliament had plummeted. Broadsheet newspapers abandoned the pages of coverage they once devoted to long reports about proceedings and shifted their focus away from what was being said in the debating chamber of the House of Commons to what was happening—or about to happen—outside; to stories written by the Lobby rather than reporters sitting inside the Press Gallery. And such journalism was much more likely to be based on anonymous sources, speculation, and exaggeration.

Back in Parliament, it was still possible to hear traditionalists moan on about how coverage in the media of what MPs had to say had become so threadbare that the 'best way to keep a secret in London is to say it on the floor of the House of Commons.' But even broadcasters were reluctant to use their new access to televise proceedings. The problem was that, aside from the gladiatorial Prime Minister's Question Time, it made for dreary—even unwatchable—television. A better way to cover politics was to book protagonists into the TV studios where they could be coaxed into saying something controversial within a tight timetable before the next ad break or update. And, best of all, the channel would own that coverage, it would have 'broken the news'—not the politicians.

# # #

Think for a moment what it must have been like for a TV editor with a limited budget and hour-upon-hour of news scheduling to fill every day.

Sending journalists out to make expensive films was costly. The cheapest and most effective route is to employ a host to hold it all together and then recruit politicians, journalists and advisers (or even ex-journalists and ex-advisers) for a panel discussion. These pundits don't have to be aggressive or demand someone resigns all the time, although it may become 'breaking news' when they do. But they have been used to

squeeze excitement and portentousness from the most trivial development, to fuel an exhausting sense of controversy as they are prodded into
disagreeing with some other studio guest, or conduct a 'paper review' of
all the stories broadcasters cannot stand up themselves.

Sometimes, it has led impartiality to mean nothing more than 'false
balance' where broadcasters give equal weight to arguments of different
validity. One of the reasons why issues like human responsibility for climate change increasingly became seen as disputed even as the science
around them became more settled was because of the TV news channels' insatiable appetite for controversy. If 10,000 scientists said climate
change was man-made and a dozen disagreed, each side was given air-
time and status. Two decades later, coverage of some of the most ridiculous claims against Hillary Clinton or the supposed economic benefits of
Brexit were given far were given far more credence than either deserved
because what seemed to matter to broadcasters was to have 'a lively
discussion' of the sort that was pioneered back in the 1990s.

This was a time when broadcasters began talking about being in the
news 'business'. Paul Jackson, a TV executive who ran Carlton TV (when
a young David Cameron was its head of communications) said: 'News is
a way of making money, just as selling bread is a way of making money.
No one believes that news and journalism are simply a service to democracy.'[76] The glut of news and repetition of limited facts meant information that might have sustained the old press for days was milked dry by the
media within hours. A story had to be huge if it was to satisfy the voracious appetite of the 'news business' so that it could lead bulletins in both
the morning and the evening. The task of journalists was to provide *new*
news, to keep moving forward, to give an existing story 'fresh legs', or
preferably find a fresh story. If news made a mistake it did not matter
much because the caravan had moved on. For some, 'not wrong for long,'
was a phrase that wavered between being a joke and a philosophy.

Sky's Adam Boulton acknowledges that 'giving people more information can have adverse consequences' and that at times the battle for
control with politics became a 'vicious cycle'. Like all good broadcasters,
he worries about 'false balance' and the dangers of polarisation. But he
adds: 'What was the alternative? A lot of this is just an inevitable consequence of the digital age.' TV channels were proliferating, video record-
ers had long since meant people could pick and choose what they
wanted. 'Some stopped watching the news altogether, others watched

more than ever,' says Boulton, 'we were giving politicians a bigger platform to get their message across ... and politics was slow to adapt.'[77]

# # #

The media's challenge for control of the agenda did not come from one
media proprietor or the introduction of rolling news on any one country;
it was global.

Political leaders began to raise concerns about the way 24-hour TV
news channels appeared to be distorting decision-making after the first
Gulf War in 1991.[78] Douglas Hurd, the British Foreign Secretary,
bemoaned how pressure from the media influenced policy on the Balkan
crisis.[79] The Secretary General of the United Nations even complained
that cable news—the so-called 'CNN effect' was beginning to operate as
a sixteenth member of the Security Council.

Indeed, the amount of news pouring out of cable TV channels in the
US was expanding fast after more than half a century when America
had very little broadcast news at all. In the 1950s, the old networks provided only fifteen minutes of news per day in a straight bulletin format.
This had risen by the end of that decade to thirty minutes, inclusive of
commercials. Even when President John F. Kennedy spoke to the nation
about the Cuban missile crisis in October 1962—the closest the world
ever came to nuclear war—the networks immediately went back to their
normal programming and there was no more news until the next day.[80]

A once-stable system was smashed to smithereens in the 1990s. By the
start of this century, the three main American terrestrial television networks—CBS, ABC and NBC—had seen their share of the audience
halve. They now faced competition from about 11,000 radio stations,
twenty national radio networks, 1,000 local television stations and 6,000
cable television systems.

Helping to drive this change was legislation Bill Clinton passed in
1996, the same year that Fox News and MSNBC were launched, to
deregulate the cable industry and change the ownership rules for local
radio stations. In line with the liberal orthodoxy of that era, the idea
was that increased free market competition from new technology like
cable, satellite and emerging internet communications would guarantee
diversity of opinion. There was no need for government to bring back
the Fairness Doctrine or regulate the news industry because, when

access to the media was no longer such a scare resource, the market would do it anyway.

This is how Rupert Murdoch put it a few years earlier: 'In the new information age, a country's prosperity will depend on the free flow of information and the resultant harnessing of its intellectual capacity. Countries that try to restrict that free flow will become technically, intellectually and economically backward.'[81]

Back then, liberal progressive types used to worry that just fifty corporations owned 90 per cent of the US news media and many supported the new law because they thought it would break this up.[82] But deregulation did not mean more competition. Just fifteen years later, the same proportion of the news media was owned by just six corporations: Viacom, Comcast, CBS, Time Warner, Disney and Murdoch's News Corporation.[83] Nowhere was this consolidation starker than in radio, the oldest form of broadcast communication. Prior to 1996, companies were not allowed to own more than forty radio stations. Eight years later one such firm, iHeartMedia—which broadcasts Limbaugh's show—had amassed thirty times the previous limit, with 1,240 stations.[84]

Although the media was still using the old technology of printed news, radio and TV, dramatic changes in the way it behaved were being driven by the production and consumption of information. News was becoming simultaneously broader and shallower. Technology had helped free journalists from old restraints of deference but it had also chained them to the wheel of rolling news. More could also mean less.

# # #

It would be wrong, silly even, to blame the media for every problem afflicting democracy in the years since. But it is also a mistake to see a disregard for facts, contempt for politics, and the polarisation of huge swathes of the electorate as a process that only began some time in 2016.

Long before the latest generation of populists began rattling the gates of liberalism, habits were being established in journalism that helped create the conditions in which they could prosper. Incubating in what is now known as the old or mainstream media were the ingredients that would grow like an algae bloom across the new ocean of information being opened up by technological change.

The likes of Boris Johnson 'chucking rocks' over the garden wall from Brussels and Rush Limbaugh sneering at the 'envirowackos' were not very different in their style or motivation to the social media 'trolls' who would later take such delight in shocking a po-faced Establishment. Brutally concise populist assaults on liberal democratic norms could be found in *The Sun* or on Fox News long before Donald Trump had ever heard of Twitter. And a brittle media elite that saw politics as a game was also already doing its bit to alienate and marginalise voices that needed to be heard.

All of this was part and parcel of the new information age. The expansion in the size and power of newspapers, the deregulation of American broadcasting, and the arrival of 24/7 TV news were themselves a function of technological change that foreshadowed the arrival of social media and cyber-warfare, bots and crypto-currencies.

It was both 'Breaking News' and the breaking of the news. It took a while to work its way through. But the madness began back then.

2

How Politics Tried to Regain Control

Giants of flesh and steel

It was the year Bill Clinton became the first Democrat in more than half a century to win a second full term in the White House and he *did* have 'sexual relations with that woman'—an intern twenty-seven years his junior.

But a piece of legislation he signed into law, with the unremarkable title of the Telecommunications Act 1996, has arguably made a far more lasting impact on history than anything else he did that year.

Running to 128 pages, the Act included reforms of telephone services and measures to deregulate the burgeoning cable TV industry. But the law also included a guarantee that the internet would remain 'unfettered by Federal or State regulation' and, crucially, Section 230 declared its platforms were not responsible for any material that appeared on them.[1] Technology that had not yet been invented—and giant corporations as yet unfounded—would be allowed to grow almost untouched by either the democratic process or the US government. Within a couple of decades, they would become powerful enough to threaten both.

Clinton, together with the Republican-dominated Congress that approved the law, was certainly making some fairly big assumptions about the capacity of free markets and free information to deliver positive outcomes. But this was a time for boldness and embracing change. At Stanford University that same year, Larry Page launched an experiment they called 'BackRub' which they would later rename 'Google'. The world's best-selling toy was Buzz Lightyear which, if its buttons were pressed in the right way, would declare: 'To infinity and beyond!' And Clinton, as he signed the Act into law in February 1996, echoed Buzz as he declared, 'Today the information revolution is spreading light all across our land and across the world!'[2]

The only real restraint placed on the web in the legislation, as well as the only aspect of it that received much attention from the media, was an attempt to limit children's access to online pornography. It is why the law is often known as Communications Decency Act and the measure enraged libertarian campaigners who wanted to keep the internet a free space without laws or borders.

Among them was John Perry Barlow, a former lyricist for the Grateful Dead who had helped found a small organisation called the Electronic Frontier Foundation. In February 1996, he spent a frustrating few days listening to global leaders talk about an internet they did not use—let alone understand—at the World Economic Forum in Davos. One night, after 'several glasses of champagne' and hearing that Clinton had signed the 'indecency provisions' into law that day, Barlow wrote his 'Declaration of the Independence of Cyberspace'.[3]

This stated: 'Governments of the Industrial World, you weary giants of flesh and steel, I come from Cyberspace, the new home of Mind. On behalf of the future, I ask you of the past to leave us alone. You are not welcome among us. You have no sovereignty where we gather.'[4]

Within hours it had lit up the internet as the declaration was emailed around by thousands of people. The indecency provisions were largely struck out on free speech grounds the following year by US courts that ruled 'the content of the internet is as diverse as human thought.'[5] It was a victory for digital libertarians that set a pattern which has seen lawmakers wary of touching tech ever since.

But people like Barlow were mistaken in thinking there was a real desire to tie up the web in regulatory knots. Progressive politicians were instinctively sympathetic to the kind of futuristic prosperity they assumed was being created by these technology entrepreneurs. They shared some counter-cultural 1960s origins and instinctively liked the idea of a borderless web that was world wide. Few could have imagined that these nice, nerdy Californians who came by their offices wearing jeans and T-shirts would one day be seen as a threat to the future of liberalism.

Indeed, through the early years of the 1990s, the centre-left had been embracing the idea of global freedom—across markets, borders and all forms of media—with the zealotry of converts. Clinton heralded the North American Free Trade Agreement with Mexico and Canada by comparing the flow of goods, people, ideas and information to an unstoppable force of nature. 'A new global economy of constant innovation and instant communication is cutting through our world like a new river,' he said, 'providing both power and disruption to the people and nations who live along its course.'[6]

In this world, regulating the web seemed about as backward-looking as, well, regulating the banks. But, more than that, a president campaigning for re-election as a 'bridge to the twenty-first century' really could not get enough of the internet in 1996. 'Let the future begin,' declared the jeans-clad Clinton as he posed for pictures alongside his vice-president, Al Gore, on step ladders as they installed internet cables at Ygnacio Valley High School. This was part of a crowd-sourced effort to connect every school in the country to the 'information super-highway', as they called it back then.[7]

The contrast with Bob Dole, the 73-year-old Republican nominee facing Clinton in the 1996 presidential election, was obvious. The Dole campaign had a website that had been designed by a student who later described how he had been roped in to do it only because the candidate 'didn't need to seem any more antiquated than he was,' adding: 'Was there a plan? Nooo!'[8]

At the end of the first TV debate, Dole tried to read out the address for his new-fangled website but got his dots, coms and orgs all muddled up, much to the derision of the Democrats. Anyone trying to guess what it might have been by typing variations of this address received a message flashing up on their screens: 'Pssst… the past is over. Click below to make the right choice for the future…' They were then directed to the tech-savvy Clinton–Gore website.[9]

# # #

Watching and learning from the other side of the Atlantic was Tony Blair, the new leader of the Labour Party and a politician self-consciously cast from the same modernising mould as the US president.

Although he had no intention of emulating Clinton's rocky first term, the way the president had stormed back for a second was studied and admired back in London as Labour prepared for its own general election. As Peter Mandelson put it: 'A major accusation against the modernisers was that we had fallen under the spell of Bill Clinton. It was true.'[10]

Blair raced to embrace the technological transformation as part of the vision he shared with Clinton for a progressive global modernity. At every turn, the Labour projected confidence and openness towards not only to free markets and an enlarged Europe but also the possibilities of what he calls this 'explosion of activity and freedom' on the internet.[11] In one of his first speeches as leader Blair declared Labour would equip Britain for the 'information revolution under way' and promised to introduce a Freedom of Information Act that 'would attack secrecy wherever it exists.'[12]

Alastair Campbell, Labour's communications chief, remembers winning a bet with a friend that he could earn Blair 'a clapline'—applause—simply by writing the words 'information super-highway' into the Leader's annual party conference speech at Blackpool in September 1996.

'I didn't really understand what the information super-highway was,' says Campbell, 'I just thought it sounded really cool and modern.'[13] In fact, so keen was he to win his bet that the phrase appeared no less than three times in the speech, as Blair—like Clinton had before—promised to connect every school in the country to the internet.[14]

Being 'cool and modern' was undoubtedly a key part of the brand for both Clinton and Blair, but the fate of governments and the business of politics did not in those days seem wrapped up with the internet.

Blair himself had neither an email address nor a mobile phone until he left Downing Street more than a decade later. Even technology such as the fabled 'Excalibur' computer system for rapid rebuttal that Labour deployed with such a flourish in the 1997 election campaign was used more as a prop to strike fear into opponents than as a real piece of weaponry. Party staff said Excalibur was a 'complete shambles' and at best 'a giant electronic dustbin'. Its chief spokesman at one stage angrily denied not only reports that the party was collecting data for commercial sale but also that the programme had, in fact, even been 'connected to the internet'.[15]

After Blair's landslide victory in 1997, Campbell nodded to the future by publishing Lobby briefings on the Downing Street website and made a reluctant prime minister do a weekly podcast. But Campbell acknowledges he was not particularly interested in the blogs that were just beginning to appear on the margins of politics: 'I didn't see how important they would become,' he says, recalling his bemusement when a journalist announced he was leaving a good job at the *Daily Express* to join the BBC's online team. 'He was telling me I should get my head round this but I fobbed him off a bit,' he says. 'I couldn't really imagine it would change the fundamentals.'[16]

But the fundamentals of politics *were* already beginning to change. For a start, both Clinton and Blair were focused to an unprecedented degree on the use of information. Clinton's appetite for polling data and focus group research was legendary. In the 1996 presidential campaign, he was said to have built 'the most sensitive radar apparatus American politics had ever seen' as he steered a course to the right on crime, welfare and spending. Mark Penn, his pollster, pioneered techniques he claimed formed the first 'psychological profiles' of key demographic groups—the big insight of which was that having children made women more likely to vote Republican.[17] The campaign duly targeted suburban 'soccer moms,' the kind who shuttled their children to sports practice while juggling a people-carrier full of other problems, with slivers of policy like more school uniforms and bans on cigarette adverts aimed at the young.

More importantly, both Clinton and Blair spent much of their time, energy and political capital in a battle for control of information with an increasingly toxic insurgent and expanding media.

Often in the fierce heat of adversity and scandal, Clinton's presidency had forged and refined techniques to manage the press and broadcast journalists who seemed to lay siege to his White House. Messages had to be carefully honed, discipline centralised, rebuttals rapid and hostile political journalists bypassed for the soft media of daytime TV sofas or women's magazines.

These were studied and then replicated so well by Campbell, that Clinton suggested—probably as a joke—that Downing Street's head of communications should work for him.[18] Campbell created an almost entirely new communications weapons system for British politics, much of which has since become standard issue for all parties. He selectively gave advance briefings to some journalists while scorning others, imposed diary grids on ministerial policy announcements so they complemented—rather than competed with—Blair, and ferociously enforced 'lines to take'. The media was monitored, 24 hours a day, by a unit based in the Cabinet Office. Briefings were put on the record and interviews granted to 'soft media' to undermine the authority of The Lobby.

It is all too easy to write—and too much has probably already been written—about how Blair's Downing Street is supposed to have become a poll-driven, spin-dried machine to manipulate voters and control the agenda. What is sometimes now overlooked is how researching public opinion and engaging with the press were once seen as necessary function of an inclusive new information age.

Back in the 1990s, it was argued that data from polling and focus groups were giving citizens a voice in politics that might otherwise not be heard among the special interests and lobbyists jostling for influence.

Blair's pollster, Philip Gould, who had spent time with the Clinton team, was forever urging Labour to emulate the Americans by creating a 'populism of the centre'.[19] And, if Blair sometimes appeared guided more by polling than by his party activists, that was a deliberate choice. Gould's 1998 book, *Unfinished Revolution*, includes an interview with Stan Greenberg, an American pollster who had worked with both Clinton and Blair, explaining why 'polls and focus groups are the best available means' to hear the public.

He said: 'It doesn't need defending. It is part of the democratisation of modern elections. … The institutions that used to be effective in mediating popular sentiment have atrophied and have lost their ability to articulate. So the trade unions, for example, just don't have the kind of base that they used to have. If you want to know what working people think, you can't turn to these organisations … there is no choice but to go to people directly.'[20]

Blair himself acknowledges that in his early days he was 'buying the notion, and then selling the notion, that to be in touch with opinion was the definition of good leadership.'[21]

Since then, he has decided this was one of several areas in his messy relationship with the information age that he got wrong. 'The time to trust a politician most is when they are telling you what you least want to hear,' he says. 'Because that is when they are telling you something they believe—it is out of conviction.'[22]

# # #

The former prime minister takes a similar view about New Labour's efforts to engage with the media. In an interview for this book, Blair says: 'Because of my own relationship with the media, whenever I'm talking about it I have to come from a position of humility and *mea culpa*. We'd lost four elections. The media had been incredibly hostile to us and so I was trying to deal with every obstacle that lay on our path to power. One of those was not just the opposition of the media but the level—the intensity—of it on the right. But I'm always very conflicted about this … It made me uncomfortable and has made me even more uncomfortable in the time since.'[23]

He was determined that what had happened in 1992, when a right-wing press pack led by *The Sun* had ripped into Neil Kinnock on a daily basis, would not be repeated. But he also saw his task as persuading a sceptical public that New Labour was different to the old Labour Party that voters had so consistently rejected. It meant placing management of the media front and centre in his political strategy, pitching an appeal directly to *The Sun*'s readers, even acknowledging that some of those nasty things written about Labour in the past maybe had a grain of truth to them.

All this was in sharp contrast to the days when the Labour Party has shied away from—or even actively boycotted—such newspapers. But, as *The Sun* itself constantly pointed out, talking directly to its millions of readers, was not only smart politics but 'democratic' too.

In 1995, the Labour leader flew to Hayman Island in Australia to deliver a speech to Rupert Murdoch and News International executives. The following year, *The Sun*—virulently antagonistic to Labour since the dawn of Thatcherism—threw its support fully behind Blair and began ridiculing John Major, the Conservative prime minister, just as it had torn into successive Labour leaders before.

Peter Mandelson cringes when he remembers, as director of communications for the party during the Wapping dispute in the 1980s, having to telling journalists from *The Sun* and *The Times* to leave press conferences. He had thought that ban was ridiculous. But this key lieutenant of Blair was also deeply unhappy with the courtship of a man who owned newspapers like the *News of the World*, which had tried to out him as gay. 'I had reasons of my own for hating the Murdoch press so I didn't like Tony and Alastair chasing after Rupert,' he says. 'But I knew its necessity so I swallowed hard.'[24]

He believes the new alliance with *The Sun* began to distort the party's agenda. 'There were different views amongst us about how to deal with the media's anti-European agenda. We were always trying to blunt it, either by arguing back against it or by making rhetorical concessions to it … You have to remember that Alastair [Campbell] was not a great Europe enthusiast in those days, certainly not compared to now, but this was hardly surprising considering what he was up against in the press the whole time.'[25]

Blair acknowledges it is a 'fair criticism' that he gave almost a seal of prime ministerial approval to the way newspapers operated in politics, 'empowering them' as he puts it, 'so when it came to something like Brexit they felt able to do what they did.'[26] But he still emphasises that the influence of the media did not change policy very much, saying: 'I was always advancing the case for Europe as much as I could.'

How about the article that appeared under Blair's name in *The Sun* on St George's Day barely a week before the May 1997 election? This said: 'On the day we remember the legend that St George slayed a dragon to protect England, some will argue that there is another dragon to be slayed: Europe. … We will have no truck with a European superstate. If there are moves to create that dragon, I will slay it.'[27]

'Ah, yes,' says Blair flashing that embarrassed smile the country used to love, 'well, yeah, you can point to pieces like that.'

When I ask Campbell about the same article, he pretends to cough. 'We wouldn't have placed that one in the *Financial Times*, would we? But people would understand why we had to do it.'[28]

Andrew Marr, who was then the liberal-minded editor of *The Independent*, could not understand it at all. He wrote: 'If people are constantly told that the EU is a scaly, fire-breathing threat, a danger which needs to be stood up to, then we cannot, as a country, stay in it forever. … How can modernity and pro-Europeanism be compatible with sentences like the one which opened Blair's article? How?'[29]

The answer, which would not become fully clear for another nineteen years, was that modernity and progressive pro-European politics were not as inextricably linked as most liberal opinion believed.

'New Danger'

When he first rose to political prominence, Tony Blair had been nick-named 'Bambi'. Partly this was because his innocent bright eyes and youth had a fawn-like quality. But it also suited the slightly cloying U-rated emphasis he placed on 'telling the truth' and 'doing the right thing'.

In speech after speech Blair contrasted himself against a worn-out grey-faced Conservative government that had won previous elections with 'lies about us and lies about what they would do.' He heralded a 'new politics, a politics of courage, honesty and trust.' He said: 'When we make a promise, we must be sure we can keep it. That is page 1, line 1 of a new contract between a Labour government and the citizens of Britain.'[30]

A quarter of a century later, Blair acknowledges this was one more mistake born of his 'desire to win' and that he was overly-influenced by the media's caricature of politics.

He says: 'We were content to play to this media notion that the [Tory] government was fundamentally dishonest as a group of politicians. The fact is that you can portray all politicians and all governments as that if you want to. ... There was a risk then, as there is a risk now, when the opposition plays to that media strain.'[31]

The Tories spotted the risk he was taking too. By the start of 1996 they had spent almost eighteen months trying to work out how to get a grip on Blair. Some wanted to portray him as 'phony Tony' or a flashy salesman. Others wanted to suggest he was a mere figurehead for old Labour. A third view eventually prevailed that said that, to attack Blair effectively, they should recognise that New Labour was different—but dangerous because of it.

The danger they identified tapped into a fear of the modernity that Blair was so keen to represent. The Conservatives seized on comments from Clare Short, a Labour frontbencher prone to speaking her mind. In one such interview, she attacked Peter Mandelson and Alastair Campbell as 'people in the dark,' adding that their 'obsession with the media and the focus groups is making us look as if we want power at any price.'[32]

During the summer of 1996, the Conservative Party launched 'New Labour, New Danger' posters with red eyes peering out from behind a curtain. But the best-known advert appeared only in newspapers and showed Blair with his eyes stripped out and replaced with demonic eyes, alongside the words: 'One of Labour's leaders, Clare Short, says dark forces behind Tony Blair manipulate policy in a sinister way. "I sometimes call them the people who live in the dark." She says about New Labour: "It is a lie. And it's dangerous."'[33]

They had planned to follow this up with a party election broadcast that portrayed Blair as Dr Faust, making a pact with a spin doctor devil who whispers: 'Do you want to know how to win the election? I can show you how.'[34] This was, however, scrapped after a furious fightback by Labour which persuaded an obliging bishop to denounce the Tories' use of Satanic imagery.[35]

The 'demon eyes' strategy had been the brainchild of Steve Hilton, a relentlessly enthusiastic and socially-liberal 27-year-old, who had helped create attack adverts against Labour five years earlier. The irony, of which Hilton was all-too aware at the time, is that his scheme to beat Blair had used precisely the same political technology it condemned as demonic. 'New Labour, New Danger' emerged from very detailed and expensive polling and focus groups, together with the latest thinking on marketing and targeted messages. Indeed, Hilton's social circle revolved around many of the Labour spin doctors and researchers—the 'people who live in the dark'—as well progressively-inclined journalists like me, he was supposed to be attacking.

But, not for the last time in his career, Hilton was onto an idea of which the destructive potential would not be immediately realised. 'New Labour, New Danger' was about more than exploiting people's natural suspicion and mistrust of change, it implied there was something inherently worthy of distrust in the relationship that politics had with the media in the new information age. And, when politicians were under relentless and unforgiving scrutiny from an ever-more expanded media, Labour's promise to be uniquely honest was never going to be sustainable.

Blair could set himself a high bar for honesty in opposition but, in office, it would inevitably trip him up. The first big scandal of his government involved the money Bernie Ecclestone had given Labour before the election and the concessions he secured for Formula 1 from the government afterwards.[36] It left Blair pleading to be given the benefit of the doubt and saying: 'I think most people who have dealt with me think I'm a pretty straight sort of guy, and I am.'[37]

Next up was Derek Draper, a former aide to Peter Mandelson whose mix of wit and mendacity sparkled in the slightly monochrome world of New Labour's message discipline. He was by then working as a lobbyist and got caught offering access to ministers, boasting: 'There are seventeen people who count in this government … [to] say I am intimate with every one of them is the understatement of the century.'[38] The prime minister's response that time was to tell his Cabinet: 'I think we have to be very careful, with people fluttering around the new government trying to make all sorts of claims of influence, that we are purer than pure.'[39]

And then there was Mandelson himself, who in his brief reign as Trade Secretary, had embraced the information age as tightly as anyone. Within a month of taking up the post in 1998, he flew to Silicon Valley so he could bring what he calls 'the whole caboodle' back to Britain.[40] But within three months of that trip, Mandelson had been forced to resign from the Cabinet when it emerged he had failed to disclose the loan he received from a fellow minister for a swanky new house in Notting Hill.

The noise generated by the media, including me, about these scandals was generally greater than any of them merited. The reason each one shook the government so much was not only because Blair had set such high standards, but also because they undermined the image of a connected, responsive modernity. Instead of being 'servants of the people', in touch with the concerns of every ordinary voter, the impression was that New Labour were more interested in the views of donors, lobbyists, their rich friends or the elite media who they met in fancy restaurants and the late-night Soho drinking clubs to which they—we—all belonged.

# # #

The issue of trust in politics is worth pausing on. Part of the puzzle for progressive leaders like Clinton and Blair at the end of the last century was that for all the soaring optimism about liberal democracy and sustained global economic growth, confidence in the political institutions delivering it—even the democratic process itself—had begun to fester.

Accounts of what happened inevitably focus on apparent betrayals of trust in individual countries. In Britain, the scandals that repeatedly rocked politics clearly played a part in shaking people's faith in politics. As late as the mid-1980s, 36 per cent of the British public still said they trusted government 'all or most of the time'. By 1996, that had fallen to 22 per cent. And in the year 2000, after three years of Blair's 'new contract with the British people' the figure was a mere 16 per cent.[41]

In the US, trust had been falling for years. The American National Election Study began in the 1950s regularly asking voters the question, 'do you trust the government in Washington to do what is right, all or most of the time?' Until the mid-1960s, around three-quarters of US voters answered 'yes'. After Watergate, Vietnam and the oil crisis, that proportion fell to about a quarter and never really recovered. Only once, immediately after the terrorist attacks on America in September 2001, has trust in the US government briefly climbed back to over 50 per cent, but nine months later it was back down in the 30s and has since fallen further to below 20 per cent.[42]

The Iran–Contra scandal under Ronald Reagan and the broken promise of 'no new taxes' from George H. W. Bush did nothing to improve public trust. Nor, it must be said, did Bill Clinton's insistence that he did not have sexual relations 'that woman'. She had a name, Monica Lewinsky, and the Leader of the Free World wanted us to believe that because her lips were in contact with his penis, it was *her* having sex with *him*.[43] When the scandal broke in the unseasonably wet summer of 1998, the White House had to lay gravel out on the North Lawn to stop it turning into a symbolically muddy morass due to the media's feeding frenzy outside.[44]

Jessica Mathews of the Carnegie Endowment for International Peace has pointed out that any US citizen under the age of 40 has lived 'their entire life in a country the majority of whose citizens do not trust their own national government.' She adds: 'Think what it means for the healthy functioning of a democracy that two-thirds to three-quarters of its people do not believe that their government does the right thing most of the time.'[45]

But this trust deficit was not confined to Britain or America. It was happening across the Western world and threatening established power everywhere from the boardroom to the battlefield and the pulpit.[46] Chief executives worried about their jobs as giant corporations were challenged by nimble technology start-ups; great armies and navies found themselves outflanked by terrorists and Somali pirates; organised religion struggled to contain grassroot congregations springing up from communities.

In Japan's 'lost decade' of the 1990s, disaffection reached near-record levels. A survey in 1995 showed 70 per cent of its citizens distrusted legislators and almost as many—65 per cent—distrusted the civil servants who had previously been credited with engineering post-war growth.[47] Confidence in the Swedish parliament fell from 51 per cent to 19 per cent between 1986 and 1996. In Germany, the percentage of people who said they trusted their Bundestag deputy to represent their interests slumped from 55 per cent in 1978 to 34 per cent by 1992.[48]

One reason may well have been that trade and migration were already changing communities faster than people could adapt, or displacing jobs from traditional industries. But accelerating globalisation went hand-in-hand with information. The speed with which news swept across the world meant that issues like terrorism, famine, epidemics, poverty and climate change were transcending borders. It was what Hannah Arendt had described, two decades earlier, as a 'common present' where everyone 'feels the shock of events that take place on the other side of the globe.'[49]

People were simultaneously demanding more from their leaders just as they became less capable of delivering. The framework for addressing the multiple crises of a 'common present' was still that of a national government. And politicians there were often either stricken by paralysis in the face of such scale or hobbled by the insurgency of their expanded media.

To the extent that those in power were capable of a coherent response, they sought to control this torrent of new information. And, for all the abuse that is still routinely poured over Blair and Clinton for their manipulation of the media, the response from the powerful in other parts of the world was generally a whole lot scarier.

For instance, Silvio Berlusconi, the dominant figure in Italian politics for almost two decades from 1994 and prime minister for most of that time, controlled the media by the simple means of owning it. Three of the seven main TV channels belonged to his Mediaset company and, when he was in power, he exercised extensive control through his power to appoint TV executives to the three state-run RAI stations too.[50]

Still more worrying for those who believed in freedom of speech and democracy was the swiftness with which China had abandoned experiments with the liberalisation the media, if not its economy. Deng Xiaoping, who had predicted 'some flies would blow in' when China opened its windows to the world, had begun swatting them after the Tiananmen Square massacre in 1989. And suppression tightened through the 1990s even as the Chinese media and internet expanded.

Clinton, having survived humiliation and congressional impeachment in his second term, was still pinning his hopes on a liberal information revolution coming down his 'super highway' to Communist China too.

In March 2000, during his final year in the White House, he made a characteristically bold and eloquent prediction: 'In the new century, liberty will spread by cell phone and cable modem. We know how much the internet has changed America, and we are already an open society. Imagine how much it could change China. Now, there's no question

China has been trying to crack down on the internet. Good luck. That's sort of like trying to nail Jello to the wall.'[51]

But the biggest battles for control of information at the beginning of this century were not yet being fought on the internet. Instead, they were taking place in the old world of print media and TV. Barely a decade after liberalism had seemed so triumphant, two new leaders were elected in Russia and the United States who were already jaded by such values. Indeed, one them didn't even care much for the idea of truth.

'Little Zaches'

The *glasnost* that had prised apart the old Soviet Union was turning out to be trickier for the new Russia than might have once been thought; freedoms that had been foaming out messily under Gorbachev were, by the mid-1990s, causing Boris Yeltsin to skid and slide.

Although the country's new democratic constitution enshrined freedom of speech and freedom of the press as fundamental rights, the economic crisis had made much of the press economically unviable. 'Newspapers are bought not to make a profit, but to fight for steel, oil, a governor's post or whatever,' said Pavel Gutiontov, the secretary of the Journalists Union.[52] And the speed with which the Soviet state-controlled media was being dismantled saw Russia's information resources—just as much as its oil and gas supplies—being carved up and sold off to the oligarchs.

Television was the most important source of information and the main stations swiftly became owned or largely controlled by media empires with agendas tailored to suit their super-rich owners like Boris Berezovsky at ORT and Vladimir Gusinsky at NTV.[53] And, as in so many other areas of the Russian economy, there was widespread corruption accompanied by organised crime and violence. Advertising revenues went missing, journalists went unpaid and Vlad Listyev, a popular pro-democracy TV presenter, was assassinated in 1995 on the staircase of his apartment building in Moscow.[54]

Berezovsky's control over ORT—the only Russian channel broadcasting to the entire country—had been credited with rescuing Yeltsin's stumbling presidential campaign in 1996. He helped orchestrate the succession in 2000 too, throwing his media resources into reinventing the short, balding KGB bureaucrat Vladimir Putin as a bare-chested horseman, a man who stroked Amur tigers and swam in freezing Siberian rivers. But Putin himself was beginning to look at Western ideas of a free press through narrowed eyes. The wounded pride that he—and much of Russia—felt over the disintegration of the former Soviet Union in the 1990s became infected and inflamed by the way the world's media, including Russia's own, had reported a vicious internal war with Chechen nationalists.

The main source of internal criticism over Chechnya came from NTV, the biggest independent TV channel. It also ran a popular satirical puppet show modelled on the UK's *Spitting Image* called *Kukly*—Russian for dolls. One sketch, entitled 'Little Zaches', portrayed Putin as the dwarf baby from an old E. T. A. Hoffman story. The hideous dwarf has a spell cast on him by a fairy to make others believe he is brilliant and beautiful.[55]

The sketch opens with an exhausted Yeltsin trying to calm the vicious baby. 'Oh, he's so unattractive and his origins, forgive me, are so dark,' he mumbles, 'God, why did this have to happen to me?' Then the fairy arrives, waving his 'magic TV comb' to beautify the baby's thin hair.

According to the sketch's writer, Viktor Shenderovich, Putin 'went mad' after 'Little Zaches' was broadcast[56] and, on 11 May 2000—just four days after Putin took the oath of office of president—a truckload of flak-jacketed and masked FSB police raided NTV. In June, Gusinsky was detained for three days in jail, where he was 'persuaded' to leave the country and sell his stake in the TV channel. Within a year, journalists were forcibly ejected from NTV's headquarters, while other parts of Gusinsky's media empire such as his *Segodnya* newspapers were simply shut down.[57]

The fairy in the 'Little Zaches' sketch was portrayed as Berezovsky. The Putin-baby bites his hand and screams that he wants to take them to an outhouse and kill them, Berezovsky replies softly—hopefully—'not all of them'. Within months of the 2000 election, Berezovsky had lost his place in the Kremlin's inner circle and began criticising the president.

But the relationship became most toxic in August 2000 after yet another blow to Russia's status.

# # #

The *Kursk* was the pride of the Russian navy, a symbol of the country's residual superpower status, a nuclear submarine the size of two jumbo jets—and supposedly unsinkable.

Putin was on holiday when the unthinkable happened and the *Kursk* sank with the loss of 118 sailors' lives. He delayed his return for five days during which the Russian government refused offers of foreign help while relations with the media descended into chaos. At one stage, a distraught mother of one of the sailors was shown on the TV channel shouting at officials before a medic approached her from behind and injected her with a sedative.[58]

An ORT presenter, Sergei Dorenko, who had once been one of the new president's loudest media cheerleaders, got hold of a transcript of Putin's subsequent meeting with the dead sailors' relatives where criticism of his handling of the crisis was repeated.

'You saw it on television?', asked Putin furiously. 'That means they are lying. They are lying! They are lying! There are people on television who have been working to destroy the army and the navy for ten years. They are talking now as though they are the biggest defenders of the military. All they really want to do is finish it off. They have stolen all this money and now all they are doing is buying everyone off and making whatever laws they want to make.'[59]

The lesson Putin drew from all this was not that it is dangerous to cover-up information or mislead journalists; the bigger risk was to allow information to go out uncontrolled. Dorenko swiftly lost his job. And, in September that year, Putin set out his 46-page 'Doctrine of Information Security'. This decreed that freedom of the press had to be balanced against the interests of the state and warned that foreign mass media could 'deform' information and represented 'one of the greatest dangers in the sphere of spiritual life.'[60] The following month, Putin was asked about criticism from Berezovsky in an interview with France's *Le Figaro*. He replied that oligarchs were using the Russian media to blackmail the state and 'if necessary we will destroy those instruments.' He then added: 'The state has a cudgel in its hands that you use to hit just once, but on the head.'[61] By November 2000, Berezovsky fled into exile amid threats of prosecution for fraud. He spent the next thirteen years living in the UK where his friend, Alexander Litvinenko, was assassinated and he was later to die himself in possibly suspicious circumstances.

Although almost sixty journalists have been killed in Russia since Putin came to power—and many more imprisoned—he has never completely suppressed the press.[62] A number of liberal newspapers and magazines have been allowed to continue publishing, albeit under conditions of self-censorship. But what Putin's early victories over Gusinsky and Berezovsky did achieve was complete control over Russia's TV where the overwhelming majority of voters got their information.

As a result, what passed for news in Russia in the first years of this century was largely being scripted inside the Kremlin by 'political technologists', a phrase suffused with artistry—the 'magic comb'—compared to the West's more surgical 'spin doctors'. The leading political technologist under Putin in his first term was Vladislav Surkov, who had been a conceptual artist, playwright and rock lyricist. He had little time for political liberalism, preferring the notion of a 'managed' or even 'imitation' democracy, but made control look like theatre.[63] Fake opposition parties engaged in fake opposition to make the president look sane by comparison, a fake justice system went through the motions of a fake legal process to maintain the semblance of the rule of law, and a fake free media made fake news for Russia's 144 million citizens to see.

In *Nothing is True and Everything is Possible*, Peter Pomerantsev describes Russian TV as a synthesis of 'Soviet control with western entertainment ... show business with propaganda, ratings with authoritarianism.'[64] When he worked for a liberal media organisation called SNOB, he suspected it was being tolerated, or possibly even run, by the Kremlin so that it could present opposition as 'hipster Muscovites, out of touch with ordinary Russians, obsessed with marginal issues such gay rights.' He concluded: 'We are just bit-part players in the political technologists' reality TV show.' The Kremlin sponsored all kinds of groups, 'beetroot-faced communists and spitting nationalists,' together with neo-Nazi skinheads, motorbike gangs and liberal human rights groups, not just to control information but to bewilder and dazzle the audience of citizens with so much conflicting information they might as well just sit back and shrug.

And when Pomerantsev later returned to London to watch the court case where Berezovsky was trying to sue Roman Abramovich for lost billions, the cycle became complete. Berezovsky, who invented Putin's image before being persecuted by him, was dismissed by the presiding judge, Mrs Justice Gloster, as an 'unimpressive, and inherently unreliable, witness, who regarded truth as a transitory, flexible concept.' Berezovsky apparently laughed as she continued: 'I gained the impression that he was not necessarily being deliberately dishonest, but had deluded himself into believing his own version of events.' A few months later he was dead.

Putin's suppression and coercion of the media to control information were a return to the norm for a country that had no real tradition of liberalism, let alone democracy. The methods he used in his first years as president owed much to Soviet and Tsarist notions of control and theatre. The fake village facades built by Grigory Potemkin along the banks of the Dnieper River in eighteenth century Russia are little different to the propaganda devoted to explaining how the *Kursk* was sunk, not by Russian technological failure, but by an American torpedo.[65]

In his first term as president of Russia, Putin's control of information remained that of a distinctly analogue authoritarian and there was scant interest in what was happening in the internet.

But it still demonstrated that the new age of information would not necessarily be either liberal or democratic. His model of authoritarianism—soon by copied by the likes of Rodrigo Duterte in the Philippines and Recep Erdoğan in Turkey—conscripted parts of the media into a nationalist credo and stuck an old iron fist into the faces of the rest.

'Dubya'

The year 2000 saw a new leader elected in Russia and George W. Bush won the race for the White House by a bitterly-disputed hair's breadth

He graced the cover of *The Economist* as 'The Accidental President', while an editorial inside the magazine bemoaned the way 'creaky voting technology' had delivered such an 'unsubstantial figure' as Leader of the Free World because of maybe just 537 votes in Florida and a 'few hanging chads'.[66]

At the outset of the campaign, most pundits predicted that his opponent, Al Gore, would canter home.[67] He seemed to understand the future; he had been the vice president in the Clinton White House which had brought rising wages and prosperity; and he was a genuine enthusiast for the bright new tomorrow being created by technology. Although he never exactly claimed to have invented the internet, Gore did say 'I took the initiative in creating' it. Indeed, nerdy 'Internet Al', with his electronic pager clipped neatly to his belt, was one of the first politicians to recognise how high-speed computing and connected networks was going to define the new century. He was the first one to utter the 'information super-highway' line that had been used to such effect by both Clinton and Blair.[68]

Bush, by contrast, appeared to be a blot on the cool, connected, progressive landscape. This president was self-consciously Texan, nicknamed 'Dubya' by his patrician family in mimicry of his Lone Star State pronunciation of 'W'—his middle initial. His White House was one where, as his former speechwriter David Frum put it, 'attendance at Bible study was, if not compulsory, not quite uncompulsory.'[69] As a candidate for the White House, he could not even say 'information super-highway' properly, asking a puzzled audience in New Hampshire, 'will the highways on the internet become more few?'[70]

Progressive politics and much of the media on both sides of the Atlantic treated his presidency with a mixture of shock, grief and derision that was not matched again until the election of Donald Trump sixteen years later. Some members of Clinton's departing staff even removed the 'W' from their computer keyboards at the White House as a childish act of technological sabotage against George W. Bush's arrival.[71]

For all this, Bush was never quite the caricature that his opponents sought to make him. He had a warmth about him that made him a far better politician than he was given credit for. He had campaigned as a moderate 'compassionate conservative' with a progressive view of education, immigration and aid to Africa. He appointed not just the first, but also the second, black Secretary of State. And, to the fury of his party's libertarian right, he oversaw an increase in the federal budget. Even the neo-conservative foreign policy doctrine of pre-emptive war that he adopted after 9/11 seemed sourced more in a starry-eyed idea of American freedom than the dark malevolence of his vice president, Dick Cheney.

But he was not a natural communicator like Clinton or Reagan and, from the outset, he was despised by sections of the media for appearing to be a bit thick. By the end of the 2000 campaign, *Slate* magazine had managed to collect enough 'Bushisms' to publish a book of them. Bush's solution to a hostile liberal press was to make himself a smaller target by carefully stage-managing events and limiting his exposure to scornful eyes.

Bush's White House held fewer press conferences, allowed fewer questions when they did, and provided less access to media. It shared the views of many conservative voters that the White House press corps was elitist, inveterately liberal and no longer deserved to be an 'exclusive pipeline to be the public.'[72] A profile of Karl Rove, Bush's chief strategist, quoted an unnamed Republican saying: 'Karl's attitude is, "We're going to change

61

Washington. They're going to have to write what we say, because it's all we're going to give them.'"[73] By 2004, even *The New Yorker* was giving the Bush White House credit for showing 'unusual skill ... in keeping much of the press at a distance while controlling the news agenda.'[74]

For much of his presidency, Bush succeeded because there was a constituency of Republican voters far away from the coastal elites who trusted him more than they did the media. Many were religious and part of the Evangelical movement sweeping US churches, others were more pessimistic and withdrawn than they had been during the 'shining city upon a hill' optimism of the Reagan years. The story that Limbaugh had been telling them on the radio—and that Fox News was now pumping through cable into their living rooms—was a simple one: they had been let down; it was now 'us against them'. And Rove had enough data on all of them to target them with messages on 'wedge issues' like abortion or gay marriage to win Bush two terms in the White House.[75]

At the same time an intellectual framework was being built by neoconservatives for whom the wandering hands, restless minds and general decadence of the Clinton's administration had symbolised the weakening of the America's Cold War resolve.[76] Even before he became defined by 9/11 and Iraq, Bush's campaign in 2000 had a strong moral, and nostalgic tone with its promise to restore 'honour and dignity' to an Oval Office soiled by Clinton. After the terror attacks of September 2001 his presidency became one characterised by what Anatol Lieven described as a 'wounded and vengeful' language.[77]

Bush's White House did not have to care too much if the leader writers of *The New York Times* and *The Economist*, not to mention international opinion, despised him. There were alternative routes to public opinion and the one he usually chose, particularly after 9/11, was Fox News. By 2002 it had overtaken CNN as the most popular cable news channel. Presenters like Bill O' Reilly kept a doormat picturing Hillary Clinton's face beneath his desk and harangued any liberal dumb enough to go on his show.[78] Opponents of the war were routinely denounced by Fox News anchors as the 'axis of weasels'. And, although it was still news-driven enough to break real stories, such as revealing Bush had been once been arrested for drunk-driving, much of its coverage was shamelessly partisan.

At one stage, during an anti-war protest in France, a confused-looking Fox reporter turned to the camera to explain to those watching back home that 'many of these people are Communists.'[79] One of its correspondents, Geraldo Rivera, announced his personal desire to kill Osama bin Laden and went out to Afghanistan armed with his own gun. Not for nothing did Gore complain in an interview in 2002 that the 'media is kind of weird these days on politics.'[80]

After 9/11, there was a simple, clear story that cut through the complexities of Middle Eastern politics, the niceties of European diplomacy, and America's own cultural battles that dated back to Vietnam and Woodstock in the 1960s. And this pugilistic, populist, resentful script was being written as much by Fox as by the White House. Fox's chief executive, Roger Ailes, is said to have sent private advice to Bush in the aftermath of 9/11, urging him to use 'the harshest measures possible.'[81] There is no reason to think that Bush would have acted very differently without this unsolicited advice from Ailes. However, as a president for whom responding to 9/11 and dealing with a whole new world of information in all its complexity was a heavy burden, Bush instinctively gravitated towards to the cleanest and clearest of lines. And the narrative Bush adopted to face the world after his country was attacked certainly resembled that flickered across cable TV on Fox News, even when the facts did not quite fit the script.

# # #

This was an administration that in 2003 had appeared to exaggerate the rescue of Private Jessica Lynch after the Battle of Nasiriyah in Iraq. Official Pentagon briefing to a credulous media told the story of how, despite being wounded by enemy gunfire, she had bravely fought on until her M-16 ran out of ammunition and was captured. It suggested she had been strapped to a bed and tortured in hospital, before finally being rescued by daring US Navy SEALs whose heroics were conveniently captured on video. Both Lynch and the Pentagon later corrected this account to say she had never fired a shot, had no bullet wounds at all and had been treated kindly by staff at the Iraqi hospital who had donated their own blood and tried to hand her over to coalition forces days earlier.[82] And, predictably, the blonde, white Lynch received far more attention than Shoshana Johnson, a black single mother who really had been shot in the same battle—and was held prisoner for longer—before being rescued.

Such episodes formed part of a pattern. The Bush administration had a Healthy Forests Initiative that opened up the wilderness to logging; a

Clear Skies Act that reduced pollution standards; and a colour-coded terror alert system for a frightened public that the then Homeland Security Secretary says he was pressured to raise in the run-up to the 2004 presidential election.[83]

In that same year, one of Bush's senior advisers did little to conceal either his contempt for liberal critics in the media or his own identity (the aide in question is universally thought to have been the chief strategist, Karl Rove). He told a journalist: 'We're an empire now, and when we act, we create our own reality. And while you're studying that reality—judiciously, as you will—we'll act again, creating other new realities, which you can study too, and that's how things will sort out. We're history's actors ... and you, all of you, will be left to just study what we do.'[84]

This remark came at the high point of Bush's hubris that saw him pose on a warship in the Gulf in front of 'Mission Accomplished' banner. Not for nothing did the comedian Stephen Colbert coin the term 'truthiness' during Bush's presidency. He described it an appeal to emotion and 'gut feeling' ahead of reason. 'People love the president because he's certain of his choices as a leader,' said Colbert, 'even if the facts that back him up don't seem to exist.'[85]

The failure to find stockpiles of Saddam Hussein's weapons of mass destruction combined with a determined military insurgency in Iraq would eventually reveal that Rove's 'new reality' had been a mirage. But it is worth remembering how large sections of the media had not needed persuasion when they suspended their critical faculties after 9/11. Dan Rather, the anchor of CBS News declared a few days after the attacks that to defeat Al-Qaeda the US would have to invade not only Afghanistan but also 'Sudan, Iran, Iraq, Syria, and Libya'. He added: 'George Bush is the President ... wherever he wants me to line up, just tell me where.'

Judith Miller was an aggressively ambitious journalist at *The New York Times* who had won a Pulitzer prize for her stories warning of the growing threat posed by Al-Qaeda to America before the 2001 attacks. She also wrote no less than sixty-four stories for the newspaper warning about the threat posed by Saddam Hussein and his alleged arsenal of WMD, often based on little more than what Iraqi exiles, hell bent on regime change, had told her. When the war began to go wrong much of the media turned on the White House, as well as likes of Miller.[86] She was forced out of the newspaper and, after a short spell in jail for contempt of court for refusing to reveal a White House source, Miller inevitably joined Fox News as a contributor.

Bush himself retreated behind Fox News and Limbaugh, besieged by the press his White House administration had once disdained. As the military mission foundered, the Pentagon tried to ban photographs of coffins from being published and prevent news coverage of their return from Iraq and Afghanistan at Dover air base in Delaware.[87] But controlling the media by holding it arm's length no longer worked. The ban was first challenged then overturned and, as the body count piled up, Bush's ratings plummeted to a record low.

By the end of his presidency, Bush was scorned by large parts of America as much as he was abroad. Aboard Air Force One before his final visit to Europe in June 2008, there was a certain wistfulness about him as he suggested his 'dead or alive, bring it on' gun-slinging language had made people think he was a 'guy really anxious for war ... and not, you know, a man of peace.' He added: 'I think that in retrospect, I could have used a different tone, a different rhetoric.'[88]

Any suggestion of an equivalence between Bush and Putin is ridiculous and perhaps dangerously wrong. Nor is it fair to compare him to other right-wing leaders elected around this time like Viktor Orbán in Hungary who delighted in being called an 'illiberal democrat'. Bush was not a card-carrying liberal, but he maintained a functioning liberal democracy. Unlike Orbán, he did not oppress minorities or undermine the rule of law. And unlike Putin, he certainly did not stage-manage elections, lock up his opponents or run a regime where journalists got murdered.

But the way Bush isolated the media and bypassed it through Fox, targeted pockets of angry pessimistic voters far away from coastal elites, and deployed the language of a vengeful nationalism after 9/11 did point the way to how, eight years after he left the White House, Donald Trump might win it. Both the 43rd and 45th presidents of the United States showed it was possible to maintain a degree of perceived authenticity with their core support that had little to do with veracity.

Indeed, for all his failings, it is worth remarking that Bush never experienced quite the same intensity of hatred and anger that surged around his chief international ally, Tony Blair. 'The US provided 95 per cent of the troops and firepower for the Iraq invasion,' said a rueful Alastair Campbell, 'but we seemed to get 95 per cent of the blame.'[89] Partly this was because there was a simplicity and a kind of naivety to Bush's stated war aim of regime change in Iraq—the violent removal of Saddam Hussein—compared to Blair's insistence that all he had ever wanted was compliance with United Nations resolutions.

Michael Moore, the American satirist and a vigorous opponent of the war, offered this explanation when he went to speak to the Cambridge Union in 2003: 'You're stuck with being connected to this country of mine, which is known for bringing sadness and misery to places around the globe,' he told the students. 'How's that feel? See, I actually hold Blair more responsible for this than Bush, because Bush is an idiot...'[90]

And, of all the labels have been attached to the former prime minister over the years, few have ever described him as being an idiot. Instead, the accusation more often thrown at him by both left and right, is that he was clever to the point of being devious.

'B-Liar'

'Unless you constantly feed the media stories,' wrote Philip Gould back in 1998, 'they will gobble you up.'[91]

This view was common currency among the teams of pollsters, strategists and spin doctors that clustered around politics in those years.

In the first five years of Blair's government, it fed the media a total of 32,766 press releases—an average of one every four minutes, day and day out, including weekends and Bank Holidays.[92] But, towards the end of this exhausting period, the story was beginning to turn from what was contained in those press releases to the process that produced them.

For instance, a memo Blair wrote to aides in April 2000, and leaked to the press after being extracted from rubbish bags outside Gould's home by an obsessive compulsive known in Fleet Street as 'Benji the Binman', proved particularly embarrassing and dominated the headlines for a whole week. It showed Blair demanding they produce a series of 'eye-catching initiatives' with which he could be 'personally associated' on a list of issues like asylum-seekers, defence, family and youth crime that could have been written by the editor of the *Daily Mail*.[93]

When Derek Draper was exiled from New Labour's inner circle after the lobbying scandal of 1998, he checked into the Priory and began seven years of treatment for depression. With this new perspective, he began to wonder if any of the press releases being produced by his former colleagues really meant anything at all.

'I had been one of the shock troops of New Labour,' he says, '[but] there was a mentality that if you got a story in the newspaper that was doing something. You know, we would announce that we were going to make all prisons focus on rehabilitation or something but then none of us had any idea what was actually being done.'[94]

Charlie Whelan, who had stood up my Tote story in 1997 before being forced to resign himself in the wake of another scandal, says: 'We were just constantly trying to feed the media to keep it quiet. I suppose that's what has always happened in politics but we were the worst generation. We were terrible.'[95]

Another senior adviser from the time suggests: 'There was a disconnect between the speed of our communications and the pace of government. It meant people would expect change faster than we could deliver it. Maybe sometimes we thought getting good headlines was getting the job done—when it was really just a small part of it; it damaged trust.'[96]

None of this stopped Blair winning a second landslide victory on 1 May 2001 against a weak Conservative Party. William Hague's Tories had adopted Steve Hilton's strategy, endlessly complaining about New Labour 'spin' and calling the prime minister 'B-Liar' long before this sobriquet appeared on left wing anti-war posters but gained a total of just one seat in the House of Commons. But turnout in that election had fallen significantly to 58 per cent, down from 71 per cent in 1997 and 78 per cent in 1992. Hilton himself had almost joined the ranks of non-voters. He spent most of that election night on 7 June 2001, in his north London flat playing music at full volume, watching Sky News with the sound turned down while telling me he had voted for the Green Party because of his contempt for Hague's illiberal and desperate efforts at 'populism'.

For all the weakness of his opponents, the media insurgency against Blair was gathering strength. Shortly before polling day, the prime minister went to BBC Radio 4's *Today* programme for an irritable interview with John Humphrys, who asked him repeatedly whether the government had met his standard of being 'purer than pure'. It culminated in this exchange:

> *Blair:* I think almost ten minutes into the interview, you've not asked me a single question on the economy, on schools, on crime, or welfare or Europe, or any of the things that I would have thought your listeners would have liked to have heard about.

Humphrys: I have dealt with a subject that you yourself said was vitally important, restoring trust in politics and I make no apology for that, and I am told by many people as you well know yourself, that this whole area of trust in politics is crucially important, and one of the reasons why I have raised it this morning is that there is a feeling on the part of many people that yours has been a government of spin, and that they can never be quite sure that those things they are being told are actually what the real situation is, or have they been turned and twisted by some of your advisers perhaps, perhaps yourself, perhaps other ministers.[97]

Humphrys was by no means alone in focusing on 'spin'. Many journalists by this stage of the Blair government had become slightly obsessed by it, and Alastair Campbell in particular. Initially at least, Downing Street's head of communications reveled in his fame. He allowed Michael Cockerell to film an hour-long fly-on-the-wall documentary for the BBC in which he starred and Blair had various walk-on parts. 'Do you often come to your press secretary's office?' Cockerell asked the prime minister. 'I do!—ah—if I'm passing. Which I happen to be!', he replied, visibly embarrassed, as Campbell made strange noises in the background.[98]

When a hostile biography was published about him, Campbell responded by highlighting the 'homo-eroticism' of its prose. Later, he wrote a long article suggesting that Paul Dacre, the editor of the *Daily Mail*, who attacked him relentlessly, really just wanted to have sex with him. 'Paulipoos, my poppet, I know you love me,' he wrote, 'scream it more gently and I might listen.'[99]

Sometimes Campbell would indulge his contempt by feeding reporters' desire for colour by giving them palpably false information just to see if they noticed. Once, he described a meeting Blair had in an eighth floor hotel room during a summit in Nice as an experiment to discover if the journalists could work out that the building they were all staying in only had six floors (they didn't). On other occasions, he would issue facetious denials to avoid having to deal with a question. I once had a story about how an embarrassed Blair had hidden horizontally on the back seat of his government limousine as it sped down a hugely unpopular bus lane on the M4 motorway to avoid traffic jams. I went to Campbell for a comment. 'It is completely untrue to suggest the prime minister has ever travelled on the M4,' he said. Huh? 'He's never used the M4. Never been on that motorway in his life. Not once. Never. I know.'

Campbell says he operated an old-fashioned 'top-down command and control system'—a phrase redolent with left-wing authoritarianism—but in his case it was more like a sheer force of will that took its toll not only on his own fragile mental health but relations with the media too. And, on occasions, Campbell's all-consuming determination to win came close to intimidation or, as he puts it now, 'conflict became the only language spoken.'

Did he go too far? 'For me, it was all about fighting to get our message across as cleanly as possible,' he says, wearily. 'I guess it did become a slightly sterile struggle.'[100] The more aggressive the media became to counteract his spin, the more Campbell felt he needed to do it. The more sophisticated he became at presenting its message, the more time the media spent deconstructing it. And so the more he spun. This endless cycle was never going to end well for anyone. Campbell's diaries from the time reflect an increasingly dark mood and are often filled with a desperate desire to quit.

Andrew Marr, the BBC political editor for much of this period, says: 'Alastair wanted to control almost everything. But he came in just at a time when the world was changing so fast it meant he could not control everything. I fear he lost all sense of proportion in trying.'[101]

The press was becoming frantic in their efforts to expose Campbell and Blair as liars. Paul Dacre, the *Daily Mail*'s editor, began to view almost any ministerial statement as part of a grand deception against his country, his readers and himself. He told MPs in 2004 that Blair and Campbell had put hostility to the press 'on a different footing,' adding, 'I think after a while the media industry came to believe that [Downing Street] was disseminating untruths and misrepresenting the truth as a matter of course.'

Other newspapers were simply degenerating into spasms of loathing. *The Express*, sold off by the Labour-supporting Clive Hollick to the pornography-enriched Richard Desmond, was becoming almost comically angry about everything. A leaked memo written by James Murray, the *Sunday Express* news editor in 2003, gives some sense of the atmosphere in newsrooms at the time: 'We need to be constantly stirring things up. We must make the readers cross…the appalling state of the railways, the neglect of the health service, the problem of teenage pregnancies, the inability of bureaucrats to get enough done properly etc etc. The middle classes feel under attack because of stealth taxes, crime, the breakdown in society and we need to reflect that. … We should always be looking for someone to blame.'[102]

Such journalism could cause real harm. Take, for example, the strange case of Dr Andrew Wakefield. A gastroenterologist, he was one of a medical team who wrote a paper suggesting there might be a link between the Measles, Mumps and Rubella (MMR) vaccine and the rising incidence of autism. Although no connection had been proven and the study involved just twelve children, Wakefield immediately began demanding the suspension of the vaccine. Media interest spiked at the end of 2001 and the beginning of 2002. The *Daily Mail*, along with Conservative MPs like Julie Kirkbride, were running the MMR story as a campaign against not only the jab but against a government they claimed was not being honest with the public.

As with many other issues at the time, the inevitable conclusion of sections of the press was that it was all the fault of Blair's lying. Stories began to circulate claiming the the prime minister and his wife had decided against giving their baby son, Leo, the jab.[103] When challenged about it, Blair refused to talk about a private family matter. Kirkbride responded by saying: 'I can only assume he has something to hide.'[104]

Just before Christmas that year, Blair issued a statement saying that any suggestion he was asking other parents to do something he would not do himself was 'offensive beyond belief'. It was then reported with confidence by *The Observer*, quoting an off-the-record source, that Leo had been given the jab. Six weeks later, *The Independent*'s Andrew Grice reported—with equal confidence and another off-the-record source—that the jab had not been given to the boy until January because he had been suffering with a cold before Christmas. For critics, this was what journalists call a 'gotcha moment'.

Peter Oborne, then political editor of *The Spectator*, declared that one or both of the journalists who wrote these contradictory stories on the MMR jab were victims of a 'deliberate heist'. He added: 'It demonstrates once again the casual and cynical approach that the Blair government has towards accuracy and truthfulness, even on a trivial matter.'[105] For the record, Grice points out that his information came from a 'non-political source'. He suggests the whole row was 'more cock-up than conspiracy.'[106] And nor can either the privacy of Blair's family or the damage being caused by Wakefield be easily dismissed as a 'trivial matter'. But uptake of the MMR vaccine fell from 92 per cent to around 50 per cent in parts of London, resulting in new outbreaks of measles—a disease that had previously been almost eradicated—and children dying.[107]

It took two years for Wakefield's claims to be incontrovertibly refuted and still more before he was struck off the medical register in 2007. He has subsequently moved to the US where he received vindication—of sorts—with his original claims apparently being backed by Donald Trump in the lead-up to the 2016 presidential campaign[108] and recycled by Russian disinformation agencies afterwards.[109] Most of the newspapers that had written endless stories doubting the safety of MMR, panicking parents or detailing Blair's alleged deceit on the issue, simply shrugged when Wakefield was discredited. This was not their problem and they were only a news cycle away from finding other controversies to feed upon. 'Not wrong for long', as they say.

The most remarkable feature of the Wakefield row, however, was the speed and enthusiasm with which the MMR row was picked up not only by anti-government newspapers but also by the BBC's flagship radio show, the *Today* programme. In the course of just ten days in February 2002, after the row about Blair's son caught fire, the programme ran versions of the story no less than six times. Its statutory requirement for impartiality was met by pitching Wakefield and his allies on equal terms against the rest of the scientific, medical and political establishment who were emphasising that the real risk was children not taking the vaccine.[110]

Rod Liddle, the editor of the *Today* programme at the time, was said by colleagues to have been particularly exercised by the story. A self-consciously edgy journalist, Liddle had been appointed to shake-up the cautious, fact-based *Today* programme and he recruited a series of scoop-hungry reporters. Even after reading reports indicating there was no link with autism, Liddle declared in print that he would not be vaccinating his own children.[111] Liddle was eventually replaced by Kevin Marsh, another journalist who had originated on the centre-left but believed a good story was one that went after the integrity of the government. In a later memoir, Marsh describes the anger he felt towards Labour and described his conviction that its spin doctors were constructing an artificial version of the truth.[112] Marsh wrote that the 1997 Labour manifesto was nothing more than a 'Potemkin document for a Potemkin party.' He added: 'For a decade, I'd seen it as my job to get underneath the "truths" that the New Labour media machine, led by Campbell, had created for the media. It had become personal.'[113]

For this to have been the attitude of an apparently left-of-centre editor of a flagship current affairs programme for the oldest and most admired public service broadcaster in the world is some indication of how poisonous relations had become in the struggle to control information, even before the Iraq War began in March 2003.

# # #

Little more than two months after the invasion, Marsh's programme was already in a stand-off with Downing Street over what Campbell thought was overly-negative and critical coverage of the conflict. The BBC was raising doubts—completely legitimately—over whether Iraq had the arsenal of chemical and biological weapons that Blair had cited as reasons for the invasion.

And then the *Today* programme ran a story that seemed to fulfil the lurid essence of Hilton's demon eyes advert six years earlier. This alleged Downing Street had secretly 'sexed up' the dossier on Saddam Hussein's weapons of mass destruction with material, including the claim that Iraq could launch missiles within forty-five minutes, that Number 10 'probably knew' was false. It said inclusion of such material in the dossier was against the wishes of the intelligence services and that Blair had chosen to make this material central to his justification of a war that was costing thousands of lives. Each of these allegations was sourced to 'senior officials in charge of drawing up the dossier.'

Marsh was no fan of the reporter who had come up with the story. He had inherited Andrew Gilligan from Liddle's regime and said his antics made him 'nervous'.[114] But Marsh acknowledged his own view that New Labour had 'created the truth' for so long was one of the reasons he was willing to give the story credence. Gilligan's infamous two-way report with Humphrys, broadcast at 6.07am on 29 May 2003, unleashed a sulphurous fight over truth between Campbell and the BBC. Many people's faith in anyone or everything—from Blair and New Labour, to the government, intelligence services, judges, and the BBC—has never really recovered from this row. And, above all, it was a controversy that went to the heart of the increasingly abusive relationship that both politics and the media were having with information.

A few years earlier I had worked with Gilligan at *The Sunday Telegraph*, where he used to describe himself as an 'anarcho-socialist'. On one occasion, an early example of surveillance technology caught us stealing chocolate from the staff canteen during the small hours of one Saturday morning. But, even by my own questionable standards of the time, Gilligan's attitude to information obtained from anonymous sources was exceptional. When he did his famous 'sexed-up' broadcast, I was at *The Times*, on good terms with Campbell and—as Marsh correctly states in his book—I swiftly developed an unhealthy fascination about the identity of the source for Gilligan's claims.

The row went on for weeks. At the Ministry of Defence, an official called Dr David Kelly came forward to admit he had met Gilligan and it became swiftly apparent to his superiors that he must have been the BBC's sole source. Along with other journalists, I got enough information from the government to name him and, I believed, discredit Gilligan's report. Kelly was not a member of the intelligence agencies, he had not been in charge of drawing up the dossier, and was certainly not in a position to know what Downing Street or the intelligence services were thinking. He was a respected MoD weapons expert, who had limited involvement with the dossier. He had also told officials that Gilligan had distorted his comments and that 'sexed up'—a phrase that reeks of desperate journalism—had been 'made up'. Then, on 17 July 2003, two days after being hauled in front of MPs to give evidence and less than two months after the broadcast, came the punch-in-the guts news that Kelly had killed himself.

There have been no less than five inquiries into Kelly's death and the Iraq War, and the report of the Chilcot Inquiry runs to 2.6 million words. None of them found that Blair, Campbell or Downing Street had deliberately falsified information about Saddam's WMD. Although the inquiries concluded that it was the intelligence services themselves who had shorn published material of caveats, most members of the public are convinced that Blair deliberately lied. Even journalists who accept Gilligan's report was way wide of the mark often still justify his reporting on the grounds that they revealed a 'bigger truth' about the Iraq War. It remains the case, of course, that the dossier was clearly wrong because those weapons were never found in Iraq.

And so, this circular argument went on and on and on it goes still. What lingers in my memory of the whole affair was how shrill and angry we all became. Friends fell out, parties split, strange alliances—like between the BBC and the *Daily Mail*—were formed. We all went too far. I took sides, just as other newspaper and broadcast journalists did. It seemed everyone was calling everyone else a liar and this was, remember, before the words 'fake news', 'Brexit' or 'President Trump' had crossed our lips.

Campbell, asked to describe Gilligan's report, told MPs: 'It is a lie, it was a lie. It is a lie that is continually repeated.' A wounded Blair told MPs: 'The allegation that I or anyone else lied to this House or deliberately misled the country by falsifying intelligence on WMD is itself the real lie.'[115] For millions of British people, however, including those who had always opposed him and some who had once supported him, Blair had become 'B-Liar'. Even the *Independent*'s Andrew Grice, who had never succumbed to the wilder fantasies about the evils of spin, says: 'Downing Street crossed the line on Iraq where I believe they were genuinely misleading on WMD and the way the intelligence reports were presented.'[116]

And the sadness of it is that Blair had good progressive reasons—about which he could never be open—to support the American-led invasion. These reasons included both ridding the world of a child-murdering dictator and stopping Bush from driving rough-shod over international law. To achieve these objectives meant trying to get a United Nations resolution authorising any military action in Iraq. In turn, this meant placing disproportionate emphasis on evidence of WMD because that was where the UN had existing resolutions. This was a progressive prime minister betting his political capital and using all his vast communications skill to make the case for war while unable to tell voters all the reasons he had for doing it; he needed the media to make his case but he could never be open about information.

# # #

On 10 December that year, Boris Johnson, who was by then the editor of *The Spectator*, hosted a dinner at an Italian restaurant. Under the banner of 'Save Andrew Gilligan', Johnson declaring that Kelly had been driven to his death by the demands of Blair's spin doctors 'to make black appear white.'[117] The dinner was organised by one of Johnson's journalists at *The Spectator*, Peter Oborne, who went on to develop an elaborate theory on New Labour's relationship with truth which he believes has helped define politics in this new information age. It leans heavily on a comment made by Peter Mandelson in 1997 when asked about his role in news management. 'If you're accusing me of getting the truth across about what the government has decided to do, that I'm putting the very best face or gloss on the government's policies, that I'm trying to avoid gaffes or setbacks and that I'm trying to create the truth—if that's news management, I plead guilty.'[118] Mandelson has since said what he meant was 'establish'—not 'create'—the truth, but that has not stopped the quotation entering legend.

Oborne believes New Labour was in thrall to a philosophy known broadly as post-modernism that has long been used by the left to challenge the idea that old prejudices about class, race, gender, and sexuality are part of a natural order. To the extent a slippery notion like this can be pinned down, it argues that almost everything people believe is a manufactured 'narrative', not built from the bricks of established truth but ephemeral constructions of language and culture, reflecting the distribution of power in a society at the time. Many critics from the right have warned that a progressive post-modern agenda threatens to rob the world of meaning and leave it 'bereft of all authority.'[119] Oborne ended up writing no less than three books on the subject. In one, he set out how New Labour had adopted the term 'narrative' to describe the story it wanted to deliver and traced the first use of the word in this way back to Geoff Mulgan, a New Labour policy thinker, in 1994.[120] In the years that followed, the word 'narrative' did indeed begin to crop up all over the place as journalists and politicians alike found it a fashionably sophisticated way to describe a strategic message in the information age.

But it is much harder to make the case that Blair was exceptional in this regard. Every American president since Jimmy Carter has been branded 'post-modern' because their efforts to communicate their message have involved media management.[121] Oborne argued that New Labour was uniquely deceitful. He describes how Continental philosophical ideas from the likes of Michel Foucault, Jacques Derrida and Jean Baudrillard were 'imported into the British political system' to undermine our 'Anglo–American school of empirical philosophy.' Blair himself seems a bit non-plussed by the theory. When I ask him if he has ever read a word of Foucault, Baudrillard or Derrida, he laughs, shakes his head and replies: 'Who?'[122]

After almost seven years of thinking about it, Sir John Chilcot's Report presented a real criticism of Blair over Iraq. It said: 'The judgement about Iraq's capabilities was presented with a certainty that was not justified … The tactics chosen by Mr Blair were to emphasise the threat which Iraq might pose, rather than a more balanced consideration of both Iraq's capabilities and intent; and to offer the UK's support for President Bush in an effort to influence his decisions on how to proceed.'[123]

What Chilcot suggested was that Blair was guilty of something more than a mistake but less than a lie. In this sense, Blair's relationship with truth is not defined by some school of philosophy, like post-modernism, but by a humbler psychological trait, usually called confirmation bias. He sought information that backed his argument for war while ignoring or downplaying anything else; blurring the distinction between what he believed—and what he actually knew. Confirmation bias is a human instinct and, when someone is engaged in politics where they are trying to make an argument, persuade people, build a case, they are more prone to it than ever. A paper published in the *Review of General Psychology* defined it as 'the seeking or interpreting of evidence in ways that are partial to existing beliefs, expectations, or a hypothesis in hand.'[124]

And, if Blair suffered from confirmation bias, then surely the media did too. Any journalism is story-telling where one fact is elevated over another: some get exaggerated, others are ignored. For Blair's critics, the failure to find WMD in Iraq was not enough. Nor were legitimate concerns about how intelligence was handled. No, the story needed to be—as Gilligan would say—'sexed up' into a vast conspiracy to trick the British people into war.

Blair was prime minister at a time when politicians and the media were coming under intense pressure from the new information age. There was more space to fill, and that meant more news, more controversy, more drama. The premium placed on commentary and opinion meant the press was more polarised. And the more a government tried to spin its way out, the more suspicious and cynical the media became. The media's determination to brand Blair a 'liar' meant that a decade after he left Downing Street, when America elected a president whose public statements was judged by an independent fact checking organisation to be false an astonishing 69 per cent of the time, no one really had a word strong enough to describe Donald Trump.[125]

When Blair first became leader, he had genuinely been excited by the progressive opportunities of the information age. More than Clinton, he really believed in this stuff. By the time he was writing his memoirs, he could scarcely credit that he had passed a law like the Freedom of Information Act that made the job of governing harder and that of his critics in the press easier. 'You idiot. You naive, foolish, irresponsible nincompoop,' Blair said of himself. 'There is really no description of stupidity, no matter how vivid, that is adequate. I quake at the imbecility of it.'[126]

These are strange and strong words from a man who suffered no real damage from this particular piece of legislation and who had not, at least in the eyes of his enemies, acknowledged his failings on more substantial issues like the Iraq War. Possibly his self-flagellation over Freedom of Information is displacement for the real rage he feels over his early enthusiasm for an era when openness was supposed to guarantee progress. For instance, the unprecedented decision to publish the intelligence dossier on Saddam's WMD in 2002 was a direct response to media demands for more information. As Campbell says: 'Tony was saying he sees all this intelligence which makes him more, not less, concerned about the threat posed by Saddam Hussein. But that wasn't good enough for the media, we had journalists saying, why don't you publish it then? Before you know it you're in this awful conflagration with the BBC, the intelligence services and the rest of it. Was it mistake? I don't know, but it was a response to the question from the media.'[127]

# # #

In one of the last speeches he made as prime minister, after a decade in office in which the early embrace he received from the media had become a stranglehold, Blair attacked the press as 'feral beasts': 'I am going to say something that few people in public life will say, but most know is absolutely true: a vast aspect of our jobs today—outside of the really major decisions, as big as anything else—is coping with the media, its sheer scale, weight and constant hyperactivity. At points, it literally overwhelms. Talk to senior people in virtually any walk of life today—business, military, public services, sport, even charities and voluntary organisations and they will tell you the same. People don't speak about it because, in the main, they are afraid to.'[128]

The impact of Blair's speech was somewhat undermined by his singling out for criticism the high-minded, low-circulation liberal *Independent* newspaper which was, by anyone's account, several places behind the likes of the *Daily Mail* in a league table of ferality. The reason for that, of course, was that even at this late stage, Blair's fear of the mass-market media was still having a chilling effect on him just as it had at the start of his leadership.

But the sense he described of being overwhelmed by the demands of the news media and the torrent of information was becoming a common theme for politicians, and journalists, as well as anyone else trying to make sense of it all.

As Jean Baudrillard—one of those post-modern thinkers—had predicted years earlier, the media had created 'a world where there is more and more information, and less and less meaning.'[129]

Politics, communications and journalism were all exercises in simplifying a world that was necessarily more complex, removing the clutter of awkward nuance, selecting a few facts to tell a story and discarding the rest.

Four different political leaders who came to power either side of the Millennium—Clinton, Blair, Putin and Bush—were all trying to manage or control this flood of information. Putin used coercion to build a dam. Bush lingered in the shallows to avoid its impact. Blair and Clinton tried to surf the wave. None of them did much for public trust.

But the information age was no longer a struggle for control just between politics and press. Instead, from the depths of the internet, a surge of energy was building that would shake the battlefield on which they had been fighting. The world was changing faster than they knew, the ground was shifting under their feet and the games that had obsessed Westminster and Washington were beginning to look a bit 'last century'.

3

How Everyone Began to Lose Control

Monkeys, first pelts and fecal matter

A man dressed in a seven-foot tall monkey costume, pledging free bananas, got himself elected as mayor of Hartlepool in 2002. 'I didn't honestly expect to win,' he said after the vote. 'It was a bit of a laugh really.'[1]

Stuart Drummond was the mascot of the town's football club, Hartlepool United, also known as 'The Monkey Hangers' on account of a 200-year-old myth about how townsfolk had caught and killed an escaped primate they had mistaken for a French spy.

He had come up with the idea of standing for election at a freezing away game where previously the mascot—'H'Angus the Monkey'—had been ejected from the stadium for simulating sex with a woman steward in Scunthorpe.[2]

To be fair to Drummond, he swiftly shed the monkey costume, reneged on the banana pledge and became a successful independent mayor who won two more terms until the post was abolished.[3] But his initial victory was a sign that the distrust—even contempt—for the process of politics was beginning to permeate from the media into the ballot box.

At the same time as H'Angus the Monkey was becoming mayor, Jesse Ventura was completing his four-year term as the Governor of Minnesota in the United States. The former wrestler had made members of the press wear passes saying 'official jackal' to gain access to press conferences while supporters had bumper stickers that said: 'My Governor Can Beat Up Your Governor.'[4]

In between these two elections, both the media and elected political leaders had worked themselves into a lather about the Millennium 'Y2K' Bug that was supposed to create global chaos when computer systems failed at midnight on 1 January 2000. The British government told families to 'stock up on food'. The *Washington Post* warned it was a 'date with disaster'. In the event, nothing happened except for a tide gauge failing in Portsmouth.[5]

Journalists and politicians had demonstrated once again they did not understand new technology, just when the public were showing they were more distrustful towards both government and media that any time since polling began.

It was logical, therefore, that the revolt against both would begin to gather pace on the internet.

# # #

In the earliest years of this century, Strom Thurmond should have been a fading memory of a dark era in American politics. Way back in 1948 he had run for the US presidency on a platform for racial segregation, declaring: 'All the laws of Washington and all bayonets of the army cannot force the Negro into our homes, into our schools, our churches and our places of recreation and amusement.'

But it was a curious—if not astounding—feature of US politics that Thurmond was still a serving US Senator on 5 December 2002. It was his 100th birthday and there was snow on the ground outside the Dirksen Senate Office Building in Washington. Inside, the atmosphere was warm, sweetened with sentiment and sycophancy. The soon-to-be centenarian Senator had invited 500 guests to his birthday-cum-retirement party. Those present included Thurmond's family and friends from South Carolina, the nation's media, as well as some of his closest Republican colleagues like Bob Dole, the former presidential nominee, and Trent Lott, the Senate Majority Leader.

There was an enormous birthday cake with 100 candles that his children had to blow out for him, as well as jokes about Thurmond's unflagging libido and fondness for young women. A Marilyn Monroe impersonator serenaded the wheelchair-bound Thurmond with 'Happy Birthday' before smearing a lipstick kiss on his ancient forehead as he reached for her, with creepy pathos, with his right arm.

Lott told those gathered that his state of Mississippi had been 'proud' to vote for the segregationist fifty-four years previously, adding that if Thurmond had won 'and if the rest of the country had followed our lead, we wouldn't have had all these problems over the years, either.'[6]

The Senate Leader's apparent endorsement of Thurmond's segregationist campaign in 1948 was applauded by some and caused an audible intake of breath in others. It was carried live by TV but, with the exception of ABC News's Ed O' Keefe, none of the network or newspaper journalists reported it. There were other big news stories that day and Lott's comments were an uneasy fit for the type of tribute piece that most of the media present had gone along to file. Thurmond had softened his racism somewhat over the course of half a century and, by 2002, he was usually treated by the media more as a relic—a curiosity—than a living symbol of anything else.[7]

But this was not about Thurmond; this was a story about Lott. It only took off when liberal blogs like Talking Points Memo and Atrios picked it up and began phoning civil rights groups for reaction. Then conservative bloggers like Andrew Sullivan's The Daily Dish joined in and, eventually, so did the rest of the media. Within a fortnight Lott was forced to resign. 'Bloggers claim I was their first pelt and I believe that,' Lott later reflected, adding: 'I'll never read a blog.'

Sullivan, who had left newspaper journalism two years earlier to write his blog, wondered whether Washington's inside-track 'socialisation' had made it hard for journalists to 'pounce on people' like Lott who they 'know, like and need as a source.' It was, he said, an advantage for the blogosphere that 'we don't give a damn and, by and large, we say what we believe.'

# # #

It is a toss-up to decide whether the fate that befell Lott was better or worse than that dished out to his fellow Republican Senator, Rick Santorum. But it certainly wasn't 'respectful or nice'. In 2003, Santorum was trying to burnish his presidential credentials with Christian conservatives as a candidate who would oppose gay marriage. 'In every society, the definition of marriage has not ever to my knowledge included homosexuality. That's not to pick on homosexuality,' said Santorum. 'It's not, you know, man on child, man on dog, or whatever the case may be. It is one thing. And when you destroy that you have a dramatic impact on the quality.'

Dan Savage, a gay activist and syndicated sex columnist responded by attacking such a comparison of 'consensual gay sex with dog fucking and child rape.' A reader known only as 'SARS' then wrote to him suggesting a competition to define 'santorum'. In a similar fashion to the Lott scandal, the bloggers were determined to keep the controversy steaming even after newspapers and TV had moved on.

It's worth quoting SARS's letter in full:

> I'm a 23-year-old gay male who's been following the Rick Santorum scandal, and I have a proposal. Washington and the press seem content to let Santorum's comments fade into political oblivion, so I say the gay community should welcome this 'inclusive' man with open arms. That's right; if Rick Santorum wants to invite himself into the bedrooms of gays and lesbians (and their dogs), I say we 'include' him in our sex lives—by naming a gay sex act after him.

> Here's where you come in, Dan. Ask your readers to write in and vote on which gay sex act is worthy of the Rick Santorum moniker. It could be all forms of gay sex ('I pulled a Rick Santorum with my straight roommate in college'), or orgasm in a gay context ('We fooled around, and then I Rick Santorumed all over his face'), or maybe something weirder ('We've bought some broom handles, and we'll be Rick Santoruming all night'). You pick the best suggestions, and we all get to vote! And then, voilà! This episode will never be forgotten![8]

More than 3,000 suggestions later, Savage announced the winning neologism was 'the frothy mixture of lube and fecal matter that is sometimes the by-product of anal sex.' This became an early example of a 'meme'. Savage created a website, spreadingsantorum.com to promote the definition that, although mainstream news outlets would never refer to it, rose in the Google rankings as bloggers who posted Santorum-related news on the site or linked to it directly. By 2006, this new definition of Santorum had displaced his official website on Google as the top result when searching for his name and the Senator lost his seat by an 18-point margin to the Democrats' Bob Casey.

Two senior US senators had been taken down or publicly ridiculed to a point beyond redemption. The advent of Web 2.0 in the early years of this century meant that the production of news was no longer controlled entirely by newspapers and broadcasting organisations.

The internet was opening up a new frontier where talk was cheap, facts were free and opinions seemed to shoot from almost every lip. These outlaw bloggers were not interested in following what was left of the tattered rules by which politics and the media existed together.

Just look at what happened to Dan Rather. Having succeeded Walter Cronkite as the anchor of CBS Evening News in 1981, he was a national figure, as respected and as respectable as journalists come. On 8 September 2004, just two months before the US presidential election, he had big story about President Bush's military service in 1973 when he had avoided the killing fields of the Vietnam War for a cushy posting in the Texas National Guard. In a prime-time slot on the *60 Minutes* show, Rather revealed documents purporting to show that Bush's record of service had been 'sugarcoated' because of pressure from above.

But right-wing bloggers, particularly Charles Johnson of the mysteriously-named Little Green Footballs, fought back and showed that Rather's supposed scoop was probably a forgery that appeared to have been written with a 2004 Microsoft Word programme. CBS retracted the story, heads rolled and, within six months, Rather himself was retired from a programme he had anchored for almost a quarter of a century.[9]

Ken Mehlman, who managed the Bush campaign in 2004, described how the rules of the game were being upended. 'Technology has broken the monopoly of the three [TV] networks,' he said. 'Instead of having one place where everyone gets information there are now thousands of places.'

YOU have the power

The internet was not just being used just to challenge Republican senators or to shame famous journalists, it was also becoming an alternative route to political action that needed the endorsement of neither the traditional media nor political leadership.

On 15 February 2003, protesters staged the biggest demonstration London had ever seen in the hope of stopping the invasion of Iraq. The million-strong march in London was part of a co-ordinated effort involving more than 10 million people in cities around the world. It did not change the mind of Tony Blair or George Bush—the invasion went ahead the following month anyway—and many of those who protested in vain that day said they lost faith in not only the Labour government but also in the responsiveness of parliamentary democracy. But the left-wing activists who organised the march through the Stop the War coalition learnt digital lessons that more than a decade later would help them elect Jeremy Corbyn as Leader of the Labour Party and keep him there despite the disdain of the political and media establishment.

Lindsay German, convener of the Stop the War Coalition, was a member of the Socialist Workers Party where she had been used to operating at the margins of politics in dusty meetings of the committed, numbering perhaps a dozen people. But now she found herself smack bang at the heart of the action in a movement of millions. German marveled at the speed with which, by simply sending group emails, they were able to mobilise and exchange information instantly with tens of thousands of supporters without any recourse to the establishment media.

'Really it's astonishing how quickly so many people become *au fait* with the arguments. You've suddenly got thousands of people who say, "oh yeah, haven't you seen that the translation is wrong," or "no, no, no, that was refuted in *The New York Times*,"' said German. 'Twenty years ago, politics was all much slower, it's a different world.'[10]

Her colleague at the Stop the War Coalition, Robin Beste, added: 'We're continually saying it: "thank god for the internet." It's very difficult to get mainstream media to relate to us at all, but I don't care anymore. ... I don't expect anything from them, so if we get something that's just a bonus. And the reason why it doesn't trouble me anymore is because we do definitely have our own networks.' He suggested the internet could help groups like his to challenge the version of reality being pumped into our minds by newspapers and television. 'There's a whole climate of truth mainstream media has created that we feel we have to counter,' he said.[11]

Anti-war groups in the US were also breathlessly excited by the potential of the internet and the power of email lists. MoveOn.Org, an email group founded in 1998 to defend Bill Clinton against impeachment grew to more than 500,000 supporters by 2002 as opposition to George Bush's foreign policy began to gather steam. Al Gore described the ability of MoveOn to use online strategies as 'Twenty-first century techniques to breathe new life into our democracy.'[12]

Eli Pariser, the group's then International Director, would later lament how this dream of 'civic connection' had been imprisoned inside the endless online echo-chambers where people with different views live in parallel but separate universes.

But back in 2002, he believed the Web would cleanse everything that progressives like him loathed most about politics and the media. 'For a time it seemed that the internet was going to entirely redemocratise society,' wrote Pariser. 'Bloggers and citizen journalists would single-handedly rebuild the public media. Politicians would only be able to run with a broad base of support from small everyday donors. Local governments would become more transparent and accountable to their citizens.'[13]

And, if he needed any more reason to be optimistic, the US presidential campaign that began the next year showed for the first time that people organising on the internet had the capacity to shake the political establishment to its foundations.

# # #

Joe Trippi remembers arriving at Howard Dean's campaign headquarters above a Vermont bar in January 2003. There were few staff, a candidate barely registering in the polls, no real database except for the names of potential supporters 'scrawled on business cards, contact sheets, and scraps of paper and stuffed in a few shoeboxes.'[14] A few months' later, Dean was the frontrunner for the Democratic presidential nomination largely because Trippi's use of the internet to build a community of supporters around his anti-war message.

By today's standards, the Vermont governor's 75,000-strong army of 'Netroots' sounds insignificant. Back then, however, it was not only unprecedented but terrifying for conventionally wooden opponents like John Kerry.

They had gathered, initially out of sight of the media, through early social networks like Meetup.com. Even Dean himself later described how he was not that impressed by his first experience of these events in February 2003. 'There were about 60 people there—I don't remember where it was. But there was a sense this "internet thing" was starting and we were starting to raise some serious money.'

A month later he went to another: 'There were something like 575 people, in a line literally out the door and around the corner and down the back—about three quarters of a block was filled with people who couldn't get in. I realised that this was going to be something much bigger than I had ever thought it was going to be. I started saying, "You have the power," because I started understanding that this as coming from people. This was not a top-down movement. People were self-organising around a mission.'[15]

Dean smashed all records for online fundraising in that year, generating more than $20 million mainly from small donors compared to the $1.6m Bush had squeezed from the internet four years earlier or the paltry $10,000 Bill Clinton had managed eight years previously.[16] The key change he made was to recognise that internet audiences were polarised. Instead of angling his website to floating voters, he tailored the message on his website to energise and monetise the Democratic party's liberal base.

The internet was not yet dominant in any field—be it fundraising, organisation or the media. Eventually, the free-wheeling chaos and inexperience of the Dean campaign, as well as the candidate's own flaws, saw him crushed by Kerry in the battle for the Democratic nomination. In turn, Bush's big money donors, Fox News-fuelled fear of terror, and the aggressive TV ads from the Swift Boat Veterans falsely casting doubt on Kerry's Vietnam War heroics, were bigger factors in the 2004 presidential election than anything on the internet.

Nor was Dean the first outside candidate to come from nowhere to surge into a lead. But he was the first one to use the internet and, according to some of those who cut their teeth in 2004, there was a special excitement about this online insurgency that politics and the media have falteringly attempted to capture ever since. Kerry and Bush may have able to replicate the internet fundraising and emails lists but 'neither developed the same kind of open, generative community where people took ownership of their own ideas.'[17]

Yellow-toothed pansies

Back in London, that presidential election of 2004 was the cause of even more angst than usual at *The Guardian* newspaper. In those days, its journalists would often indulge dark moods by heading to the suitably depressing venue of the Coach and Horses around the corner from their old offices in Clerkenwell.

On one such evening in October 2004, they were sitting around in the pub complaining about how Bush's likely re-election in a few weeks' time would have huge consequences for Britain and the rest of the world. But they did not have a say in it. In a tight race, their future might depend on just a few thousand American voters living in a handful of swing states 4,000 miles away.

Then, of course, as more pints were pulled and stale crisps chewed, one of those present had an idea. In this new age of global connection and individual empowerment, why couldn't *The Guardian's* own indomitable liberal readers contact those American voters to tell them how people in Britain and the rest of the world thought they should vote?

Ian Katz, *The Guardian's* then features editor, got his team to work. There were only a few weeks to go but a couple of clicks on digital databases revealed Ohio as the crucial swing state in the presidential elections. And, in Ohio, the single most marginal district was somewhere called Clark County. In the previous contest four years before, it had been 'balanced on a razor's edge' of just 324 votes between Al Gore's Democrats and Bush's Republicans. A list of some 40,000 independent voters was duly compiled from Clark County records and a registration website set up to match each of them to individual *Guardian* readers who would be provided with one address each and encouraged to write to their new American pen pals direct.[18]

A few of the first letters were commissioned by the newspaper from the kind of cultural or literary figure that *The Guardian* thought might impress an undecided American. Each of those published was dripping in a special kind of old world condescension.

Lady Antonia Fraser, an historian and biographer, opened her missive with some lines of poetry from Ogden Nash before lecturing Ohio about why they really should vote 'against a savage militaristic foreign policy of pre-emptive killing.'

John Le Carré, the spy novelist, wrote: 'Probably no American president in all history has been so universally hated abroad as George W. Bush: for his bullying unilateralism, his dismissal of international treaties, his reckless indifference to the aspirations of other nations and cultures, his contempt for institutions of world government, and above all for misusing the cause of anti-terrorism in order to unleash an illegal war.'

Richard Dawkins, a much-venerated evolutionary biologist of the University of Oxford, declared: 'We in the rest of the world, who sadly cannot vote in the one election that really affects our future, are depending on you.' After a ritual attack on Blair for conniving in 'Bush's lies' Dawkins went on to compare the 'gunslinging' invasion of Iraq to the actions of Tony Martin, a Norfolk farmer who had shot dead a burglar in 1999, saying 'it's not how civilised countries, who follow the rule of law, behave.'[19] This last reference might have puzzled even those voters that had heard of Martin because, in this corner of Ohio as in much of non-urban America, they believe in shooting burglars. They also like firearms so much that the official Clark County logo depicts someone holding a flintlock rifle who, on closer inspection, turns out to be an American soldier in the war of independence against Britain.

The airmail letters may have been a bit old tech but, Katz mused, 'parts of America have become so isolationist that even the idea of individuals receiving letters from foreigners is enough to give politicians the collywobbles and, perhaps, in the digital age little acorns can turn into big trees very, very quickly.'[20]

He was right about the last bit at least. The response to Operation Clark County was notable for both a speed and scale that had everything to do with a digital age that was beginning to move more swiftly than newspapers ever could. Right-wing bloggers mobilised readers across America to vent their rage at this intrusion into the election and hijack the operation by registering to write to voters themselves. A hacker got into *The Guardian*'s registration website, forcing its closure after it had matched around 14,000 readers to Clark County voters. Dozens of *Guardian* journalists found their email inboxes coming under sustained bombardment with up to 700 hundred hate-filled messages from everyday American citizens.

Here is one of the choicer replies: 'Have you not noticed that Americans don't give two shits what Europeans think of us? You stupid, yellow-toothed pansies … I don't give a rat's ass if our election is going to have an effect on your worthless little life. I really don't. If you want to have a meaningful election in your crappy little island full of shitty food and yellow teeth, then maybe you should try not to sell your sovereignty out to Brussels and Berlin, dipshit. Oh, yeah—and brush your goddamned teeth, you filthy animals.'

Another asked: 'How secure is your building that contains all you morons??? Do you have enough security?? ARE YOU SURE??? Are you VERY sure??[21]

The story was inevitably—gleefully—picked up by Rush Limbaugh and Fox News in America, as well as other newspapers and broadcasters around the world. The global scorn and attention was such that Katz could not escape it even when he visited China that month. Taking his seat at the Shanghai Opera House, he made the mistake of telling the people sitting next to him that he was from *The Guardian*. 'Hah!' they replied, 'Clark County!'[22]

But the fuse for this explosion of world-wide fame was lit not by mainstream media but amateur and partisan writers operating in a blogosphere that had scarcely existed two years previously. Significantly, given what came later, they directed a kind of venom towards individual journalists that was different—both in quality and quantity—even to the kind of material produced by talk radio and Fox.

November's presidential election in 2004 saw Bush win Clark County on a big swing against his opponent John Kerry, and the key state of Ohio, to secure his second term in the White House. Local Republicans and rival newspapers in London were quick to claim that *The Guardian*'s intervention had worked decisively in Bush's favour. Kerry had held every one of the sixteen counties in Ohio that voted for Al Gore in 2000 except the one targeted by *The Guardian*.[23]

Katz himself dismissed the idea that it was *The Guardian* 'wot lost it' as 'self-aggrandising'. But he reflected on how 'a quixotic idea dreamed up last month in a north London pub had morphed into a global media phenomenon.' He said: 'Somewhere along the line the good-humoured spirit of the enterprise got lost in translation. It's easier perhaps for British readers to recognise that a project launched in *G2*—the same section which sought to save Tory leader Iain Duncan Smith by persuading him to pose in front of a poster which read, "It rained less under the Conservatives"—was not to be taken in deadly earnest.'

Operation Clark County had never been intended to save the world from a Bush second term so much as to amuse readers who were wellused to such gentle self-mocking jokes to make a serious point. But politics on the internet was already becoming a harsh and angry place. For many years afterwards, The Coach and Horses would be boarded up as it became crystal clear that the information age really was not conducive to gentle humour at all.

Vaffanculo Day

In Italy, the comedian Beppe Grillo, whose aggressive brand of satire had so offended political leaders that he had largely been denied a platform, began using his wildly popular—and populist—blog to take aim at corrupt politicians.

Throughout 2005 and 2006, his blog regularly updated a list of all holders of public office who had been convicted, launched an online petition to demand they were banned from politics, and crowd-financed full-page adverts in printed newspapers that called for the same. His blog became one of the ten most read in the world as well as spawning hundreds of grassroot groups using the same MeetUp website beloved of Dean supporters in the US.

This culminated in Grillo organising '*Vaffanculo* Day' ('Fuck You Day') in 2007. Hundreds of thousands of Italians in hundreds of town squares simultaneously screamed 'Vaffanculo' and raised their middle finger to Italy's ruling class. 'The idea of V-Day was to give a voice to those who don't have a voice,' said Grillo. 'Because the movement starts on the web, it starts from below. We need new blood, new words.'[24]

Just a few years later, such an injection of new words and blood would see Grillo's new populist party, The Five Star Movement, topping polls as it promised to deliver a direct democracy through online referenda that would do away with much of the state or any need for politicians all together. Five Star also echoed the 'voices from below' raised against 'gypsies', 'slitty-eyed' foreigners, 'terrorist' migrants and the European Union that had been largely been ignored in post-war Italy.[25]

But when the internet and the century were still young, in that time between the invasion of Iraq and the financial crash, there was much to relish. No longer were either pompous politicians or the puffed-up media able to control the message. It meant the authentic voice of real people could be used to inform debate, invigorate stale arguments and expose the ridiculous to ridicule. The internet was fearless, a bit lawless and, well, fun.

It is hard to imagine *The New York Times* promoting Savage's definition of 'santorum' competition itself or the likes of Beppe Grillo being able to organise 'Fuck You Day' without the internet. There seemed to be no question that this disruptive technology was tearing down old barriers, empowering people and wresting control from a creaking establishment.

In the final year of the twentieth century it was estimated that fewer than fifty blogs existed on the internet. By 2007 the tracking website Technorati said it a database of over 112 million blogs with a further 120,000 started every day.[26] 'Here Comes Everybody,' as Clay Shirkey put it in his influential book predicting that change would be wrought without needing the tools hoarded away by the powerful.

In America, liberal blogs like The Daily Kos, founded by Markos Moulitsas in 2002, or Instapundit, were pioneering an aggressive and partisan approach to politics that began reaching millions of people. The Huffington Post launched in 2005 as a liberal alternative to rightward leaning news aggregators like The Drudge Report as well as providing a platform to a virtual army of amateur unpaid bloggers.

By 2006 The Daily Kos had become so influential and popular that it was able to hold its own annual convention where Democratic presidential candidates from Hilary Clinton downwards came to kiss their ring. It earned a backhanded compliment from one of its targets, Bill O'Reilly of Fox News: 'There is not a more hateful group in the country than these Daily Kos people,' he said. 'And I'm including the Nazis and the Klan in here.'[27]

# # #

In Britain, the BBC had begun noticing that more and more content was flowing in from members of the public. It had used information from unsolicited emails and photographs sent in from people who had been in Thailand, Sri Lanka, Indonesia when the tsunami hit on 26 December 2004, when very few journalists were anywhere near the scene.

But it was not until suicide bombers attacked London tube trains and buses on 7 July 2005 that the BBC's grandly-titled User Generated Content hub came into its own. Most of the bombs had gone off underground, away from the news cameras, and the story could only be pieced together by studying some of the 20,000 emails and photographs sent in by commuters, passers-by, or 'citizen journalists' as they became known. 'Increasingly, audiences of all ages not only want a choice of what to watch and listen to when they want, they also want to take part, debate, create and control,' the BBC announced shortly afterwards.

The internet's energy even began revitalise a moribund Conservative Party after Tony Blair had won his third successive general election in 2005. Tim Montgomerie had studied the success of American bloggers—of both left and right—before setting up ConservativeHome.com that year. It swiftly became seen as the authentic voice of the Tory grassroots, offering a mixture of gossip, news, policy debate, exhortations to support particular causes and candidates, as well as unfiltered pieces from party activists.

ConservativeHome was more obviously partisan than even the most slavishly loyal Tory-supporting newspapers but also independent of the party organisation. One MP was quoted at the time saying it 'has almost replaced the party membership—I don't think I've looked at the official Conservative party website for about six months.'[28]

For a hierarchical and traditionally deferential organisation like the Conservatives this presented a challenge as well as an opportunity. Under David Cameron and George Osborne, the leadership was trying to mimic Tony Blair by modernising the party, and a reinvigorated activist base was regarded as essential for achieving that. But Montgomerie, an evangelical Christian who had grown up in an army family and determinedly lived outside London, was never fully signed up to such a project. Both he and his financial backers were wary of the metropolitan elitists running the party. Although there were specific issues like gay marriage when ConservativeHome challenged its readership, it generally served to confirm the bias of those who wanted a party with a more populist message on immigration, crime, welfare and above all, Europe.

The paradox was that the Conservative Party's membership was in long-term decline and ageing so rapidly that very few of them could be described as 'active' let alone 'activists'. But technology was ensuring that those who were active, internet-savvy and a little bit obsessive were more influential than they ever had been before.

Standing alongside Montgomerie in an increasingly febrile right-wing blogosphere were others including Iain Dale, a prolific writer and publisher of political books, as well as a perennially unsuccessful applicant for a safe Tory seat. His blog regularly harried the media, especially the BBC, when he thought it had not been tough enough on the Labour government.

One such post on 22 May 2006 had a measurable impact. Dale had written a piece chiding the 'mainstream media' for failing to follow up a small story in *The Mail on Sunday* about how Cherie Blair and Alastair Campbell had donated a signed copy of the Hutton Report for Labour Party fundraising. According to Dale this was a 'sick scandal' and an instance of Labour 'profiting from the death of Dr David Kelly.' He then followed up with another blog, illustrated with a picture of Downing Street and a pile of toilet rolls along. Under the headline: 'It's Up to the Blogs to Make it Hit the Fan', he made a request: 'I'd encourage everyone reading this who has a blog to post something on it and for people to encourage any journalists they know to write about it. The whole country should be demanding an apology from Cherie.'[29] No less than thirty-six other blog-gers linked to Dale's post, and broadsheets including *The Times*, *The Telegraph* and *The Financial Times* were shamed into reheating the original story. The issue was even raised at Prime Minister's Question Time.[30]

But the most jagged rock in Britain's right-wing blogosphere was Guido Fawkes, a blog started by a self-styled 'anarcho-libertarian' called Paul Staines who had spent much of his youth working as a spokesman for unlicensed raves, telling young Tory members to experiment with psychedelic drugs and being convicted for drunk driving.[31]

Although he claimed to have calmed down after having children, his blog—as its name suggests—appeared to delight not only in breaking the rules but was bent on trying to break the whole system. Beginning in 2004, initially anonymously, Staines's most productive period lasted until the end of the decade. He eventually lost some of his edge as the Conservatives returned to power and social media emerged as a primary political platform. Guido Fawkes was not necessarily meaner than *Private Eye*, which had been publishing gossip about journalists and politicians for decades but it was more deliberately destructive and ideological. Staines often acted as a slop-bucket for Westminster journalists who could not get stories substantiated or published in their newspapers[32] and much of the time he was merely reheating it with the addition of spice and seasoning. But on other occasions the information he got hold of allowed him to claim some notable scalps—including that of at least one Cabinet minister, as well as Gordon Brown's most trusted aide in Downing Street. Although his targets were usually on the left and what he called the 'liberal establishment', Staines despised politics as a whole. 'I wanted to undermine politicians on their moral high horse,' he said. 'It was to highlight hypocrisy because they are a bunch of sleazy, under-hand lowlifes. I don't think that's generalising.'[33]

Below the line

Back at *The Guardian*, experiments with reader empowerment did not stop after the debacle of Clark County, Ohio. For several years it had been trying to bridge the gap between those who wrote the news and the citizen consumers of its journalism. Alan Rusbridger, *The Guardian*'s editor, had appointed a Reader's Ombudsman to act as an independent champion of anyone who felt they had been wronged by the newspaper.

This was a significant culture change for an industry where journalists had been taught to minimise contact with readers and avoid making corrections if at all possible. In the first decade of this century I was working at *The Times* where there was one colleague who delighted in transferring angry telephone calls to the staff canteen 'where they don't speak English.' Nutty letters could be quickly identified and transferred to the bin without even being opened if the envelope had traces of green ink, masking tape or, worst of all, glue. A very few letters to the editor, usually from people with a high degree of expertise or authority, would be selected for publication.

But Ian Mayes, *The Guardian*'s first Reader's Ombudsman, treated everyone as equally deserving of respect. His corrections and clarifications column, suffused with a gentle humour, became one of the most popular features of the newspaper. One from 2004 said: 'In a column headed "Save us from the armchair generals", the writer, having referred to the matter of gay people in the armed forces, noted that "former admiral of the fleet Peter Norton-Hill, has gone a little quiet on the subject." That is because he died in May this year.' The number of complaints and inquiries rose steadily from 5,000 a year to more than 20,000 because readers felt they were more likely to get redress. Books were published with the best corrections, T-shirts printed, and the relationship blossomed.

In March, 2006, *The Guardian* sought to extend this philosophy so that it was not just '*on* the web but *of* the web.' The newspaper launched its opinion website, the title of which was a quote from C. P. Scott, who edited the newspaper for almost sixty years, 'Comment is free'. Mayes says the idea of the site was intended as an 'extension of democracy' where everyone could have their voice heard no matter who they were.[34] In addition to an expansion in the number of written pieces, every article was opened to comments which could be anonymous and would appear on the site within seconds, unmoderated and unmediated by anyone.

All this seemed very exciting. The wisdom of crowds could correct errors of fact, powerful journalists could be held to account for their mistakes, and opinions formed inside the establishment balanced by readers outside it. Several newspapers had already opened up their articles to comments from readers but most operated a system by which moderators would view them before they were published or restricted the practice to a limited number of subjects. The BBC's 'Have Your Say' comments section strictly limited which topics could be commented upon to a few dozen a day and often these were pre-moderated with fewer than half of all messages sent being published.[35] Critics said the BBC was being too cautious and pointed out that real democratic engagement had to be more than merely encouraging viewers to send in pictures of the weather.[36]

By contrast, *The Guardian*'s anonymised free-for-all forum was a place where you could comment on everything and anything as often as you liked. Posts were only moderated if another reader complained. The egalitarian ethos extended to how they were presented: none appeared in green ink and all were given equal prominence whether they were written by an eminent professor, a serial killer, or an amateur sleuth who wanted to expose the Government deepest secrets.

One such person was Robert Lewis who set out to write a biography of David Kelly, the government scientist found dead in the middle of the British government's Iraq War crisis in 2003. Lewis described how he had joined that 'disaffected legion of disbelievers who spent their nights trawling chat rooms and internet forums…there were a lot of us about, conspiracy theories were inevitable.'[37]

A decade later, when *Dark Actors* was finally published, Lewis declared in an article for *The Guardian* that, much to his own surprise, he had written a 'tale bereft of heroes.' Dr Kelly, he concluded, had killed himself rather than been murdered by vengeful and panicked intelligence chiefs.[38]

But scroll down below the line of Lewis's article and there are dozens of comments expressing incredulity about the defection of one of their own. And, of course, they insist that Kelly was murdered. Robin Cook was murdered too, says another, the KGB has admitted it. One, inevitably anonymous, comment from someone calling themselves 'nocausetoadopt' states: 'If I do not believe anything that Governments say why should I believe this account to be true?'[39]

While those who did not believe anything were still in a minority, it was also true that they were much less likely to trust either government or the media. The information age was giving voice to an impatient freedom that was louder than before: people were no longer willing to wait for the official news to be briefed by politicians, interpreted for them by journalists, and hammered down in black ink on paper before being delivered to their doorstep or broadcast at a set time each day.

The internet, with its proliferation of blogs and message boards, meant that news or even truth itself had taken on a more ephemeral or will-o'-

the-wisp quality in which people could go out and chase it—even write it—for themselves. And the number of comments received every day by *The Guardian* soared to 20,000 a day, then 40,000, and eventually 65,000 or more. Similarly, the complaints pouring in to moderators about the comments published below the line from readers reporting abuse or hate speech were measured no longer in dozens each day but thousands.

Mayes acknowledges in his under-stated way, 'the whole process did present a bit of challenge to our liberal values.'[40] On certain subjects, in particular, *The Guardian*'s comments below the line became a deafening cacophony of loud voices and polarised opinion.

Within a decade, *The Guardian* had received no less than 70 million comments below the line, 1.4 million of which were subsequently removed by moderators. A detailed analysis of these had disturbing results for the newspaper: 'The ten regular writers who got the most abuse were eight women—four white and four non-white—and two black men. Two of the women and one of the men were gay. And of the eight women in the 'top 10', one was Muslim and one Jewish. And the ten regular writers who got the least abuse? All men. Conversations about crosswords, cricket, horseracing and jazz were respectful; discussions about the Israel/Palestine conflict were not, while articles about feminism attracted very high levels of blocked comments. And so did rape.'[41]

Becky Gardiner, the newspaper's former Comment Editor who oversaw the study, says: 'Some of our writers were taken aback by just how horrible it all was when we introduced below the line comments. I think they may have had this idea that people would just comment to say how much they had enjoyed reading the story and that's not really what happened. The problem was not just the unpleasantness, it was also that it was being doled out unequally. What we thought would break down differences in power between journalism and readers was reproducing it in different forms.'[42]

Too many readers seemed to shed all their inhibitions when they commented below the line. But above the line, some journalists were becoming inhibited about how people would react below. For them, clicking on the comments section was too often like overturning a stone where, alongside many thoughtful and intelligent comments, all manner of life forms in a slime containing misogynists, holocaust-deniers, jihadists, Islamophobes and just about every other kind of phobe. These new online town squares were not always places for Socratic debate but abuse, conspiracy and bullying by a mob that would sometimes drown out quieter voices.

Other newspapers also began to encounter difficulties. During the UK budget in May 2009, *The Telegraph* published unfiltered tweets—a so-called 'twitterfall'—directly on to its website. Within minutes, some users were posting offensive comments instead of crowd-sourced economic wisdom. 'So if I say Budget 2009 and big shitty balls in my tweet I'll appear on the *Telegraph* website,' wrote one who got a place on the homepage of one of Britain's most respectable newspapers. Julian Sambles, head of audience development at *The Telegraph* later described the experiment as 'a disappointment'.[43]

Many newspaper and media websites now severely restrict comments below the line or have scrapped the system all together. If people want a fight, they can find one on social media easily enough without it spilling over into attacking journalists. Popular Science closed down comments on articles because they 'tend to be a grotesque reflection of the media culture surrounding them, so the cynical work of undermining bedrock scientific doctrine is now being done beneath our own stories.'[44]

# # #

The proliferation of blogs, user-generated content and below the line comments in the first years of this century gave everyone the chance to register their opinion. But it was so instantaneous and easy that there already signs of people posting first and thinking later, if they ever thought at all. Abuse became normalised as the information superhighway became a mixture of *Wacky Races* and *Fury Road*.

Jessica Valenti, an American feminist writer who often receives vicious comments and violent threats when she appears in print, describes the pressure journalists are under: 'Imagine going to work every day and walking through a gauntlet of 100 people saying "you're stupid", "you're terrible", "you suck", "I can't believe you get paid for this." It's a terrible way to go to work.' She complains of a "mob mentality," adding: "To get to that place where you are used to being called a cunt every day is a terrible thing to get used to, that does something to who you are."[45]

Another *Guardian* journalist, Nesrine Malik, said it had changed the way she wrote, not necessarily for the better, because she is now 'very aware of the audience and of the gallery.' The advice she was given was to defuse anger by engaging with those commenting but that, too, can be an unsettling experience. 'They see you "below the line" and say, "She's here! She's here!" so the whole debate becomes with you rather than the article you wrote.' But Malik said it was worth keeping comments open and suggested journalists themselves, above the line, had sometimes provoked the street fights below. 'We're guilty of sharpening the tone of the conversation,' she said, because 'everyone wants as many hits as possible, as much traffic as possible.'[46]

Becky Gardiner goes further still. She believes the boiling anger sometimes seen below the line reflects the 'disconnect' between elite London-centric columnists and the humble reader. 'If you read these comments, people are saying no one is listening to them so they shout and scream to get heard,' she says. 'I would never condone the unforgiveable sexist and racist attacks some people make down there but I do think we need to ask sometimes why they are so angry.' A decade later, Gardiner believes it was possible to predict the success of the Leave campaign or of Jeremy Corbyn simply by reading below the line. 'All the journalists were writing off these comments below the line as being from mad people who don't represent our readers or the voters,' she says. 'And then they voted.'[47] Or, as one witticism had it when Donald Trump first set his sights on the White House, 'it's like the comments section running for President.'

It is important not to lose sight of how technology liberated everyone—be they gay teenagers in the American mid-West or bloggers fighting to tell the truth about Putin's Russia—from a single mediated explanation of the world. Political activists of both left and right were breathing fresh democratic life into their parties. Journalists were finally discovering that they were not just there to hold the establishment to account—they were often the establishment themselves and they, too, would be held to account.

In 2006 *Time* put a mirror on its front cover announcing its Person of the Year. It said: 'For seizing the reins of the global media, for founding and framing the new digital democracy, for working for nothing and beating the pros at their own game, *Time*'s Person of the Year for 2006 is you.' Or, as its cover put it, 'YOU, yes you. You control the information age. Welcome to your world.'[48]

What readers of the magazine were not told, however, is that it is unhealthy to stare at the mirror for too long. Sometimes, the internet was connecting people so they learnt to understand or like each other more. But they were just as likely to disappear deeper into their screens where relations with others were often corrosive and unpleasant.

And, if the millions of comments being deposited at the bottom of stories can be seen as a gauge or even a pressure valve for public opinion, it was also becoming clear that otherwise reasonable members of the public behave differently online.

Trolls and the Lulz

The famous 1993 *New Yorker* cartoon, 'on the internet, nobody knows you're a dog,' has long since illustrated the way many people understood anonymity and privacy on the web. Although, of course, system operators and platforms know a great deal about you, someone reading what you have written on the internet usually does not.

Psychologists such as John Suler have labelled this the 'disinhibition effect.'[49] It can be benign, enabling generous strangers to reach out across oceans in times of disaster or disclose feelings that might otherwise gnaw away inside. But it can be very toxic too. Below the line, people felt less constrained about expressing hostility or feel able to take on personalities that that are quite different from their own.

On the internet, you are invisible, you can grievously insult someone and you don't need to look them in the eye. You can run away—even switch your computer off—before anyone reacts. You can be making a lot of noise on a forum, but it's contained in a machine and all around you is silent.

Some regard what they write as a kind of game with different rules to real life, in the sense that it does not really matter if you hurt a person's feelings any more than it does if you crash your car on *Super Mario* or shoot a cop on *Grand Theft Auto*. People who might clap politely if they heard a speech in a hall from a famous politician or nod their heads when listening to a boring neighbour, can shout 'Fuck You!' or '*Vaffanculo!*' before popping upstairs to read their children a good night story.

Maybe they always wanted to shout 'Fuck You!' and the internet finally enabled them to do so. Perhaps it was the internet and the cloak of anonymity it offered that changed them. But either way—and it was almost certainly a bit of both—what should have been a window into the world was being crowbarred open.

Climbing inside were the extreme and the angry, people with too much time on their hands who believe stuff about secret states or assassination plots. And, long before everyone became obsessed with internet trolls, they were already flooding in to the mainstream media's comments below the line and then onto new message boards.

Appropriately enough, given how trolls like an argument, even the origin of the term is disputed. Some think refers to the dwarf-like demons of Norse legend who lurk in dank and dark places waiting to pounce on passers-by. Others suggest it is derived from the fishing term, trawling, because so much of it is designed to be like a baited hook on which to catch a reaction.[50]

# # #

The internet's capital of trolling was 4chan. Founded in 2003, it became an online playground with virtually no rules where almost everyone was anonymous but, according to 4chan's own statistics, were largely American or British young college-educated males with a nerdy interest in hacking, video games and Japanese anime.[51]

It has spawned a huge number of internet memes, the politically-motivated hacktivist group Anonymous, and straight-forward pranks that made the likes of Bill O'Reilly on Fox News look even more ridiculous than usual. On one occasion, after he fulminated against 4chan as a 'slimy scummy website', its users began cranking out its 'internet love machine' sending him thousands of incoherent messages of praise and, after someone posted his home address, many orders of takeaway pine-apple and pepperoni pizzas.[52]

Another example is from 2007 when 4chan users in the US picked up on a story from Zambia, where desperately poor children were suppos-edly getting cheap highs by breathing the fumes of 'Jenkem' made from fermented urine and fecal matter. Posters on 4chan then urged each other to send letters to local high school principals pretending to be a worried parent saying it was 'only a matter of time' before one of their pupils died of Jenkem poisoning. Success was achieved when Fox News, despite finding no evidence of Jenkem use anywhere, began imploring parents to be vigilant against what use of what it said was being called 'butt hash'.[53]

Much of what trolls do is motivated simply by 'lulz', a corruption of the text abbreviation 'Laugh Out Loud', in which they celebrate the anguish of their victims, who might be each other or the media—but also can include completely innocent bystanders such as the family of a murdered child.[54]

One such case was the way 4chan's troll army ridiculed the outpouring of online grief surrounding the rape and murder of Chelsea King, a blond Californian teenager, in 2009. Demands for nude pictures of the girl, or obscene threats to rape and kill those defending her memory, swiftly followed.[55] There are countless other terrible instances of cyber-bullying and harassment that have begun on 4chan where its notorious /b/ or /pol/ boards contain vast amounts of violent, racist, misogynistic, pornographic and sometimes paedophilic material.[56]

The light and dark side of 'lulz' sums up the conflicted relationship that many have with the internet. Techniques include 'doxxing' when a victim's contact details or addresses are published online, or 'swatting' when a hoax call is made to police telling them a hostage is being held at someone's home. What sometimes appears iconoclastic and liberating is only a click away from the malign or the horrific.

And some of most gruesome images that could be found on the internet began to appear on screens in these years. The beheading videos of Western hostages that Abu Musab al-Zarqawi popularised in 2004 were never shown by mainstream broadcasters but were downloaded by millions of people around the world. Some observers compared these 'primal, obscene and gratuitous' videos to those of violent hard-core internet pornography.[57]

But it was also possible to compare the terrorists' videos with the activities of the 4chan trolls. Both were trying to shock and elicit a reaction from other people that they could mock and defy.

Like blotting paper, the media, politics and society as a whole was absorbing the darkest material from below the line and the depths of the internet. Conventions were being tested and norms challenged. And all this was happening amid an existing battle for control of information as the world became more complex and difficult to understand.

When the US government responded by launching a YouTube channel where words of condemnation were superimposed over graphic images of ISIS's brutality, it underlined how the old men at the Pentagon failed to understand how young alienated recruits were drawn to beheading videos precisely because of their capacity to outrage the most powerful nation on Earth.[58]

Governments around the world, but particularly the US, were equally cack-handed in their response to Julian Assange's WikiLeaks which, from

November 2006, appeared to symbolise the way the liberalisation of information threatened to undermine the powerful.

# # #

Tony Blair had always instinctively tried to embrace the modernity of the information age. But, as his power ran out, Blair described how he had always clung the hope that 'help was on the horizon' and that new technology would dilute the power of traditional media. 'In fact,' he said, 'the new forms can be even more pernicious, less balanced, more intent on the latest conspiracy theory multiplied by five.'[59]

One small symbol of this involved the fate of a press officer in Blair's Downing Street who had left colleagues feeling disturbed by watching a beheading video on his work computer. When asked to switch it off, he refused, saying it was necessary to understand what was going on. A few days later, it was decided he could no longer work for the prime minister and he was moved elsewhere in the Civil Service.

As far as I know this story was never written about, even on blogs, partly because of the individual's close links with members of the Lobby. And yet I have always wondered about it: this was not illegal activity and there was no suggestion the press officer was engaged in anything other than genuine research. But Blair's media team, who had for so long prided themselves on being on the cutting edge of communications, recoiled from such material being dredged from the internet in front of them. 'We didn't know what to do,' recalls one of his bosses at the time, 'we didn't have a procedure for it so we secured a sort of managed departure.' They did not want it in their world. There was nothing politicians could do to stop it and broadcasters refused to show it but it was there anyway; they had lost control.

Beheading videos were the ultimate, darkest form of a kind of TV that had been sweeping all before it. The start of the new millennium saw an explosion of reality TV shows like *Big Brother*, *Pop Idol*, *The Kardashians* and, of course, *The Apprentice* which, in its US format, starred Donald Trump.

The powerful were initially confused about how to respond to some of these shows, which appeared to mimic democracy. In Britain, commentators wrung their hands over the prospect of distracted young people being more likely to vote in *The X Factor* than in general elections. In China, conversely, the government worried it might encourage too much voting. Beijing officials banned *Super Girl*, a local imitation of *Pop Idol*, after its 2005 season drew an audience of around 400 million people and 8 million text message votes.

But reality TV had a deeper relationship with the way politics, the media and people themselves were changing in the information age. Those watching hoped to glimpse something authentic about themselves, unscripted by the powerful, who had long since fed us our information. For those taking part, there was the chance to be contributors, creators who expose their inner life like bloggers do. Running through both TV and internet habits was a sense of energy that contrasted with the decline in election voting and newspaper readership. There was a demand for more immediate access to more information and more say over what would happen next.

Within a few years, serving MPs would start appearing on reality TV shows like *I'm A Celebrity, Get Me Out of Here* or *Big Brother*. Within a decade, a reality TV star who hosted the American version of *The Apprentice* would win the US presidency.

Blair himself won another term in Downing Street in the 2005 General Election with a strategy inspired by the individual empowerment 'real people' got on such shows or from writing blogs. The previous two Labour victories had been characterised by an exceptional level of message discipline. In the 2001 election, for instance, Blair's worst moment had been an unscripted confrontation with a voter called Sharron Storer outside the Birmingham hospital where her husband was being treated. The prime minister had looked panicked at the idea real life might intrude on the theatre of his campaign.

But Blair's victory in 2005, coming after the deeply unpopular war in Iraq and the Hutton Inquiry, saw him actively seeking more of such confrontation. Alastair Campbell christened the plan to win a third victory, his 'masochism strategy'. The political commentator Andrew Rawnsley described the Labour team's satisfaction as Neil from West Sussex demanded, 'How do you sleep at night, Mr Blair?' or Maria from Essex became so animated by her fury that she leapt out of her seat at the prime minister who was just feet away from her in a live TV studio.

Rawnsley wrote: 'Among the many things that make him the most consummate communicator of his era is Tony Blair's grasp of the celebritisation of culture and how politics can be adapted to it. For the fallen celeb, the route to rehabilitation can involve submitting to a dose of ritual humiliation presided over by Ant and Dec. For a prime minister trying to re-establish his credibility with alienated voters, redemption is sought from a tongue-lashing on TV. Mr Blair is doing the political equivalent of bushtucker trials. It is a case of "I'm A Prime Minister … Keep Me In There."'[60]

Blair was tapping into the authenticity bestowed by the unscripted interaction that we all saw on such shows or got from the internet. It enabled him to draw some final drops of trust from the electorate. But it was also a capitulation to chaos from a leader who had for long sought control of information—and now knew that battle could not be won.

Part Two

The Rise of the Alternative

4

Disablement and Dependency in the Media

They came from Nerdistan

At the end of 2007, Google News published a list of the ten most popular searches that had been made that year:

1. American Idol
2. YouTube
3. Britney Spears
4. 2007 cricket World Cup
5. Chris Benoit
6. iPhone
7. Anna Nicole Smith
8. Paris Hilton
9. Iran
10. Vanessa Hudgens

These were very different from the headlines in the old media that year. In America, these were dominated by the surge of US troops into Iraq and Barack Obama launching his historic bid for the US presidency. In Britain, Gordon Brown became prime minister and there was a run on the banks when Northern Rock was suddenly unable to re-pay loans. Across the world, there was fascination with Britney Spears who checked out of rehab to get all her hair shaved off because she was 'tired of everyone touching me'—which explains why she was third in the list

107

behind a Reality TV talent show and a video platform that Google itself had just purchased.

But it is the sixth search term on the list, and what it tells us about what was happening to digital technology, that would arguably be the most significant development that year.

On 9 January 2007 Steve Jobs unveiled Apple's take on the smart-phone—the iPhone—which would put more computing power than NASA had at its disposal during the Apollo missions straight into the hands of millions upon millions of people.[1] To date, Apple is estimated to have sold over 1.2 billion iPhones.[2] It was the year when use of Facebook and Twitter exploded across the world, when software advances enabled Big Data and cloud computing, when Kindle, GitHub, Android and Airbnb were launched, when the cost of sequencing a human genome fell from almost $100m to barely $1 million, when Intel introduced non-Silicon materials into microchip transistors, and when IBM's Watson computer showed Artificial Intelligence was no longer science fiction.

In his book, *Thank You for Being Late*, Thomas Friedman makes a convincing case for 2007 being 'one of the greatest technological inflection points in history.'[3] This was the Great Acceleration when the world was being reshaped faster than businesses, communities and governments could adapt; when people felt they were losing control.

The speed of technological change also brought a sense of unease to journalists, who were expected to observe, report or opine on such big developments. Coverage of technology in these years was often in breathless producer-friendly accounts. However, as so often in the narcissistic media industry, the real alarm being felt was not so much about the future of the world than about the future of newspapers and journalism. A slow-dawning realisation was creeping across newsrooms that they might be the last generation to have their words printed on paper.

Denis Finley, the respected editor of *The Virginian-Pilot*, said in 2007: 'I feel I'm being catapulted into another world, a world I don't really understand. It's scary because things are happening at the speed of light. The sheer speed [of change] has outstripped our ability to understand it all.'[4] Seven years later Finley quit his job citing the 'tremendous pressure' of overseeing staff cuts that had halved the size of his newsroom.[5]

Even Rupert Murdoch was struggling. He had invested $580 million in buying the social network, MySpace, as part of a plan for young people to access journalism 'on any platform that appeals to them—mobile phones, hand-held devices, iPods, whatever'—in what he described as a 'golden age of information'. But those comments, made during a 2006 speech in London, were mixed with a sense of foreboding: 'Power is moving away from the old elite in our industry—the editors, the chief executives and, let's face it, the proprietors,' he said. 'It is difficult, indeed dangerous, to underestimate the huge changes this revolution will bring or the power of developing technologies to build and to destroy—not just companies but whole countries.'[6] Within a few years Murdoch sold MySpace for just $35 million, after it had been eclipsed and destroyed by Facebook.

Media executives across the world were boasting they would become digitally-driven news organisations. Arthur Ochs Sulzberger, the publisher and chairman of the New York Times Company, said in February 2007, 'I really don't know whether we'll be printing The [New York] Times in five years, and you know what? I don't care.' His comments, inevitably made at the World Economic Forum in Davos, were intended to show his bravado embrace of technology. But, as the Pew Project for Excellence in journalism commented that year, 'his statement, like the industry, seemed to teeter between boldness and uncertainty.'[7] In the US, investors were getting nervous, with Morgan Stanley among those criticising Sulzberger's company after the share price of The New York Times fell by nearly 50 per cent in four years.

The internet was ravaging the advertising revenue which newspapers had long relied on, while income from selling papers was also falling dramatically as readers—especially the younger ones—began migrating online. And no one really had a clue how they were going to monetise a website readership that was getting its news for free.

Revenue from small ads, 'the classified section', had provided American newspapers with more than a third of their income at the start of the century. But a single, ugly-looking website that began as an email circular to a group of friends in San Francisco was spreading like a virus across the US—ten cities by 2000, eighteen by 2003 and thirty-two by 2004. Everywhere it went newspapers' profits plummeted. Revenue from classified ads in the US fell from $19.6 billion in 2000 to just $4.6 billion twelve years later: a drop of about 77 percent in little more than a decade.[8]

At the convention of the American Society of Newspaper Editors in 2006, a photograph of Craig Newmark was flashed up and the audience was asked if they knew who he was. Very few hands went up. But his website, Craigslist.org, was selling everything newspapers had once sold, plus casual sex and prostitution, usually without charging vendors a penny. 'The shocking thing is that this was someone who was not only a threat to steal their business but was in the process of doing it," said Jay Rosen, a Professor of Journalism at New York University. 'What industry could survive in which you don't know the name of the person who is taking away your business? They're mystified. They don't know who this guy is and where he came from. And it just shows—that it's easier for Craig to learn journalism than it is for these guys to learn the Web.'[9]

Just as most journalists had tried to keep themselves insulated from direct contact with their readers or viewers, they had also showed little interest in the other set of customers, advertisers, who provided the money that paid their wages. I landed my first job at the age of 18 cold-calling local businesses to sell them overpriced ads for the now defunct *Oxford Journal*, but I never once spoke to a journalist. A few years later when I became a journalist myself, I scarcely spoke to anyone in an advertising department that was kept strictly separate from editorial. Even now I don't quite know why. The high-minded types will tell you it was because journalism should not be tainted by commercial pressures and mixing too freely with the people selling adverts might compromise professional integrity. I suspect people from the advertising department concluded we were just snobs.

But there was another reason why the media did not see Craigslist coming: this was not only about advertising, it was also about computing. By Newmark's own account, people like him came from 'Nerdistan'. As a child he put quantum physics ahead of popularity, 'didn't realise that wearing thick black glasses taped together and a pocket protector was not attractive'[10] and had 'some problems getting along with other kids.'[11] The children who grow up to be journalists would not generally notice the boy in the corner who is good at coding unless they wanted him to explain how to make their computers work.

They should have paid more attention, because those kids from Nerdistan were bulldozing the foundations of print journalism. After the likes of Craigslist destroyed classified advertising, then came Google and Facebook.

Google had started as an academic project at Stanford University in 1996 to rank the importance of different websites in internet searches at a time when its founders, Larry Page and Sergey Brin, still disapproved of the corrupting potential of advertising. In an academic article they wrote two years later, extolling the virtues of their new system, they warned: 'Advertising funded search engines will be inherently biased towards the advertisers and away from the needs of consumers.'[12] But, as the new century began, they needed money to scale their business and launched Google's AdWords system to sit alongside searches, almost as a service to help people find what they were looking for. And, in the years to come, Google found it could be even more helpful with AdSense that targeted adverts according to location, previous searches and a whole ocean of other data users were making available. Income rose from $40 million in 2001 to $10 billion in 2006 to $55 billion in 2013.[13]

Newspapers were not losing only classified adverts but also the bigger display ads that were so lucrative. By the 2010s much of this revenue began going to Facebook that saw revenues shoot upwards from $764 million to 2009, to $7 billion in 2013, $11.5 billion in 2014, and $17 billion in 2015.[14] Mark Zuckerberg, its founder, had initially resisted making the same mistake of rivals like MySpace in having too many adverts, damaging the user experience. But, having seen off the competition, and with access to data on users' location and searches through their smartphones, Facebook had a tool that could target adverts back to those phones with a precision never seen before on a site that was proving addictive to hundreds of millions—then billions—of users the world over.

The old print media saw revenues crash. Advertising income for US newspapers fell from $63.5 billion in 2000 to about $23 billion in 2013. In the UK too, advertising revenue almost halved over this timeframe.

The big tech companies themselves take a pretty robust line on all this. Some of them privately point out that newspaper owners could be pretty ruthless and should not expect too much sympathy just because someone had invented a more competitive product.

When I visit Google's Mountain View headquarters in Silicon Valley, Richard Gingras, the company's Vice President, tells me: 'Frequently I hear the statement that the challenges in the newspaper business were because of Google and Facebook. That's not factually correct. What happened? The internet changed the marketplace of information. ... The advertising market moved with those behaviours. ... Some in the industry have adapted—and others have not.'

What few would deny, however, is that a hugely competitive, immensely powerful and often highly lucrative newspaper industry was, by the end of the first decade in this century, looking like it was holed beneath the waterline; the computer technology that had helped revive print journalism in the last years of the twentieth century was now threatening to scupper it.

The lingering prestige of media brands meant big deals were still being done. For all Murdoch's gamble on MySpace, the business he really understood was newspapers and in April 2007 he overcame entrenched opposition to buy the *Wall Street Journal* for an eye-watering $5 billion. Two years later Murdoch announced an $8.4 billion write-down, a $6.4 billion quarterly loss and NewsCorp stock was worth about 60 per cent less than it had been before. Far from being the ruthless exploiter of technology he once was, or the tycoon boldly embracing the digital future he had hoped to be, some people thought Murdoch was sentimentally pumping his fortune into a failing industry. Yes, he might have a reputation as a wrecker of standards over the years, but he was at least 'a newspaper man'.

This is how *The New Yorker* described him in 2009: 'Murdoch is accorded a sneaking gratitude for his willingness to make heavy investments in the newspaper business, at a time when everybody else seems to be disinvesting. Who cares if he's not being rational?'[15]

The alternative to an old-fashioned media mogul like Murdoch was the likes of Sam Zell, a billionaire property developer, who paid $8.2 billion in 2007 for a highly leveraged takeover of a sprawling media empire that included the *Los Angeles Times*, *Orlando Sentinel*, and *Chicago Tribune*. Some people wondered how he ever planned to make his money back. Zell delivered a speech to *Sentinel* staff setting out plans to shift the newspapers into a much more ruthless white-knuckled commercial operation that would leave their jobs on the line. He then had this exchange with one of his journalists:

> Zell: I want to make enough money so I can afford you. You need to, in effect, help me by being a journalist that focuses on what our readers want and therefore generate more revenue.

> Journalist: But what readers want are puppy dogs. We also need to inform the community.

> Zell: I'm sorry, you're giving me the classic, what I would call, journalistic arrogance of deciding that puppies don't count. Hopefully we get to the point where our revenue is so significant that we can do puppies and Iraq, okay?

There was laughter from some of the audience and a smattering of applause from his acolytes as the new owner turned away and muttered something, words that were caught only by the camera.

Zell: Fuck you.[16]

Dark light from a dying star

Throughout this period there were, of course, endless laments about the finances of the media and the future of journalism in the digital age. But what was strange was how few extrapolated out from their own plight to think what this digital revolution meant for the rest of the country or the world.

Friedman asks why it was that he—like so many others—completely missed the significance of 2007, this seemingly 'innocuous year'. His answer was simple: 2008. 'Yes, right when our physical technologies leapt ahead … all of the rules, regulations, institutions and social tools people needed to get the most out of this technological acceleration and cushion the worst—froze or lagged. In the best of times social technologies have a hard time keeping up with physical technologies, but with the Great Recession of 2008 and the political paralysis it engendered, this gap turned into a chasm. A lot of people got dislocated in the process.'[17]

And some of the most dislocated people on the planet were those in the media who had been swaggering around for the previous couple of decades as if they owned them. The financial crisis in 2008 was the trigger for the bloodletting to begin in earnest on newspapers. Zell blamed the chaos on Wall Street as his Tribune Company duly tipped into bankruptcy in 2009, listing debts of $13 billion. More than 4,200 people have lost jobs with the company since the purchase, while resources for the newspapers and television stations owned by the group have been slashed.[18]

Jobs in newspapers began to disappear across much of the world and the redundancies continued long after the economy as a whole stabilised. Although there are no definitive figures, it is estimated that staff numbers in newsrooms shrank by a third in the US, from 55,000 jobs in daily newspapers in 2007 to 38,000 by 2013.[19] And in the UK the number of jobs in mainstream journalism is said to have fallen by a similar proportion—between 27 and 33 per cent—between 2001 and 2010.[20] In both countries, these cuts began to eat into budgets for expensive foreign coverage, in-depth political coverage or investigative journalism.

Even as the world was becoming more inter-connected through a globalised economy and information system, coverage of it was shrinking as the media began a long retreat into a narrower, more inward-looking culture. It was not that there was less news, far from it. In Britain, national newspapers were double or even triple the size they had been thirty years previously.

James Harding says when he became director of BBC News in 2013, he was taken aback to discover the Corporation's different channels were producing 'four seconds of news for every second of the day.'[21]

But the amount of foreign news was falling precipitously. Between 1998 and 2011, a time when the US—a global superpower—was fighting two wars, at least twenty American newspapers and other media outlets eliminated all of their foreign bureaus, while the size of those remaining shrunk dramatically.[22] For much of this time I was based in Washington, DC as correspondent for *The Times*, whose foreign pages were—and are—among the best-resourced. Even there, before the newspaper retreated behind a paywall (in July 2010), it sometimes felt as though we were chasing clicks as editors back in London scraped together news lists from reading popular websites overnight. For instance, I ended up writing stories the next morning from Washington about how Paris Hilton had been jailed tearfully in Los Angeles, over 2,500 miles away, the day before for no other reason than I was on the same continent.[23]

Coverage of politics in US newspapers was becoming patchier too. Senator Chris Dodd described how, when his career began, more than a dozen reporters from outlets in his state of Connecticut were regularly working in Washington. By the time he retired in 2010, that number had fallen to zero.[24] The consequence was that no Connecticut newspaper or television station had a reporter in the capital covering national politics at a time when respect for Congress was plummeting to an all-time low—and Dodd himself was taking money from some of the companies embroiled in the subprime mortgage crisis.[25]

Those journalists still in work were left were producing more news, faster than ever, and with fewer resources as they filed for print and online editions, filmed videos or posted continual updates while virtually chained to their desks and their Twitter feeds. One study showed staff at

Murdoch's *Wall Street Journal* produced 21,000 stories in the first six months of 2010, as many as they had in an entire year a decade earlier, even though they had 13 per cent fewer staff.[26] 'The bottom line culturally is this,' said the Pew Research Centre's 2008 report, 'in today's newspapers, stories tend to be gathered faster and under greater pressure by a smaller, less experienced staff of reporters, then are passed more quickly through fewer, less experienced, editing hands on their way to publication.'[27] Another study for Pew in the city of Baltimore during 2010 concluded that 'fully eight out of ten stories studied simply repeated or repackaged previously published information.'[28]

Peter Baker, the *New York Times*'s chief White House correspondent described how he used to have 'the luxury of writing for the next day's newspaper' when he could make calls, access information and provide context: 'Today, as much as you want to do that … when do you have time to call experts? When do you have time to sort through data and information and do your own research? Even with a well-staffed news organization, we are hostages to the non-stop, never-ending file-it-now, get-on-the-Web, get-on-the-radio, get-on-TV media environment. …We are, collectively, much like eight-year-olds chasing a soccer ball. Instead of finding ways of creating fresh, original, high-impact journalism, we're way too eager to chase the same story everyone else is chasing, which is too often the easy story and too often the simplistic story—and too often the story that misses what's going on.'[29]

And if that was true for a newspaper with the highest standards in the world, imagine what it was like lower down the food chain. Rather than being the seekers-after-truth they had once hoped to be, former colleagues of mine in the parliamentary Lobby admitted they were spending less time talking to sources or discovering facts, and more time processing those available on the internet and therefore, by definition, already known.

A serving political editor on a British national newspaper describes it like this: 'The culture we used to have of getting and protecting exclusives began changing a decade or so ago and has now gone. It's now news if someone says something—anything—even if it has been said before. We're not really adding to knowledge about what's going on but feeding the machine. We're not thinking about how it looks tomorrow in the paper but how it will look in a few minutes. We're not informing our readers but racing against each other. For instance, when we go on foreign trips, it's about staying close to the pack instead of finding out what's really going on. We're there just so that we can file online a little bit faster—which is the same time as everyone else—but better than if we were back in the office reading it on the wires. It all seems a bit pointless, really.'[30]

Much of investigative journalism was in any case by this time sinking into a mire of phone hacking, entrapment and 'blagging'—impersonating third parties to obtain confidential information. The victims were not always the powerful, the rich and the famous but also the relatives of British soldiers killed in Iraq, survivors of the '7/7' bomb attacks on London, as well as the murdered schoolgirl, Milly Dowler.

But it is too simplistic to regard the phone hacking scandal in Britain as being caused just by low standards and morals among certain journalists. Much of it was driven by technological change that both opened new opportunities to harvest information as well as left newspapers' finances so squeezed that some reporters felt they could no longer do their jobs any other way. Instead of building relationships with contacts, following leads, speaking to numerous sources, reporters—or the private detectives working for them—were told to get exclusives on the cheap and while never leaving their desks.

One reporter, Richard Peppiatt, gave evidence to the Leveson Inquiry into the ethics of the press[31] about his time at the *Daily Star*, where resources were so limited they had to invent bylines. 'I recollect one day there being just myself and two other reporters to write the whole newspaper,' he said. 'We were forced to use pseudonyms just to make it appear to readers there were more of us. Any fact checking etc. goes out the window when you have such a heaving workload.'[32] Matt Driscoll, a former sports reporter on the *News of the World* described to the inquiry how his newspaper had blagged the medical records of Alex Ferguson from his doctors and then agreed not to use the information provided he started co-operating with them on other stories. 'At the time I felt uneasy about such methods,' he told the inquiry. 'It seemed that any method that could stand a story up was fair game. It was also clear that there was massive pressure from the top to break stories.'[33]

Large parts of the profession had ceased producing original material altogether. Nick Davis's book, *Flat Earth News*, describes the never-ceasing production line of what he called 'news factories' as journalists filled papers with a tide of became known as 'churnalism'—recycled, unchecked material often cut and pasted straight from a press release or plagiarised from the web and news agencies. He cites a study at Cardiff University which found that 60 per cent of the stories even in Britain's quality press were largely copied from news agencies or PR material and that only 12 per cent were generated solely by the newspaper's own reporters.

Like dark light from a dying star, Britain's national press still dominated the political conversation, with newspapers like the *Daily Mail* regularly lashing out at institutions more trusted than itself—the police, the judiciary, schools, business, universities, the NHS and the BBC. Even in its apparent infirmity, with advertising revenues and circulation falling, the old press seemed more vicious than ever as it sought to maintain a weakening hold on digitally distracted readers by being shriller, louder and nastier.

By 2009, as *The Sun* prepared to switch its endorsement from Labour to the Conservatives, its circulation dipped below 3 million and would continue to fall over the next decade. The newspaper began to target Gordon Brown with a series of largely spurious stories designed to show he was disrespecting British troops serving in Afghanistan. He was supposed to have fallen asleep at the Festival of Remembrance, failed to bow at the Cenotaph and misspelt the name of a dead soldier when he was writing a letter to his mother.

Brown had many difficulties as a person and as a prime minister in this period. But the anger he expressed about how *The Sun* treated his motives on an issue that is always the most eviscerating for leaders—the decision to send soldiers into war—was justified. In a passage in his memoirs that bears a remarkable similarity to Tony Blair's parting shot at the press, Brown wrote: '*The Sun* and the Conservatives wanted people to believe that lives were being lost not just because of alleged mismanagement of the war but because we did not care. No longer the first port of call for up-to-the-minute news, with TV and social media operating on a 24/7 cycle, newspapers needed another unique selling point—hence their rising tide of sensationalism. It was not enough for *The Sun* to allege that I had made a mistake; it felt compelled to report an ulterior motive ... [that] we were not just misguided but malevolent.'[34]

In January 2009, America was preparing to inaugurate Barack Obama, a new president who said he was seeking bi-partisan solutions to unite the country across party lines. The response from the likes of Rush Limbaugh and Fox News was to dig deeper trenches. Limbaugh told his listeners that he had been asked to write 400 words on his hopes for the

Obama presidency. He responded: 'I don't need 400 words, I need four: I hope he fails.' Next came the anti-tax Tea Party movement that helped defeat Obama's Democrats in the 2010 midterm elections. From the outset, it was actively promoted by Fox News—and in particular its presenter Glenn Beck—while one of its producers was caught on camera urging the crowd to shout louder during a Tea Party rally.[35]

Even as an alternative space for right wing news, views and conspiracy theories was being created on the internet, much of spade-work was still being done by those early agents of the ever-expanding information age, the partisan traditional media like Talk Radio and Fox News. They made it respectable to discuss repeatedly debunked claims such as the myth that President Obama's Affordable Care Act would mean government-appointed 'death panels' to decide if it was worth keeping elderly patients alive. One academic study into how such misinformation spread concluded: 'In most cases, the claims were made in conservative outlets on cable news, talk radio, and the Internet, highlighting the importance of increased media choice in promoting the dissemination of misinformation.'[36]

Back in Britain, *The Daily Telegraph* won deserved plaudits for its exposure of MPs' secret and sometimes corrupt expenses claims, with the result that five parliamentarians were jailed. But this was not exactly investigative journalism in the best tradition of Watergate. The newspaper paid £150,000 in 2009 for a computer hard drive containing more than 2 million documents that had previously been hawked round other newspapers, including *The Times*.

The scandal was drawn out by the newspaper for weeks as, drip-by-drip, detailing each painful item of claims. It was not so much what the *Telegraph* revealed than how it appeared to confirm to a furious public that MPs were all crooks and liars. A decade when politics had been treated like failing contestants on Reality TV went into a food processor along with the electronic data of ludicrous or trivial expenses claims—a duck house, a bath plug—where it was chopped and sliced into so much gloop and gunk.

# # #

I returned home from America around this time, disorientated, to find British politics had changed and I no longer fitted in at *The Times*. Within a year, shortly after the 2010 election, I left to work for the Labour Party as Communications Director. And it was not long before we were in open conflict with my former employers at News Corp over phone hacking. This time it was journalists' turn to go to jail. Among those successfully prosecuted was Andy Coulson, a former editor of the *News of the World*, who had subsequently been appointed communications chief for the Conservative Party.

Miliband had shown genuine courage in forcing the resignation of Rebekah Brooks as News Corp's Chief Executive and helping prevent its takeover of the remaining stake in BSkyB. In doing so, he broke the eighteen-year spell that Murdoch had cast over British politics when no-one dared take on the press. Tom Newton Dunn, *The Sun*'s political editor, is alleged to have made the prospect of retaliation explicit with direct threats to a senior member of staff from the Labour leader's office. 'You made this personal about Rebekah,' he was quoted saying. 'we're going to make this personal about you. We won't forget.'[37] There were also reports that Murdoch himself flew to London to berate staff for failing to do enough to stop Labour, which was then committed to better press regulation and limiting the number of newspapers anyone could own, telling them 'the future of the company is at stake.'[38]

Newton Dunn himself vehemently denies ever making such a threat. He certainly never threatened me. Executives at the newspaper also dismiss suggestions that Murdoch ordered his journalists to ramp up the attacks on Miliband, as 'a typical left-wing fantasy'. One said: 'We threw a lot of stuff at poor old Ed but that's because we thought he would ruin the country and that's what our readers, who are the salt of the earth and not stupid, believed too.'[39] Miliband himself, who continues to battle News UK's bid for broadcast media expansion, these days takes wry pleasure in reading evidence from its executives who insist that any idea newspapers like *The Sun* ever seek to influence their readers' political views is greatly 'overplayed'.[40]

For all this, there was still much to be admired in Britain's raucous tradition of press freedom, as well as the huge variety in journalism and the political affiliation of broadsheets, broadcast media and tabloids. But newspapers must take some share of the blame—or perhaps credit—for spreading ignorance on subjects like immigration. A 2013 poll showed that British voters believed 31 per cent of the population is made up of immigrants and that 24 per cent are Muslims. In reality those figures are

13 per cent and just 5 per cent.[41] Have newspapers like *The Daily Mail* and *The Sun* caused their readers' ignorance or merely reflected it? The UN High Commission for Human Rights certainly believes it is the latter, saying elements of the UK press had been guilty of 'decades of sustained and unrestrained anti-foreigner abuse, misinformation and distortion.'[42]

This, together with the years of rough treatment dished out by Murdoch's newspapers to the left, meant there were plenty of people who could scarcely contain their glee over the crisis that engulfed his tabloids during the phone hacking scandal. For many, the hobbling or even demise of the newspaper industry was a cause for celebration. And there was a view among progressives in general—from Islington to Silicon Valley—that these ugly death throes symbolised a destruction of old media power that would usher in a more democratic and tolerant age.

But in Britain almost all the national newspapers were still standing years later, despite predictions of mass closures. Even when the *News of the World* was shut by Murdoch in 2011, it was effectively relaunched the following year as the *The Sun on Sunday*. In America, Fox News faced significant challenges from streaming video, social media and so-called cord-cutting, as eyeballs shift from TV to smartphones for news, but in 2017 was still raking in billion-dollar profits each year.

Instead, the brunt of the pain from the digital revolution has been borne in Britain by its local and regional newspapers, which had been previously been the most trusted form of print media. They were becoming hollowed out with advertising income dropping sharply by 54 per cent from £2.74 billion to £1.28 billion between 2007 and 2012.[43] The number of journalists in regional newspapers had already been squeezed before the financial crash, but afterwards it went off a cliff, falling from 13,000 to possibly 'half that figure' seven years later, according to the *Press Gazette*.

Takeovers by grim, soulless media chains became commonplace as plummeting revenue and circulation for local newspapers shook these pillars of their communities loose from their local owners. By 2008, the four biggest regional publishers in the UK—Trinity Mirror, DMGT, Johnston Press and Newsquest Media Group—had almost 70 per cent market share.[44] Concentration of ownership was even more intense in broadcast where, aside from the BBC's dominance, four companies—GCap, Bauer, Global, and GMG—controlled 77 per cent of commercial radio stations.[45]

Such media conglomerates warned the only way any local provision could be maintained in the face of mounting cost pressure was through economies of scale and centralising many functions. The government and the broadcasting watchdog agreed, allowed ITV to scale back its regional news coverage while rules on media ownership were further relaxed.[46]

The consequence was the rise of 'zombie' newspapers and local radio stations, often with journalists based in hubs far from the communities they once served, scraping the bottom of social media and the internet for free content. In America, Clearchannel, which bought up hundreds of local radio stations and syndicated Limbaugh, was being accused of homogenising and centralising news production to save expenditure on local journalism. Many outlets went into a destructive cycle of reduced quality, falling circulation and staff cuts that left them as little more than empty shells—unloved by the community they were no longer able to serve.

In Britain, David Montgomery, a legendary management villain in national newspapers, bought up the DMGT's 100 remaining local titles in 2012 to form Local World and told a parliamentary committee how he intended to save them by embracing a digital future: 'We have to go truly digital, so that in three or four years from now I think that much of our human interface will have disappeared. In line with other digitised businesses, we will have to harvest content and publish it without a human interface. Journalists collecting stories one by one is a highly unproductive process ...we cannot sustain a model that is from the Middle Ages virtually, where a single reporter covers a single story, comes back to the office, writes it up. All of that is highly wasteful.'[47]

Within a couple of years, Local World, which by then consisted of just eighty-three local titles, was itself sold off to Trinity Mirror. Its vision for its 200 regional newspapers, five nationals and a takeover plan for the *Express*, is scarcely more inspiring. A senior executive explained it to me like this: 'We want to put everything in one big bucket. The idea is for 80 per cent of stories to be the same across the group with just a bit of dressing to distinguish them for each other.'

Gareth Davies used to be a reporter on one of those Trinity Mirror titles, the *Croydon Advertiser*, where he had won weekly journalist of the year on four occasions. After quitting in despair he spoke out after seeing his former paper had run 'listicle' stories filling consecutive pages headlined: '13 things you will know if you are a Southern Rail passenger,' and '9 things you didn't know about Blockbuster'. He said 'a paper with a

121

proud 147-year history' had been 'reduced to being a thrown together collection of clickbait written for the web.'[48]

There are still many outstanding local newspapers, including the one where I got my first job as a reporter: the *Newbury Weekly News*. It remains a proud, independently-owned operation that is rooted in its community. This paid-for publication, packed with original reporting, comes out every Thursday—known as 'pig and paper day' because that is when the market is in town. But even there, circulation is less than half what it used to be, while a much-reduced staff now operate from a corner of what used to be the advertising department. And the survival of papers like the *Newbury Weekly News* is becoming the exception to a rule in which local papers have either been hollowed-out or closed.

In the US, more than 500 newspapers have shut down, including big city titles like the *Rocky Mountain News*, the *Baltimore Examiner*, and the *Pittsburgh Tribune-Review*. Across the UK, there is a similar picture where there has been a net loss since 2005 of around 200 local newspapers[49] including the *Northampton Mercury*, which was 295 years old and claimed to be the oldest in the UK.

The question is, what happens when newspapers are gone?

What happens in the desert, stays in the desert

Port Talbot lies sandwiched between the sea and the South Wales valleys where they once dug for coal. The steel works are under perennial threat of closure. A leisure complex on the sea front was destroyed in a fire a few years back and the site still sits empty behind blue hoarding. The M4 slices across the town on 45-foot concrete stilts towering over terraced houses. This is a place that is all too easy to write off, especially when no one is writing about it.

After almost eighty-five years of existence, the *Port Talbot Guardian*, appeared for the last time on 1 October 2009, leaving the town part of Britain's ever-expanding news desert. There is still the Trinity Mirror-owned *South Wales Evening Post* but this is based 10 miles away in Swansea and has just one reporter covering a string of towns and villages, with a combined population of around 150,000 people. Even when the *Post* had an office and more staff in the town, it had always been the *Port Talbot Guardian* that was regarded as the 'weekly bible', chronicling the school plays, clubs, court cases, crimes, road closures, sport and planning applications that used to fill papers such as this. 'It did the nitty-gritty of life in the town,' says Malcom Rees, who worked on both papers in the 1960s when no less than eleven reporters were based in Port Talbot itself. 'The *[Port Talbot] Guardian* was personal to people because they relied on us to know what was happening—it bound us all together.'

Rachel Howells is a local journalist and academic who has studied the effect of the paper's closure on Port Talbot.[50] In 2014, the Welsh government tried closing Junction 41 of the M4 in an effort to speed journey times for everybody except people who used it to get to this town. Although such a humiliating decision had been covered by regional TV and the *Post*, Howells interviewed local residents in focus groups and found many were deeply confused about what was happening with one participant saying he only found out about the closure 'from graffiti sprayed around the town.'[51]

Around the same time, rumours flared in parts of Port Talbot that pet dogs were being systematically stolen from a council estate and then killed in fights. Gossip and fear smouldered for weeks before police persuaded the *Post* to run a prominent story pointing out the dog-killing was an invention. 'Word of mouth, stumbling upon information, and social media were dominant news sources,' Howells wrote. 'This has resulted in frustration, anger and powerlessness.'[52]

It became harder for people not only inside the town to discover what was going on, but outside too. Mentions of Port Talbot, the stories and lives of tens of thousands of people began to fall away. The exception was a few days in 2016 when it looked like the steel works would shut and journalists descended on the town for a few days, only to leave again. What happens in the news desert, now stays in the desert.

Coverage of council meetings had almost dried up even before the *Port Talbot Guardian* closed. Howells's analysis of hundreds of news stories on planning issues in Port Talbot over four decades showed that journalists had still got lots of their stories from attending committee meetings, or at least looking at the agenda and interrogating officials, until the 1990s. But such reporting had declined since then to the point when, in 2013, 100 per cent of planning stories about Port Talbot were lifted straight from the council's press releases. Civic engagement was also corroded. After the newspaper stopped publishing in 2009, turnout in elections fell from above the national average to below, while levels of volunteering— which had been remarkably high in Port Talbot—began to drop steadily every year since the *Port Talbot Guardian* stopped rolling off the presses. According to Howells's survey, barely half the town knew their MP was Labour, even though this had been the case since 1922.

In 2010 Howells set up an online local news service called the *Port Talbot Magnet*. But, over fish and chips on the seafront, she describes how difficult it was even to gain access to the council offices to report on this withered local democracy. 'At the beginning it was difficult to get them even to send us their press releases or tell us what they were doing. It was as though they didn't really want us there. We asked if we could live stream council meetings but they said "no" because some of the councillors had come to think of their meetings as being private affairs. When we started going to meetings, we would have to be accompanied to the chamber by a member of council staff. It was quite intimidating—so no wonder hardly any members of the public try to go. But it was always worth it: at one committee meeting we found out about problems at an open-cast mine at Margam where the owners had allowed to fill with water that residents were concerned could flood the houses below. I saw, again and again, how difficult it is to live effectively as a citizen, to know what's going on and have your voice heard, inside a news black hole. The people of Port Talbot probably know more about Donald Trump 5,000 miles away than they do about what is happening on their local council.'[53]

One of Port Talbot's most recognisable residents is a man called Barry Kirk, or 'Captain Beany' as he prefers to be known. He spends much of his time dressed in a baked-bean coloured superhero costume raising money for charities or a similarly orange suit and bow-tie as the curator of the Baked Bean Museum of Excellence. The museum is housed in his third-floor council flat where every spare surface is painted in the exact shade of tomato sauce and dedicated to his collection of ageing tins of baked beans, some of which occasionally explode, from around the world. In 2015, the same year he had sixty baked bean shapes tattooed on his orange-tinted head, he stood for Parliament and won a respectable 1,137 votes.

For most of his three decades as Captain Beany, his charity work was sustained by local newspapers. 'I was never out of the papers in the old days and that may have helped me establish a sort of legendary status,' he says wistfully. 'But it's harder now. There is nothing tangible which people can hold in their hands to know what's going on. There is no focal point in this town, not even a noticeboard. I have to do a lot of it through social media with my Facebook group. It's brilliant! I call it the "Captain Beany Appreciation Society."'[54]

But there are other Facebook groups for the people of this town such as 'Neath Argue and Debate'[55] that do not provide a service so much as a pit in which its 10,000 members can fight. It offers a warning to people joining that it 'does not pander to your need for safe space and political correctness' while, before being accepted as a member, it gives new recruits a hint about what it's like inside by asking: 'Someone calls you a cunt, how do you react?' Howells says that many of these local groups are like the 'wild west', with baseless rumours and a fair amount of anti-immigrant sentiment roaming freely alongside scraps of real information.[56]

Howells is reluctant to attribute the anger she detected in Port Talbot and the loosening of the ties that once bound this community together solely to the newspaper closing down. When she, and volunteers including Captain Beany used to hand out printed copies of the *Port Talbot Magnet* to shoppers, she noticed a curious effect: if the news was bad, local residents were less likely to pick up their free newspaper. 'When there was talk of the steelworks closing, people just wouldn't want to know. They were fed up with everything, it was as though they'd had enough doom and gloom already,' she says. 'It's easy to say that civic life declined in this town because *The Guardian* closed or because the journalists went away. But equally you could argue the newspaper died because people were becoming disengaged from the news here.'

# # #

In the small hours of 24 June 2016, it was announced that the people of Port Talbot and Neath, despite receiving massive grants from Brussels, had voted by a margin of more than 10,000 to leave the European Union. Howells and her colleagues from the *Port Talbot Magnet* were the only media present at the count.

She describes the scene like this: 'We sat on a little table, ate some biscuits and did some live-streaming from the count. It was a strange atmosphere with no cameras or any other media, a bit like being in a library. When the result came in, the Leave people—mostly elderly and retired—were very happy. But I think that night was very demoralising for the two young lads I had with me who had so wanted to be journalists and felt they had a stake in the future. The problem round here is that if people read anything it will be papers like *The Sun* and the *Daily Mail*. There is no strong local voice saying anything different.'[57]

A few months after the referendum, Howells decided to close the *Magnet* amid falling advertising revenues and plummeting morale. 'I was subsidising the newspaper with my time and money, holding it up artificially,' she says. 'From the outside everything looked okay. But it wasn't.'[58]

The woman with 'three breasts'

The media's finances were being wrecked by the flight of advertisers to Google and Facebook, but it was also becoming dependent on those same platforms. And the consequence was to debase journalism and damage democracy still further.

Media executives embarked on an almost mythical quest to replace their lost readers and revenues with new audiences and income that were 'digital'. A 96-page report written for *The New York Times* on how it could—should—become a 'digital first organisation' was leaked to rivals a few years ago.[59] It questioned which 'print-based traditions and their demands on our time' could be abandoned for more internet work. For example, the report cited the 'packaging, promoting and sharing our journalism'—even though none of that had anything to do with original reporting or discovering facts.

On one level, they were succeeding because more people than ever were consuming, and engaging with, their journalism. Even as *The New York Times*'s circulation slipped below 1 million in 2009 amid cover price increases and newsroom cutbacks, it was able to point to a vast increase in readership—the number of 'eyeballs'—on its website. Newspapers like *The Guardian* that had once measured their audience in the hundreds of thousands now could do so in millions and it began to shift reporting resources from Britain to its new global horizon of America and Australia.

The problem, however, was that they were getting only digital pennies to replace print pounds. It was estimated that every dollar in new revenue newspapers got from online advertising was being offset by losses ten times as great from print advertising.[60] Even this began to be worth less to newspapers as the money moved to companies that had the data. In 2003 publishers received most of the money advertisers spent on their sites but by 2010 that proportion had fallen to just 20 per cent.[61] As Google and Facebook siphoned off bucket-loads of advertising revenue, newspapers were trying to keep the lights on with nothing left in the tank but fumes.

For some, particularly at the quality end of the market, the solution was to introduce paywalls that forced readers to take online subscriptions but in these years there was little co-operation from Google that insisted publishers offer at least three free articles a day if they wanted visibility on the internet.

Most newspapers concluded that they had no alternative to working with Google and Facebook. But these firms were proving to be fickle, even capricious, masters as they carved the grooves into which the future of journalism would be made to fit. One month might see algorithms tweaked to favour video over words or to promote articles without complex graphics so they could be uploaded on smartphones. The next month might see media that had responded to such changes with fresh investment then lose even more money because Facebook was pushing updates from friends and family ahead of news in its feed.

Franklin Foer, the former editor of *The New Republic* magazine in the US put it this way: 'Over the past generation, journalism has been slowly swallowed. The ascendant media companies of our era don't think of themselves as heirs to a great ink-stained tradition. Some like to compare themselves to technology firms. This redefinition isn't just a bit of fashionable branding. As Silicon Valley has infiltrated the profession, journalism has come to unhealthily depend on the big tech companies, which now supply journalism with an enormous percentage of its audience— and, therefore, a big chunk of its revenue. ... Dependence generates desperation—a mad, shameless chase to gain clicks through Facebook, a relentless effort to game Google's algorithms. It leads media outlets to sign terrible deals that look like self-preserving necessities: granting Facebook the right to sell their advertising or giving Google permission to publish articles directly on its fast-loading server. In the end, such arrangements simply allow Facebook and Google to hold these companies ever tighter.'[62]

Chris Hughes had made nearly a billion dollars helping his former roommate at Harvard, Mark Zuckerberg, create Facebook. He then helped Barack Obama's presidential campaign, where his official title was 'online organising guru', dominate internet activism in 2008. When Hughes bought *The New Republic* in 2011, Foer thought the magazine had found the liberal benefactor it needed to get through a turbulent digital era and was persuaded to return as editor. But, within a few months, Hughes had installed his own 'data guru' to increase the odds of getting viral hits by 'listening to the data' and mimicking the rest of the internet. At one meeting with staff, the digital expert was greeted with stony silence as he asked: 'Chipotle has run out of pork and it's all over social—what can we generate?'

Hughes was only imitating a new breed of digital news organisations—the likes of BuzzFeed, the Huffington Post, Upworthy and the ill-fated Gawker—which were being built on a system of monitoring traffic and trending topics.

Such digitally-native sites specialised in headlines known as 'clickbait' that are often defined by what is known as a curiosity gap. The classic formulation is to begin with the phrase 'You'll Never Guess ...' before adding lines such as '...Why People Are Sharing This Facebook Photo Of Two Women Holding Each Other,' or '...What These 00s Stars Are Doing Now,' or the simple '...What Happens Next.' Often clickbait is laced with a primal appeal to sex or violence—'This Man Thought He Could Get Away With It, But Then She Showed Up.' Many entice readers to click through lists, '10 Problems Only Short Girls Understand'— and most are decorated with hover buttons, multiple images and pop-ups. BuzzFeed would sometimes test dozens of different headlines on audiences to discover which was most likely to be shared over smartphones and had the most virality. Pictures of cats were, apparently, often a key factor—'29 Cats Who Failed So Hard They Won.'[63]

And, where the likes of Buzzfeed and Gawker led, much of the 'legacy press' followed. They were becoming organisations that survived by capturing people's time and attention before selling it to advertisers. Some of this was no more than doing what the media had always tried to do by writing clever headlines, designing pages and getting stories. Nor was the degradation confined to the internet, as anyone who has endured the *Daily Express*'s endless, repetitive front pages on health cures for its elderly readers, the death of Princess Diana and house prices, can attest. But whereas the link between a successful piece of journalism and revenue had always implicit and imprecise, data metrics meant it was becoming a science in which more clicks and more shares equalled more advertising revenue.

This exacerbated the problem of the media 'piling in' on the story of the day as the need for clicks meant news got simultaneously faster and bigger. Such algorithmic news did not necessarily mean bad journalism—some of the best pieces written this century were produced by sites like BuzzFeed and the Huffington Post. But it certainly broke down the barrier that once existed between editorial and advertising, with BuzzFeed designing viral campaigns for companies that are difficult to tell apart from its other output. And also, sometimes, it built a new barrier against the kind of worthy reporting that paternalist editors had once thought was good for the readers.

Instead, journalism was becoming a commodity, the commercial value of which could be measured exactly and traded in an increasingly efficient market.

# # #

I had remembered Nick Denton at university as someone mysteriously known as 'Floods', possibly on account of his trousers being several inches too short so it looked like he like he was expecting to get his ankles wet. But, when I met him again in the US a few years later, he had developed into a preternaturally self-confident evangelist for the future as the founder of Gawker. His vision was one where journalists could be outsiders, 'beholden to no-one but the readers,'[64] running the stories you wouldn't find in the mainstream media.

In 2011, Denton declared the system of web metrics worked for everything but 'the worthy topics,' adding: 'Nobody wants to eat the boring vegetables. Nor does anyone want to pay [via advertising] to encourage people to eat their vegetables. But, anyway, look at me. I used to cover political reform in post-communist Eastern Europe, which had been my subject at Oxford. And now I tell writers that the numbers (i.e. the audience) won't support any worthiness. We can't even write stories about moguls like Rupert Murdoch or Barry Diller unless it involves photographs of them cavorting with young flesh.'[65]

Although Gawker itself was later sued out of existence after publishing a sex tape featuring the not-so-young flesh of the former wrestler, Hulk Hogan, Denton left his mark on the media. He pioneered the use of 'The Big Board'—the screen that hung over Gawker's newsroom so that the traffic and rank of its best-performing stories could be seen by all. As one observer put it at the time: 'Write an article that makes it onto the Big Board and you're liable to get a raise. Stay off it for too long and you may need to find a different job.'[66]

In time, such use of metrics began creeping into even the highest-minded editorial decisions as screens flickered across news desks around the world with numbers and dials showing how readers behaved.

The 'below the line' comments at *The Guardian* were about the bottom line as much as they were about reader empowerment. Becky Gardiner, the newspaper's former comment editor, says: 'There was an editorial motive for it all but the dirty secret was that there was also a commercial one. If you engage the readers you increase their value to the advertising department; the time people spend on the site and the level of engagement is measured and it is something a newspaper can sell to advertisers.' A senior editor at the same newspaper suddenly began finding that his skill and expertise was being discounted by an 'algorithmic time and motion study' that he felt was just as humiliating as anything done to production line workers in the 1920s. 'I put up a story today on EU reform,' he said, 'but the news desk said the story wasn't worth it because the last time I wrote something like that we got a poor online response. It doesn't matter how important the story is, metrics matter more.'

Foer resigned from *The New Republic*, along with most of his editorial staff, after being told by Hughes that the magazine was now a 'technology company'. He was replaced with a recruit, inevitably, from Gawker.[67] In America, there were reports that the big chains owning much of the regional press, McClatchy and Gannett, were introducing click targets for journalists to reach each month,[68] while Trinity Mirror briefly tried to do so in parts of Wales.[69]

For many media organisations, including some of those that counted themselves as being among the most respected in the world, the job of journalism was becoming a humiliating and ceaseless effort to maximise clicks. This had an inevitable impact on quality.

David Weigel, a *Washington Post* journalist, complained about a series of internet hoaxes that were making their way into newspapers at this time, saying: '"Too good to check" used to be a warning to newspaper editors not to jump on bullshit stories. Now it's a business model.'[70] Ryan Grim, the Washington bureau chief for The Huffington Post, acknowledged: 'The faster metabolism puts people who fact-check at a disadvantage. If you throw something up without fact-checking it, and you're the first one to put it up, and you get millions and millions of views, and later it's proved false, you still got those views. That's a problem. The incentives are all wrong.'[71] Joshua Benton, director of the Nieman Journalism

Lab at Harvard, said: 'You are seeing news organisations say, "if it is happening on the internet that's our beat, the next step of figuring out whether it happened in real life is up to someone else." This is journalism as an act of pointing—"look over here, this is interesting."'[72]

Katharine Viner, the editor of *The Guardian*, has said that because 'Facebook and Google swallow digital advertising,' the digital journalism produced by many news organisations 'has become less and less meaningful.' She added: 'Publishers that are funded by algorithmic ads are locked in a race to the bottom in pursuit of any audience they can find—desperately binge-publishing without checking facts, pushing out the most shrill and most extreme stories to boost clicks. ... On some sites, journalists who learned in training that "news is something that someone, somewhere doesn't want published" churn out ten commodified stories a day without making a phone call.'[73]

One example of this kind of journalism involved the curious case of a Florida woman calling herself Jasmine 'Tridevil' made headlines around the world in September 2014 when she posted pictures of herself with a third breast. The clue, perhaps, should have been in her name.

Claiming she had got the implant surgery to make herself unattractive to men and hoping to land a reality TV show contract, her story appeared in media ranging from *New York Magazine*, BuzzFeed, *The New York Post*, *The Toronto Sun*, Fox News, CBS Tampa, *The Daily Mirror*, *The Week* and *The Daily Telegraph*.

It was, of course, invented. Tridevil's website was registered by someone named Alisha Hessler, a Tampa massage therapist who bore a striking likeness to Tridevil, albeit with one obvious difference. Her own website boasted it was the 'provider of internet hoaxes since 2014' and that she was a 'specialist in massage for three breasted women'. And, oh yes, she had recently filed a stolen baggage complaint at the local airport that listed a '3 breast prosthesis' among the lost items.[74]

As the fact-checking organisation, Snopes, later put it: 'Multiple media outlets took her claims at face value and ran it as a straight news story with no corroboration (other than self-provided images that could easily have been faked): they contacted no one who knew or had seen Ms Tridevil, they sought no third-party photographs of her, they didn't verify the story with the doctor who supposedly performed her unusual enhancement surgery, nor did they probe her obvious pseudonym to determine her real name and background.'

The reason why so many respectable news organisations would run it anyway is because it was flying around the internet and the prospect of a few hundred thousand clicks was too tempting to waste time with checks.

The text of *The Telegraph*'s story about Hessler provided a good illustration of what journalism had become. The only sources quoted apart from Tridevel/Hessler were those it could salvage from a search of social media: 'Tridevil has written on her Facebook page that she has a number of TV and radio interviews coming up, but a few days ago added: "I'm nervous as Hell. I'm prepared for people to judge harshly and tell me to kill myself lol." So far, social media users have been unable to decide what they think about Tridevil. One user wrote, "you are a hero in my books". While another commented, "you're stupid for doing this. There are other ways to become famous."'[75]

The triple-breasted woman story was one of those studied in a report by Craig Silverman at Columbia University. He pointed out that while the original stories had been widely shared and read—generating 1.5 million views for BuzzFeed—subsequent corrections and debunking had scarcely registered. 'Journalists have always sought out emerging (and often unverified) news. They have always followed on the reports of other news organisations. But today the bar for what is worth giving attention seems to be much lower,' he wrote. 'Within minutes or hours, a claim can morph from a lone tweet or badly sourced report to a story repeated by dozens of news websites, generating tens of thousands of shares. Once a certain critical mass is reached, repetition has a powerful effect on belief. The rumour becomes true for readers simply by virtue of its ubiquity. … There is little thought or incentive to follow up. The potential for traffic is also greatest when a claim or rumour is new. So journalists jump fast, and frequently, to capture traffic. Then they move on.'[76]

Peter Oborne, the journalist who had so often accused the British government of lying over the Iraq War, then turned his still smoking guns of moral outrage on his own newspaper, the *Daily Telegraph*. He claimed it had suppressed revelations about HSBC's tax affairs because it did not want to upset a major advertiser. But Oborne's long resignation letter in 2015 also suggested the newspaper's 'click culture' and its story about Jasmine Tridevil may have helped tip him over the edge: 'Stories seemed no longer judged by their importance, accuracy or appeal to those who actually bought the paper. The more important measure appeared to be the number of online visits. On 22 September *Telegraph* online ran a story about a woman with three breasts. One despairing executive told me that it was known this was false even before the story was published. I have no doubt it was published in order to generate online traffic, at which it may have succeeded. I am not saying that online traffic is unimportant, but over the long term, however, such episodes inflict incalculable damage on the reputation of the paper.'[77]

Malcolm Coles, *The Telegraph*'s 'Search Engine Optimisation' consultant, was later caught on a video leaked to the Guido Fawkes blog, telling a conference about how the newspaper put clicks ahead of brand. Displaying a slide of a headline that read, 'Bow down to Kate Middleton's new baby,' he said: 'This is a terrible headline for the *Daily Telegraph*, which is a quality news organization. ... We had literally run out of headline ideas. But it was amazing, it shot to the top of Google. And stayed there for ages [because] up against all the other fairly staid ones it stood out. It's not great from a brand point of view, but for a click though rate getting these slightly quirky headlines in the news box means they tend to stay there for quite a long time.'

Coles went on to claim that the *Telegraph* had published 13,000 articles along the lines of 'what time is the FA Cup final?' He explained the trick to maximize clicks was to add in an additional part of the question such as 'and what channel is it on?' and then 'some interesting fact.'

As one traumatised *Telegraph* reporter put it to me: 'The mantra during this era was to maximise clicks and shares. The website would cover anything that others were doing that was being shared widely, no matter how old or how poor quality it was. Everything was supposed to have at least four different types of shareable content embedded like graphs, pull quotes, picture galleries, polls. And we did literally dozens of stories headlined "how to make the perfect cup of tea." For all of us who had great respect for the paper—on the basis that it had been woven into the fabric of British society for more than 150 years—it was a deeply dispiriting period. You would lose literally hours of your day, not in pursuit of truth, but in generating digital excrement.'[78]

The alternative sphere

Even as the early idealism around the internet began to evaporate in the first decade of this century, there were still plenty of people who saw it as a route to free their minds from the constructs of powerful forces that sought to tell them what and how to think.

Some wanted to escape the propaganda of an authoritarian state, others wanted liberation from a sexist or racist culture, while still more saw the enemy as wealthy and ideologically-motivated media barons. And, when they looked for a philosophical underpinning for all this, many turned to the work of Jürgen Habermas.

He had grown up in Hitler's Germany and described his own father as a 'passive sympathiser' with the Nazi regime.[79] Fascinated by the Nuremburg trials and horrified in equal measure at how the minds of his fellow-citizens had been so twisted, Habermas developed a theory of the 'public sphere'. This was a place where free and rational people could have 'discourse—the unforced force of the better argument'—to reach a common position and influence affairs of a democratic state for the better. He described how the 'bourgeois public sphere' of educated liberal men meeting in London's coffee houses in the eighteenth century had been corrupted through the power of mass media in the hands of the state or wealthy capitalists able to distort public opinion.

Habermas's most important book was translated from German into English in 1989, just when the internet became a reality for American and British academics.[80] And a whole school of thought soon sprang up around the idea that the internet finally offered a chance to achieve the Habermasian ideal by creating a truly public sphere where everyone could participate in democratic discourse without the barriers of sex, race, class or power getting in the way of their voice being heard. Yochai Benkler's influential book from 2006, *The Wealth of Networks*, held out the promise of a unified or 'networked' public sphere where citizens could stop being passive recipients of 'received wisdom' from their biased TV and newspapers and become, instead, active participants in a more democratic, open and prosperous age.[81]

And, on the face of it, enabling people to find more out about each other across barriers of race, class, religion, geography, politics and language seemed like a nice idea. The biggest concern appeared to be whether everybody would get access fast enough to this amazing new resource, as well as the usual fears from libertarians that heavy-handed regulation by the state would spoil all the fun.

But Habermas himself, by now an old man, had remained silent. And when he did speak about the internet in 2006—the same year that Benkler's book was published—he infuriated his followers by suggesting it might not be quite as useful as they thought. Although Habermas recognised it can 'undermine the censorship of authoritarian regimes that try to control and repress public opinion,' he added: 'In the context of liberal regimes, the rise of millions of fragmented chat rooms across the world tend instead to lead to the fragmentation of large but politically focused mass audiences.'[82]

Howard Rheingold, one of the chief Habermasian cheerleaders for the internet, wrote an angry blog denouncing his former hero. He said that by referring merely to 'chat rooms', Habermas had shown he did not get the digital age where—'as millions of people know'—there is a vibrant public sphere of blogs and message boards. He suggested that since Habermas 'clearly does not understand a phenomenon that is central to the applicability of his theory in the twenty-first century' he should have decided to 'leave that work to younger scholars.'[83]

This is about as rude as rude can be in the academic world. And whether or not a German philosopher in his late seventies should get every nuance of the internet does seem to be rather beside the point, not least because the thrust of Habermas's argument has worn far better in the past decade than that of his critics. Of course, there were endless bloggers, YouTubers or people contributing below-the-line comments on *The Guardian* who would say they were opening up democratic participation and decision-making. But far from being a public sphere for reasoned discourse to reach consensus, the internet was increasingly fragmenting debate into 'alternative spheres' where different groups of people no longer always agreed even on the same facts.

The old media had many faults, not least the way it was already loosening respect for truth through the 1990s. But it was at least a relatively straight-forward exchange in which people buying the *Daily Mirror* in Britain or tuning into Rush Limbaugh in America probably knew what kind of bias they were getting.

But in the early years of this century, concern began to be voiced that the internet was encouraging people into a second—more hidden—dimension of bias. People began to filter the torrent of information and news coming at them by using their 'bookmarks' or 'favourites' to read only what they liked—and remove the bits they found disagreeable, boring or annoying. This was the 'Daily Me', a term popularised by Cass Sunstein, a Harvard law professor who later worked for Barack Obama.[84]

There is a vast body of psychological literature demonstrating how in-group bias works. The most famous and disturbing experiment was done with refugee children amid the bitter religious and ethnic divisions of Beirut in the 1960s.[85] Psychologists divided 11-year-old boys at a residential camp into two teams called the Blue Ghosts and the Red Genies. The study had to be abandoned after fighting broke out with knives stolen from the camp kitchen but, remarkably, this had nothing to do with Muslims and Christians because each team was more-or-less evenly divided between each. Instead, it was simply about being Blue or Red.

Sunstein's own research confirmed that the more people interacted in their group with people like them, the more polarised they became with other groups. One experiment involving different groups showed each ironed out internal differences to adopt purer positions when they debated with other members. For example, progressives who initially worried that action on climate change might hurt the poor came to toe the line after discussing the issue with like-minded people for only fifteen minutes. In other words, if you put a bunch of progressives together they become more left wing, while a group of conservatives will become increasingly right wing.

'Countless versions of this experiment are carried out online every day. The result is group polarisation, which occurs when like-minded people speak together and end up in a more extreme position in line with their original inclinations,' wrote Sunstein, who added: 'Given people's new power to create echo chambers, the result will be serious obstacles not merely to civility but also to mutual understanding and constructive problem solving. The Daily Me leads inexorably also to the Daily Them. That is a real problem for democracy.'[86]

In other circumstances, the free media might have been expected to arbitrate between two sides of an argument and protect a democratic public sphere. And there are countless examples of principled, fact-based journalism from the regulated fairness of British broadcasters to the quality press of the United States that have tried to do just that.

But the media itself had generally become more polarised and fragmented, as well as less worthy of trust, over the previous decades. Then came the disablement of newspapers as revenues went out with the digital tide and never came back. Finally, its dependency on a trickle of income from chasing the clicks and shares gave the old media a perverse incentive to abandon what was left of its standards and amplify whatever trends it could find from new media.

As for Habermas, who had spent so much of his career warning that the operation of monolithic mass media had corrupted the public sphere, he ended up suggesting that this same media might need propping up with government subsidies to save a descent into something even worse.

He said: 'When reorganisation and cost-cutting … jeopardise accustomed journalistic standards, it hits at the very heart of the political public sphere. Because, without the flow of information gained through extensive research, and without the stimulation of arguments based on an expertise that doesn't come cheap, public communication loses its discursive vitality. The public media would then cease to resist populist tendencies, and could no longer fulfil the function it should in the context of a democratic constitutional state.[87]

The digital age, far from building the kind of unified consensus in the 'public sphere' that Habermas said was essential for a healthy democracy, was devastating the best of the media and creating consensus only within bitterly opposed 'alternative spheres'.

5

Tyranny and Temptation in Politics

Analogue politicians

Gordon Brown had waited more than a decade to become prime minister and, by the time he finally succeeded Tony Blair on 27 June 2007, he
was no longer quite the New Labour moderniser he had once been.

Brown's style and temperament had hardened into the opposite of—
or even a rebuke to—his predecessor. In the words of the campaign
posters that briefly went up that year, the new prime minister was 'Not
flash, just Gordon'. Those posters swiftly came down again as Brown
called off an early election and he never regained his reputation for
either strength or stability.

But there was another measure that appeared to confirm he was neither a leader for the future, nor for very long: his initial indifference,
bordering on hostility, to fashionable ideas of digital democracy and
voter empowerment.

He had become leader of the party without a contest after his political
machine had pre-emptively crushed any potential challengers from both
the right and the left of the party. And, even before he took over from Blair,
one of his lieutenants in the Cabinet had dismissed Downing Street's voter
participatory experiments with 'e-petitions' as a stunt dreamt up 'by a
prat'.[1] A few months' later, Brown's first speech to the Labour conference
as leader—a long one of almost 8,000 words, setting out the challenges in
years to come—contained just one reference to the internet.

Spencer Livermore, who was Brown's chief strategist when he entered Downing Street, points out that Brown was 'steeped in conventional, traditional press operations' with gnarled warriors of spin like Charlie Whelan and Damian McBride running his communications through newspaper journalists in the Lobby. Livermore admits: 'For reasons of old habits, scepticism and total ignorance, we couldn't really have been less digitally-aware if we had tried.'[2]

Brown himself acknowledges he 'wasn't an ideal fit' for twenty-first-century political communications and 'an age of social media [that] elevates public displays of private emotion.' He wrote in his memoir: 'I was born forty years before the World Wide Web and arrived in parliament twenty years before the advent of Twitter … During my time as an MP I never mastered the capacity to leave a good impression or sculpt my image in 140 characters.'[3]

He would, of course, prefer to be remembered for achievements like the 2009 London G20 summit, when he managed to secure agreement from the world's major economies on measures to stabilise markets amid the global financial crisis 2008. Within a few days that success had been wiped from the front pages by a grotesque effort to gain a foothold in the new digital media world. Damian McBride wanted to set up a website called RedRag modelled on the Guido Fawkes blog, but somehow Guido Fawkes itself got hold of his emails. The subsequent row exposed the dark belly of the execrable media operation run by McBride that, by his own account, had always involved a bit of smearing even against MPs in his own party.[4] But it also showed how locked in he was to the old newspaper world of trading scraps of information and rumour.

'Gents,' began the first leaked email from McBride, discussing the kind of content they could run on Red Rag, '… a few ideas I have been working on …' He went on to list a series of false rumours or previously-denied allegations, including sex claims about a senior Tory MP's wife—most of which he had gleaned from his friends in the Lobby. Twenty minutes later, he got a reply from Derek Draper: 'Absolutely totally brilliant Damian. I'll think about timing and sort out the technology this week so we can go as soon as possible.'[5]

Draper, previously disgraced for his part in a 1997 lobbying scandal, had been readmitted to the ruling circle of the Labour Party because he had spotted the importance of having digital media. He had proposed setting up a series of left-of-centre blogs and websites to counter the success of the right in this area. But Draper had never asked McBride to send him these emails and emphasises he knew, even then, that many of these smears were unpublishable. 'My view was that Labour needed an internet strategy,' he says, 'and I saw this as my way back in to that very seductive place of power and certainty I had once enjoyed.'[6] The consequence, as he acknowledges, could not have been more counter-productive for both these objectives. McBride was forced to resign, Draper disappeared for a second time, and Brown was left trying to find a new way to conquer the internet.

Brown had previously gone 'viral' on YouTube only with a video of him picking his nose during Prime Minister's Question Time.[7] But, one week after the Red Rag row, and as the storm over MPs' expenses gathered around Westminster, Brown chose YouTube to announce cuts in parliamentary allowances. It had huge impact for all the wrong reasons. Coverage focused on his unnerving habit of smiling at random moments utterly unconnected with what he was saying.[8] Mention of 'young people' was suddenly accompanied by a huge grin, as if someone had told him that is how youth expected people to relate to them on the internet. Parliamentary sketch writer Simon Hoggart in *The Guardian* compared it to 'the smile a 50-year-old man might use on the parents of the 23-year-old woman he is dating, in a doomed attempt to reassure them.'[9] Unsurprisingly, the video has since been used in media training to illustrate the danger of inauthenticity on digital platforms.

John Woodcock, who was then one of Brown's chief media advisers, is keen to point out none of this was his idea. He says: 'It was a disaster, he looked so weird. It was a disaster too because this was the wrong topic—too serious—to do a stunt like this. And chiefly it as a disaster because it was so badly done, people could smell the inauthenticity.[10]

# # #

The new leader of the Conservative Party, David Cameron, was fifteen years younger than Brown and busy draping himself in the mantle of modernity that had fallen from Blair's shoulders. Cameron had already described Brown as 'the roadblock stopping Britain from meeting the challenges of the future,' adding: 'He is an analogue politician in a digital age. He is the past.'[11]

The Tory leader had a glistening, slightly moist, self-confidence that would have enabled him to slide effortlessly inside any era. Not for nothing did Steve Bell, *The Guardian*'s cartoonist, always portray him as wearing a condom on his head.[12] He launched 'WebCameron' on YouTube at the party conference in October 2006. The inaugural video showed him shirt-sleeved, scraping plates into a bin as his wife readied their children for school. 'Watch out BBC, ITV, Channel 4. We're the new competition,' he whispered into the camera. 'We're a bit wobbly, but this is one of the ways we want to communicate with people properly.'

In 2007, Cameron flew to the Google Zeitgeist conference in San Francisco—his costs met by the tech giant. After beginning with an explanation to this progressive liberal West Coast audience that he really wasn't like the gun-loving, gay-hating American conservatives, he launched into an almost embarrassingly effusive paean of praise for what was already one of the world's largest corporations: 'You are responsible for a large portion of the wonders of our modern world from the technology we use, to the products and services we rely on, to the innovations that improve the quality of billions of people's lives … Perhaps the greatest accomplishment of all is not something specific to any of the individual organisations represented here, but something that is the collective result of all your endeavours. And that is the new world of freedom we live in today.'[13]

His speech went on to suggest the internet would enable the human race to move beyond the 'bureaucratic era', in which overbearing governments had told people what to do for the last 100 years, to a 'post-bureaucratic era where true freedom of information makes possible a new world of responsibility, citizenship, choice and local control.'

Alongside him on the trip to California was the restless figure of Steve Hilton, the brains behind the 'demon eyes' advert that had caused so much trouble in 1997. He had returned to politics as Cameron's all-powerful strategist after spending a few years helping big corporations like McDonalds improve their image. Hilton was by then married to Rachel Whetstone and the couple were joint godparents to Cameron's eldest son. But Whetstone, a straight-talking and formidable Tory adviser had left politics in 2005 to become a successful executive with Google. When they came to visit me in Washington, a pregnant Whetstone fell asleep on the sofa as Hilton railed against the journalists back in London who were just 'too stupid' to understand how revolutionary Cameron would be.

At the heart of the modern Conservative programme, he said, was the idea of using digital technology and freely available information to rein-vent the relationship between citizen and state. And the speech Hilton had written for Cameron in California summed it all up perfectly; if only people would just pay attention.

However, the policy measures Cameron proposed were modest compared to the heights to which Hilton's rhetoric soared. He offered a bit more online transparency on spending and promised to make government data available on the internet so that people could hold service providers to account with things like 'crime maps'. George Osborne, the Shadow Chancellor who was never far from a Tory modernisation project, had himself travelled to California to meet tech entrepreneurs in 2006 and his aide, Rohan Silva, began working closely with Hilton to come up with some digital policy ideas. They settled on the idea of bringing 'nudge theory' into government to achieve change without passing laws or imposing draconian regulations.

The front cover of the Conservative Party manifesto in 2010 declared it was 'an invitation to join the government of Britain.' Inside, it stated: 'We believe in people power and today the information revolution gives us the practical tools to realise that philosophy.' But, aside from passing references to innovation, Silicon Valley and freedom of information, the people-powered agenda appeared to be much more about directly-elected police chiefs, recall mechanisms for corrupt MPs, and the recruitment of 5,000 full-time community organisers as part of an agenda to create a 'Big Society'.

And when Cameron became prime minister, the reality of his government was a disappointment for anyone hoping he would create some digitally democratic nirvana. There were undoubted improvements in mundane government websites, including making it easier to file a tax return. But each year he was in power, Whitehall granted a diminishing proportion of Freedom of Information requests. At the same time, the release of open data was criticised for being patchy or late,[14] while the Big Society agenda to empower citizens collapsed amid spending watchdog investigations into the waste of millions of pounds in public money.[15] Hilton alienated civil servants by forcing them to attend 'design-thinking workshops', advocating the abolition of most of their jobs, and proposing ideas like creating more sunshine through the use of 'cloud-bursting technology'. And, when he did not get his way, Hilton told friends he had been 'betrayed by Dave' and left to join Whetstone in California.

His mistake was to think that someone like Cameron, rooted in the Home Counties and the Establishment, was ever going to instigate a post-bureaucratic age or radicalise the concept of citizenry. Hilton was more useful to Cameron for his old skills as an advertising and marketing man than as the thinker of big thoughts.

The Tory leader had already said his party must stop 'banging on about Europe' and 'move to the centre, meeting the priorities of the modern world.' Hilton helped him re-brand the party with strikingly different language about the environment, open data and personal empowerment, as well as pictures of him hugging huskies on a glacier or riding his bike into work. It gave the media something else to talk about at a time when the Tory leader was already worried about his party sliding into an inward-looking nationalism. But it was always a shallow conversion; a paint job at best.

Ed Vaizey, who served over six years as Cameron's minister for the digital economy, was far from convinced it meant anything at all. He tells me: 'This agenda was really about positioning us as "with it" and young. But I am not sure there was a great deal of follow through. Cameron liked doing prime ministerial things and George [Osborne] was a master-manipulator of Whitehall turf battles. They weren't really interested in the relationship between citizens and the state, and I think there were missed opportunities.'[16]

Few people, probably not even those yearning to read more government data, would have switched their vote on the basis of the Conservatives' digital policy offer. And, even the much-vaunted internet campaign innovations were more for show than anything else. WebCameron, for instance, got an average of just 15,000 views for most of its videos, compared to the 7 million people who still watched the evening news in 2010. And when *Wired* magazine produced an admiring five-page profile of the Tory digital team at the 2010 election, it was told to interview Charlie Elphicke, the party's candidate in Dover who was a bit of poster-child for connectivity because he had a 'Facebook group with 71 fans'. Slightly embarrassingly, it discovered Elphicke was not using the party's expensive online Merlin system for canvassing returns but sheets of paper printed off from a now-defunct database.[17]

Craig Elder, who was the Conservatives' deputy digital director at the time, says: 'In 2010 the medium was at least part of the message. We felt lots of the stuff we did—WebCameron and so on—would allow David Cameron and the Conservatives to be presented as more modern than people might otherwise have thought. But looking back, it didn't have much depth—and more importantly it was usually only reaching the party faithful or the politically obsessed. Floating voters wouldn't have seen much, if any, of it at all.'[18]

Spencer Livermore, who had left Brown's side by 2008, watched through the fingers of his hands subsequent efforts by the Labour Party to adapt to the new environment. He says: 'Over and over again we had been told this would be the moment when the digital age met politics. But the elections of 2001 and 2005 had been fought through broadcast and newspapers in the air and a decent operation with canvassing and leaflets on the ground. In the end, it was the case in 2010 too. But that didn't stop people pushing Gordon to do things like his YouTube video. The trouble was that you couldn't move for people telling you in 2008 and 2009 how Barack Obama's digital campaign had transformed everything. And I think that got in everyone's heads.'[19]

Much of the 2010 campaign was dominated by the press, and particularly the broadcast media as the UK enjoyed its first ever TV debates. And, if there was one story people remember from this election it was Brown's off-camera remarks, caught a by Sky News microphone. As he left Rochdale where he had spoken about immigration to a pensioner called Gillian Duffy, he was heard telling aides that he thought she was a 'sort of bigoted woman'.

But 2010 was also described as the 'Mumsnet election' as party leaders queued up to submit themselves to live WebChats with readers of the site.[20] But Justine Roberts, Mumsnet's co-founder, says it was more than a desire to address what had been identified as a key group of voters. 'They all wanted to appear modern and on the ball,' she says. 'The problem was some of them thought they could pigeon-hole the readers. Gordon Brown went on and on about childcare tax credits without realising that women might also want to talk about the economy. Eventually the readers got so fed up they all started asking him his favourite biscuit. Cameron showed that he was at least listening.'[21]

Ultimately Brown and Cameron were both analogue politicians. Just as Blair and Clinton had before them, they saw some political advantage in being associated with such modernity. Cameron, in particular, was entranced by technology because it made him look good and provided cosmetic cover for an unmodernised Conservative Party. But he had neither the inclination nor the policies needed to embrace it properly. The only real difference between them was that Cameron was better than Brown at faking it. And, as Livermore suggests, both were casting envious eyes across the Atlantic at Obama for whom it all seemed to come so naturally.

Yes, we can! No, you can't!

Just 24 hours after Barack Obama had beaten John McCain to win the 2008 US presidential election, Silicon Valley's progressive legions gathered in a euphoric mood under the crystal chandeliers and vaulted ceilings of San Francisco's Palace Hotel.

The slogan of their summit was 'Web Meets World'. Organisers announced that the internet's 'greatest inventions are, at their core, social movements' which can be used to solve global problems. They added: 'To that end, we're expanding our program this year to include leaders in the fields of healthcare, genetics, finance, global business, and yes, even politics.'[22]

One such invitee, Arianna Huffington, the formerly conservative but now liberal founder of the Huffington Post, used her panel to declare: 'Let me put this bluntly: were it not for the internet, Barack Obama would not be president; were it not for the internet, Barack Obama would not have been the Democratic nominee.'

She got applause for saying the efforts of a vigilant blogosphere had 'killed off' the style of fear-and-smear politics characterised by Bush's years. This time the fear-mongering had failed because, she said, 'the idea that Barack Obama was a strange socialist terrorist was not believable when the truth kept intruding into peoples' rooms.'[23]

Joe Trippi had run the 2004 Howard Dean campaign described in Chapter 3 that had first tried to harness the power of the internet for politics. He pointed out that one in eighteen of all Americans had signed up on the internet to organise, fund raise, communicate with each other or share information about Obama. This vast online army, said Trippi, would make the new president extraordinarily powerful. 'Congress will get caught between a rock and hard place if it refuses to go with his agenda. It won't be [up against] just the president but millions of connected people.'[24]

The metrics for Obama's campaign were, indeed, jaw-dropping at the time. Even though more Republicans were connected to the internet in 2008, studies showed that this new medium was disproportionately benefitting the Democrats, with voters who got their news online more likely to vote for Obama or give him money.[25] He received $500 million in donations via the internet, smashing all records for online fund-raising. His campaign established its own social network, MyBarackObama. com—known as MyBO—with over 2 million accounts that had posted 400,000 blogs and organised 200,000 events.[26]

Such success was no accident. It had been built, like many of the best technological innovations, by learning from earlier failures. Joe Rospars had been an amateur blogger in 2004 who dropped everything and rented a van with some friends so he could hitch a ride on the free-wheeling Dean campaign. 'It was chaos,' he says, 'we were telling people just to show up in Iowa and knock on some doors. There was no data, no message, no strategy.'[27] In the ashes of Dean's campaign, however, Rospars systematically worked through the lessons learned for this new form of internet-driven politics. Three years later, Rospars was Obama's chief digital adviser in a campaign that for the first time turned Howard Dean's dreams into a brutally effective reality.

'We built these tools for people to organise their events and ended up with tens of thousands of groups which snapped together perfectly,' says Rospars.[28] At times, the Obama campaign was still assembling the rocket as it was taking off, at others it was trailing in the wake of the enthusiasm of his activists. For instance, the campaign only began putting money into the Idaho caucuses after local people had built such a head of steam for his candidacy it became clear he could win it.

'Yes we can!' they shouted at rallies, and for a heady few months, they did. The language he used was similar to that of digital entrepreneurs like Mark Zuckerberg, who was expanding Facebook out of college cam-puses with the aim of making a better, 'more open and connected' world. It felt as if Obama, with the energy and excitement surrounding his historically-charged candidacy, was ready to lead this changing world. And it was not the policies that Obama espoused which seemed radical so much as the inclusive, empowered means by which they would be achieved. 'It's different, not because of me,' he said, 'it's different because of you.'

I remember hearing him speak after his crucial first win in Iowa when the ecstasy of his supporters thundered around the hall so loudly that even Obama's baritone struggled to be heard. The start of his speech was interrupted several times by wild cheering of the sort I had never heard at a political rally before: 'You know … they said … they said … they said … this day … would never come … They said our sights were set too high. They said this country was too divided; too disillusioned to ever come together around a common purpose. But on this January night—at this defining moment in history—you have done what the cynics said we couldn't do: you came together as Democrats, Republicans and independents to stand up and say that we are one nation, we are one people, and our time for change has come.'[29]

# # #

The reality of the Obama presidency, however, was very different. Far from being one of bi-partisan unity on the change America needed, it was characterised by deepening polarisation, legislative gridlock in Washington, the emergence of the Tea Party Movement and, eventually, the Alt Right. America was of course fighting two wars and battling the effects of the global financial crisis, so it was never going to be easy.

But the biggest disappointment for many of his supporters was Obama's retreat from the online movement he had created. Just when Trippi was telling the San Francisco tech conference that Obama would use the power of 'millions of connected people' to break partisan gridlock, many of those activists were bombarding the Obama campaign with questions. One frustrated volunteer from Pennsylvania said: 'We're all fired up now, and twiddling our thumbs! Nowwhatnowwhatnowwhat?'[30]

David Plouffe, the campaign director, emailed the list asking them what they wanted to do and more than half a million replied. Some 86 per cent said they wanted to help Obama pass legislation through grassroots support, 68 per cent wanted to help elect candidates who shared his vision and, most remarkably of all, more than 50,000 of respondents said they wanted to run for elected office themselves.[31]

But none of that happened. Obama's team, including Plouffe, balked at proposals to take a 'Movement 2.0' into the White House. They were returning to the insider politics they understood, which meant pushing the new president's agenda through the 'traditional channels' of reaching out to members of Congress, offering them jobs in the administration, positions on committees or cash for their districts.

Once the election was over, MyBO, Obama's vast, effervescent online network for change—was renamed Organising for America (OFA) and tipped into the grinding political machinery of the Democratic Party. 'Yes we can!', a chant still echoing around the great cities of America, was replaced with a regretful slight shake of the head that told them, 'No you can't.' And rather than turning out hundreds of thousands of voters at rallies for Obama's health care reform, the activists simply switched off.

When healthcare reforms ran into trouble, the White House belatedly asked them through the OFA to sign a vapid 'statement of support' for the health care reforms. But only 300,000 out of the 13 million answered a late plea to make phone calls backing watered-down reforms. In the 2010 Congressional elections, the Democrats lost the ground war and control of both houses in Congress. In the years that followed, activists complained Obama was sometimes thin-skinned in his dealings with them, bristling when criticised, or dismissive of their efforts to be heard at a time when the White House wanted them to be little more than an online version of traditional cheerleaders.[32]

Rospars is among those who thought a mistake had been made. After the election he went back to his business, Blue State Digital, saying he felt that was the best way to 'keep the flame of our approach alive ... there was some risk of it being tossed aside.'

He adds: 'There was a lot going on, not least with the economy collapsing at the time. Although people made a good faith effort to try to use the energy from the campaign to benefit the whole party, if you look at the political strategy from the time, it was pretty clear the president and his staff were focused on the inside game. He wanted to get things done and, temperamentally, Barack Obama was never going to deploy a grassroots army at politicians in his own party just to get what he wanted. But was there an opportunity left on the table? For sure.'[33]

Others had always been more sceptical about Obama's commitment to digital empowerment. Zephyr Teachout, another veteran from the Dean campaign, warned as early as 2007 that 'some very smart people have figured out how to organise your excitement.' She added: 'The subtext is "you don't have the power."'[34]

Perhaps this was inevitable from a campaign that had been determined to avoid the freak-show chaos of Dean four years earlier and a new president whose preternatural calm was a sharp contrast to political activists on the internet. And there were real concerns that Obama risked replacing the old pressure from lobbyists, donors and big media proprietors with that from the fired up partisan activists who populated the message boards of the Daily Kos and were already beginning to dominate social media. As one former Obama staffer puts it: 'We live in a democracy that elected Barack Obama to be a president not a representative of an email list.'

And yet, looking back, it still feels that there was a special opportunity as so many people got so excited about what was essentially a pragmatic, evidence-based and centrist politician calling for change through consensus. Obama was a once-in-a-lifetime candidate who both inspired people and plugged politics into the technology that was transforming the world. It is hard not to wonder what might have been possible if the president and his activists had together continued to dominate politics on the internet.

Instead, Obama went into the White House and shut the door.

# # #

The new president did not give up on the information age, far from it. Obama can justifiably claim to have been America's first digital president who, by 2012, had amassed 28 million followers on Facebook, attended Google hang-outs, released playlists of his favourite songs on Spotify, launched his own app, used his own messages on Twitter to bypass an occasionally critical mainstream media, and created the United States Digital Service so that technology could be used to improve government.

But all these were the actions of a corporately tech-savvy president rather the insurgent leader of an online army. The new administration had a trifecta of executive positions modelled on corporate best practice: chief technology officer, chief data scientist and chief performance officer. Obama nurtured relationships with the new billionaires in Silicon Valley like Steve Jobs at Apple and Mark Zuckerberg at Facebook, supporting policies they wanted, such as net neutrality, which prevented internet service providers discriminating against any of their applications or platforms.[35] He took Brian Chesky, the chief executive of Airbnb, with him when he went to Cuba, perhaps to symbolise how America's technological revolution was now more meaningful than the Caribbean island's political revolution more than half a century before.

Flooding into the space he vacated were a different set of activists, particularly from libertarian right, who lacked the moral leadership and progressive purpose that had seemed so strong in 2008. Conservative billionaires like the Koch brothers helped pay for the online coordination of the Tea Party movement's hundreds of seemingly spontaneous meetings to oppose Obama's stimulus plan and healthcare proposals.[36] False stories—about Obama's real place of birth, his religion, and his plans for so-called 'death panels' to determine whether elderly people qualified for care—flew free across the internet before landing in Fox News panel discussions and talk radio.

The activists of the Tea Party helped define Obama in the minds of millions of Americans, and, after he left office, they helped unpick much of his legacy. Whether their rise could have been slowed or even halted if Obama had put more effort into empowering his own grassroots network is a question that seemed to haunt him in some of his end-of-office interviews. He still hankers after it, saying 'one of his big suggestions' for Democrats now is 'how do we do more of that ground-up building?'[37]

An Arab Spring and a Russian Winter

If the new president was getting cold feet about digitally-powered democracy in the United States, nobody told the young people clamouring for the same thing across North Africa and the Middle East.

The Arab Spring began in December 2010 when Mohamed Bouazizi, a Tunisian street vendor whose wheelbarrow of fruit and scales had been confiscated by the authorities, set fire to himself in protest. Within months, the governments of Tunisia, Egypt and Libya had been toppled, while those of Yemen, Bahrain and Syria were wobbling too.

Although there has since been much debate about whether social media drove or merely accelerated these revolutions,[38] they swiftly got bundled up and branded with the digital hype of the time. Protesters spray-painted the logos of Californian tech corporations on to walls of ancient Arab cities while a baby girl in Egypt was even named 'Facebook Jamal Ibrahim' in tribute to the role the network played in organising the protests in Tahrir Square.[39]

Obama himself got very excited about the possibilities that the web would ensure that 'repression will fail and that tyrants will fall,' through its ability to help people organise non-violent protest. 'Satellite television and the internet provide a window into the wider world,' he declared. 'Cell phones and social networks allow young people to connect and organise like never before. And so a new generation has emerged—and their voices tell us that change cannot be denied.'[40]

Within a couple of years, the Obama administration's passion for the Arab Spring had cooled as the revolutions splintered into factions, terror and violence. Islamic militants killed the US ambassador in Libya, the democratically-elected president of Egypt was removed by an allegedly American-backed military coup, while the death toll of Syria's civil war climbed to over 100,000. As Marc Lynch, a critic of the web's polarising role in the mayhem, remarked: 'There is something very different about scrolling through pictures and videos of unified, chanting Yemeni or Egyptian crowds demanding democratic change and waking up to a gory image of a headless 6-year-old girl on your Facebook news feed.'[41]

# # #

But Washington's boasts about how the technology developed in Silicon Valley would spread liberal democratic values through the world had not gone unnoticed in countries where the authoritarian leaders had long been troubled by the prospect of uncontrolled information. By 2008, China had already completed construction of its Great Firewall of censorship to block blacklisted websites and platforms such as Google and Facebook. It was part of the wider Golden Shield project to conduct surveillance over citizens' use of the internet as well as nurturing the country's own increasingly lucrative tech industry, which included firms like Tencent and Alibaba.

The Arab Spring is said to have alerted Chinese authorities to the 'existential threat the internet posed' to their regime. And, little more than a decade after Bill Clinton warned that seeking control over the internet would be like trying to 'nail jello to the wall,' the country's new president, Xi Jinping, and his internet tsar, Lu Wei, showed that with a big hammer and a sharp nail, almost anything could be achieved.

The scope for anonymous posting shrank dramatically as new rules were introduced requiring users to register online accounts with their real names and phone numbers.[42] The number of Chinese security officials policing the internet swelled to an estimated 30,000–50,000 while a 'troll-army' of another 250,000–300,000 *wumaodang* or '50-cent party members' got paid tiny sums to influence social media discussions in support of the government's position. Companies also began hiring their own self-censorship teams, knowing if they did not immediately remove material deemed offensive they faced being shut down. By 2013 it was estimated that a total of 2 million people were employed by both the state and commercial organisations in monitoring the internet.[43] At the same time a chilling effect swept across the Chinese web as the regime began arresting celebrity bloggers before shaming them on national television.[44]

Lu began proselytising for his philosophy of 'internet sovereignty' by which countries could set their own rules rather than accept the libertarian free-for-all that had blown across their societies from the west coast shores of northern California. Governments with an authoritarian streak that have since taken note include those in Thailand, Laos, Saudi Arabia, Serbia, Turkey and the United Arab Emirates.[45] But the country that really pricked up its ears was Russia.

# # #

In 2011, with the Arab Spring in full flower, Vladimir Putin was eyeing a return to his country's presidency. He had obeyed Yeltsin's democratic constitution by stepping down as president in 2008, while staying on as prime minister. But a deal struck with Dmitry Medvedev, his slightly more liberal successor, meant the two men would swap jobs when victories for their United Russia Party had been secured in parliamentary and presidential elections in December 2011 and March 2012. Although the results of those elections were never really in doubt, evidence of no less than 7,000 instances of polling station irregularities was posted on an interactive website by Russia's independent election watchdog, the Movement for the Defence of Voters' Rights—or 'Golos'.[46]

Mass protests erupted in Moscow, some of them organised on Facebook where Alexei Navalny, a nationalistic anti-corruption blogger on LiveJournal who routinely condemned Putin's party as one of 'crooks and thieves', had emerged as a figurehead. 'There are enough people here to seize the Kremlin,' he yelled into a microphone with a degree of unjustified hyperbole, at one such rally, 'we are the power!'[47] After numerous arrests, cyberattacks, raids and imprisonments, Navalny would use his fame to build multi-million strong followings on Twitter and YouTube. And he acknowledges that whatever impact he has had would not have been possible without the web, saying: 'Probably you can call me a person of the internet.'[48]

But Putin, who had long since suspected that the US had fostered the earlier 'colour revolutions' on what had once been Soviet soil in Georgia and Ukraine, was less worried about how to deal with leaders like Navalny than the capacity of this Western technology to build movements without having identifiable ringleaders who could be locked up.[49] Putin explicitly blamed Hillary Clinton, the then US secretary of state, for fomenting the Moscow protests, saying: 'She set the tone for some of our actors in the country and gave the signal. They heard this and, with the support of the US State Department, began active work.'[50]

The Kremlin is said to have taken particular interest in remarks made by Alec Ross, the innovation adviser at the US State Department on a visit to London in 2011, where he described the internet as the 'Che Guevara of the twenty-first century' and declared that authoritarian regimes 'are now more vulnerable than they have ever been before ... because of the devolution of power from the nation state to the individual.'[51]

During the Moscow protests, it had become painfully apparent to the FSB—Russia's state security police—that all they could do in response to the crowd-recruiting power of the web was to deploy 30-year-old technology by sending a fax to the social network, VKontakte, vainly ordering it to block the websites of protest groups.[52] In March 2012, Sergei Smirnov, the deputy director of the FSB, admitted they had yet to find ways to tackle the social networks, saying they were being 'used by Western special services to create and maintain a level of continual tension in society with serious intentions extending even to regime change.'[53]

The fate of Viktor Yanukovych, Ukraine's president and Putin's ally, terrified the Kremlin. On 21 November 2013, after he announced that plans for new links with the EU had been shelved in favour of closer ties with Russia, a young activist opposed to the regime opened his Facebook account and posted the following message: 'Come on guys, let's be serious. If you really want to do something, don't just "like" this post. Write that you are ready, and we can try to start something.'[54]

After more 600 replies, he posted again, suggesting protesters congregate on Kiev's Maidan Square and bring some warm clothes. Within days the 'winter encampment' had grown to tens of thousands without any mainstream political leadership and, after violent clashes with riot police, Yanukovych was eventually removed from office.

# # #

Back in the Kremlin, Putin had strengthened his grip with laws enabling authorities to filter the internet and blacklist the sites it did not like through a full-scale censorship agency, Roskomnadzor[55] And when Edward Snowden leaked the US government's surveillance capabilities, Putin had the excuse he needed to pass new laws requiring Western internet companies like Google, Apple, Facebook and Twitter to store their data within the Russian border. The intention was not, of course, to protect the country's civilians from US surveillance so much as to ensure that Russia's security forces could access it too. And the great joy for the Kremlin was that the world's most prominent critic of state surveillance had fled to Russia itself to escape prosecution. Before long, Moscow was hosting a Russia–China cyber security forum, with Lu Wei in attendance, where these two great powers declared their 'digital sovereignty' over the American multinationals.

Alexey Kovalev, who was then working as a senior editor for a state-run broadcaster, describes how the limited leeway he had enjoyed disappeared soon after. 'New managers came in, telling us "patriots first and journalists second,"' he says. 'They rarely tell you what to write but you develop a sort of sixth sense, a kind of self-censorship, on what they will find acceptable.'[56]

He has since set up a blog to debunk false information coming from the Kremlin called Noodle Remover—the name is inspired by the Russian saying that when you deceive people you are 'hanging noodles from ears'. On a Skype call from Moscow, he says that each year a number of opposition websites are banned by Roskomnadzor, on spurious grounds, such as the discovery of extremist content in a below-the-line comment. The ban will often be issued by a remote provincial prosecutor's office, thousands of kilometres away from the journalists who are unable to defend themselves. But when the censors tried to block him 'they were so incompetent that they typed in the wrong URL and I just carried on.'

Kovalev says: 'Although they would like to be more like China—and it is getting worse each year—they are so useless and corrupt, so reliant on the internet themselves for their car navigation systems and foreign bank accounts, that I don't think we'll ever get blanket censorship.'[57] Instead, a more effective tool is to use automated social media accounts, known as 'bots' to make material disappear from people's social network feeds using Western technology. Kovalev describes it like this: 'I recently uploaded a YouTube video and got 3,000 "dislikes" in just a few minutes. That sort of bot activity will have a huge influence on the algorithm and will mean very few people will ever see that video. It is a very common form of harassment in Russia. If you get a thousand dislikes on Facebook your account can be blocked for weeks. Moscow City Hall has its own bot army working for it, there is a whole industry around this. Look, I can go downstairs to a shop now where there is a vending machine and buy 100 likes for an Instagram picture right now. I can go online and buy 1,000 Twitter bots for the price of two coffees. This is not Russian censorship but Western technology. And none of them—YouTube, Twitter, Facebook—do anything about it.'[58]

# # #

Putin's digital strategy was not just for domestic use, it was for export too. Russia had already used cyberattacks to shut down the internet—a so-called Distributed Denial of Service attack—of its perceived enemies in the former Soviet republics of Estonia and South Ossietia. The next step was to become a combatant in what it regarded as the information war being waged by the West.

Pavel Zolotarev, a retired Russian general, was quoted in *The New Yorker*, saying that old 'grandfather-style' methods of seeking to influence Western journalists were ineffective: 'We had come to the conclusion, having analysed the actions of Western countries in the post-Soviet space—first of all the United States—that manipulation in the information sphere is a very effective tool...all of a sudden, new means have appeared.'[59]

Putin replaced his former political technologist, Vladislav Surkov, with Vyacheslav Volodin, a hardliner who began a new policy of systematically monitoring and manipulating social networks. Pro-Putin youth groups were already seeking to disrupt the conversation on social media and the Kremlin had recently established a 'school of bloggers'. But the Russian president wanted more action—and urgently.[60]

In 2013, the independent newspaper, *Novaya Gazeta*, exposed an operation in a St Petersburg suburb where employees were paid 25,000 rubles a month to post comments on blogs and articles. It was soon being described as a 'troll farm'. Further leaks from this farm, including a paper discussing how to avoid being spotted by American readers, showed they were not just targeting Russian public opinion.[61] The work was not particularly glamorous, nor were 'trolls' in their original anarchic cyberpunk form.

Instead, they were what Kovalev calls 'failed journalists and hard-up language students' doing dreary, repetitive work in the name of the state. He says most of them are not particularly political and points out how a lot of them appear on other forms of social media moaning about the boredom of their jobs. The St Petersburg 'troll farm', now named the Internet Research Centre was expanded to 250 people who worked in twelve-hour shifts and were required to post 135 comments a day.

In an interview with the US-backed Radio Free Europe, Marat Burkhard, a former employee, described how there was different department for targets such as Ukraine, Facebook and English-speaking sites like the BBC and CNN, which got 'bombarded' with posts. Burkhard said they would work in teams with a 'villain' who crudely stirs controversy before being brought back into line by others who provide factual support for the Government's position with links and pictures or graphics.

He said: 'The funniest [instruction] was when US President Barack Obama chewed gum in India and then spit it out. "You need to write 135 comments about this, and don't be shy about how you express yourself. Write whatever you want, just stick the word Obama in there a lot and then cover it over with profanities." In the assignment, there's always a conclusion you've got to make—it's already written that Obama is a black monkey who doesn't know anything about culture.'[62]

The work of such state trolls, as well as that of mainstream state-funded propaganda outfits like the TV channel Russia Today and the news agency Sputnik, was increasingly amplified by tens of thousands of bots that relentlessly pushed messages through the echo chambers of social media. The objective was not just to undermine those who had just imposed sanctions on Russia after the annexation of Crimea or scorned the fairness of Russia's elections but also to throw back in the face of the West the idea that liberal democracy was anything special.

After the 2014 referendum on Scottish independence resulted in a narrow victory for the 'No' campaign (in favour of staying in the UK), self-styled election observers from the Russian Public Institute of Electoral Law produced a dossier packed with spurious irregularities. These included asking why video equipment was banned from polling stations, complaining counting halls were too big to see what was happening, and pointing out how the traditional black ballot boxes used in Britain were not transparent.

The allegations were first reported by Sputnik, which directly linked them to controversy over a referendum held in Crimea in 2014 over whether the region would be part of Ukraine or Russia. The accusations were promptly posted on a Facebook account called 'Rally for a Revote'. Videos purporting to show proof of ballot-rigging were pushed by social media accounts from the St Petersburg troll farm. Before long, an online petition with 100,000 names was delivered to First Minister Nicola Sturgeon demanding another vote 'counted by impartial international parties' while protesters carrying saltires descended on the Scottish parliament.[63] Soon afterwards, Sputnik opened its first UK bureau in Edinburgh, headed by Oxana Brazhnik, who had no previous journalistic experience but was a former political adviser to the Kremlin's Volodin.[64]

Douglas Alexander, the former Labour Cabinet minister, recalls a supermarket conversation with a voter in his Paisley South constituency at this time: 'The conversation began inauspiciously with her explaining that she would never vote for me again "because of the referendum". I then suggested regardless of how we had voted, surely we could all now come together on the basis of the decision that, as Scots, we'd reached. She was having none of it, saying: "But that's not the decision we reached." I asked her if she thought it was a conspiracy. "Yes," she replied, because everyone she knew had voted for independence. Exasperated, I asked her what she did for a living. "I'm a senior Social Worker," she replied. And where did she get her news? "Off Facebook, every night," she replied.'[65]

# # #

But Putin himself would probably measure the effectiveness of any cyber warfare according to the impact it made on his chief target: the US. And by such a metric, probably the most important piece of its weaponry was not the troll farm, it was hackers. In 2013, the Russian military announced that it was forming 'information operations' battalions staffed by graduates from the country's leading technical universities. The next year, it began recruiting young programmers with social-media ads depicting a soldier putting down a rifle and turning to a keyboard, accompanied by a heavy-metal soundtrack.[66]

Later that year, Russians intercepted and posted on YouTube an embarrassing phone conversation between American diplomats in which one could be heard declaring, 'Fuck the EU'. Then a hacking group known as the Dukes successfully gained access to the US State

Department systems for a 24-hour period.[67] According to European and US intelligence service officials, the hacker teams then turned their attentions to undermining Angela Merkel, the German chancellor or helping Marine Le Pen's *Front National* in France.[68] Most importantly of all, American intelligence agencies say the Russians gained access to the email system of the US Democratic Party and, later, the account belonging to John Podesta, chief of staff at Hillary Clinton's presidential campaign.[69] These resulted in the hugely damaging disclosures during the presidential election. US security experts admitted afterwards they had been caught flat-footed by the scale and sophistication of such cyberattacks. 'The Russians got much smarter since the days of rent-a-crowds and bogus leaflets,' one official was quoted saying.[70]

The reason for such complacency was that America regarded this Silicon Valley technology as its own. The people working for these tech companies were friends and allies of the Obama administration. In 2012, even as the Kremlin was re-arming for a cyber-war in the future, the president was more concerned with how he could use Facebook to win himself a second term.

When voters became data

When Obama began his campaign for re-election, the instruction was to 'get back to the we' that had defined the grassroots movement four years previously. But this was now a one-way relationship. Although the president knew he needed people to knock on doors, persuade their friends and donate more than ever, the idea that they would be given a real stake in how America was governed had evaporated.

Matthew McGregor, a member of his online team, says: 'The path to victory in 2008 had run through self-organising, make-it-up-as-you-go along local enthusiasm and trial and error of new campaign techniques. It worked for that time. In 2012, after four years of hard governing, the clearer path to victory was through clinical use of data, more control over message, and much more careful management. It wasn't as pretty, but it was what worked. The Electoral College doesn't include points for style.'[71]

Obama's campaign director in 2012 was Jim Messina, who had arrived late in 2008 after a long career as a behind-the-scenes fixer in the Senate. He had little of the starry-eyed vision about people-powered politics that characterised some of his colleagues and, during Obama's first term in the White House, Messina clashed frequently with grassroots activists campaigning on issues such as health care, gay rights and immigration.[72]

Instead of empowering people, he set about measuring them by mining vast seams of data. Messina spent an unprecedented $100 million on technology at the campaign's Chicago headquarters, hired an analytics department five times bigger than that of 2008 with an official chief scientist who had once crunched huge data to maximize the efficiency of supermarket sales promotions, and did 66,000 computer simulations every night to work out where to put ads the next morning.[73]

All potential swing-state voters were allocated four numbers: the first, on a scale of one to 100, represented the likelihood that they would support Obama. The second assessed the chances of them using their vote. The third evaluated the consistency with which they maintained their views. A fourth estimated how persuadable they were on a particular issue.[74] As one admiring academic study put it later: 'the campaign didn't just know who you were; it knew exactly how it could turn you into the type of person it wanted you to be.'[75]

What the scientists were up to in their cordoned-off section of the Chicago headquarters known as 'The Cave' was a closely-guarded secret, with one staffer referring to the numbers they produced as 'our nuclear codes' and the key advantage they had over the Republican candidate, Mitt Romney.[76] Just as sports teams like the Oakland Athletics in baseball had used the Moneyball approach of analytics and data to become more competitive, the Obama team was using techniques gleaned from social science experiments.[77] These aimed to identify and reach supporters with weak voting habits who were most likely to be persuadable.[78]

Using demographic information was not new in elections. Bill Clinton's campaigns in America and those of Tony Blair in Britain had targeted particular socio-economic groups—'soccer moms' in the US, or the so-called 'Worcester Woman' or 'Mondeo Man' in the UK. What was different was the sheer scale, the level of individual granularity, and above all, the innovations in how they harvested data.

# # #

Romney's team were initially puzzled when Obama buying ads in fringe markets, on marginal stations, and at odd times. Campaign messages that had traditionally been placed either side of TV news would appear during late night re-runs or shows like *Sons of Anarchy*, *The Walking Dead* and *Don't Trust the B—in Apt. 23*.[79] But Obama's campaign had done deals with cable TV providers so that it could access the bills they sent out and individual viewing histories. If target voters were watching zombie movies at 3am, the campaign knew how to find them.[80]

Still more significant was the way it harvested data from Facebook, which by then had a user base approaching 1 billion. Whenever someone logged in to the Obama re-election site on Facebook, 'targeted sharing' protocols instantly ingested all the information they stored—home location, date of birth, interests and, most importantly of all, network of friends—directly into the campaign's database. Algorithms would then rifle through the contents to find voters it needed to persuade or people who it could mobilise or maybe solicit donations from as part of a $1 billion online fundraising drive.[81]

If that sounds familiar, it is because a very similar process is at the heart of the scandal that later erupted over the British firm, Cambridge Analytica. Its access to millions of Facebook accounts, which it allegedly used to help elect Donald Trump, only broke the rules because Facebook had changed them in 2015 to stop apps getting information about people's friends. Obama was doing much the same in 2012 with full permission from Facebook. This is what Carol Davidsen, director of data integration and media analytics for Obama for America, said: 'We ingested the entire US social graph. We would ask permission to basically scrape your profile, and also scrape your friends, basically anything that was available to scrape. We scraped it all.'[82]

And this is what Messina said at the time: 'It allowed us to use Facebook to persuade people. We figured out a simple truth: what your friends and family and neighbours say is more important to your consumer decisions and your political decisions than anything else. So in the final six days of the campaign, 6 million people logged onto to Facebook through BarackObama.com and they saw a 20-second Michelle Obama video—because everyone loves Michelle Obama—and at the end of the 20 seconds we had matched our data with their data and we gave each of them five of their best friends who are undecided voters and we said click here to send them a video, click here to send them information and of those 78 per cent voted for Barack Obama.'[83]

The use of all this data helped the campaign not just to appeal to voters with broad policy pronouncements but to micro-target individuals.

A tailor-made message could be delivered to each of them with scientific precision. Messina said his favourite story of the campaign was from Wisconsin ten days out from polling day: an Obama volunteer was knocking on doors on one side of the street and the Romney campaign was knocking on doors on the other.

He said: 'The Obama volunteer was asked to hit two doors. One was an undecided voter and she knew exactly what to say. The other was an absentee ballot and she was told to make sure they filled it out and returned it. On the other side of the street, the Romney campaign was knocking on every single door. Most of the people weren't home, and most of the people that were home were already supporting Barack Obama. ... That's what data can do.'[84]

An incumbent president carrying the battle scars of four years in the White House, Obama was never going to run for re-election with a campaign based on hope, change and individual empowerment. And yet the level of desiccated calculation was a very sharp contrast to the idealism that had swirled around Obama's candidacy in 2008. The campaign in 2012 elevated analytics to the place once occupied by heart and soul as Messina coined little metric-inspired aphorisms such as 'low-information voters think about politics less than four minutes a week.'[85]

In a nod to Obama's earlier incarnation, Messina claimed such number-crunching methods contained a human dimension by taking everyone's views into account and made it more likely voters would be contacted in a way they wanted.[86] But none of this was really about giving ordinary people a bigger voice in a new digital democracy, it was about turning voters and the magic of the ballot box into giant matrices, thousands of rows and columns of data running across a screen. And politics doesn't need to listen to what people are trying to say if technology can discover what it needs to win their vote while they slump in front of cable TV.

The micro-targeting of voters both reflected and drove the polarisation of voters into alternative spheres that had been gathering pace in the early years of this century. Previous campaigns were pulled to the centre because they had to tailor messages for the main news bulletins— or place ads either side of them—that would appeal to as broad a spectrum of opinion as possible. But, as the centre became squeezed, campaigns became increasingly focused on energising and expanding their base. While Republicans sent an eighteen-wheeler truck—'Reggie the Registration Rig'—to NASCAR motor racing events and country-music shows to mobilise conservative voters, Obama's team adopted a much more analytic approach to registering voters from African-Americans, Hispanics, the young, and highly educated whites—who backed him overwhelmingly.[87]

In 2012, the world's most powerful progressive politician was not worried about Russian cyber warfare. Nor was he particularly concerned any more about the information age leading to a loss of control over the agenda or the polarisation of voters. Instead, his team was harnessing the power of technology to control electoral outcomes better than any had done before.

# # #

As for Messina, he showed considerable skill in presenting himself after Obama's victory as someone possessing the recipe for the 'secret sauce' needed to win elections, even though he was not a data scientist himself.[88] Among all the commercial clients scrambling to hire his services was another blue-chip political campaign: David Cameron's Conservative Party.

Initially, there was some scepticism about whether the analytic alchemy of Obama's campaign in 2012 could easily be transplanted to Britain, where there were stricter data privacy laws as well as a ban on TV advertising and limits on campaign spending. But the Conservatives were investing heavily in identifying their target voters and finding new ways to reach them. Craig Elder, who was brought back from the private sector to head the party's digital strategy in 2013 and given a seat at the top table for the coming election, describes how Facebook was immediately identified as a key part of their plan.

He says: 'By 2015, Facebook reached around 55 per cent of the entire UK population and it was becoming about a lot more than just a platform for "young people"—Facebook was now used by mums, dads, and grandparents too. In addition, its advertising and data targeting capabilities meant we could really focus who we were talking to, and where—namely undecided voters in the marginal constituencies that would ultimately decide the election—and tailor our communications to make sure people were receiving the messages most relevant to them.'[89]

A vast and unprecedented effort was also being made by the Conservatives in getting good data with which to work. Elder says that as early as 2013, the party was surveying as 40,000 people each in around 100 key constituencies. This was then narrowed down 'to find the few thousand voters per constituency we really needed to focus on.' He adds: 'By the time of the election, we knew not only who our potential voters were, but what the issues were that they cared most about and how they preferred to be reached.'[90]

Andrew Cooper, Cameron's pollster and chief strategist at the time, says target voters were placed in thirteen different buckets and then granular information on each was then used to decide which, of 2,000 different campaign messages, would be sent to them. By the end of the campaign, he says, Messina claimed to 'have 1,000 pieces of data on every voter in the UK.'

This is how Cooper describes the micro-targeting process in key seats: 'If someone really cared about David Cameron remaining prime minister, they would get ads focusing on the difference between him and Ed Miliband. If someone did not like David Cameron they would get stuff from Boris Johnson or a reminder that only the Conservatives were promising a referendum on Europe. We knew whether they were most open to a knock on the door, a letter, an email or an online ad. We did a lot of impact testing on samples of about a thousand at a time to see what messages worked best and which were remembered.'[91]

Labour's campaign, of which I was part, was significantly less data-driven and micro-targeted. The party's digital operation was run by Matthew McGregor, who had just returned from working on Obama's re-election campaign. But, unlike Elder over at the Tory headquarters, McGregor was never fully integrated into our strategy team. Instead, he was told to prioritise online fundraising and the mobilisation of activists ahead of direct communication with target voters. The official figures show the Tories spent £1.2 million—compared to Labour's £16,454—on Facebook ads pumping campaign messages into the news feeds of key voters in marginal constituencies during the run up to the 2015 general election.[92] McGregor believes the real figure for Labour spending was closer to £200,000—with some of it obscured by accounting practices—but suggests the Conservatives still 'outspent us by a factor of at least twenty to one' over the course of two years.[93]

McGregor says: 'We did spend on Facebook and ran some smart ads. Being outgunned to such an extent mattered. There were a whole range of people we needed to speak to and we were not reaching them—it was like saying we won't do any interviews on ITV for the course of the election campaign—an entire channel of communication was virtually closed to us.'[94]

Labour's spending was more focused on the traditional 'ground game' of street-by-street canvassing that saw it repeatedly boast about having '5 million conversations' with voters during the 2015 election campaign. On the evening of 7 May 2015, reports from the ground operation had been overwhelmingly positive. Hope bubbled through the party's headquarters, where I had spent most of the day, that those millions of doorstep conversations might help edge Ed Miliband over Downing Street's own doorstep in an election that pollsters said was almost tied.

And then, a few seconds after 10pm, the exit poll came out. I remember turning to see colleagues' hands instinctively covering their mouths and their eyes widening as if witnessing a fatal traffic accident. The TV monitors across our suddenly silent war room were showing the Conservatives gaining both votes and seats. It was another apparent triumph for chilly metric methods as Cameron went on to secure, unexpectedly, the Conservative Party's first parliamentary majority for twenty-three years.

The next morning Cooper tweeted this message: 'Big data, microtargeting and social media campaign just thrashed "5 million conversations" & "community organising."'

A vast loophole had appeared in British electoral law. Political parties are not allowed to buy TV and radio advertising by law, but there are no such restrictions on online advertising where an increasing proportion of voters were getting their news. It meant not only could parties avoid bans on advertising but they could also target ads to a very narrow group of people. Moreover, strict campaign spending limits for each constituency could be circumnavigated by buying Facebook ads targeted on voters in particular marginal constituencies as the line between national and local budgets became blurred.

David Cameron may well have won regardless. But, on his way back to Downing Street, he had climbed through that loophole.

The brand of authenticity

It is a strange experience to go from being a journalist, speculating on what might be happening in politics often based on little more than a hint, to sitting at a table where politicians are breathtakingly honest about what is really going on, who they hate and what they truly think. It is therefore ironic that I spent so much of my four-and-a-half years working for the Labour Party trying—and largely failing—to persuade people that Ed Miliband was authentic.

After becoming leader of the party in 2010, Miliband was quicker than most to understand that the expectation of voters was changing in the new digital age. He instinctively grasped that people who were now getting their information through social media wanted something different than sound-bites clipped at exactly eighteen seconds to fit the lead-in for the 10 o'clock news. He set out to be a change candidate; anticipating some of the rage felt by those left out and left behind by globalisation, challenging thirty years of free market orthodoxy and standing up to powerful interests—including Rupert Murdoch and Paul Dacre's *Daily Mail*.

Yet Miliband was also too conflicted, too conventional and perhaps too constrained to be an insurgent. It is not easy attacking an out-of-touch elite consisting of bankers and Old Etonian prime ministers when, sometimes even in his own mind, that same elite included Oxford-educated former Cabinet ministers like him. His polite, sometimes awkward, demeanour contained little of the tell-it-like-it-is swagger of leaders who relish confrontation with their critics. And, for all his genuinely courageous struggles with the press, he spent much of his time trying in vain to win the game it told him he should play.

When I go back to visit him in the much smaller Westminster office he now inhabits, Miliband describes those years like this: 'I suppose I was caught between an old way of doing politics—which I did not love, nor was very good at—and a new way of doing politics, which I did occasionally but too infrequently. I wanted people to think I could be prime minister but I didn't want to be seen as simply another establishment person. I was trying to say I could be different. Maybe I was a bit of a bridge between the old and the new in this regard because the politicians that are going to win in the future are the ones that go out there and don't just look like they're trying to win votes.'[95]

I had many similar conversations with him, about him, when he was leader. From the outset, a brutal press was intent on portraying him as weak, weird or both. And polls consistently told us that people did not know what Miliband stood for. All this was unfair on Miliband, who is a deeply decent human being. But 'authenticity' is a brand, its intangible qualities are defined by the eye of the perceiver and, for all our efforts, we just could not alter them. At times, Miliband decided the way to overcome his negative ratings was to earn authenticity by 'doing politics differently'. He toyed with an idea similar to reality TV in which he immersed himself in the struggles of people's lives, spending a whole day at a small business selling windows in his Doncaster constituency and, later, a night on the wards of Watford's general hospital. He tried to break out of the risk-aversion afflicting so much of politics by standing on a wooden crate in town squares taking questions from all-comers that sometimes included beery hecklers who had stumbled out of nearby pubs. He did big speeches without notes or autocues and attempted to adopt a gentler, more enquiring tone into the weekly House of Commons shouting match of Prime Minister's Question Time.

But all these initiatives were abandoned in the face of the media's disdain and contempt or—in the case of the note-free speeches—public calamity when he forgot a key passage on the deficit at Labour's 2014 conference. Indeed, many of Miliband's most notorious moments, such as when he allowed himself to be photographed eating a bacon sandwich, had come when he attempted to achieve authenticity through spontaneity.

Eventually, and probably belatedly, he delivered a speech seeking to make a strength of not being great 'at eating a bacon sandwich' saying principles and ideas mattered more than a slick image. 'If you want the politician from central casting, it's just not me, it's the other guy,' said Miliband, 'if you want a politician who thinks that a good photo is the most important thing, then don't vote for me.'[96]

And yet we continued to spend a lot of time and money trying to improve his image so he could do what politicians from central casting are meant to do. We even took advice from a theatre director who told us strength was shown on stage as much by the way actors around a powerful figure behaved as by anything he did himself. If Miliband was to be filmed talking and walking, he was taught to stay one pace behind whoever he was with so they would turn and lean deferentially towards him. On greeting someone, Miliband was told to offer his hand while keeping his arm close to his body, so people would be seen to reaching out to him. I wrote ludicrous memos saying he should be seen striding purposefully through Parliament at the head of a V-shape with deferential aides trailing either side in his wake (that lasted about a week).

But none of this really suited someone who was simultaneously too serious and too self-mocking to engage in a theatrical role. Often, efforts to project him as a stereotypical 'tough' or 'down-to-earth' leader—only exposed Miliband to further scorn.

Spencer Livermore, who returned to politics to run the 2015 campaign, says: 'Our biggest problem with Ed was that he was neither authentically prime ministerial nor authentically insurgent. Every time he tried too hard to be one or the other, he stumbled.'[97]

One example was when Emily Thornberry was hastily sacked from his team for posting what appeared to be snobbish tweets showing pictures of white vans parked next to houses displaying the English flag in November 2014. It was then briefed to the *Daily Mail* that Miliband had 'never been so angry,' that he thought people should fly the Cross of St George 'with pride' and whenever he saw a white van outside a house, he felt 'respect'.[98]

When one prominent member of the House of Lords saw this, he is said to have told colleagues: 'I don't know about you, but when I see a white van outside, I just feel relief because it means the plumber has arrived.'[99]

# # #

This tension between the demands of the digital age and the conventions of the old media was putting severe strain on political parties, particularly the one I was working for at the time. Just when social media was dissolving the distinction between public and private lives by demanding ever more informality and information, it also opened up new routes for an unforgiving and unrelenting old media to dissect every discrepancy between words and deeds.

For instance, consider this cycle of despair. We decided that allowing ITV cameras in to film Miliband and his family 'relaxing at home' during the election was an opportunity to show viewers the 'real Ed'. But by this stage we had almost lost sight of what that was, so neuralgic had we become about concealing his most left-wing instincts from voters or preventing him ever being seen eating sandwiches. Our media team sought to choreograph every moment of the visit down to the plastic toys his children would walk in carrying. It did not stop Sarah Vine, a *Daily Mail* columnist, using the film to attack the Miliband family for having such an austere kitchen it might have been modelled on Soviet-era flats.[100]

Another newspaper columnist, ever keen as she was to show off her connections, tweeted that she knew the Milibands had a 'lovely' second kitchen and only used the one shown on TV for the preparation of 'tea and quick snacks'.[101] Miliband, in a spasm of honesty, then admitted the second kitchen was just 'for the nanny'. The verdict from the media—both old and new—was that we had cynically sought to portray Miliband as normal and the whole operation had backfired into an authenticity disaster. It was hard to disagree.

And yet other world leaders were managing to bypass mainstream media by embracing the intimacy offered by social media. Obama recorded a video with BuzzFeed showing him posing and making faces in the mirror under the title of 'Things Everyone Does but Doesn't Talk About'. Jens Stoltenberg, the Norwegian prime minister, made a video in which he recorded himself driving voters around while pretending to be a taxi-driver. We thought hard about this too. One idea was to embrace the now iconic image of him eating bacon sandwiches by releasing a video of him preparing one. I suggested he get a dog and call it 'Gromit' because *The Times*'s cartoonist, Peter Brookes, had successfully caricatured him as the plasticine 'Wallace'. But Miliband was usually easily dissuaded whenever someone, probably correctly, pointed out how hard the press would whack him for it.

We did, however, experiment with Miliband doing YouTube video interviews during the 2015 election such as one with the 'beauty vlogger' Louise Pentland, known as 'SprinkleofGlitter'. Another, with Russell Brand, promptly went wrong when pictures of Miliband leaving the comedian's house were posted on Twitter long before the interview came out which somehow became front page news. I have subsequently been told that Brand was personally involved in undermining it in this way which, if true, demonstrates the risk politicians take when they step into this world. But it could have been worse: Brand, who had previously been in rehab for sex addiction, had initially insisted he wanted to do the interview sprawled across his bed.

Since losing the election Miliband has emerged as an unexpectedly liberated star of social media. He has become an outspoken and often spontaneously funny personality on Twitter, while also recording a successful podcast series. When I interviewed him for this book, he seems much more at ease with himself and comfortable in his own skin than he had in the hundreds of interviews I had supervised before.

He insists it would not have possible to show this side of himself when he was running to be prime minister, saying: 'As leader you can't say Donald Trump is an absolute moron like I've done recently—I mean, even Jeremy Corbyn doesn't say that! I was operating in a political war zone.' But Miliband also recognises that he is by nature 'maybe too cautious,' adding: 'There is a judgement call to be made about how constrained you are and I wish I had been a bit less so.'

There were those in our team who argued that authenticity, of a sort, could have been achieved if Miliband reflected a version of real people's thoughts and feelings back at them. Sometimes, it felt as if polling and focus group results were becoming a guide to what he should say, rather merely a test of whether what he wanted to say would work. But our relationship with data and metrics was as conflicted as it was with the potential of social media. This was apparent in the disagreement between the two US consultants hired by the Labour Party. Stan Greenberg, a veteran from Bill Clinton's first presidential campaign, said we should be aiming to attract potential Conservative switchers by reassuring them on issues like the deficit and immigration, while making more retail offers like freezing energy prices. David Axelrod, who had been Obama's chief strategist, was dismissive of what he termed 'vote Labour and win a microwave' policy offers. Instead, he advocated a bigger message that would energise and motivate a coalition, including new voters, to come together as it had in America in 2008 and 2012. In the end, neither side really prevailed. Greenberg allowed his polling to be used as a comfort blanket that persuaded Miliband he was still on a narrow path to victory. Axelrod was kept at a distance after gloomily sniffing the air and making it clear he did not smell a movement building so much as an impending defeat.

Douglas Alexander, who had worked directly with Blair, Brown and Miliband both in Government and as Labour's General Election coordinator, does not mince his words.

He says: 'There are certain truths that technology does not alter. The opinion polls throughout Ed's leadership consistently indicated that the majority of voters did not see him as a potential Prime Minister. ... You can have a targeted online and ground campaign, you can have 5 million conversations but if people don't believe or relate to the messenger or the message they are not going to be persuaded.'[102]

Part of the problem was that the 'centre ground' in politics no longer seemed like a broad plain filled with moderate views so much as a spiky median point where people's anger was precariously balanced between competing hatreds. Although voters might have loathed bankers or scorned Cameron for being 'posh', they were also inclined to blame their falling living standards on people defrauding the welfare system, Europe and, above all, immigrants.

Miliband, himself the son of Jewish refugees from the Nazis, did not go into politics to campaign against migration. He was critical of Tony Blair's focus group-driven approach and would often open meetings on difficult subjects by saying 'the best place to start is by setting out what I really think.' Quite often, those discussions would demonstrate that if there was one subject he cared about more than anything it was the role of markets in creating economic inequality. But when he was leader, he was consistently discouraged by polling evidence from talking too much about it. At one stage, he was even told that focus groups thought 'equality' only referred to the rights of foreign migrants to claim welfare. Another important speech was almost cancelled all together because an aide thought the venue, Brighton's Regency Pavilion with its famed domes and minarets, would lead to voters thinking he was speaking 'outside a Mosque'.

# # #

He did, however, make at least four set-piece speeches about immigration. All of them, at Miliband's insistence and to his credit, included lines about how immigration had benefitted the economy as a whole. There was nothing in these in his speeches on the subject that was even a faint dog whistle to racists. Miliband also tried to make them as much about economic equality as he could. But my view—then and now—was that each time we intervened on this issue we ceded more territory to those in the media and in politics who wanted to pretend immigration was the cause of people's problems. We did not win any votes back from Ukip by telling people they were right to be worried about immigration and then offering a set of policies designed to tackle low pay of people already living here—and immigrants.

In his first such speech, Miliband asserted that immigration had directly affected wages in low-skilled jobs and told the story of 'a chicken factory in my constituency in Doncaster' where Eastern European workers had undercut existing terms and conditions. He added: 'There are lots of stories like this of wages having been pushed down. They are the hidden stories of Britain, they are the stories that make people angry, they are stories that politicians have ignored for too long.'[103]

It was only after he had stopped speaking that we discovered the usual fact checks had not been made and almost every aspect of the story was mistaken: the factory was in Selby, almost 40 miles distant from Doncaster; it made sauces which had very little to do if anything with chickens; and no one was quite clear if there were still any migrant workers there or not. Our press office resorted to issuing a series of deliberately obscure instructions on how to find a non-existent chicken factory to national media, who began descending on Doncaster that day believing they were on the trail a story that suited its anti-immigration frame for politics so well.

Looking back on his leadership, Miliband rejects my suggestion that we failed to do enough to counter this prevailing narrative. 'You can't right every wrong about political debate from opposition, you have to pick your battles.'[104] But when I point out that economists reject the claim that immigration has had any meaningful impact on wages, it is clear that this is a subject on which we still have an honest disagreement. I get the familiar sense of him speaking to conflicting constituencies as he talks about how 'the collision of highly deregulated labour markets and high levels of immigration' meant that both 'migrant workers' and 'workers already here' are being exploited.

'That was our main focus and I think that was right and I also think it was right to talk about the issue of immigration more generally. I was always incredibly careful as you know to do so in a way that I felt was true to what I believed. That is to say I was proud to be the son of immigrants, that I believe immigration benefits the country overall in a myriad of ways and it is vital we defend our openness and diversity as a country. I also said that immigration does have different effects in different communities, whether that was to do with the pace of change or migrant workers being exploited by unscrupulous employers as a part of the labour market, and we couldn't pretend that wasn't happening.'[105]

Immigration was, of course, a neuralgic issue for Labour at a time when Nigel Farage's Ukip was taking chunks of votes from all the mainstream parties and Gordon Brown's unfortunate encounter with Rochdale pensioner Gillian Duffy in 2010 was still fresh in people's memories. But there was no real evidence, despite the efforts of the Home Office, then under

Theresa May, to show that immigration had significantly reduced wages. The best estimate is that in the lowest-paid jobs it may have reduced income by just 1 per cent over a period of eight years.[106]

It was not Ed Miliband or the Labour Party that were particularly at fault, so much as politics as a whole. The leaders of all the mainstream parties believed immigration was necessary and beneficial. Few politicians defied the polls and the press that demanded endless new initiatives on immigration. In Cameron's case that meant making empty promises, that he knew he could not keep, to limit the number of people arriving in the country to less than 100,000 a year.

Collectively, Britain political leaders offered little or no resistance to a virulent new strain of nationalistic, nativist politics—surfacing like skin lesions across both old and social media—that only a few years earlier would have been deemed far-right, even racist.

The Owl of Minerva spreads its wings

On the night of the 2015 General Election I wandered for hours around St James's Park outside Labour's headquarters to avoid the tears of colleagues inside. Alongside me was Marc Stears, Miliband's chief speechwriter. We spent a while watching nightshift workers build what we morbidly thought looked like a hangman's scaffold in the park but turned out to be a platform to celebrate the VE Day anniversary. And we talked about how devoid of meaning politics had seemed not just that night but over the past five years.

Stears, as a former professor of politics at the University of Oxford, is one of the few people in the world with a quotation from Hegel to suit every occasion. This time it was, 'the owl of Minerva spreads its wings only with the falling of the dusk.'

Apparently, it means that we can only really understand the meaning of a time when it is almost over—and then, the bird of prey is upon us. Stears explains this was more than the one-minute-past-ten exit poll disaster we had witnessed back in the office, but the way politics itself had become so utterly dried out, disillusioning and disconnected.

He says: 'Democracy used to provide moments when the powerful could catch a glimpse of, or at least be forced to look at, everyday life. But that election night in 2015 I felt the divorce between citizens and the elites was almost complete. We had been working together at the top table of politics and we couldn't see people sitting at their kitchen table anymore. This was the Labour Party, created to give people a voice, and what was extraordinary was how far we had been cut off from the ordinary. And if voters felt they were being treated just like numbers, then frankly, that's because they were.'[107]

The 2015 election was the dusk of the time when politics was still predictable. For all the fuss later about how the polls had got the result wrong, the two key indicators showing Labour was behind on the economy and leadership had always pointed to a likely Tory victory. Google's chief, Eric Schmidt, was busy building a new campaign database that was supposed to make Hillary Clinton unbeatable in a 2016 presidential run.[108] Jim Messina was looking forward to working wonders for Clinton, too, while telling interviewers he had never had any doubts about a Tory victory because his modelling had predicted it.[109] And a political, media and business establishment decided that although Cameron had promised a reckless referendum on Europe, it did not really matter because the prime minister was a proven winner who would not let the British people self-harm.

All this was the product of an algorithmic approach to politics by which data analysis experts appeared to be able to control campaigns by turning voters into dots on a screen. The growing dependency of political leaders on such metrics was slowly separating them from the essential purpose of democracy which is to give people a chance to decide—or participate in—how they are governed. Far from creating a new era of empowered digital citizenship, it was enabling democratic political leaders to disconnect from everything but their data.

If the old media had been first disabled by digital technology and then become dependent on it, politics was going through the same process in reverse. The unquestioning belief in the infallible magic of metrics to deliver victory and power meant older political instincts withered away. Politics was coming to resemble professional wrestling: quite fun if you liked that sort of thing but, beneath all that oiled-up muscle and posture, fake.

In the half-light of May 2015, Donald Trump—a reality TV star who long since had been inducted into World Wrestling Entertainment's Hall of Fame—was preparing to announce his candidacy for the White House. Eurosceptic campaigners were beginning to stir and consider how they could take Britain out of the EU. Somewhere in cyberspace there were Russian hacking teams known as 'Cozy Bear' and 'Fancy Bear' trying to burrow their way into Democratic Party computers.

Mainstream politics had effectively locked itself in a windowless room with only a laptop, while populists or even more sinister figures prowled outside the gates.

And darkness was coming.

6

Three Shocks to 'The System'

The Embarrassment of Metrics

Night had not yet fallen on the damp summer's day of 23 June 2016, when David Cameron gathered his exhausted team together in Downing Street at the end of another campaign.

The referendum on Britain's membership of the European Union had been the most hate-filled political battle any one of them could remember. The poison of racial politics and immigration had infected open wounds that sliced across the country. But, with polling stations closing in just a couple of hours, staff inside 10 Downing Street were beginning to believe they had done just enough to scrape victory. A long table had been set up, laden with trays of moussaka and lasagne; glasses of wine and elderflower cordial were being poured.

Craig Oliver, Cameron's head of communications, described how a relaxed prime minister floated around the room dressed in a casual blue shirt which was untucked at the waist. The final polls were pointing to a Remain victory, the markets were buoyant and, perhaps most of importantly of all, Jim Messina—who liked to tell people he had 'never lost'—thought they had won this one too.

In his account of the campaign, Oliver wrote: '[Messina's] looking confident, telling me his model says it will be around 52–48 for Remain. Close, but I'll take it. His prediction has extra force, because he is one of the few who called the general election right. ... There isn't a single indicator that suggests we should be worried.'[1]

But this time Messina had got it wrong. As the night wore on, it became clear that the Leave campaign had won by 52 against 48 per cent, the opposite of the outcome he had predicted. Britain had voted to leave the European Union and Cameron would be leaving Downing Street.

Later that year Messina advised Spain's centre-right People's Party as it emerged victorious in elections before heading back to the US, where he was was doing his best to help Hillary Clinton defeat the menacing figure of Donald Trump. The polls began to tighten, but Messina was unperturbed. 'Dear panicking Dems, she will win,' he tweeted on 21 September 2016, before accusing Trump of running the 'most incompetent campaign in history.'

Seven weeks later, Clinton refused to leave her hotel suite on the top floor of the five star Peninsula Hotel in Manhattan. The unthinkable had happened. Trump was elected as the 45th President of the United States. Equally distraught that night in the Peninsula was the man who had been the 42nd President. 'It's like Brexit,' lamented Bill Clinton, 'I guess it's real.'[2]

Messina just had time to get on the wrong side of another defeat in the Italian referendum on constitutional reform in December 2016 before another British General Election was called in April in 2017. Once again, Messina was brought in by the Conservatives to run the data analytics. When a couple of polls began to suggest Jeremy Corbyn might do better than anyone—possibly including the Labour leader himself—expected, the man with all this data at his fingertips swiftly offered more reassurance.

'Spent the day laughing at yet another stupid poll from YouGov,' Messina wrote on Twitter, before challenging the polling firm's general manager to a charity bet. A week later, on 8 June, Theresa May's House of Commons majority was wiped out by a resurgent Labour Party, just as YouGov had predicted, and Messina's Twitter account fell silent.

The political landscape was being churned up across the developed world. Populist tunes were being sung once more about a better and largely mythical yesterday, when the people were not ruled by an out-of-touch or corrupt elite. The far right, in the form of Marine Le Pen's Front National in France and the AfD (Alternative für Deutschland) in Germany, was on the march again. Narrow-minded nationalists were in power in Poland and Hungary. An angry left—Syriza in Greece, Podemos in Spain and the followers of Bernie Sanders in America—were, in some ways at least, howling at the same moon.

But there was something particularly emblematic about these three votes—two in Britain and one in America—in the way that they not only challenged the political Establishment, but made fools of them too.

It is slightly unfair to focus solely on Messina's flawed forecasts because he was not alone: prime ministers and presidents, journalists, professional political consultants, talking heads on TV, markets and polling companies, all shared in this embarrassment. For instance, Nate Silver, a big data analyst who had been spot-on with his predictions in some previous contests, wrote an apologetic blog shortly before the US presidential election, explaining why he put Clinton's chances of becoming president at a mere 85 per cent when others assessed her chances at between 92 and 99 per cent.[3]

Silver was known in the US as an analyst who had taken the data-driven 'Sabermetrics' approach to baseball—depicted in Michael Lewis's book *Moneyball* and the film of the same name—into political forecasting. By 2016, however, even some of the most enthusiastic exponents of using data to scout and analyse baseball players were beginning to develop doubts. They included John Henry, the owner of the Boston Red Sox, who had employed Bill James—considered the father of Sabermetrics—to help the team win the World Series in 2004, 2007 and 2013. In February that year, Henry suddenly announced he was going to set less store by analytics.

'We have perhaps overly relied on numbers,' he said. 'Perhaps there was too much reliance on past performance and trying to project future performance.' Asked why he had decided to change tack, Henry replied with a single word answer: 'Results.'[4]

Some worried whether the use of analytics in baseball was discovering misleading and coincidental correlations, such as that the rise in the incidence of autism almost exactly matches increased organic baby food sales. And, as data flooded into sport and coaches' offices, the very success of teams like the Red Sox bred imitation. Once everyone started using Sabermetrics there was no competitive advantage; it was no longer a wizard's wand but simply another tool, the use of which should be determined by skill and judgement.

Sport was beginning to understand the limits of the Moneyball approach because it is hyper-sensitive to the fine margins that make the difference between defeat one week and victory the next. Politics is tested less often and therefore is more prone to over-learn the perceived lesson from a previous cycle. And, after Obama's victory in 2012 and Cameron's unexpected majority in 2015, analytics were still seen as an electoral smart-bomb.

In the build-up to Britain's referendum campaign, pro-Europeans in the Conservative, Labour and Liberal Democrat parties were trying to put their short-term interests aside so they could work together. But George Osborne, the then Chancellor who oversaw such strategic matters for the Tories, fretted about whether such co-operation could damage the digital advantage his party had established over its opponents. Osborne wanted specific guarantees that Labour would not get sight of his party's state-of-the-art analytic modelling.

Peter Mandelson recalls 'slightly tortured' discussions with Osborne over the Conservatives' insistence that 'our access to the secrets of the Tories' algorithms' be restricted in the referendum campaign. The strategist behind the creation of New Labour now believes such episodes should have served as an early warning about the reliance the Remain campaign was placing on data analytics. 'You are led to believe that they are in possession of some special secret sauce. But it does not tell what voters are really thinking and politicians can too easily be left with a tin ear.'

Mandelson dismisses the idea that data was the reason Obama won in in 2012 or why the Tories were victorious three years later. 'The reason Ed Miliband lost in 2015 had nothing to do with data, it was to do with voter perceptions, with strength versus weakness,' he declares, jabbing an accusing finger in my direction. 'You don't need Jim Messina and his data to tell you that, you just need a brain.'[5]

But Osborne was firmly wedded to the scientific approach, regarding Messina's return to Britain in almost messianic terms. The Remain campaign had lined up Dan Wagner—who had done much of the analytics for Barack Obama in 2012—but Osborne was determined to wait for Messina, telling colleagues: 'I'm not putting my country's future and my career in the hands of some person I've never even heard of.'[6] The campaign was left frustrated that 'Jim's second coming' was delayed until the end of December 2015 and that data was not available until April, meaning mail shots to 14 million voters were fired off blindly to random postcodes. By that time, Mandelson was not the only person in the Remain campaign beginning to wonder if Messina was value for money.

Nonetheless, the strategy for the Britain Stronger in Europe campaign was designed around Messina's metrics. Andrew Cooper, the Remain campaign's pollster, was told to segment voters into different groups, just as he had for the general election the year before. On one side were the 'ardent internationalists', 'comfortable Europhiles' and 'engaged metropolitans', while 'strong sceptics' and 'EU hostiles' were placed the other side. In between were the 'disengaged middle' and the 'heart versus head' groups. Messina and his team then used the 1,000 pieces of data he claimed to hold on every voter in the country to ascribe each of them a score, on a scale of one to 100, for the likelihood they were a Remain supporter and another estimating their propensity to vote. Adverts and mail shots were then tailored accordingly, with sixty-three different versions of the Remain campaign's referendum leaflet sent out to voters, depending on what issues analytics indicated they cared about most.

This use of data can be far more intrusive and personal than people outside politics realise. For instance, officials on the Remain campaign discovered they could use the tool to look up individual names—including themselves, friends, celebrities and enemies. One of them described to me how they took great pleasure in checking the name of Boris Johnson, who was assigned by Messina 'an 84 per cent probability of voting Remain' on account of factors such as being a well-to-do and educated resident of the hyper-liberal London Borough of Islington. This may explain why his neighbours—not to mention the Prime Minister—felt such a sense of betrayal when Johnson became one of the leaders of the Leave campaign.

But for all the merriment that playing around with Messina's metrics created, tightening polls and structural problems with the strategy were causing brows to furrow in the Remain campaign. Cooper says: 'One of the biggest group-think errors we made was to believe that, because certain types of people who favoured Brexit had not voted in previous elections, they would not vote in the referendum either. We got blindsided by that.'[7]

Will Straw, the Remain campaign's director, says that the campaign's polling under-estimated the strength of motivation among some Leave-leaning voters who had traditionally stayed at home at elections. 'On the night I was hearing stories of middle-aged men walking in off the street at polling stations in places like Stockport demanding to know how to vote Leave. They were in their forties or fifties but had never voted before,' he says. 'We did not see that coming. The country was having two separate conversations which went right past each other. We were not talking to the same voters as Leave; we were mostly talking to our voters while they were mostly talking their supporters. We didn't really have a feedback loop.'[8]

In America, during that same tumultuous year, there were also misgivings inside Hillary Clinton's campaign over its reliance on data. The Facebook-fuelled campaign of Bernie Sanders, who for years had been treated as an oddity for being the only declared socialist in the Senate, had already run her closer than anyone—including her analytics team—thought was possible in the primaries. Her husband, Bill, and John Podesta, her chief of staff, were among an older group who distrusted 'the model' which drove so many decisions. But Robbie Mook, her campaign manager, was zealous in his adherence to the scientific approach. One senior staff member said: 'It was hard to fight with him because no one wanted to sound like a Luddite in the face of the data.'[9]

Mook's team had built a secret and highly complex computer algorithm named 'Ada' after the nineteenth-century pioneering female mathematician, Ada Lovelace, who is credited with helping create the first computer. It controlled every strategic decision including how to deploy the candidate and the placing of TV ads, as well as micro-details like the location of campaign offices, what doors volunteers knock on or what phone numbers they dialled. One staffer on the campaign, says: 'Data directed everything. In training sessions we were told to tell volunteers that "our data shows" that there are enough people with political values close enough to Hillary that we do not need to win over new voters. We explicitly told volunteers not to waste time trying to convince swing voters.'[10]

Operated by the campaign's (human) analytics chief, Elan Kriegel, and a team of no less than sixty data scientists at the campaign headquarters in Brooklyn, Ada was said to be several times more powerful and sophisticated than any previous system. Much like the candidate herself, the algorithm was sometimes accused of being chilly and fact-based but both were recognised as capable of grindingly hard work: if Obama's team in 2012 had run 66,000 computer simulations every night, Ada did 400,000. And if Ada told Clinton it was safe to stay away from Michigan and Wisconsin, that trumped any local anecdote or seasoned political operative.[11]

Clinton did not visit Wisconsin once in the election—the first time a major party nominee had avoided it since 1972—and largely stayed away from Michigan too. Stories abound like the one about a woman who turned up at in a Clinton campaign office in Flint, Michigan, asking for a lawn sign and offering to canvass, only to be told these were not 'scientifically' significant ways of increasing the vote. She never came back.[12] On the morning of the vote on 8 November 2016, Ada's internal models predicted a Clinton win in Michigan by five points. At lunchtime, Democrats on the ground who voiced concern were assured 'the model' still had Clinton winning by a clear margin. But that night she lost Michigan, Wisconsin and Pennsylvania—most of the so-called 'blue wall' of states that had voted solidly Democrat since 1992—by a combined margin of just 79,316 votes. Hillary, Ada, Robbie and Jim had all been disastrously wrong and 'The Donald' would be the next president.

Back in Britain, less than six months later, another slightly robotic female leader also had an overly-optimistic idea of her chances of victory as she embarked on a similarly highly-centralised data-driven campaign.

Despite being—by instinct and practice—a cautious politician, Theresa May had called a snap election in 2017 because she seemed certain to get a thumping majority. The team that had delivered Cameron his victory in 2015 was reassembled, with Lynton Crosby brought back to direct the campaign, Messina to do the analytics, while Craig Elder and his colleague, Tom Edmonds ran the digital media strategy. May had a twenty-point lead in the polls when she called the election and was targeting Labour constituencies with working class-friendly policies lifted straight from Miliband's supposedly terrifyingly left-wing manifesto of 2015.

When Messina first ran his model for the General Election of 2017, he predicted she would win 470 seats, a majority of 290.[13] But Elder sensed early that something was wrong. The digital operation he had nurtured so painstakingly along with Edmonds in 2015 had suffered from neglect. The email list had dwindled from 1.4 million names to 1.2 million by the time they returned two years later. Emails to this list got stuck in spam filters for hours because algorithms were picking up that messages to dead accounts had been unopened. It meant an email to Conservative activists urging them to get out the vote on polling day, supposed to have been sent at 1pm, was not received until 4am the following day. Although Tory ads attacking Corbyn's record on security chalked up millions of views, the YouTube channel that had once featured David Cameron's pioneering videos had been reduced to a dumping ground for unedited and largely unwatchable twenty minute-long speeches by Cabinet ministers. Theresa May's Twitter account was moribund, her Facebook 'likes' were barely a third of the 1.2 million achieved by Jeremy Corbyn, and digitally-native news sites such as BuzzFeed mocked the Conservatives' desperately bland efforts on Instagram.[14]

Worse still, Elder felt the party was targeting the wrong set of voters. He says: 'We were trying to win in Leave-voting Labour areas where there had not been a Tory candidate on the streets for a long time. Digitally, it felt like we had not rolled the pitch at all—we had not done surveys and other research that we had done before 2015 to identify those vital persuadable voters. To be brutal, it felt like all too often we were trying to talk to the wrong voters in the wrong places about the wrong things.'[15]

Messina was paid a premier-league grade salary, rumoured to be £100,000 a week during the election but his optimistic modelling forecasts led to overreach from the beginning of the campaign.[16] There was excited talk in Tory headquarters of targeting any Labour seat with a majority of less than 8,000.[17] Vast sums were spent on advertising targeted at the Facebook feeds of Labour voters in traditional Labour seats that the Tories thought they could persuade, only to discover they should have been fighting a defensive game in once rock-solid Conservative constituencies like Kensington and Canterbury.

Although the election of June 2017 left Conservatives as the biggest party and May clinging on in Downing Street, she lost her Commons majority. When the results of the exit poll were published, the silence that fell over the Tory war room was as profound as that in Labour's headquarters two years earlier. On this occasion, the stillness was apparently broken only by the sound of someone vomiting.[18]

Much of the blame for a catastrophic seven-week campaign has settled on old-school political failings such as May's own performance and a manifesto that terrified once-reliably Conservative sections of the electorate. But Nick Timothy, her former joint chief of staff and the co-author of that manifesto, believes the prime minister made mistakes because she had become too reliant on opinion-based research, as well as on 'campaign consultants' who told her to start 'hogging the limelight' and to build the campaign around her rather awkward personality. He claimed that Messina's final modelling, 'suggested we would win 371 seats, giving us a majority of 92'[19] and that the Conservative campaign had 'failed to notice the surge in Labour support, because modern campaigning techniques require ever-narrower targeting of specific voters.'[20]

As with Trump and Brexit, one of the reasons why highly-paid political consultants failed to realise what was happening was because they were locked into such models. They played into the hands of insurgent campaigns which presented themselves as the alternative to politics-as-usual, that roared with defiance against the elite political opinion that had written them off.

The Ukip leader, Nigel Farage, used an eve-of-poll rally in June 2016 to declare: 'This referendum is the people versus the Establishment'[21] In the same year, Trump released a video on Facebook in which he warned: 'The Establishment, the media, the special interests, the lobbyists and the donors—they're all against me.'[22] Corbyn opened his election campaign in 2017 with a remarkably similar statement: 'Much of the media and establishment are saying that this election is a foregone conclusion. They think there are rules in politics which, if you don't follow by doffing your cap to powerful people, accepting that things can't really change, then you can't win. But of course, they do not want us to win.'[23]

But almost every losing political campaign makes an appeal to voters telling them to ignore the pollsters and the pundits. Usually, they still lose (and, in Corbyn's case, still did). The difference this time, with each of these campaigns, was they spectacularly out-did expectations.

And perhaps the reason they did so was because some of them had become as good, or even better, at using the same analytic methods than the people who invented them—the political class they claimed to despise.

Insurgent Analytica

Dominic Cummings is an intense and slightly wild-eyed figure, prone to quoting Otto von Bismarck or Warren Buffett when you least expect it. In September 2015, he had been appointed director of Vote Leave and was beginning to assemble a team to fight a referendum most people assumed he would lose.

At the time, Cummings was reading Philip Tetlock, an American academic who had spent twenty years studying 28,000 flawed expert predictions on everything from the likely collapse of the Soviet Union to the existence of weapons of mass destruction in Iraq. Tetlock described how pundits were more likely to appear on TV if they had a know-it-all self-confidence and fondness for big ideas. But he then added this also made them much more likely to be wrong, even suggesting that such experts were no better at predicting political futures than the proverbial 'dart-throwing chimp'.[24]

Tetlock is often misinterpreted as having denigrated expertise altogether. He has been horrified at the way populists subsequently seized on his book and Tetlock says no one should take his work as 'proof that knowledge itself is somehow useless'.[25] But Cummings did not need help to understand the subtlety of the argument: far from rejecting analytics, he believed getting the best out of them would make the difference between defeat and victory. In an admiring review of one of Tetlock's books published nine months before the referendum, Cummings described how numerate people, so long as they were humble enough to be open-minded and update their opinions, were those who really knew how to use big data. He said one of the things he did as a consequence of reading Tetlock was to 'hire people with very high quantitative skills'—because, as he put it, 'physics, mathematics, and computer science are domains in which there are real experts.'[26] In school, they would have been called 'nerds'. But for Cummings, they held the keys to victory.

The science and maths wizards that he hired compiled a colossal database on the voting public which he claimed was better than anything Messina had put together and was built from scratch.[27] Vote Leave did this, he says, by scraping information about voters off the web in ways that, 'if you haven't got a maths or physics PhD, you're not going to understand.'[28] Michael Gove, one of the leaders of the Leave campaign, admits he could never really get his head around it all. 'I knew a lot of work was going on,' he says of all the 'astrophysics' that went into the campaign, 'but I didn't have the smarts to understand every stage of it.'[29]

It is interesting to note that, despite setting itself up as an insurgent revolt against technocratic experts, the Leave campaign was run by was someone who thought much of the political establishment was too poorly educated, or possibly too stupid, for him to bother explaining any of this to them. As such, this was an extremely elite form of anti-elitism.

More controversially, since the referendum, *The Observer* newspaper has implied that the data operation run by the Leave campaign was not just hard for the average politics or economics graduate to fathom, but designed in such a way that anyone scrutinising it would never be able to understand exactly what had happened.

Cummings has written thousands upon thousands of words on his blog on the referendum, but is notably opaque about how the campaign scraped so much personal data about voters off the web or built data files so fast from scratch. The only method he described properly was an online football competition where he offered people a £50 million jackpot if they could predict the results in the Euro 2016 tournament in exchange for their contact details and a rating of between one and five for how likely they were to vote Leave.[30] Clever though that was—the mathematical chances of getting the scores in all fifty-one matches was infinitesimal and he had insurance just in case—it does not explain the apparent depth and quality of his data. Cummings has firmly denied doing anything improper, but in an email to Carole Cadwalladr, the indefatigable *Observer* journalist who has pursued this story, he made an interesting concession: 'The law/regulatory agencies are such a joke the reality is that anybody who wanted to cheat the law could do it easily without people realising.'[31]

What is not disputed is that Cummings poured 98 per cent of his advertising budget into digital communication, including vast spends on Facebook ads that were, he said, largely under the control of 'people whose normal work was subjects like quantum information.'[32] A total of £2.7 million went to a previously obscure Canadian-based digital agency, AggregateIQ, that sits outside British jurisdiction. A further £750,000 was funnelled into the same firm through small offshoot campaigns including a youth group called BeLeave run by Darren Grimes, a 23-year-old fashion student, which received no less than £675,315.[33] Cummings said his spending enabled Vote Leave, remarkably, to put out 1 billion targeted digital ads during the ten-week campaign—the bulk of these weighted to targeted Facebook messages in the final few days.[34]

The rival and unofficial Leave.EU campaign, centred around Ukip's Nigel Farage and Arron Banks, claims it built a social media audience with 800,000 likes on Facebook and a weekly reach sometimes in excess of 20 million people. It has been linked to Cambridge Analytica (CA), a firm that became infamous for obtaining, in murky circumstances, a treasure-trove of Facebook data on tens of millions of voters from academic researchers who never received permission to use it for commercial purposes. In May 2018, CA announced it was closing down, although even that announcement was treated with justifiable suspicion amid signs it had simply been rebranded under another name.[35] At the time of writing the issue of how campaigns got their data is among those being investigated by the UK's Information Commissioner who has said she is investigating thirty different organisations, including Ukip, Facebook, CA and AggregateIQ.

Alexander Nix, the firm's former chief executive, has insisted it did not work for Leave.EU, despite his staff appearing on the platform at the campaign's launch and claims in press releases under his name that CA was doing so. Nix described all this as merely the result of 'slightly over-zealous PR.'[36] The firm was, however, paid around $6 million to do work for the Trump campaign in 2016 and claimed to have played a 'pivotal role' in his election. CA boasted that it had developed psychometric profiles of 230 million US citizens using 4,000–5,000 separate pieces of data collected on each of them.[37]

Nix's talent for self-publicity saw him travel the world saying things like advertising 'Mad Men' now needed to listen to the 'Math Men'.[38] He was trying to sell what he claimed was a new secret weapon in data analytics called psychometric, or psychographic, targeting. This seeks to match the 'big five' personality traits—Openness, Conscientiousness, Extroversion, Agreeableness and Neuroticism—with data such as that obtained from Facebook to understand the most primal fears and desires of consumers, or 'voters' as they are known in politics.

A villain straight from central casting—slim, blond, bespectacled and Old Etonian—Nix appears in promotional videos describing with a cut-glass accent how the firm's expertise in psychometrics will change poli-tics. In one such appearance, Nix shows how he might use these methods to campaign against restrictive gun laws in the US. Pointing to a slide of a vulnerable-looking woman, he says voters with 'highly neurotic' per-sonality traits will respond to a 'fear-based message' and 'the threat of burglary'. On the screen behind him, an image of a dark, gloved fist is shown smashing a window.[39]

There is peer-reviewed, academic research that showed algorithms trawling through Facebook data of users' 'likes' could find connections with much deeper—and private—personality traits. For instance, a 2013 study showed 'predictors of male homosexuality' included 'liking' the musical *Wicked*, Mac Cosmetics and *Desperate Housewives*. Strong predic-tors of male heterosexuality included liking the Wu-Tang Clan, the bas-ketball player Shaquille O' Neal and 'being confused after naps.' Although it might not be immediately clear whether these tell-tale signs were the result of scientific research or slightly dated stereotypes, researchers claimed that these markers enabled them to predict sexuality with 88 per cent accuracy.[40]

CA certainly persuaded some people it was on to something big. Robert Mercer had become a billionaire at a company called Renaissance Technologies by using self-learning algorithms to beat the rest of Wall Street. He was keen to replicate this success in politics so that he could propagate his extremely right-wing views on wealth and welfare. Steve Bannon, then chairman of the right-wing website Breitbart, which had been backed by Mercer, persuaded him to invest $15 million in CA's psychometrics. Rebekah Mercer, his daughter, a co-owner of Breitbart and later a member of Trump's transition team, was given a seat on CA's board. Mercer is then said to have insisted that, as condition for making big donations, CA be employed by the presidential campaigns of first Ted Cruz and then Trump.[41] And, if that is not all tangled enough, Facebook says it has discovered 'certain billing and administration connections' that link AggregateIQ, the Canadian firm employed by the Leave campaign through its parent company, to CA and its parent company SCL—which has its roots in sinister military 'psy-ops'.[42]

But it is very unclear what work exactly CA did for the Trump campaign—or if any of it was effective. The data it is alleged to have harvested from Facebook was three years old by 2016 and the Trump campaign has explained it preferred more up-to-date voter files from the Republican National Committee. A Channel 4 News recording, showing Nix boasting to undercover reporters how CA could do 'sting' operations involving ex-spies and honeytrap Ukrainian prostitutes, begs the question why, if his firm could really fix elections by mind-reading millions of voters, it would need to deploy such crude, old-fashioned methods? Even Nix himself, having initially claimed that CA's work for the Trump campaign drew on psychographics, backed away from this position a few months later, insisting CA had destroyed the Facebook data and had only helped the campaign in the more prosaic, if still important, work of analysing the Republican dataset and crafting ads.[43]

A pattern has emerged of CA, and Nix in particular, making big boasts which are then withdrawn under scrutiny. It is quite apparent that Nix has not always told the truth; what is less clear is whether to believe him when he contradicts himself. But he is not exceptional in this regard: political consultants offering cure-all solutions and secret formulas are often compared to snake oil salesmen and this reputation is perhaps most deserved in the field of data analytics, which few politicians or journalists properly understand. As Steve Bannon—a board member of CA at the time, has pointed out, data does not need to come from a terrible breach of security because it is there to be scraped by anyone who wants to do so. 'Facebook data is for sale all over the world,' he said.[44] Data brokers with names like Experian, Acxiom and Epsilon have spent years gathering information from public records such as voters lists and court documents, buying it from commercial sources like retailers and magazine subscriptions, scraping it off what can be seen by anyone on social media, or extracting information from the tracking devices known as cookies that are placed on every visitor to many websites.

Facebook acknowledges it does not know how much of its users' data is being hawked around the market, not least because it used to encourage organisations like the 2012 Obama campaign to access the accounts of users' friends. Together, all this data forms an often highly-detailed picture of people who thought they were private citizens. The 'secret sauce' being touted around politics by the likes of Nix may not have had any more ingredients than what could be bought with a few clicks on the data market.

# # #

Whatever the truth about CA, what can be stated with more confidence is that Trump would not have become president without using data analytics to target voters with ads.

Brad Parscale, a straggly-bearded 6ft 8in former basketball player does not look much a typical political data analyst, and, indeed, he isn't. Parscale had never worked on a political campaign before and apparently only became Trump's digital director because he had once designed a website for one of his hotels. But his lack of experience was also an advantage.

The uptight and inward-looking Clinton campaign spurned offers of assistance from tech companies. But Parscale gratefully accepted the help of what he described as 'teams of people' already set up within Facebook who had been identified as Republicans. 'I understood quickly that Facebook is how Donald Trump was going to win,' he said. 'Twitter was how he talked to American people but Facebook … was the highway that he drove on.'[45]

In an interview with CBS, he described how they were embedded in the Trump campaign: 'Facebook employees showed up at our offices every day. … I said to them, "I want to know every single secret, button, click, technology you have; I want your people here to each me how to use it.'''

Facebook disputes whether it is fair to say its staff were 'embedded' in the Trump campaign but recognises its experts have spent longer thinking about what kind of content goes viral and what ads work than anyone in politics. And sharing such insights with the Trump campaign was why the campaign became so good at using Facebook's platforms. Facebook taught Parscale how to reach clusters of voters such as micro-targeting what he described as 'fifteen people in the Florida Panhandle that I would never buy a TV commercial for' by using Facebook tools such as Custom Audiences. Facebook's taught him how to find more voters like the ones the campaign was already targeting using a tool called Lookalike Audiences. And Facebook taught him how to vary with minute alternations made in the design, colour, background and phrasing in order to maximize their impact before being rolled out to broader audiences.[46]

And, unlike CA's Nix, Parscale does not appear to have been exaggerating about his social media skills. An internal paper from Facebook's data scientists said Trump's ad campaigns 'were more complex than Clinton's and better leveraged Facebook's ability to optimise for outcomes.' Clinton ran 66,000 different variations of Facebook ads during the campaign, which sounds like a lot until it is compared the Trump's total of 5.9 million. Indeed, there were days when Parscale varied ads more often than Clinton did in the course of the whole campaign.[47]

Some of these Trump ads were so-called 'dark posts' which cannot be viewed by anyone but the recipient unless they are shared. 'Only the people we want to see it, see it,' said Parscale. Often, such dark posts were aimed not at persuading people to vote for Trump but rather demoralising or disillusioning those inclined to vote for his opponent. In the run-up to the election, a senior official on the campaign was quoted saying: 'We have three major voter suppression operations under way. They're aimed at three groups Clinton needs to win overwhelmingly: idealistic white liberals, young women, and African Americans.'[48] One was an animation in the style of *South Park* that highlighted bitterly-contested remarks she had made twenty years earlier about young members of drug gangs. 'Hillary Thinks African Americans are Super Predators,' said the ad, as cartoon text popped up. The aim was to lower voting among black people. 'We've modelled this,' said the official. 'It will dramatically affect her ability to turn these people out.'[49]

Another technique which appears to have been deployed in support of the Trump campaign was the use of automated social media accounts (bots) to drive messages into voters' newsfeeds or to confuse and conceal others. According to the research from Oxford University, an army of pro-Trump bots overwhelmed similar automated accounts supporting Hillary Clinton by a margin of five to one in the final days of the presidential election; at least a third of tweets backing Trump came from such bots, and the busiest 100 of them on Twitter 'generated around 450,000 tweets at an average rate of 500 tweets per day.'[50]

There is no proof that Trump's campaign directly paid for bots, although his habit of retweeting those that were supportive of him, no less than 150 times in the first three months of 2016 according to one analysis, may suggest a degree of synchronisation.[51] At the same time, sudden leaps in the numbers of fake accounts following or liking Trump's personal social media accounts have provoked suspicions he bought—and may still be buying—bots to boost his image. Indeed, a programme called 'Twitter Audit' consistently shows millions of his online fans are not real people at all.[52]

Since the presidential election much of the focus has been on alleged Russian interference, including the hacking of Democratic National Committee emails, as part of a disinformation campaign seemingly designed to undermine US democracy and, in its latter stages, to help get Trump elected. Efforts included systemic use of trolls, bots and fake social media accounts including one called 'Blacktivist' which used its 360,000 likes—more than the verified Black Lives Matter account on Facebook—to urge African Americans not to vote for Clinton.[53] Russia's troll farm in St Petersburg is also reported to have bought at least 3,000 Facebook ads that were seen by 10 million voters and reached as many as 150 million US voters with social media content.[54]

But for all this, the Russian operation was still relatively tiny. For instance, its spending on Facebook ads in the final days of the election was just $46,000 compared to a combined total of $81 million by the Clinton and Trump campaigns. Antonio Garcia Martinez, one of the Facebook engineers who built its advertising system, is among those who believe the real problem with social media and advertising was made in northern California rather than cooked up in the Kremlin. Facebook's algorithms, he said, would have ensured Trump's divisive, viral quality messages were much more likely to be shared. 'Facebook users in swing states who felt Trump had taken over their news feeds may not have been hallucinating,' he said. 'Plotting Russians make for a good story, and external enemies frequently serve an internal purpose, but the trail of blame often leads much closer to home. It's right there, topped by a big, blue bar on our smartphone screens.'[55]

# # #

Even Jeremy Corbyn's unexpected electoral success in 2017 owed a bit more than he would generally like to acknowledge to the data-driven techniques of political consultants, digital platforms provided by American capitalist monopolies, and some suspiciously centrist Labour staff who have been steadily purged from the party's payroll.

Patrick Heneghan, the party's campaign's director and a veteran of four previous general elections, was one of those still working at the party's headquarters, an anonymous building called Southside—but known as 'the dark side' to Corbyn's inner circle. He had regularly infuriated key figures in the Leader's Office like Seumas Milne and Karie Murphy but there was a further stand-off in April 2017 when he produced a list of key seats at risk in the expected Tory landslide which the Southsiders said needed to receive extra funding. Corbyn's team thought Heneghan was diverting resources to his friends and their enemies in the parliamentary party. They demanded more money be spent on getting their left-wing allies elected for the first time.

The Southsiders, however, were still useful to Corbyn's team because the party staff had developed data tools and a digital plan that showed how much they had learnt from the 2015 defeat. A six-figure sum had been invested and more than a year spent creating new software, known as Promote, that could match data gleaned from commercial suppliers or canvassing with Facebook's own data to target ads with pinpoint accuracy. The party spent £1.3 million buying digital ads, often through outside organisations. Although this was still less than the Conservatives, Heneghan believes Labour had closed the technology gap with the Tories or even overtaken them because they 'did not have the kind of advanced weaponry we had.'[56]

The party also spent £100,000 buying an advert which reached 7 million Snapchat users reminding them to vote in the final three days of the election. More than 1.2 million people clicked on a link to view maps showing where they could do so. 'For a month before that I had two members of my staff spend all day, every day, typing in the location of every polling station in the country,' recalls Heneghan. 'It wasn't glamorous work but it was the only way we could do it.'[57]

Steve Howells, a political consultant who was brought in by Corbyn to help run his communications during the election campaign, acknowledges social media was a 'key ingredient' in their success, with the leader's Facebook likes and Twitter following increasing by as much as a third to well over a million in the course of the seven-week long campaign. He says 'smart, tactical use of paid-for digital advertising' reached parts of the electorate that might otherwise have failed to hear Labour's message.[58] It was not just paid-for advertising that achieved this success, Labour's messages, like those of Trump, were more viral and travelled further and faster as a result. Sam Jeffers, co-founder of the 'Who Targets Me?' project that examines the social media feeds of thousands of volunteers said organic sharing among voters meant that Labour's online ads were being seen in 464 constituencies as opposed to only 205 for the Tories.[59]

But a civil war was being fought in the party even during the General Election. And when the weapons were digital it was inevitable they would be deployed in these battles too. Momentum, the pro-Corbyn grassroots organisation, worked with veterans of Bernie Sanders's presidential campaign to create an app that directed activists to the nearest marginal seat. Initially, at least, this appeared to exclude some moderate Labour MPs with small majorities fighting for their political lives and whose communications often sought to distance themselves from the Labour leadership.[60]

At the same time Labour Party staff had realised they could target Facebook ads to reach just a few people with a degree of precision. And it was not always used just to campaign for votes. For instance, Corbyn's aides sometimes demanded big spending on Facebook advertising for pet projects which Southsiders regarded as a waste of money. What happened next, according to two former party officials who spoke on strict condition of anonymity, showed just how good they had got at microtargeting. 'They wanted us to spend a fortune on some schemes like the one they had to encourage voter registration,' says one ex-Southsider. 'But we only had to spend about £5,000 to make sure Jeremy's people, some journalists and bloggers saw it was there on Facebook. And if it was there for them, they thought it must be there for everyone. It wasn't. That's how targeted ads can work.'[61] Another former staffer confirms that such ads would be aimed at people who were 'likely to care most about those issues like left wing people living in London including, I suppose, Jeremy's team'. The ex-official emphatically denied one suggestion I had heard that resulting savings were then diverted to the Southsiders' priorities of shoring up Labour MPs. But, either way, Corbyn's team were receiving 'dark posts' that were tailor-made for them by their own party while most voters saw different content.

Inevitably, when dealing with operations that few people in politics or the media understand, there is a risk of Cambridge Analytica-type exaggeration about what data analytics can do. But Facebook and social media advertising is consistent theme of all these elections and it does not seem like hyperbole to suggest it may have become the most effective tool for reaching voters that has ever been used in democratic politics.

No one really doubts that elections in the future will be decided at least in part by the capacity of campaigns to pay for the best data, the most sophisticated analytics and huge spending on social media adverting. Hillary Clinton is probably right when she warns Democrats that the lesson of her failure is not to 'abandon data but obtain better data, use it more effectively, question every assumption and keep adapting.'[62] Even in 2017 when Theresa May's campaign was imploding, Scottish Conservatives unexpectedly won more than a dozen seats with a highly data-driven campaign that used different techniques to Messina.

And, while it appears that Cambridge Analytica exaggerated its capacity to swing elections, the potential is only going to grow for a wealthy individual like Mercer one day to use psychometrics to gain a crucial marginal advantage in elections, just as he has used big data analytics to gain an advantage on Wall Street.

The three contests examined in this chapter—the referendum on membership of the EU, the US presidential battle in 2016, and the British General Election of 2017—show how fast politics and the rules of the game were beginning to change in the new information age.

And, in many cases, it left people baffled by the results.

In the deep, dark cave

Tom Steinberg had spent most of his working life trying to harness the power of digital technology to make the politics a little bit more accountable, open and democratic. He set up Downing Street's e-petitions website in 2007 and founded MySociety which included sites like FixMyStreet for people to report potholes and TheyWorkForYou which laid bare the varying rates of productivity among MPs.

On the morning of 24 June 2016, he woke up to discover that Britain had voted to leave the European Union. Like most liberal left types he was devastated by this news. But his immediate reaction was to seek out a better understanding of what had just happened. The trouble was, he did not know people who had voted for Brexit—and nor were they to be found in the one place someone like Steinberg would naturally turn to look: on social media.

Later that morning, he posted a message complaining he could not find 'anyone who is happy' on Facebook despite more than half the country voting for Brexit and 'the fact that I'm *actively* looking to hear what they are saying.'

He added: 'This echo-chamber problem is now SO severe and SO chronic that I can only beg any friends I have who actually work for Facebook and other major social media and technology to urgently tell their leaders that to not act on this problem now is tantamount to actively supporting and funding the tearing apart of the fabric of our societies. … We're getting countries where one half just doesn't know anything at all about the other.'[63]

The shock felt by so much of the political class after the victories of Brexit and Trump was not merely because they had been unexpected, it was also because those who had voted for such outcomes had simply since disappeared from view.

A subsequent autopsy saw these electorates being sliced and diced across almost every demographic. Well-heeled journalists travelled from Westminster or the prosperous coasts of the US to explore the heart of darkness in 'the North' and the so-called 'fly-over states'. Some concluded the split was about social class and economic opportunity, with poorer, less educated white voters in Britain's northern towns or the American Rust Belt swinging towards Brexit and Trump. Others saw it as a cultural clash between liberals who have the mobility to be from 'anywhere' and those left behind 'somewhere'.[64] Still have shown how it reflected age, pointing out that older voters disproportionately backed the inward-looking offers of Brexit and Trump—while younger voters who grew up in the internet age with open and outward-looking values overwhelmingly preferred Remain and Clinton.[65]

But, in the bitter aftermath of both these votes, just about everyone could agree that both Britain and America were more divided than at any time in the past fifty years. And it was also clear that social media was not necessarily making the world 'more open and connected', as Facebook's mission had promised, but giving people the means to close their eyes and their minds to any view they did not like.

Little more than a year before Steinberg had woken up to news of Brexit, Rebecca Roache, a philosophy lecturer, had been similarly devastated when she discovered the Tories had won the 2015 General Election. Her response was not quite as open-minded as that of Steinberg. In a blog for a University of Oxford site, ironically dedicated to practical ethics, she announced she had 'unfriended' any Conservative she could find on Facebook.

She wrote: 'One of the first things I did after seeing the depressing election news this morning was check to see which of my Facebook friends "like" the pages of the Conservatives or David Cameron, and unfriend them. (Thankfully, none of my friends "like" the UKIP page.) Life is too short, I thought, to hang out with people who hold abhorrent political views, even if it's just online. I'm tired of reasoned debate about politics. ... I don't want to be friends with racists, sexists, or homophobes. And I don't want to be friends with Conservatives either.'[66]

There are endless other examples of this phenomenon. For instance, during the US presidential election the Huffington Post delighted in showing its readers how they could use a simple search-and-cleanse tool on Facebook to remove anyone who supported Donald Trump, adding: 'The unfriend button has never been more important.'[67] Although Facebook does not publish data on the extent of these purges, one survey showed fully 24 per cent of Democrats—and a further 9 per cent of Republicans—had removed people from their social media circle as a result of the presidential election in 2016.[68]

Social media executives point out that there is also a lot of intolerance offline, in what some of them refer to as the 'meat world'. One says: 'The problem here is people, not people using Facebook.' But there are also good reasons to think that the internet, and social media in particular, has made such polarisation worse. At the very least, it indulges what seems to be a basic instinct to surround ourselves with others like us, or known to us.

Indeed, one of the paradoxes of the most advanced technology human beings have ever created is that it is underpinned by instincts that predate the invention of the wheel or even the discovery of how to make fire. On social media, we are encouraged to build a group identity through those we 'friend' and 'follow'. The content we 'like' and 'share' communicates our good standing with other members perhaps in a similar way that ancient Britons did when they painted their bodies with woad or wore antlers on their heads. And, if someone wants to be friends or like us back, we experience the warm and very public glow of being acknowledged by the co-habitants of our online cave just as our hunter gatherers ancestors perhaps once gathered around to admire someone's painting of a mammoth.

In the early years of this new age, such polarisation was at least a free choice, like buying the *Daily Mail*, watching MSNBC or unfriending people who voted Tory. By the second decade of this century, however, the internet was potentially driving people apart in a new and dangerous fashion. Eli Pariser was the former director of the online grassroots organisation, Moveon.org, that had done so much to help get Barack Obama elected in 2008. He began warning that the algorithms of Facebook and Google were learning from the reams of data being generated to keep people on their platforms by giving everyone more and more of what they already like. He said this meant we were not only disappearing deeper into caves to hear the same views but were also locked inside our own 'filter bubbles' that invisibly imprison us with ever-more amplified versions of our own thoughts.

And often, it is the worst form of us that we heard: intolerant, angry, in search of instant gratification and attention-seeking.

# # #

In the US, interest in the filter bubble idea began to surge during the presidential election in November 2016—about which almost 9 billion pieces of content, likes or comments had been posted on Facebook.[69] The *Wall Street Journal* began offering online readers the chance to read about highly polarised issues like guns, abortion or healthcare through a 'Blue Feed' for Facebook liberals and a 'Red Feed' for Facebook conservatives.[70]

And, after the vote, it became a go-to reason for everyone trying to work out how the man they so despised had become president. 'The "Filter Bubble" Explains Why Trump Won and You Didn't See It Coming,' said a *New York* magazine headline the day after the vote.

And here's what Brian Eno, the ageing rock star, told *The Guardian* in 2017: 'I thought that all those Ukip people and those National Fronty people were in a little bubble. Then I thought: "Fuck, it was us, we were in the bubble, we didn't notice it." There was a revolution brewing and we didn't spot it because we didn't make it. We expected we were going to be the revolution.'[71]

Barack Obama used his post-presidency interviews to say the 'optimistic feeling' he had about social media when he was using it to win elections had been dissipated by the way powerful forces had learnt how to manipulate algorithms. 'Whatever your biases were, that's where you were being sent, and that gets more reinforced over time,' he said. 'That's what's happening with these Facebook pages where more and more people are getting their news from. At a certain point you just live in a bubble, and that's part of why our politics is so polarised right now.'[72]

Pariser himself was more sceptical, suggesting that while the bubble surrounding US liberals had been a direct cause of the shock they felt at the outcome of the presidential election, 'my guess is that talk-radio, local news, and Fox' had more to do with why some older, poorer—and less digitally connected—voters had unexpectedly plumped for Trump.[73] Indeed, several academic studies since 2016 suggested people who rely on social media are overall more, not less, likely to see content with which they disagree.[74]

But that did not quite settle the argument. Anyone who has used YouTube, for instance, knows how it recommends and lines up the next videos.[75] Zeynep Tufekci, an internet specialist at the University of North Carolina, described her experience after watching videos of Trump rallies during the 2016 presidential election. The next ones lined up for her by YouTube were those featuring 'white supremacist rants, Holocaust denials and other disturbing content'. Similarly, watching clips of Hilary Clinton and Bernie Sanders saw her being autoplayed left conspiracy videos about secret government agencies.

She said: 'Videos about vegetarianism led to videos about veganism. Videos about jogging led to videos about running ultramarathons. It seems as if you are never "hard core" enough for YouTube's recommendation algorithm. ... Given its billion or so users, YouTube may be one of the most powerful radicalising instruments of the twenty-first century.'[76]

Other studies have shown how consumption of false news was heavily concentrated in the US elections among a small group of voters. One found that almost 60 per cent of visits to fake news websites came from the 10 per cent of people with the 'most conservative online information diets'. And it found that Facebook users were 'differentially likely' to consume such false news.[77] Most people are not that interested in politics but the filter bubble effect appears to exist, perniciously, on the extreme edges of debate where it helps create new political eco-systems nurtured far out of sight from the mainstream consuming with its own diet of alternative facts.

Alt-Right, Alt-Left

By 2016, young white supremacists no longer had to wear pointed hoods or get swastikas tattooed to their foreheads. Instead, they found each other online using symbols from their childhoods like Pepe—a curious but previously innocent cartoon frog adopted as a meme on 4chan—or projected themselves as characters from *The Matrix*, a 1999 science fiction movie.

Pepe was suddenly popping up everywhere, appearing, for instance, as a huge green anthropomorphic frog, with Donald Trump hair and an ironic expression, standing on one side of a border fence as a Mexican family with a baby gaze on forlornly from the other. In another image, Pepe is shown wearing SS uniform.[78]

The endless references to *The Matrix* and red pills are similarly obscure and disturbing. Neo, the hero of the film, is offered a choice: he can take a blue pill that will allow him return to the soft comfort of a make-believe computer-generated world; or he can take the hard choice and swallow a red pill that will reveal the truth. When young conservatives or libertarians talked of being 'red-pilled', it meant they were rejecting the norms of democracy, as well as perhaps rebelling against their parents, to discover their version of an alternative truth.

These red-pilled internet warriors became known as the alternative right—the 'alt-right'. It was a phrase coined by Richard Spencer, a white supremacist who likes to claim 'we memed the alt-right into existence,'[79] but the movement only crawled out from the depths of the internet when Donald Trump announced he was a presidential candidate in 2015.

And by then, it wasn't always easy to distinguish the real racists from the common troll doing it for the 'lulz'. Digitally-native memes and humour gave darker motives an edgy, cyber-punk patina. In some eyes, it made them cool.

The first sign that some of the trolls amusing themselves on sites like Reddit, 4Chan or its offshoot 8chan, were getting ready to migrate over into politics came with an episode known as 'GamerGate'. In 2012, the feminist critic Anita Sarkeesian was musing in an online post about whether video games might 'reinforce and amplify sexist and downright misogynist ideas about women.'[80] Over the course of the next few months, she became the unwitting catalyst not only for a new video game called 'Beat Up Anita Sarkeesian' but an entire movement. She received multiple threats of death and rape, while her parents' home was identified along with suggestions that they should be killed too.[81] And, having once been stirred, the mob did not take long to find its next target.

In 2014, Zoë Quinn's jilted boyfriend, Eron Gjoni, posted a 9,000-word online manifesto accusing her of sleeping with a journalist in return for a positive review for a video game she had designed. One of the more printable online threats she subsequently received on 4chan, Twitter, Facebook and Reddit over the next year, read: 'I am going to hunt you down and behead your ugly face, you disgusting, cheating feminist whore. See you soon, slut.' Quinn is clear that the 'typhoon of shit' unleashed on her was less to do with 'a bad break up and a video game review that never existed' than the new 'landscape of the internet.'[82]

She added: 'I feel like one of the few people not surprised by Trump's election. I called it the second he announced his candidacy. ... I had been years-deep in the muck, and I saw my attackers start shifting to support him.'[83]

New terms of abuse that were trialled in GamerGate were deployed repeatedly in aid of Trump when the presidential contest began. They included terms such as 'snowflakes' to describe sensitive young people; 'cucks' for men craving female approval (or 'cuckservative' for a moderate conservative); and 'Social Justice Warriors' for left-wingers and feminists. And the trolls who attacked Sarkeesian and Quinn in GamerGate were soon out in force in the 2016 election. In July that year, Jessica Valenti, a feminist writer who had felt uncomfortable about the tone of comments she received below the line on *The Guardian* a earlier, fled from social media all together after a rape threat was made against her daughter, aged just five.[84]

Social media personalities like Milo Yiannopoulos were also forged in the misogyny of GamerGate before becoming tools of the alt-right movement in the 2016 presidential election. Yiannopoulos, raised in the

Home Counties and formerly of the *Daily Telegraph*, was the gay, bottle blond star technology writer of Breitbart until he eventually lost his job for making pro-pederasty comments.[85] Breitbart itself, chaired by Steve Bannon until he left to join Trump's team in the final months of the presidential election, was being built into a multi-media network with bureaus in Los Angeles, Washington, London, and Jerusalem, a daily radio programme on Sirius XM, as well as a cash supply from the deep pockets of Robert Mercer. And, as *The New York Times* put it, Breitbart had a comments section that 'dwarfs the comments at this newspaper by roughly a factor of ten, even as those readers/commenters/trolls remain, to most of the outside world, a mysterious horde of indistinct origin and uncertain intent.'[86]

# # #

Breitbart's importance in 2016 was underlined by a gigantic collaborative study undertaken by Harvard and MIT which compiled a database called Media Cloud of more than 2 million election stories published by approximately 70,000 media sources.[87]

Its purpose was to discover how news travels and its results were published in an extraordinary and rather beautiful map that looks like a planetary system engulfed in a red and blue coloured dust cloud.[88] Each speck of dust represented sites linked to each other by fine lines denoting online shares. The red colour indicates a story that was shared by conservatives, blue a story shared by liberals. The more each website's stories were shared on platforms like Facebook, the bigger these specks grew so that largest formed planet-like circles. On the 'liberal' side, there are large spheres coloured a light shade of blue, The Huffington Post, CNN, *The Washington Post*, *Politico* and *The New York Times*. But there was only one big planet on the 'conservative' side, a huge deep red glob—far larger than Fox News—labelled Breitbart.

While the big names of the centre-left media continued to dominate liberal debate, Breitbart, surrounded by other conservative sites like Fox News and the Daily Caller, was at the apex of 'a discrete and relatively insular right-wing media ecosystem whose shape and communications practices differ sharply from the rest.'[89] Breitbart acted as a bridge between the mainstream and more extreme content such as that found on conspiracy sites like Infowars, American Renaissance and Gateway

Pundit or even the overtly fascistic Daily Stormer. The Harvard–MIT report concluded that Breitbart effectively had hollowed out the centre-right of the American media—once dominated by newspapers like *The Wall Street Journal*—leaving it 'more conducive to the echo-chamber, information-cascade, and filter bubble effects often discussed as risks of the online environment.'[90]

One of the academics who conducted the study was Yochai Benkler, whose 2006 book *The Wealth of Networks* had heralded the internet's capacity to open up politics. This study, however, suggested that it was the far-right forcing its way in. 'Whether that's "democratising" or not,' said Benkler, 'depends on how much emphasis you put on people being able to contest an election versus how much you put on civil rights, protection of minorities, rule of law.'[91]

Changes in Facebook's algorithm in 2012 and 2013 to increase the amount of news in its feed favoured the clickbait viral headlines being produced by the partisan conservative media that sought to shock, surprise or reinforce an existing prejudice. It meant Facebook had become the gateway into an alternative right wing reality for this group of US voters.[92]

By 2016, there were thousands of Facebook-native Trump support pages, bouncing the same stories and memes between them. Most had just a few hundred members, but a few were sometimes able to generate more traffic through 'likes' and shares than long-established media players. For instance, Make America Great, managed by Adam Nicoloff from his home outside St Louis, had content that was shared, commented on or liked more than 4 million times in July 2016, beating the Facebook page of USA Today.[93] This dense, interconnected eco-system of news meant that statements that sounded utterly bizarre to outsiders could become common currency inside. In August that year, when Trump called Clinton 'the devil' at a rally in North Carolina, a poll in the state showed 41 per cent of his supporters believed his rival really was Satan.[94]

The paradox here is that the alt-right has exploited the liberalisation of the information age and its borderless communication to galvanise a bitterly illiberal agenda; one that demands controls over the movement of goods and people; that proselytises an intolerance and hatred of others; that utterly contradict the high ideals of the web.

# # #

There are other examples of this phenomenon in extremist politics around the world, such as the so-called 'fachosphere' in France. They share not only an aggressive stance towards their enemies but also a sense of outrage that their voice is 'ignored' by a 'lying' liberal mainstream media (MSM). The far right has spawned on social media in the UK too. A group called Britain First reached 2 million Facebook likes after its videos attacking Muslims were Tweeted by Donald Trump in November. It was eventually banned Facebook in March 2018 for breaching 'community standards'.

But the biggest new space in British politics was being carved out on the left. Though very different from the women-hating neo-fascists that populate the alt-right, sites like The Canary, Another Angry Voice, Evolve Politics, and Skwawkbox have still been characterised as being part of a vocal 'alt-left'. Like the extreme right, they define themselves in opposition to the hated MSM. And, as with the groups proliferating on social media in the US, their success has been driven by shares that bounce their stories around within insular filter bubbles and ideological echo chambers. Some of the Facebook groups set up to support Jeremy Corbyn are deliberately closed so that its members can avoid having to listen to heretical opinion or, in some cases, being subjected to scrutiny. Even open groups like 'We Support Jeremy Corbyn'—a public page with 68,000 members—bans links to right-wing newspapers. It also explicitly tells people to stay off debating Brexit—the single biggest challenge facing the UK—because 'this has proved a very divisive issue and we'd like to keep the main group clear for supporting JC.'[95] The page administrators then provide a link to an off-shoot group, closed to the public, where members can fight over Brexit without giving the appearance of disunity, before signing off with this cheery message: 'You may feel this isn't a democracy and you are right. This is Facebook.'[96]

Much of the material being pushed by these groups in the 2017 election included highly-effective YouTube videos produced by the Labour Party or Momentum, that reached well beyond the alt-left cave. 'Daddy, why do you hate me?'[97] was the title of one such film focusing on school cuts and student fees that achieved 5.4 million views in just two days. But most of the pro-Corbyn content poured forth from bloggers or the websites that were suddenly flourishing in the shelter of Facebook; unseen by the bulk of the country's voters and un-noticed by most journalists in the mainstream media.

Another Angry Voice—known as AAV—is a blog written by Thomas G. Clark, a part-time English tutor from Yorkshire. He proudly claims to have had three of the ten most shared political articles on Facebook during the 2017 British General Election campaign, 'including both of the top two.' After years of relative obscurity when he measured views in the thousands, he says that in the final week of the campaign, AAV 'generated almost one million likes, comments and shares.'[98] The day after the election, Clark gave himself a deserved pat on the back as he wrote a piece describing himself as 'one lone wolf guy making more Facebook noise than the pages of every UK newspaper except the *Daily Mail* and the *Independent*.'[99]

Clark has attributed the success of his journalism to it having less 'cognitive dissonance' than a reader of the traditional left-of-centre press might encounter. 'When you follow something like *The Guardian* or *The Mirror*, one minute they're posting good stuff that holds the Tories to account, and the next they're posting anti-Corbyn stuff that goes way over the line,' he explained.[100]

Part of me wants to celebrate this. Having fought on the frontline of politics when I was working for Ed Miliband, I would have loved to have had a vast social media army reinforcing Labour's messages and loyally protecting the party leader's back.

But Sunny Hundal, who had pioneered left-wing blogging for many years at a site called Liberal Conspiracy before closing it in 2013, is among those who fear the alt-left media is going too far. He says: 'We tried to be balanced and offer space to different opinions; we wanted to show the left was a broad church of people. The new sites have grown up on social media since Facebook's algorithms were changed to favour very click-baity headlines. A lot of them are now in an echo chamber where they are taking extreme positions, defending Jeremy Corbyn at all cost no matter what he does, pushing people to be more and more radical. But there is a real risk of extreme polarisation which rejects anyone who says anything different. They now have real power and need to show some responsibility because, when you see them taking potshots at people like those at the BBC, you realise what they can become.'[101]

In my angry, fraught and often desperate days as a Labour spinner, I would make daily—even hourly—complaints to the BBC in an effort to influence its coverage. Sometimes, it does show signs of a bias towards power, or at least conventional wisdom. But the real reason I complained was because I knew its editors and journalists really cared about getting a story right and unlike the press, the BBC—together with other broadcasters—has a duty to try. Even if they told me to 'fuck off' as BBC or ITV editors (sometimes justifiably) did, I knew they had listened.

The alt-left's regular assaults on the BBC has been completely different in scale, tone and consequences. Mere sight of those three letters seems to trigger an almost Pavlovian response of foaming rage about bias. In this, they share symptoms previously only seen consistently in the columns of the *Daily Mail*. According to one analysis, of the fourteen news stories on The Canary's homepage on the eve of the election, half were pieces condemning news outlets for the thought-crime of being unfair to Corbyn. One even attacked the BBC's 'shocking stunt' of tweeting the front page of *The Sun* when that is what it does for all national newspapers, every day.[102]

Particular venom was reserved for Laura Kuenssberg, the BBC's first female political editor. The Canary went for Kuenssberg so often it gave her a special tag on the website.[103] It promoted a petition on the campaign website 38 Degrees calling for her to be sacked that it had to be taken down, 35,000 signatures later, after becoming a magnet for misogynist abuse.[104] The Canary has also been censored by the independent press regulator for falsely claiming she was speaking at the Tory party conference.[105]

For what it's worth, I don't think The Canary intends to promote misogyny. And the website's defenders will point out that Kuenssberg was ruled by the now-defunct BBC Trust to have once, unintentionally, quoted Corbyn out of context.[106] Nor does the alt-left need to take any lectures on 'fake news' from critics like *The Sun* which have been misleading and dividing people for a lot longer. But the treatment meted out to Kuenssberg by sites like The Canary has seen her booed, jeered and shouted down for asking perfectly fair questions at Labour events. After receiving specific threats, the BBC decided she needed to have a bodyguard when she went to the party's annual conference in 2017.[107]

The sadness of this is that Kuenssberg herself was once an evangelist for social media as tool for breaking down the barriers between journalists and their audiences. In 2008, she made a formal submission to the BBC's board of directors about why reporters like her should be using Twitter. Eventually, six months' later, she won the right to start tweeting without having each one of her 140 characters approved by her bosses.

And when she began working in UK politics, her brief was about empowering people to make themselves heard.

Sitting in a cramped BBC office while Kuenssberg's piece from the evening news blares out, slightly disconcertingly, from the TV on the table behind her, she still seems fired up by the memory.

She says: 'What I was excited about was the opportunity for punters to be part of politics. The whole idea was to allow the voices of people outside this weirdo Palace of Westminster to be heard. That was my whole ethos—that people deserve to know what is being done in their name—and I used Twitter to get their stories and let them ask questions. I thought the whole social media thing might be really positive with people interacting with each other politically. Some of that has happened—the atmosphere now is so grim it's easy to lose sight of the way grassroots campaign groups have been able to grow online.'[108]

But weariness creeps into Kuenssberg's voice as she talks about her own experience and admits to using social media less than before. 'I've tried to pull back and I've thought about coming off it all together. Partly, that's because it's uglier out there now; it's like a playground where people want to shout each other down. I don't read the comments people write about me, it's not worth it. I can't be arsed to get into spats where people fighting online have already made their mind up and, if I got sucked into that I wouldn't have time to do anything else—sometimes all people want is to have a pop, why give them the satisfaction of answering back?'[109]

She believes that social media has 'both reflected and enabled' the polarisation of politics, leaving broadcasters like her 'who get sacked if we make stuff up' caught in the crossfire as both sides seek to discredit them. 'I don't want to sound like a girl guide but I really, really believe people have a right to quality information. It's important we don't get pushed around—and we won't. I have never treated a story differently because of this stuff.'[110]

# # #

Kuennsberg was by no means the only or even the chief target of the trolls. And some corners of their online lair have become a source of abuse of Labour women MPs like Jess Phillips or Stella Creasy, just as the likes of Diane Abbott have long since been targets from trolls from

Britain's racist alt-right. Still more disturbing is the way Corbyn supporters on social media appear to have nurtured a strand of anti-semitism that has always been present on the extreme left. A closed Facebook group, called Palestine Live, with which Corbyn himself briefly engaged, included links to Holocaust denial myths, along with bizarre conspiracy theories about the Rothschild family or Israel's involvement in the 9/11 and 7/7 terror attacks.[111] Other closed groups, such as 'The Labour Party Forum' and 'We trust and support Jeremy Corbyn's Labour' have been found by the *Sunday Times* to have anti-semitic and violent postings including one saying: 'The holocaust was a big lie!'[112]

Labour MPs who happen to be both Jewish and female have had it worst of all. In April 2018, Ruth Smeeth read out to the Commons just some of more printable social media interactions she had received:

Hang yourself you vile treacherous Zionist Tory filth. You are a cancer of humanity.

Ruth Smeeth is a Zionist—she has no shame—and trades on the murder of Jews by Hitler—whom the Zionists betrayed.

Ruth Smeeth must surely be travelling 1st class to Tel Aviv with all that slush. After all, she's complicit in trying to bring Corbyn down.

First job for Jeremy Corbyn tomorrow—expel the Zionist BICOM smear hag bitch Ruth Smeeth from the Party.

#JC4PM Deselect Ruth Smeeth ASAP. Poke the pig—get all Zionist child killer scum out of Labour.

You are a spy! You are evil, satanic! Leave! #Labour #Corbyn.

Your fellow traitor Tony Blair abolished hanging for treason. Your kind need to leave before we bring it back #Smeeth Is Filth.

The gallows would be a fine and fitting place for this dyke piece of Yid shit to swing from.[113]

Jeremy Corbyn himself probably does not have a racist cell in his body but some of his supporters should be jailed for such abuse. And too many more of his fans casually dismiss the outrage over anti-semitism as just another smear or a media conspiracy to get at their leader. An 'MSM' columnist—and long-time Labour party member—Janice Turner, described the cultish intolerance of the alt-left bubble. She wrote: 'For Corbyn and his supporters there are only sides. Enemies and allies; traitors (crush them!) and the righteous. Either you are 100 per cent

Corbyn4PM or you hate the disabled, support genocide in Iraq, think benefit claimants should die. There is no room for debate, compromise, legitimate concerns, doubt. Any means is justified by the socialist end, even Holocaust denial.'[114]

In this alt-left echo chamber it was logical for Laura Pidcock, a Labour MP often mentioned by Corbyn's supporters as his possible successor, to tell Skwawkbox she had 'absolutely no intention of being friends' with any Tory MP because she regarded them all as 'the enemy'.[115]

The symbolic 'unfriending' that follows any dissent or deviation is as devastating for the faithful as ex-communication must once have been for a devout Catholic. When, in March 2018, one of the alt-left media's leading lights annoyed the leadership of the Labour Party for daring to suggest it should stay true to its principles of internal party democracy, Jeremy Corbyn swiftly expelled him from his personal filter bubble. That night, Aaron Bastani tweeted plaintively: 'Unfollowed by Jeremy Corbyn Twitter account for saying the General Secretary should be elected. Sad! (Hopefully several hundred hours of dedication and commitment will make up for having such an outrageous opinion!)'[116]

How resonance beat reason

Just days before the 2016 EU referendum, a poll was published showing the attitudes of Remain and Leave supporters towards different groups. Remainers said they trusted academics by a margin of 68 to 19 per cent, economists by 63 to 22 per cent, and the Bank of England by 61 to 27 per cent. By contrast, just one in four Leave supporters had faith in the opinions of academics, while other professions, including economists, charity leaders, religious leaders and of course politicians, fared even worse.[117] In other words, the Brexit voters trusted pretty much no one.

These were the kind of numbers that emboldened the usually cerebral Michael Gove to declare, in answer to a question about the leading economists lining up against Brexit, that people 'have had enough of experts from organisations with acronyms saying that they know what is best and getting it consistently wrong.'[118] Since the referendum, Gove has tried to row back on these comments. He suggests he was not denigrating expertise itself so much as 'those who consider, or declare, themselves experts' but whose track record showed they were not very good at their job. In an interview for this book, he acknowledges that his views on the subject had more impact than he perhaps intended. 'It was not a conscious thing that I had intended, it was much more spontaneous than that,' he said, 'the irony, of course, is that I often cite experts to justify what I'm doing.'

Gove then adds: 'My aim at that point was to try to say that these people had been wrong in the past and they're wrong now. They had said "trust us" in the run up to the 2008 crisis and when the tide had gone out, we could see who was naked. I just think it is wrong to claim that because you work for the IMF we must automatically accept what you say. My argument would be, "justify yourself, let's look at the evidence."'[119]

But the referendum campaign was not characterised by a sober and considered examination of the evidence. Dominic Cummings, Vote Leave's director, has said Brexit would have been lost if the likes of Gove and Boris Johnson, had not 'picked up the baseball bat marked Turkey/NHS.'[120] The most contentious, and false, claims suggested that Brexit would result in a £350 million-a-week bonus for the NHS and that Turkey was about to join the EU, 'opening the floodgates to 77 million Muslim migrants'. But it no longer seemed to matter whether what being said was true or false

In the days after the referendum, many Brexit campaigners like Iain Duncan Smith walked away from promises that the Government would find the extra money for the health service.[121] And Johnson, whose own family has Turkish heritage, swiftly reverted to his former position of trying to help the country join the EU. But none of this bothered Cummings, who wrote proudly on his blog that he had spent huge sums targeting these messages through Facebook because Turkey and the NHS had been the 'most effective argument with almost every demographic.'[122]

In one speech, Gove claimed that Turkey and four other countries could join the EU as early as 2020, leading to 5.2 million extra people moving to the UK. He said it was 'clearly unsustainable' to ask the NHS to look after a new group of patients 'equivalent in size to four Birminghams'.[123] In another, he warned Turkish migrants would raise the threat of terrorism.[124]

I ask Gove if he was entirely comfortable making claims that appealed to some very low sentiments. He pauses for a long time. Eventually, he replies: 'I know what you mean, yes. If it had been left entirely to me the Leave campaign would have a slightly different feel. I would have to go back and look at everything I said and think whether that was the right response at the right time. There is a sense at the back of my mind that we didn't get everything absolutely right. It's a difficult one.'[125]

# # #

It was a 'difficult one' because, in this fight, smashing voters over the head with baseball bats seemed to be the only strategy on offer. The Remain campaign's own weapon of choice was hyberbolic claims and terrifying numbers about the economic consequences of leaving. Although these were more evidence-based, there was a degree of what might be called technocratic hysteria in the way they were delivered. For instance, George Osborne claimed that a Brexit vote would trigger immediate spending cuts in an emergency budget. As I write this almost two years later, no such emergency budget has happened—although continued austerity and post-Brexit economic malaise have had their own impact.

One small instance serves as an illustration of how the referendum degenerated. When I helped out Ed Miliband with a speech in March 2016 he hoped to use for setting out a progressive case for membership of Europe to solve big challenges of the future, we were told by the Remain campaign it was not primary-coloured enough to be noticed. 'This is a nuclear arms race to get to the top of the [broadcast] bulletins,' said one member of their top team, as he urged us to delete entire sections and replace them with some attack material about the Leave campaign's 'secret agenda'. They may have been right about the state of the media debate because Miliband's speech disappeared without trace. But, by the end of the referendum, what had been dubbed 'Project Fear' by the Leave campaign was being given even less credence by voters than the bogus claims made by the Brexiteers.

And, in the vanguard of the rebuttal was none other than Steve Hilton, who has popped up in so many other chapters in this book. He flew back to Britain from his new home in Silicon Valley to attack his old boss, David Cameron, over immigration. His argument was carefully calibrated to suit the febrile, distrustful temperament of the voters he was visiting. Hilton said he knew how politics worked and had himself created famous scare-mongering adverts for the Tories in the 1990s. He warned that no one should believe all these 'phoney figures' that they were all getting so sick of hearing. Hilton even implied voters should not really trust anyone, neither himself or the prime minister for whom he used to work, because 'it is literally impossible to know what will happen in the future.'[126]

Discrediting the Remain campaign's experts was clearly a strategic gain for Brexiteers. But Hilton was tapping into a deeper mistrust and anger among voters that meant facts did not matter so much as they once did. In a series of TV appearances, Hilton—tanned, T-shirted and yoga-honed after four years of Californian luxury—went on to rail against the 'elites of bankers, bureaucrats and accountants' who had let so many migrants in. Without any apparent sense of irony, he complained they had imposed their will on 'our country'—or those he described as 'real people, in the real economy.'[127]

At the time of the referendum, Gove, an instinctively polite and self-consciously thoughtful politician, held the rather grandiose post of Lord Chancellor that required him to wear knee-high breaches, black stockings and buckled shoes on ceremonial occasions. He was also pursuing a programme of prison reform that had much of the liberal establishment purring. When I go to see him, he is sitting in the swimming pool-sized office he gets as a Cabinet minister. I ask if he really regards himself as an anti-Establishment figure. This time, Gove replies without a flicker of hesitation: 'Yes. All my life. It's a cast of mind. I associate the Establishment with being smooth and I would see myself as spiky rather than smooth and, one of the criticisms of me—entirely understandable—is that I am inclined to cross the road to have a fight in certain areas. I think that's anti-Establishment. It might seem preposterous to you, but that's how I see myself.'

He says there is a temperamental difference between the likes of David Cameron and George Osborne when compared to people like himself or Hilton—even though they all went to private schools and Oxford. 'George and Dave, smooth; me and Steve spiky,' he says, 'George and Dave posh; me and Steve *arriviste*.' Although Gove says he would not have voted for Trump, he acknowledges similar forces were at work electing the American president just five months after Brexit and admits to having discovered a 'streak of populism' in himself.

He says: 'My view is that the Sirs and Dames and the captains of industry more often than not tend to be complacent. ... If you are the chairman of a FTSE company, then I tend to think you're probably wrong.'[128]

Gove goes so far as to suggest this has led him to be attracted to some radical left-wing communitarian ideas he describes as 'blue Labour'. It is, he says, an argument that 'the interests of capital have triumphed over those of the working classes, the interests of the City of the rest of the country, the interests of the mercantile over the industrial.' He adds: 'I have found myself in the position of thinking there is a lot of truth in that. It's about reminding Versailles about the rest of the country, an element of knocking on the plate-glass window and saying, "you know."'

Arron Banks, who funded Farage's unofficial Leave.EU campaign, would regard all this talk of facts, progressive ideas, and avoiding too much association with Trump as ridiculous pussy-footing. If he could not buy Versailles with the money he keeps in tax havens offshore, this self-styled 'bad boy' would not have been tapping on plate-glass windows, but breaking them.[129] His analysis of what happened in the referendum was best summed up when he was asked to compare it with the US elections. 'The Remain campaign featured fact, fact, fact, fact, fact. It just doesn't work. You have got to connect with people emotionally,' he said. It was, Banks added with pride, what explained 'the Trump success.'[130]

# # #

Hillary Clinton, like the leaders of the Remain campaign, was not good at making an emotional connection. She had perhaps spent too many years seeking to obscure the full truth as she picked her way through the minefields of scandals involving her and her husband. But that was also because she was desperate to avoid being branded a liar. Donald Trump, by contrast, just did not care.

Early on in the contest, when he was still seeking the Republican nomination, Trump told a campaign rally in Iowa that such was the loyalty of his supporters, 'I could stand in the middle of Fifth Avenue and shoot somebody and I wouldn't lose any voters. It's like, incredible.'[131] For all the doubts and dysfunction that afflicted his campaign, he disorientated opponents, deflected proper scrutiny from the media and deceived his supporters with apparent impunity. Trump's genius was that he realised what others mistook as iron rules of politics had only ever been made of paper like the framed—and fake—*Time* magazine covers featuring himself that decorated his golf courses.

The fact-checking website, Politifact, has examined hundreds of claims made by the president. Just 5 per cent of them were judged to be wholly true, with the vast bulk of them—69 per cent—deemed either mostly or entirely false.[132] Such a record should have been fatal for the prospects of someone getting elected as parish councillor. But Trump found, perhaps to his own surprise, that it did not stop him becoming president.[133] In the peculiar circumstances of 2016, anything could be true if enough people believed it. As one of Trump's spokespeople said, in about as pure an expression of post-modernism that you can get, just after the election: 'People that say "facts are facts"—they're not really facts. ... Everybody has a way of interpreting them to be the truth, or not truth. There's no such thing, unfortunately, anymore as facts.'[134]

Clinton's own account of the campaign contrasts what she regarded as her play-hard-but-by-the-rules approach with an opponent who was taking 'the war on truth to a whole new level.'[135] After the election, the finger of blame was immediately pointed at so-called 'fake news'. Much of this false content came from the partisan ideologues of the alt-right, some of it from teenage satirists in their bedrooms and still more from the now infamous Macedonian fake news entrepreneurs or Russian trolls. Their motives became as indistinct as they echoed and merged into each other. BuzzFeed produced an analysis a few days after the election showing that in the final three months of the campaign, the twenty best performing fake news stories—such as one about the Pope endorsing Trump—generated more shares and likes than the top twenty stories from traditional news outlets.[136]

But the focus on fake news also let the traditional—mainstream—media off the hook. What is striking about the votes of 2016 is how the old and new media were hugely influenced by each other. For instance, an analysis of the 100 most popular pieces of Brexit content shared online during the UK referendum showed they were usually the work of long-established news outlets 'that relied on exaggeration rather than fakery.'[137] The most successful story—attracting 464,000 shares, comments, and interactions on Facebook, as well as many millions of views—was a half-baked report in the *Sunday Express* a few days before the referendum claiming Brussels planned for the NHS to be 'KILLED OFF'.[138] Britain did not need Macedonians producing false news stories when our own indigenous industry was doing the same thing under the mastheads of old Fleet Street.

In the US presidential election, much of the most toxic coverage for Clinton that was endlessly shared in the online echo chamber also originated in the supposedly liberal mainstream media. The MIT–Harvard

Media Cloud study shows that roughly four times as much of their coverage was devoted to Clinton's scandals—such as her private email server—than to her policies. At the same time, it dedicated one-and-a-half times more space to discussion of Trump's policies than the multitude of scandals in which he was implicated.[139] Some of this, of course, was the consequence of fair-minded journalists doing their job of providing scrutiny to both candidates. It is also the case that Trump's messaging—'Build the wall!'—was a clearer talking point for the media to pick up on than the earnest fifteen-point plans that Clinton was producing. But the disparity is so great that it is hard to escape the conclusion that much of the media, supposedly so hostile to Trump, got suckered.

After the election, Trump's team pointed out that only 20 per cent of American voters use Twitter but the vast majority of voters were hearing about his tweets because CNN and the rest of the mainstream media could not get enough of him. 'It was like owning *The New York Times* without the overhead or the debt,' said Michael Glassner, who was Trump's deputy campaign manager. Jennifer Palmieri, Clinton's communications director, complained that every time she tried to talk about economic policy, the press just wanted her to respond to whatever Trump had just said or tweeted—they 'only covered her when she talked about him.'[140]

The media, with its new dependence on data and metrics, could see the dials move dramatically whenever they wrote or talked about him. Les Moonves, the chief executive of CBS, was at least honest about what was happening when he made an early assessment of Trump's candidacy back in February 2016: 'It may not be good for America, but it's damn good for CBS.'[141]

Trump was helped in this task by Julian Assange's Wikileaks which published a new batch of leaked emails from the email account of Clinton's chief of staff, John Podesta, almost every day from July 2016 until the election in November. The media lapped up every excruciating detail of Clinton's campaign. Assange himself, holed up in the Ecuadorian embassy in London, denied they had come from Russian hackers. But he also boasted to *The New Yorker* 'about the way he often bent the truth' to protect himself, to cover his sources, or to maximise impact.[142]

For some of those who had once worked closely with Assange during previous data dumps, the Podesta leaks seemed to be an act of vengeance against Clinton for the tough stance she had taken towards him when she was US secretary of state.[143] Ian Katz, the former deputy editor of *The*

Guardian, says: 'He started as a kind of information anarchist who believed that corrupt political and corporate structures could be exploded by breaking their grip on information. But over time it began to seem like he was using his leaks more and more to prosecute his own personal vendettas. ... I suspect he will go down in history as a deeply flawed but hugely significant figure in the shaping of the information age—the man who exposed the frailty of the data-based state, who ushered in a new era of data-driven journalism, maybe even the man who put Donald Trump in the White House.'[144]

But if Assange had taken on many of the same characteristics as the journalists he professed to despise, and then played them expertly, he shared that tendency with Trump himself, who is both a creature and creation of the old media he so often condemned.

Before taking office, Trump is said to have told aides to think of each day as an episode in a reality television show in which he vanquishes rivals. It has been estimated that the president, who starred in fourteen series of *The Apprentice*, spends at least four hours a day—sometimes much more—watching television, 'marinating in the no-holds-barred wars of cable news.'[145] He has also shown himself to be a highly-proficient social media troll himself, delighting in causing outrage and provoking reaction. Beginning soon after he has turned on Fox News at 5.30am, he fires off Twitter salvos, complaining about plots against him from the 'deep state', scorning climate change experts, and insulting opponents. 'Bad!', 'SAD!' or 'WikiLeaks! I love WikiLeaks.'[146]

Like any good reality TV star, Trump came across as more real than anyone else on the show, displaying what seemed to be genuine emotion—pride, joy, anger and contempt—when others, particularly Hillary Clinton, appeared to feign it. When tapes emerged of Trump saying of women that he would 'grab them by the pussy' it did not, remarkably, prove fatal to his bid to be president. His campaign went into meltdown, but for his core supporters, his comments were on-brand: he was already a celebrity misogynist and serial groper standing on a platform of political incorrectness against a feminist who sought to be the first woman president of the United States. 'When you're a star they let you do it,' he said in that Access Hollywood tape. 'You can do anything.'[147]

# # #

For many years in the UK, Boris Johnson seemed to have similar gravity-defying powers. He not only knew how to press the media's buttons, he discovered some that really should not have existed. His career as Brussels correspondent for the *Daily Telegraph* in the early 1990s had taught him that facts did not matter if he could make people laugh. After transitioning from journalism to politics, famously fearsome journalists would chuckle over his semi-scripted fumbles and indulge his repeated lies, whether they were about extra-marital affairs or his plans to stand for parliament, because he was different—he was 'Boris', a popular light entertainment brand.[148]

But this conventional media game also masked a deeper digital-era appeal to voters disillusioned by air-brushed, metrics-driven, spin-dried politicians. Just as few people would have thought a gold-plated billionaire property developer could become a champion of the American Rust Belt, Johnson was an unlikely figure to lead a populist revolt against in the UK. After all, his whole act was elitist: he went to school at Eton and university at Oxford where he was president of the debating society for students who want to dress up in white tie and pretend to be MPs. He was also a member of the notorious Bullingdon Club dining society. But, whereas Cameron sought to ban any use of photographs of him decked up in its ludicrous club uniform, Johnson would still go up to fellow former members years later at parties, shouting: 'Buller! Buller! Buller!'[149]

For Johnson, such fearlessness in the face of convention conveyed a type of authenticity that helped conceal his dishonesty. He had always played the odd-ball outsider, foreign born and funny-looking along with that faint edge of being a scholarship boy which, apparently, still matters at Eton. He was what Lynton Crosby, the Tory strategist described as a 'multigrain politician in a white bread era'[150] and, if few people believed that Johnson always told the truth, he nonetheless resonated with a similar type of authenticity to his fellow populist on the other side of the Atlantic.

As for that third big shock—Jeremy Corbyn's success in wiping out Theresa May's majority in 2017—there is an obvious difference in that even the Labour leader's biggest critics do not accuse him of routinely telling lies or misleading voters. Instead, much of what Corbyn has said has been remarkably and disarmingly honest. What infuriates his opponents in the media, the Tory party—and in his own party—is that it seems to work for him.

Does he want to increase tax? Yes. Would he nationalise the railways and the public utilities? That too. Would he use nuclear weapons if Britain was attacked? No. Why didn't he condemn the IRA at the height of the Troubles? 'I condemn all bombing,' he says, 'I condemn what was done by the British Army as well.'[151]

The new information age was turning out to be an era when the facts no longer mattered—even when they were true. Like Trump and Sanders who were into their 70s when running for the presidency, Corbyn is relatively old—68 at the time of the 2017 election—having spent much of his career on the political margins accumulating a record that some people might dislike but few could deny was consistent.

And it may be significant that, in contrast to Tony Blair, Bill Clinton and David Cameron, who had all sought to use their relative youth to project optimism about the future, the elections of 2016 and 2017 were restorative offers: 'take back control' by Vote Leave; 'make America great again' from Trump; or a return to the good old days of the 1970s from first Sanders and then Corbyn, with his promises of British Rail, free higher education and the return of free school dinners.

From the outset, when he first won the leadership in 2015, Corbyn's team showed an instinctive understanding for the way movements could be built online. The fierce loyalty of supporters in his grassroots movement, Momentum, together with the alt-left news sites, prevented the old media monopolising the supply of information. Although the proportion of terrified *Sun* and *Daily Mail* readers who voted Tory in 2017 rose dramatically even compared to 2015, it was noticeable that the charges against him received less traction in broadcast media than those against Miliband two years earlier.[152]

Like Trump and the Leave campaign, Corbyn could not have done as well as he did without the technology that allowed him to bypass established routes to winning support. And, of course, it is also true that they were all helped by facing some pretty dismal opponents.

But equally, none of these campaigns could have succeeded without leaders like Corbyn and Sanders on the left, and Johnson or Trump on the right, whose brand and record often defied reason while nonetheless resonating online as something new—an 'alternative' to the politics and media with which people had become so disenchanted.

These were the three severe shocks to the system. By the summer of 2017, they had left democracy itself hanging off its hinges.

Part Three

Delete

7

Crashing Democracy

Missing the story; a media failure

Sweating in his dark suit and tie outside the remains of Grenfell Tower, a reporter from Sky News was doing his best to interview a man who had just berated him for at least five long minutes.

When Ishmahil Blagrove finally paused for breath, Jason Farrell jumped in with the kind of question that journalists always ask when faced with death and disaster.

Farrell: How do you feel?

Blagrove: What do you mean how do I feel? How do you feel? ... You are just down here for some feeding frenzy looking for some sensationalist news that might help you make your career and give you a nice news report ... If I had my way I would not be out here talking, you would be the first person I would seize. You! The Media![1]

It was 15 June 2017. The previous day, a fire had begun in one of the tower's flats and swiftly engulfed the entire building. For months afterwards, its blackened concrete was the most jolt-inducing sight in London, a monument to the seventy-one people—overwhelmingly poor and mostly immigrants—who had died there in the Borough of Kensington and Chelsea, one the wealthiest places on the entire planet.

A few minutes earlier, Jeremy Corbyn, fresh from his General Election success, had been given a hero's welcome by the crowds that seethed around Grenfell. Journalists like Farrell found themselves lumped in with the Establishment.

> Farrell: So, what do you want to happen now?
>
> Blagrove: What do I want to happen? I want there to be a revolution in this country. I say fuck the media, fuck the mainstream.

Their exchange was being filmed on a camera phone by onlookers and it later, inevitably, went viral on social media. But Blagrove was not necessarily typical of Grenfell's angry citizens. He was a long-time activist who would become the convenor of the Justice4Grenfell group, contributing columns for *The Guardian* and received offers to make a film from both Channel 4 and the BBC. Most satisfyingly of all, he got himself denounced as a 'rabble-rouser' by the *Daily Mail*.

Blagrove, someone who claims to have grown up heckling people at Speaker's Corner in Hyde Park,[2] now had an audience of hundreds of thousands and credibility that the 'MSM' lacked. By the end of the interview, he was playing to a crowd both online and in the street as more people began gathering around him. The journalist tried to lighten the mood:

> Farrell: I like you anyway.
>
> Blagrove: I like you too. I like you fried, oiled, any way I can have you, motherfuckers.

It was unfair on Farrell, who has led important investigations into banks and pharmaceutical companies, to be tarred with the same brush as the worst of the media. More justifiable was criticism of the *Daily Mail* which, that morning, had pre-empted any sort of inquiry by naming and publishing a picture of the 'Ethiopian taxi-driver' whose faulty fridge, it claimed, was responsible for starting the fire.[3] Farrell is proud that Sky News used the interview with Blagrove that evening. He said: 'We gave him a voice and rightly so. He would have been more justified in being angry if we hadn't been there listening to him.'[4]

There were many other exchanges like this outside Grenfell Tower in the days that followed. Jon Snow, the enduringly liberal face of Channel 4 News, got yelled at by a local man demanding to know: 'Why weren't you here before? You only come when people die.'

Snow later expressed shame at not knowing more about the impoverished world of tower block tenants and highlighted figures published that year showing just 14 per cent of Britain's senior journalists had gone to comprehensive schools.[5] 'I felt on the wrong side of the terrible divide that exists in present day society,' he said. 'We are too far removed from those who lived their lives in Grenfell.'[6]

But the media's apparent failure to connect the people to the powerful was not merely a function of it being part of some remote elite. As we have already seen, the information age has not been good to organisations that had traditionally gathered and curated information. And the story of what happened to local newspapers in West London would be a familiar one to anyone living in towns like Port Talbot or countless other communities.

# # #

Back in 1990, the area surrounding Grenfell Tower was covered by at least ten local reporters.[7] But after years of staff cutbacks the *Kensington and Chelsea Chronicle* was finally closed by its owners, Trinity Mirror, in 2014. A free newspaper, *The Kensington and Chelsea News* was revived in 2015 with one reporter expected to file stories for this and two other newspapers. He worked from home, 150 miles away in Dorset, and visited the borough only twice in two-and-a-half years.

He told the BBC that the only story he ever published about Grenfell Tower was written up from a council press release announcing the installation of the cladding which was subsequently blamed for the raid spread of the fire.[8] In July 2017, even while Grenfell was still the subject of global media attention, this shell of a local newspaper was shut down too.

There was, however, real information on the internet, if journalists had only been around to look for it. A blog written by Edward Daffarn, a 55-year-old social worker who had lived in Grenfell Tower for sixteen years, had warned repeatedly of the high risk of serious fire and loss of life in one of these tower blocks because of the high-handed misman-agement by the company contracted by the local council to look after the buildings.[9]

Grant Fella, a reporter on the *Kensington and Chelsea News* back in its heyday, said: 'Without a doubt we would have found that blog. ... I'm convinced that if the paper I worked on existed today there is no way that Grenfell could have happened. We would have been part of that community at the time; we felt part of the community.'[10]

As Peter Preston, the late, great editor of *The Guardian* said after the fire: 'Without journalists to raise a ruckus, scandal slides by unchecked.'[11]

The Grenfell fire also exposed the limitations of new hyper-partisan media too. Two days after the fire, the alt-left site, Skwawkbox, which is run by someone called Steven Walker from Liverpool, ran a false story for which it claimed to have 'multiple sources'. This stated that the government had issued a D-Notice censoring the MSM from reporting the true casualty numbers from the fire at Grenfell Tower and then repeated allegations that the death-toll could be as high as 200.[12]

Parts of the 'MSM' took a little too much relish in pointing out that Skwawkbox's story was utterly false. The *Daily Telegraph*, for instance, ludicrously decided their rebuttal of a one-man blog was worth putting on its front page.[13]

# # #

The contempt, even hatred, felt by many people towards the mainstream media in Britain did not suddenly appear in 2016 or 2017 and nor was it all whipped up by left-wing activists like Ishmahil Blagrove.

Its roots can be found in the behaviour of newspapers and journalists over the past three decades as they have stirred fear, prised looser a fragile grip on truth and generally spread distrust of every institution, including the media itself. The antics of phone-hacking red top tabloids, the viciousness of the *Daily Mail*, and even the snooty inside-game reporting of broadsheets have all damaged the country and frayed its democracy. There are still, of course, great exceptions where the media has served democracy well. For those who think Britain cannot get much worse than it has under Theresa May should remember that Andrea Leadsom might have been Tory leader and prime minister had she not self-immolated in a half-hour interview with Rachel Sylvester from *The Times*.[14]

But too often the old press in Britain has undermined democracy even as it hides behind values like freedom of speech to resist even the lightest dusting of statutory regulation—when they would be rushing to demand it in any other industry caught up in so much scandal and corruption. Small wonder, then, that by 2016 only 22 per cent of the British people trusted the British press, the lowest rating anywhere Europe.[15] Although ratings for broadcasters in the UK have fallen too, they are generally more trusted than newspapers—probably because they are regulated by rules requiring them to meet standards for accuracy and impartiality. In

2017, 57 per cent of people named the BBC as the one source of news they would most trust, albeit in a poll that it had, not untypically, commissioned about itself.[16]

Many journalists writing for newspapers do not always even trust themselves. When I was working for the Labour Party, a number of political correspondents (or, on occasions, their spouses) privately apologised for what they had been writing. One of them described to me the effect of routinely filing misleading stories about Europe and immigration during the referendum: 'We were just having a bit of laugh really because we all thought Remain would win in the end and everyone would be okay. It was what Boris [Johnson], [Michael] Gove and the rest of them were up to as well; they didn't know what to do with themselves when they won. Usually I don't mind writing shit because it's just a way of earning a living but Brexit was so seismic—we'll have to live with it for so long—I beat by myself up for a year or so afterwards. I keep telling myself I will resign soon. That's what keeps me going.'[17]

Tom Newton-Dunn, the political editor of *The Sun*, is another suspected of being more reasonable than his virulently anti-European newspaper, not least because his phone was covered in a large 'Vote Remain' sticker throughout the 2016 referendum.

It might, therefore, be a source of comfort for Newton-Dunn (although I am pretty sure it is not) to know that his newspaper has lost some of its former power. Twenty years after Tony Blair flew halfway around the world to bend his knee to Rupert Murdoch, Corbyn felt confident enough not to invite *The Sun* to Labour Party press events in the 2017 election. And when *The Sun* published allegations in February 2018, saying that Corbyn had been recruited as an informer by Communist spies in the 1980s, the backlash from the alt-left on social media was so strong that a Tory MP stupid enough to pick up on the claim swiftly had to make a grovelling apology on Twitter.[18]

Corbyn's strength on social media serves a dual purpose. His team post pictures of snowball fights on his office balcony or Instagram shots of chocolate marshmallows, celebrated as proof that he has that intangible 'authenticity' that his predecessors, Gordon Brown and Ed Miliband, lacked.

Large sections of Corbyn's online support is doing no more than venerating their leader and celebrating their idealism. They are less 'Leninist' than 'Lennonist'—so-called because their natural habitat is at festivals, singing along to John Lennon's *Imagine*. But others operate like a paramilitary cyber-army and launch co-ordinated trolling attacks on individual journalists.

I got a sense of it at a meeting in London organised by the far-left site, Counterfire, where speakers talked about the imperative to establish their 'own channels of communication' to counter the 'lies and cynicism of the MSM'. One of them even criticised John McDonnell, the shadow chancellor and a proud Marxist, for 'getting too close to the *Financial Times*' because its magazine had run a largely positive cover story on him that week. They are used by Corbyn almost as a bulwark against having to give the sort of straight answers to difficult questions on which claims of authenticity should surely be based. One journalist, who insisted on speaking anonymously, complains: 'I might ask Jeremy Corbyn ask about his position on Brexit and he'll reply by saying, "Well, what I really want is world peace." I'll try again, and he'll say, "I find it very strange that you don't seem interested in asking me about world peace." You never know if the trolls will emerge—and what began as a perfectly reasonable question will end up with me then being attacked for hating world peace. It goes through the online mangle and becomes a manufactured outrage about the interviewer's alleged views.'

And it is not trolling that makes it harder for journalists, it is the sheer volume of conflicting information, often from polar opposite positions, that threatens to overwhelm. Every minute of every day there are hundreds of thousands of new posts on Facebook and other forms of social media, far exceeding anything the BBC and the rest of mainstream media can produce. What gets shared, what goes viral, and what is seen as 'authentic', is often the content that is most strident, loudest or weirdest. It's why my daughter tells me lots of her friends think Corbyn is 'cool', along with—even more bafflingly for me and her—Jacob Rees-Mogg, a fogeyish Tory MP who tweets in Latin and has his own 'Moggcast' on the ConservativeHome site. My son shows me how ArsenalFanTV works: after every football match Robbie Lyle, who runs the site and seems like a gentle soul, posts a video of himself talking to supporters. But his biggest hits on YouTube are always when the team has lost because his most strident regular interviewees—known as DT and Troopz—can be guaranteed to scream abuse at the manager, the board of directors and anyone in hearing range. 'Liverpool 4 Arsenal 0. Arsène Wenger is Finished!!!' received 2.3 million views. What might have once been one shouty man in a crowd is now an internet sensation; viral because it is divisive, angry, mad.

In political journalism there is a similar cacophony as everyone shouts at everyone else on Facebook and Twitter, as well as in the streets. Conspiracy theories and hatreds that were frozen out in the far fringes of politics are now thrusting themselves on to the stage. Some journalists think social media has helped raise the standards of their profession. Kevin Maguire, *The Daily Mirror's* political commentator, says: 'In the old days people on *The Sun* or the *Daily Mail* could write whatever they want and not really give a toss. Nowadays we're all constantly held to account on Twitter. It has made us better as a group in accepting mistakes and correcting them.'[19]

But Maguire, a life-long Labour supporter, always liked a scrap. Britain's broadcasters, by contrast, have a statutory duty to be impartial. And they admit it feels as if they are on a narrower, more precarious, path even as both the news and journalists themselves run ever faster to catch up.

Robert Peston, ITV's political editor, is in Cardiff on his way to inter-view the prime minister when I phone him. I ask if it is still possible for the media to perform its gatekeeping duty in a democracy. He says: 'Today there are lots of information bubbles, alternative realities, com-peting truths. Many are in fact prejudice and ignorance masquerad-ing—either in social media or on the printed page—as reality. I will always aspire to be one of those trusted arbiters of what is objective reality. But I increasingly fear that is vanity on my part, that the horse may have bolted.'[20]

Laura Kuenssberg, the BBC's political editor, is racing out of the door to get to a dinner when I ask her the same question. She says: 'There is so much more stuff—more and more information on TV, social media and everywhere,' she says, 'There is always space for people to find some-thing which can back up any position.'[21]

And in the midst of all this haste and fury, many British voters are now turning away from the whole spectacle. According to one study published in 2018, trust in the media as a whole—including broadcast, press and digital platforms—was flat at 32 per cent but fully a third of people said they were consuming less news and one in five were avoiding the news completely.[22]

# # #

In his reflections on the Grenfell fire, Jon Snow recognised the anger directed towards the media elite in West London during the summer of 2017 was similar to that he had experienced at Trump rallies in America the year before. Snow described how, at one such event in North Carolina, he had been herded into the back of the room with other journalists while Trump, accompanied by 'whoops of derision and joy' from the crowd, jabbed his finger at the media and declared they were 'bad people, the worst people in the world.'

And, once such statements are wiped clean of their usual bile, they show that Trump was tapping into something that many people felt to be true. There is good evidence that the American media has also become deeply disconnected with the rest of the country. One study showed that a map of the 150 US counties with the most newspaper and internet publishing jobs very closely resembled one showing those Hillary Clinton won by a margin of 30 points or more.[23] As Steve Bannon, the former chairman of Breitbart, then still working in Trump's White House, put it: 'The media bubble is the ultimate symbol of what's wrong with this country. It's just a circle of people talking to themselves who have no fucking idea what's going on.'[24]

But such a bubble, largely covering the prosperous cities on the east and west coasts of the United States, also reflects how the disablement or disappearance of old local newspapers has also had a deep impact on the functioning of democracy. Official US government figures showed how an American newspaper workforce of 455,000 reporters, clerks, sales staff, designers and the like in 1990 had shrunk to 174,000 by 2017.[25] In the 1990s, the San Jose *Mercury News*—the newspaper that covers Silicon Valley—employed 400 union-recognised journalists. By 2018, the number working for the *Mercury* and other titles in the area was just 41.[26]

Another map of the areas that switched most dramatically from voting for Barack Obama in 2012 to backing Donald Trump in 2016 closely corresponds to another, showing a slowly expanding 'news desert' stretching across the waistband of America where local papers have closed down.[27] Perhaps it merely reflects the economic decline of those areas. But the loss of city and community newspapers creates vacuums where stories like the American opioid epidemic in Middle America—or even the rise of Trump himself—are missed.[28]

And those vacuums are being filled online by rumour or prejudice that reverberate across the internet without anyone to stop them. For instance, a false claim about Muslims imposing Sharia law and stoning a woman to death in Dearborn, Michigan, was repeated by voters 700 miles away in St Cloud, Minnesota during the presidential campaign of 2016.[29]

Immediately after that election, trust in the US media was at an all-time low with just 32 per cent of Americans—and a mere 14 per cent of Republicans—having any faith in what major news outlets told them.[30] Since then the trust rating has recovered dramatically on the left. According to Gallup, confidence among US Democrats in the mass media to report the news 'fully, accurately and fairly' jumped from 51 per cent in 2016 to 72 per cent this year. Republicans' trust was unchanged at 14 per cent. That margin—72 to 14—suggests trust in the media is now one of most polarising issues in America.

This deep divide in US media and politics means that no matter how furious viewers of CNN or readers of the *Washington Post* get about Trump, his hardcore support—in similar fashion to that of Jeremy Corbyn in the UK—is insulated from it. Their information world is enclosed within a social media filter bubble revolving around Breitbart and Fox News. A survey in 2018 showed Fox News beat all its rivals to be the single most trusted source of news, with a rating of 24 per cent. Some 60 per cent of Republican voters identified it as such; and only 3 per cent of Democrats.[31] And fringe websites, including those of the alt-right, have been given press accreditation at the White House. And, within that echo chamber, everyone seems sure that anyone else is lying but them.

As Grenfell showed, the greatest fault of the media may have less to do with what it reports than what it does not. This is what was troubling James Harding, the director of BBC News, as he watched TV one evening in 2016. He described feeling 'bombarded by the news' and 'bewildered' by the speed with which events—post-Brexit political turmoil in Britain, a terrorist atrocity in France, a coup in Turkey—were now tumbling over each other. Harding said he craved explanations of the 'why' as well as the 'what' and, at the end of 2017, quit the BBC to found a start-up that would attempt to do news at a more considered pace. As he put it, the danger for the media is that 'while we're busy reporting the news every day, we may be missing the story.'[32]

In the past twenty-five years, hour upon hour of broadcast coverage has been devoted to stories about the threat of terrorism, the fear of crime and the fighting of wars. Tens of millions of words have been written about failing public services, the financial crisis and falling living standards. A voracious, expanded media has obsessed about politicians and celebrities having sex, people cheating the benefits system, and Britain being invaded by hordes of immigrants. Some, if not all, of these were important stories.

But for an industry that also spends an inordinate amount of time talking about itself, it is strange that the media has paid comparatively little attention to probably the biggest story of this period: the change in the way people receive and use information.

The same force that has been so disruptive to the media and the consumption of news is also transforming every aspect of our economy and society. And, if much of the media was culpable for missing this story, politicians are guilty of much worse.

Missing the point; a political failure

Inside a factory that sprawls long and low on a road skirting the west side of Indianapolis, a man in a suit is telling workers they are about to lose their jobs.

'Fuck you!' shouts one of them. Others begin jeering as they hear their jobs are heading 1,500 miles south to Mexico. Another turns away in disgust and walks out into the freezing night.

'Listen, I've got information that's important to share as part of the transition,' says Chris Nelson, the president of Carrier, which owns the plant, 'so let's quieten down, thank you very much.'[33]

The viral qualities of this video, filmed shakily by a Carrier employee on his phone, are obvious: here was a member of an executive elite telling members of the working class that they were all done. Nelson was using technocratic language that suggested their lives and communities were little more than figures on a balance sheet: 'Relocating our operations to Monterrey will allow us to maintain high levels of product quality at competitive prices so we can continue to serve this extremely price sensitive marketplace.' And he was delivering these words in the middle of a US presidential election where one candidate in particular appeared ready to put American jobs first.

Less than twenty-four hours later, Breitbart had seized upon the video[34] and shortly afterwards on 12 February 2016, Donald Trump had started tweeting: 'I am the only one who can fix this. Very sad. Will not happen under my watch!' The future of the Carrier plant in Indiana, which has been making air conditioning and heating furnaces systems since the 1950s, stopped being a local story and became one of the hottest issues in the most bitterly contentious presidential election anyone could remember.

Bernie Sanders, who was contesting the Democratic nomination with Hillary Clinton, had always been opposed to any trade deal he judged benefitted multinational corporations more than workers.[35] Clinton, on whose husband's watch the NAFTA treaty—blamed for exporting jobs to Mexico—had been signed, tried to talk of re-negotiating or re-evaluating trade deals, as well as creating more of the 'jobs of tomorrow', like looking after elderly people.[36]

But Trump was promising to save the jobs of today—or even bring back those of yesterday. Declaring he would be 'the greatest jobs president God has ever created,' Trump rarely missed an opportunity to kick out at Carrier as a symbol of how global trade deals had screwed the forgotten American worker. He warned he would 'tax the hell' out of the firm and predicted that, after he won, it would call him and say, 'Mr President, Carrier has decided to stay in Indiana.'[37]

And, a couple of weeks after the election the president-elect appeared to have been vindicated. Trump flew in to announce that, even before he had entered the White House, he had reached an agreement for the Carrier plant to stay open for at least ten years. In return for seven-figure tax breaks and grants, Trump declared most of the jobs at Carrier would be saved. The deal-maker-in-chief then paraded himself victoriously through what he described as 'this big, beautiful plant'.

But there was a wrinkle that went largely unremarked upon at the time. Carrier said it was making a $16 million investment in that factory to keep it competitive, automating more of the production line and, as its executives acknowledged, 'what that ultimately means is there will be fewer jobs.'[38] Indeed, two waves of redundancies later, almost half the manufacturing jobs at this factory have gone and few doubt that more will follow.[39] 'Trump came in there to the factory last December and blew smoke up our asses. He wasn't gonna save those jobs,' said Brenda Darlene Battle, who'd been working at Carrier for twenty-five years. 'The ones that really supported him are quiet right now. Some of them got let go yesterday, too.'[40]

This is not an exceptional story about Trump so much as an illustration of the way politics has operated in recent years. A system that was supposed to represent the interests of citizens has all too often just 'blown smoke up asses', scapegoated outsiders, and wilfully ignored piles of evidence about where the true problem lies. Just as with a media that has hyperventilated about almost every story but the one staring it in the face, politics has spectacularly failed to address the single biggest driver of change this century: the revolution in information and technology.

# # #

A number of studies have shown that the jobs disappearing across the 'Rust Belt' of America were not headed to Mexico or being exported to China so much as being replaced by computer-operated machines—'robots'. One such paper attributed just 13 per cent of manufacturing job losses in America to trade or outsourcing—and the rest to enhanced productivity because of automation.[41] Indeed, another academic paper, enticingly entitled, 'Did Robots Swing the 2016 US Presidential Election?' suggests that the more voters were exposed to the risk of their jobs being automated, the more likely they were to vote for Trump.[42]

Technology and outsourcing have often been part of the same story. Many industrial jobs that had once been done in the American Rust Belt have moved to countries where technological advances, not least in communication, mean production can be carried out cheaply while still being directed from the US. But, in the years running up to the 2016 election, when international trade was making all the headlines, this process had already levelled out. By then, automation was the real threat to jobs. Even as Trump was placing the Carrier plant front and centre in a campaign where he rarely mentioned technology, Andrew Puzder, a fast food executive and Trump's initial choice to be labour secretary, was explaining the advantages of replacing people with robots. 'They are always polite, they always upsell, they never take a vacation,' he said, 'they never show up late, there's never a slip-and-fall, or an age, sex or race discrimination case.'[43]

In 2013, a widely-cited study compiled at the University of Oxford's Martin School suggested that 47 per cent of all the jobs in America were ripe for automation over the next two decades.[44] Another report estimated 30 per cent of British jobs could be automated by the 2030s.[45] More recent work suggests the job loss figure could be lower. A 2018 OECD study of dozens of developed countries said only 14 per cent of jobs were certain to go—but a further 32 per cent faced a better-than-even risk of disappearing too.[46]

What these reports all agree on, however, is that a colossal upheaval in the economy and labour market is underway. It is one that is already challenging orthodox theory that technological advances ultimately create more jobs than they destroy. According to another paper from the University of Oxford, just 0.5 per cent of American workers are employed in the high-value digital industries that have emerged since 2000.[47] The photography company Kodak filed for bankruptcy in 2012 with the loss of 47,000 jobs. That same year Instagram—a company with just thirteen full-time employees—was sold to Facebook for $1 billion.[48] Facebook's 2014 purchase of Whatsapp for $19 billion came when it had just fifty-five employees, meaning it paid a thumping $345 million for each one of them. The real value of companies like Whatsapp was not in the skill or size of its workforce, but in preventing an upstart rival becoming a competitor, as well, of course, as selling ads to its users and mining them for their data.

There are shelves groaning with the weight of books (if they are not being published electronically) written with varying degrees of dystopian despair on this subject.[49] And, if even a small fraction of their worst predictions are right, any low-paid worker stacking shelves should be grateful that they still have a job at all. Many of these books include warnings that robots, big data and 3D printing are destroying manufacturing jobs, damaging industries like the media and music where content is reproduced for free, and threatening other professions too.[50] The University of Minnesota has produced a map of America that shows the most common job in each state over recent decades. In the 1980s and early 1990s when industrial jobs began to disappear, the most common job was secretary. But much of what secretaries did got computerised. By 2014, the common job in no less than thirty states was 'truck, delivery and tractor drivers.'[51] And how many of them are going to be left when Google or Uber wheel out their driverless vehicles?

Increasingly, economists think the reason why wages have been stagnant has much less to do with immigration or foreign competition than the digital technology atomising workforces and forcing them out of well-paid secure jobs into the precarious 'gig economy'.[52] The share of national wealth going to workers has fallen by around 6 per cent in the UK and 10 per cent in the US over the period in which automation and information has done so much to change people's lives.[53] And that was before firms like Uber and Airbnb began steadily shifting risks—owning a car or a home—on to self-employed workers who do not even get to be called staff. Companies like Mechanical Turk and TaskRabbit represent an even scarier future where humans will compete against each other to perform mind-numbing tasks—filling in forms, writing online reviews—that often pay just a few pence an hour because it is not worth getting a robot or algorithm to do them.

Fears that technology will destroy jobs or generally undermine the human condition are, needless to say, as old as the Luddites who attacked the mechanical looms in Lancashire's cotton mills during the first decades of the nineteenth century.[54] The Luddites are now taught in schools as being symbolic of a misguided backward-looking worldview standing in the way of economic progress that has created such vast riches and benefits for much of the human race.

But the reason why those benefits were shared at all is because there is a democratic tradition—almost as old as the Luddites—of fighting for better working conditions, living standards and the dignity of those affected by change.

Those Luddites did not have many democratic rights at the start of the nineteenth century but 'voted with sticks and stones' against the machines. The government sent its cavalry, sabres drawn, into crowds demanding votes at Peterloo in Manchester in 1819, killing eighteen and maiming many more. But eventually even propertied MPs had to take notice of the strikes, protests and pain. Parliament was shamed into passing laws to protect young children working in factories and mines, legalise trade unions, educate the poor and widen the franchise for voting. The exploitation of workers inspired Karl Marx to write *The Communist Manifesto* in 1848 and led to the realignment of British politics with the emergence of the Labour Party. In the United States, too, democracy provided a genuine check on the advance of unfettered free market capitalism with 'trust-busting' laws that broke up the monopolies and limited corporate power in the late nineteenth and early twentieth centuries.

Across the world, wherever industrial technology advanced there were strikes, riots and reform because the technology of the industrial revolution connected people, empowered them and, through all this upheaval, catalysed the process of democratic politics itself.

But in the revolution of the new information age over the past twenty-five years, democracy has been noticeable only by its absence as elected leaders have largely disengaged from issues that will determine the future of their countries and their citizens: the use of new technology; the regulation of the internet; the ownership of information.

Gargantuan corporations, larger than any the world has ever seen—Google, Microsoft, Facebook, Amazon, Apple—shake the ground on which nation states were built, cutting across borders and challenging governments' capacity to raise tax. They are accused of re-wiring our brains, corrupting our children, providing a safe haven for paedophiles and extremists, spawning terrorism, trashing our privacy and, of course, harvesting for free the most valuable asset of all—our data—usually without our knowledge.

Governments have allowed private firms to extract information—the oil of the digital economy—worth hundreds of billions of pounds. This time, it has not been have pumped out of the ground but out of citizens. Worse still, this vast transfer of wealth and power has happened without touching the sides of democratic debate, until it is perhaps too late to stop it.

The 'new grooves of how people live, how we do business, how we do everything,' as the tech writer Jaron Lanier put it, have been carved into the future by private corporations in the pursuit of vast profit without, for the most part, proper political debate or legislation.[55]

The tremors of economic and social change have already shaken politics. Although it is often forgotten that most of those backing Brexit and Trump were relatively well-off—part of a traditional Tory or Republican vote[56]—it is still true that neither campaign would have won if slogans like 'Take Back Control' and 'Make America Great Again' had not had real appeal to a decisive slice of blue-collar voters angry about the decline of communities and the decay of hope.[57] These were people for whom an 'earned identity' through work was being denied them as their fragile footholds in the economy were washed away. They were turning to older forms of identity—based on race, nation or religion—that harked back to an earlier, better time when they felt 'great' or at least had more 'control'.[58]

The solutions offered by this new breed of populists are, of course, either ugly or false. Sometimes, they are both. Trump's promise to scrap trade deals and build walls will not stop jobs being automated, especially given that he is providing tax breaks for firms to do just that.[59] A Brexit deal that ends freedom of movement of migrants between Britain and

Europe will not raise the wages of low paid workers but its impact on trade will almost certainly make the whole country poorer, with industrial towns hit first and worst.[60]

But the response of many progressive politicians to the decline of these communities has been scarcely more edifying. Left-leaning US Democrats have begun lurching towards new forms of trade protectionism, while Britain's Labour MPs who should—and usually do—know better have too often connived with anti-immigration policies.

# # #

In the final days of the 2016 referendum, polls showed that voters preparing to back Brexit thought 20 per cent of the UK's population—around 14 million people—were EU immigrants. Those voting Remain thought the figure was much lower, at just 10 per cent. What is remarkable is that both groups were wrong to the tune of several millions of people. The true figure was just 5 per cent—and lower still in most of the regions that supported Brexit. Similarly, just 14 per cent of voters knew that the proportion of child benefit being sent back to other countries by migrants living in the UK was 0.3 per cent. Nearly four in 10 voters got the figure grotesquely wrong—saying it was between 40 and 100 times higher than reality.[61]

Immigration was to Brexit what trade deals were to Trump. And, in the face of such scary populism, progressive politics has generally shrunk away. By the end of the US presidential election Clinton was sounding almost Trumpian on NAFTA, while in 2017 the Labour Party was insisting that the abolition of free movement of people to and from Europe had to be included in a Brexit deal.

Such politicians say it is elitist and patronising to tell people in blighted working-class communities that they are wrong. Maybe so. But it strikes me as even more patronising to pretend that you think they are right— and that you have solutions—when you don't.

In the 2015 General Election I worked on, Labour had a key pledge— and even a souvenir mug—promising 'controls on immigration' when we were not really offering control so much as a package of perfectly respectable social democratic measures to prevent the wages of workers being undercut, be they from Britain or abroad.

The following year in the EU referendum, the Remain campaign felt hobbled by David Cameron's failure to negotiate a concession from Europe on immigration. Will Straw, the campaign director, described to me how he was desperate to address the issue that was motivating so many voters and felt the data analytics were defying common sense. 'Downing Street came back and told us the data was clear that we will lose if we try anything,' he says, 'they just wanted to put their fingers in their ears.'[62] A source close to Cameron dismisses this, saying it was far too late to change the dynamic of the argument with a policy such as compensating areas with particularly high numbers of migrants. When they tested this policy 'in focus groups', the source said, 'people literally laughed.'[63] That is not entirely surprising given that Cameron himself had spent the previous decade attacking the EU, campaigning against immigration and promising—falsely—that he could cut numbers coming in to less than 100,000.[64] Indeed, as Oliver Letwin, Cameron's policy sage, later acknowledged, all parties had made a 'terrible mistake' over the past decade for failing to make the case for how immigration benefits Britain 'in every sense'.[65]

What has really been missing is an honest analysis about what is causing wages to stagnate in the north of England or jobs to disappear in the American Rust Belt. Such an analysis could and should face up squarely to the challenges from a technological revolution that is still gathering pace. Instead, the three great shocks to the system examined in the previous chapter saw politics dominated by myths that claim everything is the fault of Mexican workers, Chinese trade deals or Romanian immigrants.

Nor was this confined to the votes of 2016 and 2017. A failure to say anything meaningful about this upheaval has been endemic over decades. Look at sections on digital technology in the different parties' election manifestos in the UK between 1997 and 2017 and you'll find most of them include variations of the same four policies: rolling out access to the internet or broadband provision across the country; stopping children watching porn or videos of violent acts; a vague plan for digital delivery of government services; and an even woollier commitment to help the tech sector to make Britain a 'dynamic economy of the future'. Tony Blair remarked that he could not see much difference between those being offered in 2017 and those he was pursuing when he left government a decade earlier.[66]

Technology has moved at breakneck speed, and politics has been dragging its feet.

When Ed Miliband was invited to speak at a Google Big Tent conference in 2013, he decided that instead of the usual big tech fawning that had become standard practice from politicians at such events, he would attack the company for paying 'just a fraction of 1 per cent' of its UK revenues in tax. I went to elaborate lengths to ensure there was an empty chair in the front row—by having a staff member sit in it until the last minute—so that the TV cameras could show Eric Schmidt, the firm's chief executive, was boycotting Miliband's speech. We wanted a public debate and, for a few days, we got one.[67] Behind the scenes, policy advisers had begun looking at whether there could be a tax on revenue rather than the profits that companies like Google sent offshore. But Ed Balls's shadow treasury team were reluctant to let us start inventing any new taxes.

And, by 2015, there was no mention of Google or any of the big technology firms in Labour's manifesto—let alone a specific measure that might make them pay a penny more to the UK Exchequer.[68] A few months later, George Osborne, the then Chancellor, hailed with great fanfare a new tax deal that had 'sweetheart' stamped all over it: Google would pay a marginal rate of 3 per cent on its earnings—compared to a corporation tax rate set at 20 per cent.[69]

Two years on from that election, there was widespread admiration for the radicalism of Labour's 2017 manifesto. But the party had little to say about the towering new capitalist corporations like Google, Facebook or Amazon. Instead, Labour's sights were trained on the operators of 200-year-old technology—the private railway companies that, even added together, are worth 0.01 per cent of these tech businesses.[70]

The political disaster that was Theresa May's manifesto of 2017 was mitigated a little because she bravely tried to tackle unpalatable challenges like the cost of social care for the elderly. And, for a politician who had shown scant interest in technology over the previous twenty years of her parliamentary career, she should be given some credit for adding a couple of new policies to the usual list. These were a promise that young people would get the right to remove their social media post history at the age of eighteen (in case, perhaps, they were thinking of a career in politics), as well as some fuzzy ideas giving citizens more rights over their own data through a 'digital charter'. But these were neither significant campaign issues nor, at the time of writing, has much been heard about either of them since.

# # #

One reason for the lack of political engagement is that the technology firms themselves had become a powerful and very effective lobby. Lord Younger, the minister in charge of regulating intellectual property rights, complained in 2013 that he did not have the influence with David Cameron that Google enjoyed. 'I am very aware of their power, put it that way. I am also very aware, I think, that they have access, for whatever reason, to higher levels than me in No. 10, I understand.'[71] At the time, Rachel Whetstone, the wife of his chief strategist Steve Hilton, was a senior Google executive. Later, when she moved to Uber, both the Prime Minister and the Chancellor are said to have been co-opted by her to lobby the London mayor against measures that might have restricted its growth in the capital.[72] Whetstone is a highly effective operator and prefers to avoid the limelight. On this occasion, however, she ended up with her face plastered across the sides of London's traditional black cabs in protest at Uber's power and influence.[73]

She is only one of dozens of former political aides to have taken senior posts with technology firms. Tim Chatwin, once Cameron's head of strategic communications, jumped ship to Google in 2011. So too did Verity Harding, a political adviser to Nick Clegg while he was deputy prime minister. Ed Balls's two most senior advisers as shadow chancellor both went off to tech firms after the 2015 election: one to Facebook and the other to Uber. Coming in from the opposite direction were Amy Fisher, once Google's communications chief across Europe who became head of press for the Conservative Party, and Joanna Shields, who went from running Google in Europe to a seat in the House of Lords and a ministerial job in charge of internet safety.

In the US, Sheryl Sandberg, who had been chief of staff to Treasury Secretary Larry Summers in the 1990s took executive roles at Google and then Facebook. But the revolving door really began to spin with Obama, the tech president. David Plouffe, his former campaign manager, turned up at Uber before being hired to run Mark Zuckerberg's charitable foundation, while Jay Carney, his press secretary, went to work for Amazon. There was always a particularly warm relationship between Google and the Obama administration. Eric Schmidt, the company's former chief executive, had been an adviser and donor to Obama in 2008 and was later given a seat on his Council of Advisors on Science and Technology. Indeed, White House officials met representatives from the company 427 times—more than once a week—during his eight years in office.[74] Technology executives object to the idea that their Washington lobbyists—running up bills of $50 million a year—captured the White House.[75] They point out how they are asked to come in to offer advice. 'We know about stuff that politicians don't,' says one. It is also true that many of these hirings were because of a large degree of shared values between politicians and the tech firms, so much so that when Obama left the White House, his former aides headed to Silicon Valley in such numbers they could have been mistaken for a column of refugees.

But the admiration was mutual. This is what Barack Obama wrote about a trip to Google's headquarters before he became president as he gazed into a screen that showed global patterns of the internet: 'The image was mesmerising, more organic than mechanical, as if I were glimpsing the early stages of some accelerating evolutionary process, in which all the boundaries between men—nationality, race, religion, wealth—were rendered invisible and irrelevant, so that the physicist in Cambridge, the bond trader in Tokyo, the student in a remote Indian village and the manager of a Mexico City department store were drawn into a single, constant, thrumming conversation, time and space giving way to a world spun entirely of light.'[76]

# # #

Obama, with those stars still in his eyes, went on to revolutionise the use of social media in his successful presidential campaigns, name check Google in half his State of the Union speeches, and make concerted efforts to utilise Silicon Valley's expertise in solving some of America's deep-rooted problems.

But, in his final year of office, a World Bank report declared that tech companies were widening income inequality and wealth disparities, not improving them.[77] And, in a tearful farewell address to the American people in January 2017, Obama spoke with grim conviction about new divides of wealth, the polarising influence of social media and the prospect of more 'economic dislocations' not from Mexico and China, 'but from the relentless pace of automation that makes a lot of good, middle-class jobs obsolete.'[78]

As secretary of state in Obama's administration, Hillary Clinton invested tens of millions of dollars to promote a global 'Internet Freedom' policy she hoped would symbolise the modern era as much as the Berlin Wall had symbolised the dark days of the Cold War. 'The new iconic infrastructure of our age is the internet. Instead of division, it stands for connection,' she said.[79] A few years later, when asked about the impact of structural unemployment caused by automation, she said: 'I don't have a quick glib answer for you. There are no easy fixes.'[80]

By the time Clinton was running to succeed Obama as president, exploitation of the internet was driving democracy backwards and dividing countries across the world, including her own. And, after her defeat, Clinton warned it really was time that politicians do something about all the jobs being lost to robots and automation, saying: 'The future is coming right at us, and honest to goodness, I just think everybody ... should be demanding that public officials start coming up with some approaches to how we're going to protect human beings and our lives from this.'[81]

Tony Blair also acknowledges that it was possible for people in power to be dazzled by the allure of technology. 'It all looked progressive because they tended to be socially liberal and tolerant, open minded and creative—those are great virtues,' he says. 'I remember meeting Mark Zuckerberg in Davos when Facebook was only just beginning and thinking, "he's very quiet and shy but, my God, he's going to change the world."' With a slightly wistful shake of the head, Blair now suggests if he was still in government, he would be totally focused on finding solutions to the challenge technology is setting democracy and, in fairness, he published more workable policy ideas in this area in 2017 than any British political party has in the previous decade. 'These companies—these tech titans—they operate as vast and separate spheres of power and influence,' he says. 'And you have to say up to now they have been creating more problems than they solve.'[82]

Ed Miliband, who was never particularly in interested in this subject when I worked for him, now presents a successful podcast called 'Reasons to be Cheerful' and tweets regularly. He suggests politics in general has 'too often been caught between Luddism and getting starry-eyed' about technology. He says: 'It is not a question of either resisting it or saying—fantastic—it's the Brave New World; it's about not ignoring the economic effects of some very big changes.'[83]

Even some of those who may have reaped short-term political benefit from the upheaval acknowledge there is a deep-rooted problem with technological change. Michael Gove says: 'It is undoubtedly the case that this has led to a wrenching effect.'[84] After the 2017 election, there were confused reports that Jeremy Corbyn was planning to impose 'a robot tax' to pay for the retraining of displaced workers, as well as looking at ways to give more power to gig economy workers such as those controlled by Uber. Concrete policy on such issues, however, has not quite lived up to the briefing.[85]

In any case, by the spring of 2018—after a quarter of a century during which the internet's information revolution has dramatically disrupted the economy, work and culture—there were signs that politicians had begun to stir.

Perhaps that was because by then the impact of this fundamental economic change had begun to disrupt democracy itself and—particularly for progressive politicians—it was threatening to take away their jobs too.

Missing its own Mark; a technological failure

'Hi, we're trying to raise awareness of Women in Analytics, would you like some pie?' I am standing inside Facebook's Menlo Park headquarters, said to be the largest open plan connected office space in the world. And two women, in analytics, are staring at me intensely.

'Pumpkin? Or Key Lime?' one of them asks insistently. 'We have both,' says another. I make what I hope is the strong choice: Key Lime. Tom Reynolds, who works in Facebook's policy communications team, is one of the refugees from Obama's White House Silicon Valley has taken in. He tries to halve a piece of Pumpkin but gives up and eats the whole thing. New members of the 'Facebook family' usually gain weight—'the Facebook 15,' when they join.

Food is everywhere—goat curry, chicken gyoza, vegan sushi, ice cream. More pie. And it's all free. So is the kind of home-made art that usually decorates artisan coffee shops. 'All children are artists, remain an artist when you grow up,' says an annoyingly inspirational banner stretched across a wall. Directly above us is a nine-acre roof garden with artificial hillsides, 100,000 sustainable plants and strange triangular swings where staff sometimes practice meditation. And, of course, no one wears a tie. Mark Zuckerberg did—for a whole year—but that was just because it was a 'personal challenge', that the founder of Facebook embarked upon in 2009 in one of his annual acts of self-improvement.

Writers have found it easy to sneer at super-nice, super-nerdy Silicon Valley for years, even though this has usually been accompanied by a justifiable sense of awe. Menlo Park has a deliberately rough-hewn feel to it because Zuckerberg wanted to convey the idea that the new world they were building was only half-finished and the flicker of that earnest early-internet idealism is still there. Women and African Americans are under-represented in analytics and I like Facebook for trying to raise my awareness.

This is a company that, for all its faults, has helped create an internet that has, more than at any point in our species' history, empowered and connected billions of individuals to live freely and love who they want. And it is worth remembering that having corporations talk about doing good or promoting democracy should still be refreshing for anyone old enough to remember how the world's biggest businesses used to behave. In short, this is not 'Trump Country' and I do not believe that Democrats like Tom Reynolds work at Facebook simply because Women in Analytics feed him pumpkin pie.

Yet, even as he was speaking, it was also possible to sense that something was amiss—if not rotten—in Menlo Park. By all accounts, the staff at Facebook were as devastated as any other group of overwhelmingly liberal voters by the result of the 2016 presidential elections. In the months afterwards, however, they also had to deal with the accusation, or even realisation, that they were to blame for Donald Trump's victory.

What so many had thought of as a ubiquitous and slightly bland social network they used to keep in touch with friends and family, share photos and videos or find out what's happening in the news, was suddenly being portrayed as an open sewer pouring falsehood and hate into their homes—accused of polarising voters to the point where they lost their compass—and exposed as the vehicle of choice for Russian trolls intent on interfering with US democracy.

# # #

All this is said to have hit Zuckerberg, who had never really concealed his generally progressive instincts, very hard. When Barack Obama visited Facebook's headquarters back in 2011, the then president told the assembled staff that rich people should pay more tax. 'I'm cool with that!' shouted Zuckerberg. 'I know *you're* okay with that,' replied Obama, smiling.

A few yards on from the free pie is a giant chalk-covered blackboard that announces it is 'The Facebook Wall' and implores passers-by to

'Write Something…' In February 2016, just as Donald Trump's racially-charged run for the White House was gathering pace, Zuckerberg discovered someone had crossed out the words 'Black Lives Matter' on the Menlo Park wall—and replaced them with 'All Lives Matter'. Zuckerberg issued a memo to staff, telling them that such 'disrespectful' and 'malicious' defacement had to stop. 'Crossing something out means silencing speech, or that one person's speech is more important than another's. Facebook should be a service and a community where everyone is treated with respect,' he said.

At the very least, this incident serves as a metaphor for how the open social network that Facebook once was, has become riven by questions of free speech, tolerance and whether it needs to take responsibility for the extremism that has incubated on its pages. But some people say that Zuckerberg's memo was where all the trouble began.[86] When the memo was leaked to the website Gizmodo, conservatives began to ask whether this northern Californian nirvana was biased against them.[87] Further leaks to Gizmodo claimed Facebook's news curators on the 'Trending Topics' team were routinely weeding out right-wing stories from its news feed. Facebook, under-fire from Fox News and Breitbart, responded by sacking the whole team and leaving decisions about what appears in people's news feeds entirely to the algorithm.

According to legend, this then led to Facebook being overwhelmed by a tidal wave of fake news including that written by Macedonian teenagers, alt-right ideologues and Russian trolls.[88] Zuckerberg's high-handed and complacent initial reaction to the election of Trump did not help. 'The idea that fake news on Facebook influenced the election in any way is a pretty crazy idea,' he said.[89]

But, in the months that followed, and after a long chat with his friend Obama, Zuckerberg sought to row back. He chastised himself and his company in public for their failings and, by the beginning of 2018, Zuckerberg announced his personal challenge for that year would not be about improving himself so much as Facebook.

He wrote: 'The world feels anxious and divided, and Facebook has a lot of work to do—whether it's protecting our community from abuse and hate, defending against interference by nation states, or making sure that time spent on Facebook is time well spent … This may not seem like a personal challenge on its face, but I think I'll learn more by focusing intensely on these issues than I would by doing something completely separate.'[90]

Gone were the flippant annual resolutions to wear more ties, run more miles and read more books. Zuckerberg wanted to show he was serious about saving his creation. The algorithm was tweaked to emphasise 'meaningful interactions' from friends and family ahead of click-bait. The mission statement was changed from making people more 'open and connected' to the more purposeful one of giving 'people the power to build community and bring the world closer together.' More fake accounts were closed, while users were given the chance to rank news sources on the basis of trust and enticed out of their filter bubbles to read 'related articles'.

As we walk around Menlo Park, Tom Reynolds tells me, time and again, that Facebook's 'community' of more than 2 billion people matters a lot more to Zuckerberg than the billions of dollars he makes selling ads to them. 'Mark wants to get this right. He does this for the right reasons. When we get things wrong, he constantly tries to make them better,' he says. 'Sure, we have shareholders and investors. But that isn't what drives decisions here—it's like the mission is the head, the business is the tail.'

In 2017, Facebook was the world's fifth biggest corporation with a capital valuation approaching $500 billion and revenue of $13 billion—more than triple what it was making at the start of 2015.[91] Reynolds emphasises that what drives the corporation is not profit, but a sense of values. 'These are not American values or Western values, these are first and foremost Facebook values,' he says. 'The idea that underpins Facebook is authentic communication, to connect people with their friends and family, to share information. … What the Russians did runs counter to that philosophy, it ran against the idea of democracy and civic engagement which we believe in as a company.'

But, even as he talks about 'values" and 'community' the contradictions are welling up inside almost every sentence. Facebook makes its money by extracting as much data as possible from its 'community', before monetising it with advertisers who use that data to target their messages selling users anything from training shoes to white supremacy.

False news travels so far and so fast on Facebook because it wants to keep users' attention for as long as possible—so it can extract more data and sell more ads—even if that means feeding members of its 'community' information that is addictive, misleading and takes them deeper into polarising echo chambers where the 'values' are not democratic at all.

Therefore, Facebook's business model is based on giving people a seemingly free service where users can stay in touch with each other in return for allowing effective and unprecedented surveillance—of memories, friends, secrets—by anyone willing to pay the company to advertise.

If the purpose of Facebook really is to build community and bring the world closer together, it has been missing the mark. Indeed, through the course of 2017, some of those who had helped create Facebook with Zuckerberg said they had begun to fear it. Sean Parker, a billionaire founding president of the company, said the objective had always been to 'consume as much of your time and conscious attention as possible' by giving users 'little dopamine hits' through shares and likes. But he added that the 'unintended consequences' had been to change people's relationship with society, each other and the economy. 'God only knows what it's doing to our children's brains,' he said.[92]

Then Chamath Palihapitiya, who had been Facebook's vice president for user growth and who was close to its leadership, spoke of his 'tremendous guilt' at having helped create 'tools that are ripping apart the social fabric.' He told Stanford University students about an incident in India earlier that year when false messages on WhatsApp—owned by Facebook—had led to the lynching of seven people.[93] 'That's what we're dealing with,' said Palihapitiya. 'Imagine when you take that to the extreme where bad actors can now manipulate large swathes of people to do anything you want. It's just a really, really bad state of affairs.'

Those bad actors included the Russian trolls who seemed to have worked out how to produce viral material that had flown around Facebook's ideological echo chambers. One analysis in October 2017 suggested that just six fake Russian accounts on Facebook produced material that was viewed 340 million times, far in excess of the ads paid for by the Kremlin.[94]

Facebook's response to all this was to insist that new laws and regulations were unnecessary because, having always followed Zuckerberg's dictum to 'move fast and break things,' the company was now going to move even faster to fix things too.

But the crashing noises coming from Facebook had only just begun. In March 2018, a couple of days after my visit to Menlo Park, the story broke that Cambridge Analytica had harvested data from 50 million—or, as it turned out later, 87 million—Facebook users before offering its sinister-sounding services to the causes of Brexit and Donald Trump.

The previous chapter has already looked at whether this really had much effect on the result of those votes in 2016. The more lasting impact of the row over Cambridge Analytica may be on the future of Facebook and possibly the internet itself. That is because what the Cambridge Analytica scandal did was throw a shaft of light on to the murky way such platforms harvest and monetise data on billions of individuals.

# # #

Facebook is not a social network so much as an analytics business that makes its money selling its users' attention to advertisers. In the same way that some political consultants claim they can win elections through their analysis of voters' data, Facebook tells its customers (the real ones who pay it money to advertise) how they can influence minds because it knows so much about each member of its 'community'. It has even shown some advertisers how it can identify when teenagers feel 'insecure' or 'worthless'.[95]

When Facebook is so ready to put all this at the service of almost any organisation willing to pay, it does make you wonder why a political campaign, with Facebook staff working with it as the Trump campaign had, would need to use the services of Cambridge Analytica at all, let alone pay for old data harvested off an app three years earlier.

Facebook has pages devoted to its 'success stories'. Until they were removed during 2018, these included a section for 'government and politics' boasting about how Facebook had been able to influence elections. It described the company's role helping David Cameron in the 2015 General Election. Under the headline, 'A Real Vote Winner', it said: 'Using Facebook's targeting tools, the [Conservative] party was able to reach 80.65 per cent of Facebook users in the key marginal seats. The party's videos were viewed 3.5 million times, while 86.9 per cent of all ads served had social context—the all-important endorsement by a friend.'[96] In Scotland, it had 'triggered a landslide' for Scottish Nationalists using Facebook's 'powerful targeting tools' like Custom Audiences and Lookalike Audiences.[97]

Those tools, Custom Audience and Lookalike Audiences, were the same ones that the Trump campaign said it had learnt to use so successfully in the 2016 election. Indeed, almost every notable result in elections or referendums over the last few years seems to have involved heavy use of Facebook's targeting tools.

Ricken Patel, as the founder of the online activist community Avaaz, is someone who knows all about building momentum behind online campaigns. He can see how Facebook advertising is distorting the political playing field and told me: 'What Facebook has done is rent out the internet. What used to be a highly meritocratic medium where what appealed to people the most would win, has now become a place where it's sold to the highest bidder. You can get millions of views for just a few thousand dollars.'[98]

Beyond the potential power of micro-targeted advertising, there is another level of concern about Cambridge Analytica related to privacy. But again, the problem is less the breach that allowed Facebook's data to be accessed by a third party like Cambridge Analytica, than how anyone was allowed to gather so much data in the first place.

When he was still a student at Harvard in 2004, Zuckerberg was chatting to a friend on an instant messaging system about his new website. The transcript was later leaked to a blog called Silicon Alley Insider:

> Zuck: yea so if you ever need info about anyone at harvard
> Zuck: just ask
> Zuck: i have over 4000 emails, pictures, addresses, sns
> Friend: what!? how'd you manage that one?
> Zuck: people just submitted it
> Zuck: i don't know why
> Zuck: they "trust me"
> Zuck: dumb fucks[99]

Most of us have said stuff when we were younger that is embarrassing later in life and Zuckerberg has made one of his now-customary abject apologies for writing those messages. But Facebook's file of data on each of its users has not been confined simply to emails, pictures, addresses, or even their likes and comments. It has learnt from users' smart phones where they are, from the posts they read and those they do not read, from when they stop scrolling down and when they start again, from the other sites they visit and even from the messages they type but delete before sending.[100] In 2016, it published a list of ninety-eight data points on each user ranging from their political leanings to the square footage of their homes and even the likelihood that they will be moving soon.[101]

Nor were its files on people limited to information provided by users when visiting the site. Facebook is said to create 'shadow profiles' of users and non-users based on data mined from friends or from offline information purchased from brokers like Experian. In some cases, these profiles have led to strange and slightly creepy algorithmic connections such as when a woman, whose father left her family when she was six years old, had his then-lover suggested to her as a Facebook friend forty years later.[102]

Facebook is not unique in its pursuit of data and its practice of what has become known as 'surveillance capitalism'.[103] Apple and Microsoft also collect huge amounts of data, although this appears to be largely used to improve their products. Amazon's artificially intelligent 'Alexa' home assistant not only tells you the weather forecast but listens to people's conversations and then sends the data back to Amazon's Seattle headquarters for analysis.[104] One problem it is encountering, according to an engineer working on the project, is working out how much data to harvest—and how long to listen to perhaps intimate secrets—without users realising that the device may be spying on them.[105]

But Facebook's real rival for data is, needless to say, Google. There are some obvious differences between the two corporations. For instance, when someone types the words 'car insurance' into search, Google does not need particularly sophisticated or sinister analytics to work out that it might be worth sending them some adverts for different car insurance firms. But Google also harvests monstrous amounts of data from its users. It tracks people as they move across the internet, monitoring not only their searches and browsing history—including those that have been cleared—but also the contents of their Gmail, the location of every Android phone and everyone using Google Maps, as well as whatever videos they watch on YouTube. Google tracks people so well, it usually knows where they might go next—or what they might want to buy and believe—perhaps even before they do.

Both Facebook and Google have made their money through selling their users' attention to advertisers. Between them, they account for more than 70 per cent of traffic on the internet as well as taking the bulk of advertising revenues. And both use much of that data to find more and more ways of getting increasing numbers of people to engage for as long as possible with its platform in order to sell ever more advertising. None of this is necessarily bad. Both companies can tell inspiring stories about how they have challenged established thinking or helped small businesses and new ideas reach their intended audiences.

But some of those who used to work for the company have turned away in disgust. James Williams, who quit Google in 2015 and headed to the UK after a decade working for the company's advertising search systems, is now among those warning that this battle for our eyeballs is changing the way media and politics have functioned. Having watched voters in the EU referendum back Brexit and then his own country elect Donald Trump as president, Williams warns that the 'attention economy' is tilting democracy towards emotional, impulsive, identity-based outrage that works as well as for Jeremy Corbyn and Bernie Sanders as it has for Nigel Farage.

When I talk to Williams in Oxford, he describes how his worries 'about what was being lost' had grown all the time he was at Google. He says: 'There was a disconnect between the high-minded values of making the world a better place and being incentivised with a quarterly bonus for getting people to buy more stuff. I guess that's what they mean when they said a "bad system will beat good people every time."' He fears that social media is now leading to a 'polarisation not so much of information but of identities where different groups believe only they are the authentic expression of "the people."'

The same year of Brexit and Trump, a study found that people touched their smart phones, on average, 2,617 times a day or more than 100 times an hour, even allowing for a certain amount of sleep.[106]

Sergey Brin, one of Google's orginal founders, once talked about how he wanted the company to become the 'third half of your brain' which might sound wrong to most ears but, given that it came from the lips of an unfathomably wealthy mathematical genius, had much of Silicon Valley nodding along.[107] Eric Schmidt, Google's chief executive, said: 'The Google policy on a lot of things is to get right up to the creepy line and not cross it.'[108]

# # #

It is a twenty-minute drive from Menlo Park to Mountain View. On the way, you pass Stanford University, where many of the tech billionaires studied, and the once-suburban city of Palo Alto where most of them seem to live.

Google's global headquarters are not quite as fancy as those of Facebook. At the time of writing, a major new build is apparently being planned but, in its relative dowdiness, there is a sense that Google might be a bit more mature than its social media rival. There are still touches that grate, such as putting all the help-yourself-for-free sugary soft drinks behind frosted glass to encourage 'healthy habits'—or the 'lawn statues' designed to resemble equally unhealthy children's treats—a Kit Kat, an Oreo cookie, a jelly bean—that celebrate each new version of its Android mobile phone operating system.

But when I sit down to talk with Richard Gingras, Google's vice-president for news, he has what sounds like a grown-up answer to questions about whether his company has a responsibility to root out the fake information flying around the internet. At least he does not depend, like Zuckerberg, on yet another latest iteration of the company's 'values'.

He says: 'Do we have a sense of responsibility to ensure there is good information out there? Sure we do, and not just because that's the right thing to do. The relevance and value of Google search is dependent on there being a rich corpus of knowledge on the web. If it becomes sub-par you use Google search less. And our ad platforms are successful only if publishers are successful. If we don't have a sustainable ecosystem of knowledge that's good for society, it's not good for Google's business.'[109]

Gingras bats back, in similar fashion, questions about whether Google's secret algorithms are designed to maximise profits or improve that corpus of human knowledge, saying: 'I have worked here a long time and I've never been in a discussion where people are skewing the algorithms towards areas that are more revenue producing than others. It's all about user satisfaction. That is a key metric for our business and for our mission.'

Google has been keen to disentangle itself from the mess over at Menlo Park where Facebook groups seem to have provided the shelter where extremist content can flourish. In the course of 2017, it tweaked its algorithm to give more weight to authoritative sources after it emerged that a search query asking, 'did the Holocaust really happen?' took users to a neo-Nazi site saying it had all been made up. At Mountain View, Gingras contrasts the walled gardens of social media with the way Google is open to the winds of competition that have blown previous internet market leaders off their perch. 'If users don't trust us another search engine is just a click away. I know this well from when I ran the Excite search engine which was number two in popularity to Yahoo. But Google came out of nowhere, offered a better product and knocked Yahoo off its perch, and Excite as well.'[110]

When I mention that there does not seem to be any democratic input into the process, Gingras shakes his head in frustration: 'What does that really mean? Google is democratic in the sense that billions of users vote with their clicks every day ... People have alternatives to Google. If users don't trust us another search engine is just a click away.'[111]

But what Gingras is describing is surely not democracy, but a market. And it is a market where Google almost monopolises search and Alphabet—its parent company—had grown to a mammoth $817 billion capital value in 2018. Much of this argument is familiar to anyone who listened to media owners like Rupert Murdoch explain why he was just giving the public what they want—if they did not like it they could stop buying *The Sun* or switch off Fox News.

Google says much the same. 'What's really happened over the last twenty-five years?' Gingras asks, before answering his own question. 'The internet happened. We put a printing press in the hands of everyone. ... It has both democratised the production of content and dramatically changed how people consume information. And yes, not all the information is good or created with good intentions. However, if one supports freedom of expression it also means accepting there will be information out there which each of us in our own way will find uncomfortable.'[112]

A key difference, of course, with the media is that Google and other internet platforms generally have little, if any, liability for material—no matter how extreme or shocking—that they link to or host. This is a legacy from the 1996 Telecommunications Act mentioned in Chapter 2 and is a legal regime that has largely been reproduced by most Western democracies in the years since.

Google, along with other technology firms, have argued that what they do is so complex, fast-moving and global in scale governments are unable to regulate the internet more effectively even if politicians wanted to do so. And, in the absence of a regime as draconian as China, where at least 2 million people are employed in censoring the internet, they may well be right.[113]

Gingras says: 'The marketplace does work. When you talk about over-sight you have to be very careful and define what that means. What is the purpose? What kind of oversight? How do you audit this? Who oversees the overseers? Who decides who they are? Do you want parliament to determine the algorithm in a political process?'

I mumble something about how people might expect public policy makers to be at least able to understand it. Gingras shoots right back: 'I hate to go into the complexity of it but it's too easy for people to make simplistic judgements based on headlines they might read in the press. If we're not doing the right thing by our users, they will not be our users.'

One of the regulations that does exist in Europe is the 'right to be forgotten', which allows users to request that embarrassing data about them is erased from search results. But even this has generally been adjudicated upon by Google itself in what seems to be an implicit acknowledgment by the European courts that they are not competent to decide such matters.[114] Similarly, a German law threatening huge fines against social media failing to remove 'hate speech' has also effectively been implemented by the tech firms, with Facebook hiring more than 1,200 new staff—a sixth of its global 'community operations team'—to monitor posts in the country.[115]

According to critics, the big five technology firms are no longer merely market participants, they are 'market makers,' exerting real control over the terms on which others can provide services and possibly poised to replace the government as the *de facto* regulator. For instance, Amazon has increasing control of commerce by providing the infrastructure for a range of businesses and industries, while Airbnb is already controlling rental markets more effectively than local government in many cities.[116]

As such, they represent a challenge not only to regulatory authority—including those of democratic government—but also to employment and social cohesion. The next wave of jobs to be affected by technology will not necessarily be production lines or even hotel workers losing out to Airbnb. Instead, it will be about data, with some suggesting that even blue-chip professionals like lawyers and doctors might be displaced by algorithms that can crunch through millions of cases and clinical outcomes faster than any human.[117]

And once again that does not seem to fit with the ideals of those working for these tech firms. Although there are some right-wing libertarians like Peter Thiel with dark ideas about the nature of the state, the vast majority of them are just straight-forward liberals. In 2016, donations from Silicon Valley favoured Hillary Clinton over Donald Trump in 2016 by a margin of twenty to one.[118] When you sit down with any of them, they chatter excitedly about doing good, changing the world and I often leave meetings at these big tech firms thinking they may still be our best hope. If many of those I meet in Silicon Valley used to work for Obama, in Britain's tech firms I keep bumping into former colleagues from the Labour Party. These companies are also packed with scientists whose training makes them recoil from the idea that they are spreading the fakery of Trump or the stupidity of climate change denial. And staff at the tech firms will usually deny that they are opposed to all regulation, as well as pointing out, fairly, that it is a nonsense to pretend there is none.

But they often look pained and puzzled when mention is made of a new law proposed by those dumb politicians who, as one put it to me, 'don't know their apps from their elbows.' Sometimes, they will still come out with the mantra that 'technology is neutral but people are not'—so often used by Eric Schmidt when he was Google's chief executive[119]—a phrase which remains a close relative of the National Rifle Association's even more offensive slogan 'guns don't kill people, people do.' And, in the same way that politicians do not understand algorithms, much of the language used by Silicon Valley to describe its values is platitudinal and naïve.

Their mission statements were often written when their founders were running internet experiments in garages and denying they would ever do anything so grasping as make money out of advertising.

Google's corporate code of conduct still begins with the words: 'Don't be evil.' But it is clearly inadequate for a giant corporation that now has profound influence—on economies, politics and society across the planet—to define its moral purpose purely in the negative. Northern Californian values are comparatively friendly but they are not universally applicable. For instance, post-war Germany has never tolerated the use of Nazi symbols or language in the way that American notions of 'free speech' continue to do. In Britain, the role of the BBC and other regulated broadcasters means they have a legal obligation to make a heroic effort, several times a day, to discover the best version of truth.

But when I talk to Google's Gingras about further regulation, he cites the free speech amendment of the US Constitution as if it were there for everyone in the world, including benighted Europeans like me.

'Not all regulation is good regulation. Not all regulation is equal. A lot of regulation can be focused on maintaining the status quo and locking out the future. The consequences may be worse for our society. You have to look very hard at what you're trying to regulate and what that means. You have to decide what is the right approach which has the best effects. When you look at "fake news and misinformation"—most of that information is completely legal—if government is going to try to control that, is it going to try to control fee expression? In the United States the word "truth" is not in the First Amendment for very good reason.'

One seasoned British political figure recalls meeting a Google executive and asking whether he feared new regulation. 'My biggest worry is that the penny will drop with people in power and they'll realise that it doesn't apply to us because we're an American company,' replied the executive.[120]

A former senior figure in Facebook tells how executives back at Menlo Park failed to heed warnings about what was happening outside America as populists, extremists and authoritarians showed they could use the internet just as well as pro-democracy protesters. 'They were all in a bubble, I was trying to get through to them but when they thought about politics, they thought about how they could get a better balance of Democrats and Republicans working for them. They weren't really very interested in what was happening anywhere else.'[121]

Even in Britain, the global power of these Californian corporations can leave politicians feeling inadequate. Ed Vaizey, who was David Cameron's minister for digital policy for six years, describes how he tried to get meetings with the big tech companies to discuss ways of improving regulation: 'The big tech companies couldn't really give a stuff about what we think. They quite liked getting access to Number 10 but when it came to getting any progress on the digital charter policy I was drawing up, they would at best send an underling along to a meeting who would then say absolutely nothing. I got the impression they were not in the slightest bit interested.'[122]

In April 2018, when Zuckerberg was dragged before a Senate committee to answer questions about Facebook's data breach to Cambridge Analytica, the real revelation was the incapacity of even America's most powerful elected representatives to hold him to account.

Senator Roy Blunt was very keen to tell Zuckerberg how much his 13-year-old son, Charlie, liked Instagram, 'so he'd want to be sure I mentioned him while I was here—with you.' When 84-year-old Senator Orrin Hatch asked the Facebook founder how it was possible to 'sustain a business model in which users don't pay for your service,' there was a look of complete bemusement on Zuckerberg's face. 'Senator,' he said, pausing for a second, 'we run ads.' And then a slight smirk appeared that might have said 'dumb fucks', had he still been a student at Harvard.

# # #

At the time of writing this, Zuckerberg's net worth is said to be roughly $74 billion. And, as someone who got rich by renting out other people's personal data to advertisers, he has gone to great lengths to protect his own privacy. For instance, he spent $30 million buying all four houses surrounding his Palo Alto home[123] and up to $200 million on moving anyone else off his estate in Hawaii because, according to a local official, 'privacy is a bigger issue to him than anything else.'[124]

In Silicon Valley, the extreme wealth and power of a technology industry that is supposed to be all about connecting people, grinds hardest against the poorest. At one stage, there were protests at bus stops in San Francisco where luxury coaches with tinted windows would pick up Google workers while local workers waited for the city's own creaking public transport system. Homelessness has soared with property prices and investors buying up houses to rent out on Airbnb. The local newspaper is filled with complaints about 'lice-covered' homeless people defecating in the streets or sleeping on the BART trains that loop around the city.[125]

But those trains do not go anywhere near Cupertino, at the southern end of Silicon Valley, which is where its third, and most lavish, great technology campus can be found. This is a giant glass and steel ring resembling a space ship—indeed visible from space—with a one-mile circumference. It belongs to Apple, cost $5 billion to build, and contains a 100,000-square-foot fitness and wellness centre including a two-story yoga studio covered in distressed stone carefully selected to look like Steve Jobs's favourite hotel in Yosemite.[126]

Jobs, already clearly frail from the pancreatic cancer that would kill him four months later, turned up at a meeting of Cupertino City Council on 7 June 2011, to pitch his plan for what he promised would be the 'best office building in the world.'

A video of the proceedings still exists and it serves as an illustration of how shrivelled democracy can be in the face of vast new power. The council leader opened proceedings by stating, to applause, how honoured they should be to have 'Mr Steve Jobs' himself present the planning application. A few minutes later, after the Apple chief had taken them through his plans that would surely lead to higher house prices and increased traffic as well as years of disruption as this cyber-age palace was built in the midst of this community, Jobs announced he would be happy to take some questions. The only moment of real awkwardness came from a council member called Kris Wang.

The exchange went like this:

Wang: Hi Steve.

Jobs: Hi.

Wang: Quick question—I think people are concerned to know if city residents can have benefit from this new campus?

Jobs: Well, as you know, we're the largest taxpayer in Cupertino so we would like to stay here and pay taxes.

[Nervous laughter from council members]

Jobs: That's number one. Because if we can't, we go somewhere like Mountain View. We take our people with us and give up and over the years sell the land here. We go away and take the largest tax base with us. That would not be good for Cupertino—

Wang: No…

Jobs:—and it's not good for us either.

Wang: … of course not.[127]

She asked a follow up question about whether there might be free wifi. Jobs said he took an old-fashioned view that maybe it was something the council could pay for with all its taxes. Another member of the council wondered whether Jobs might open an Apple store in the town which, he said, was so proud to host the company's army of 12,000 employees. No, said Jobs, there was not enough traffic—there weren't enough civilians— in Cupertino for that.

Desperation for tech dollars has seen other elected representatives prostrate themselves in even more embarrassing fashion. In 2017, an Amazon competition to find the location of its second HQ triggered a stampede of deference. Fresno offered to give the corporation control over how taxes were spent. Boston offered to set up an 'Amazon Task Force' of city employees working on the company's behalf. Stonecrest, Georgia offered to annex a 345-acre site from its centre, name the new town 'Amazon' and make Jeff Bezos the mayor.[128]

In Europe, Apple, Google, Amazon and Facebook have routed their revenue through countries like Ireland, Luxembourg, the Netherlands which offered them low rates of corporation tax. But the European Commission ruled in 2016 that Apple's marginal rate on the profits of just 0.005 per cent was totally inadequate and ordered it to pay €13 billion in back taxes to Ireland. Tim Cook, who succeeded Jobs as the company's chief executive, said the decision was 'total political crap ... I think it clearly suggests that this is politics at play.'[129] The word, 'political', is now thrown around by tech companies as an insult. But surely all that had been 'at play' was democracy? And maybe that is what had made Cook so cross.

Some dystopian visions of the future depict these tech titans as feudal robber barons in their high castles, too powerful to be governed by 'political crap' or nation states as they occasionally toss tech trinkets to a servile, surveilled population of 'digital sharecroppers.'[130] As ever, such a vision contradicts the reality of those well-meaning, earnest people who work in Silicon Valley and still think they are making lives better. Indeed, what robber baron ever gave away most of their money to help feed and cure the world's poor as Bill Gates, the founder of Microsoft, has done?

At the last count, the Bill and Melinda Gates Foundation, which has received matching donations from the investor–philanthropist Warren Buffett, was worth $43 billion—which is a lot more than the combined GDP of the poorest dozen countries in Africa.[131] On the margins, among development and health scholars, it is possible to find muted criticism over its priorities or suggestions it might be too focused on technological solutions that benefit Microsoft.[132] But it would take cynicism to new depths to really doubt the motivation or effectiveness of the Foundation's data-driven spending that has undoubtedly had a profound impact treating infectious diseases like HIV/Aids, polio and malaria. It has earned Gates and his wife the Presidential Medal of Freedom that Barack Obama presented to them in 2016, as well as the kind of media that elected politicians only ever get in their dreams.

This is how an article in *Forbes* magazine, under a headline describing them as 'The World's Greatest Philanthropists,' began in 2015: 'Bill and Melinda Gates have given away over $29 billion, more money than anyone in the history of humanity. But the way in which they have given away that money—turning philanthropy into their full-time professions—is equally unprecedented, their close friend Warren Buffett told a packed room of 200 billionaires, leaders and social entrepreneurs.'[133]

The problem is not that Gates, or any of the other tech titans—most of whom are setting up their own charitable foundations—is immoral or misguided. It is that they have vast power and wealth while they have also been given a free pass from detailed scrutiny by either the media or politics or most of the past twenty-five years.

Public trust in Gates, if not Zuckerberg, is unlikely to fall below that of any elected politician any time soon and nor is there very much that anyone could do about if it did. If Gates wants to eliminate malaria in Africa, he may have the capacity to do so. But other billionaires may want to pursue other goals with both their wealth and their technology. And, at the moment, there would be very little that democracy can do about that either.

Barack Obama was not only the 'tech president' whose values were in tune with the bulk of people working in Silicon Valley, but he was also a very smart guy. He continued to read and think when he was in the Oval Office and once said his favourite philosopher was Reinhold Niebuhr.[134] Writing in the 1930s when totalitarianism held sway across much of Europe, Niebuhr always argued that good people can do very bad things when they are in groups that are given vast power. 'There is less reason to guide and check impulse, less capacity for self-transcendence, less ability to comprehend the needs of others, and therefore unrestrained egoism than the individuals who compose the group [might] reveal in their personal relationships.' Any supremely powerful organisation—be it the state or a corporation—that is given untrammelled power will go wrong, said Niebuhr, 'however social its intentions or pretensions.'[135]

For all the good intentions and claims of Silicon Valley, there was a fundamental contradiction between the liberal values of these digital behemoths and the very illiberal—even undemocratic—consequences of their activities. And those who believe in democracy have done remarkably little about it.

8

Can Democracy be Rebooted?

Whatever happened to Derek and Steve?

Back in the 1990s, when progressive politics was speeding along what was still called the 'information super-highway', I spent many a late night and early morning with two of the characters whose strange careers have flickered through the pages of this book.

Derek Draper was the self-styled 'New Labour storm-trooper' who got caught boasting about how he would sell access to the powerful. He later re-emerged briefly as the author of Prime Minister Gordon Brown's digital strategy, only to crash and burn a second time when emails were leaked implicating him in a plot to smear opponents.

Steve Hilton was the creative genius behind the Tories' 'demon eyes' attack adverts on Tony Blair and a marketing expert for big firms like McDonalds, who later became David Cameron's policy guru and tried to replace the civil service with a digitally empowered citizenry. When that didn't work, he turned on Cameron and metastasised into a Brexit-backing, corporation-bashing, Trump-loving populist living in—of all places—the heart of Silicon Valley.

At the time of writing 2018, Draper is a psychologist working with business leaders and reluctant to talk about his old life at all. When I meet him at his north London practice the daylight is fading and he asks me if I want to lie on his old-fashioned therapist couch. Draper seems genuinely puzzled why anyone should still be interested in politics or, as he puts it, why they should want to persuade voters of their 'version of the truth' when people are so divergent, complicated and contradictory. 'I didn't vote in the last election. Political activity, thinking about all this stuff, it's just not for me anymore and I've turned away from it,' says Draper. 'In my more cynical moments I think maybe we should all just mind our own business.'

As for Hilton, he and I stopped speaking at some point between my decision to work for the Labour Party and his to back Brexit. Last I heard, he was living in Silicon Valley's billionaire enclave of Atherton with his tech executive wife, his yoga regime and a clutch of chickens.[1] He sometimes complains that he cannot go out very much because everyone in Silicon Valley is so liberal and he still refuses to have a smart phone.[2] But on Sundays he flies down to Los Angeles where, in a studio that Fox News built just for him, Hilton hosts a show called *The Next Revolution* on which he attacks the elites, the big corporations and the 'Washington swamp'.

In a Fox News opinion piece in March 2018, Hilton reiterated that 'The Wall' needed to be built to protect him from 'the minority of illegal immigrants who are violent criminals,' before taking aim at what he says are the pro-immigration policies of California's Democrats. 'They are literally prepared to release convicted child sex offenders, drug dealers and other violent criminals on to the streets,' he said. 'As a resident of the Bay Area, this affects me personally. It offends me personally.'[3] Some of his old friends back in London say that he wants to stand for election as governor of California one day as a 'positive populist' candidate.

Neither Draper nor Hilton have, by themselves, changed the course of history and perhaps I have written too much about both of them already. But they were players in the game and their strange careers—advertising, spin, lobbying, digital policy, psychology, cable TV host and populist proselytising—stand as totems of how the new information age has developed over this past quarter of a century. In the 1990s, neither would have thought that democracy itself was in danger or predicted they would be doing what they do now. But both Draper and Hilton, in different ways, are reflecting a fashionable view that democracy no longer responds properly either to the demands of its citizens or the challenges of the age. One seems to have had his politics burnt out of him and been left with no opinions on anything; the other is still inflamed with his opinions on everything.

'It's just a mirage,' says Draper. 'Don't delude yourself that you have that much control over anything really.'[4] Hilton believes that we have 'a democracy in name only, operating on behalf of a tiny elite, no matter what the electoral outcome.'[5]

And part of me worries that both of them might be right.

Is democracy still fit for purpose?

Claims that the system is rigged against the many and that power is exercised only by a privileged few are not exactly new; they have been the rallying cry of radicals and populists, particularly those on the left, for generations. But the idea that democracy has simply stopped working was examined in some detail by an academic study published in 2014 that tracked how well the views of US citizens on 1,779 policy issues were reflected by their government over the previous twenty years. It concluded that, compared to economic elites and special interest groups, 'the preferences of the average American appear to have only a minuscule, near-zero, statistically non-significant impact upon public policy.'[6]

This research has since been criticised by other scholars[7] but it definitely touched a chord. The authors, Martin Gilens and Benjamin Page, were cited by Hilton in a book he wrote the following year that recounted his Downing Street battles with the British Establishment—or the 'Deep State' as he now refers to it in his new Trumpian incarnation.[8] Gilens and Page even appeared on Jon Stewart's *Daily Show*, which is good going for a pair of political science scholars.[9]

Writers like Stephen Pinker make a strong case that liberal enlightenment values have done pretty well over the past couple of centuries for a human race that is generally healthier, better educated and richer than ever before.[10] Perhaps the current panic is merely the result of the media's negativity bias and the pessimism of a self-critical liberal elite. But, having been in the thick of both the media and politics for the past quarter of a century, I think the rotting smell that permeates democracy means the decay has gone deep.

It comes from the way idealistic hopes about the potential of the new information age have turned sour as the impact of technological upheaval has been too often ignored, not only by journalists chasing clicks and politicians chasing votes, but also by the behemoth corporations striding out across the world with such adolescent self-confidence from Silicon Valley.

Online, there is a clamour for people's attention as they are bombarded with images of wealth and happiness they do not have. Some are lured deep into echo chambers where blaming others—Mexicans, Muslims, migrants or 'the Jews'—becomes not shocking but normalised because everyone there seems to agree. Others prefer just to participate in screaming matches with opponents on Twitter. Offline, in the real world of a globalised economy turbo-charged by automation and digitalisation, people are discovering they have little control over systems which leave them getting less, just when they had been encouraged to expect more.

This was the source of the nationalistic populism of Brexit and Trump in 2016. America, that had elected its first black president in 2008, chose to replace him with a white billoinaire misogynist who promised to ban Muslims entering the country. As for Britain, even Margaret Thatcher had accepted in her Bruges speech that the UK's 'destiny is in Europe.'[11] But twenty-eight years later, it voted to leave after a poisoned referendum in which Nigel Farage unveiled a poster depicting a line of refugees with the headline 'Breaking Point', just hours before Labour MP Jo Cox was murdered on the streets by a neo-Nazi shouting 'Britain first'.

In the heady days of 1989 Francis Fukuyama had predicted 'the end of history' as free market liberal democracy took root across the world.[12] By the time Trump was elected, he was saying that he feared for democracy's future.[13] History, it seems, is back—and it's in a terrible mood.

Steven Levitsky and Daniel Ziblatt, two Harvard political scientists, have pointed out that democracies have often died before, not at the point of a gun in military coups, but through voting. They warned that 'the guardrails of American democracy' were weakened as Trump breached the 'norms'—the unspoken rules that hold it together—by painting Hillary Clinton as a criminal, tacitly endorsing violence against journalists and warning that if he lost it would be because the ballot had been rigged. And on their scorecard since the election, the president has continued to rattle those rails.[14] To take just one example: in August 2017, a twenty-year-old man ploughed his car into a crowd of people, killing a woman and injuring several others. His motive was apparently that they were protesting against a white supremacist neo-Nazi rally in Charlottesville, Virginia. The democratically-elected president of the United States declared that rally included 'some very fine people'. When asked about the murder and maiming, Trump explained: 'I think there's blame on both sides. And I have no doubt about it.'[15]

CAN DEMOCRACY BE REBOOTED?

Britain and America, once the most stable of democracies, are now bitterly divided. In the UK, the split between Leave and Remain voters has deepened since the referendum to the point where it is stronger for many people than any party affiliation.[16] In the US, although Barack Obama and Trump managed to handle a peaceful transfer of power in 2017, the way both sides—supporters and opponents of the president— have delegitimised each other since raises a question mark over whether that will still be possible in the future. Online adverts for the National Rifle Association feature its spokeswoman, Dana Loesch, warning the media, teachers and Hollywood liberals that 'the only way we save our country, and our freedom, is to fight this violence of lies with a clenched fist of truth.'[17] In another video, depicting her dressed in black next to an hourglass, she declares: 'To those who bring bias and propaganda to CNN, *The Washington Post* and *The New York Times*, your time is running out. The clock starts now.' She then turns over the sand timer and the screen turns dark.[18]

Tony Blair, who knows better than most what it is like to be hated in politics, told me after a recent visit to the US he had been 'stunned' by what he had found was a 'complete separation of people from one another.' He warned: 'You get to the point where people think if we let these other people run the country they are going to destroy it, so we better keep power. They just want to pull you down so you just want to keep them out. I don't where that ends … But it's contrary to the spirit of democracy.'[19]

Nor should the Anglo-Saxon focus of much of this book obscure how this is a global crisis for democracy. Take just one example: Aung San Suu Kyi, a winner of the Nobel peace prize, had emerged from house arrest to become the elected leader of Myanmar in 2016 and a powerful symbol of how a developing nation could peacefully transition to democracy. But the next year, in the same month that James Field was ramming his Dodge Charger into a crowd of terrified people in Charlottesville, she turned her back as her country's military massacred fleeing members of the Rohingya minority.[20] In its annual report at the start of 2018, Freedom House declared that democracy faced its most serious crisis in decades as its basic tenets, including the rights of minorities and freedom of the press, came under attack. It said a total of seventy-one countries had seen democratic decline in 2017, with countries that had once seemed to herald a bright new liberal future—Egypt and Turkey,

Hungary and Poland, Brazil and Venezuela, India and South Africa—falling into the hard hands of authoritarian nationalistic rulers, the sticky fingers of corrupt regimes, or in some cases both.[21]

The technology of the information age is often close to the scene of the crime. Nationalist Buddhist priests in Myanmar find Facebook is the best way of spreading genocidal hatred against Rohingyas.[22] The legions of trolls used to suppress opposition in the Philippines—where Rodrigo Duterte's 'keyboard army' work through the night to keep their vicious president popular—could not have been deployed without the web.[23] New challenges to the nation state loom as cryptocurrencies or encrypted messaging build a market where criminals and corruption may be beyond the reach of the law. Already, social media platforms have become a 'tool of terror', with groups like ISIS using them to recruit terrorists, as well as laundering money and buying weapons on the dark net.[24]

And then there is Russia, where Putin's hackers, trolls and bots had unexpected success in gaming Silicon Valley's algorithms to inject democracy-corroding propaganda into the 2016 presidential elections. The cries of outrage at the idea that anyone might interfere in US elections will stick in the craw of all those Caribbean, Latin American and Middle Eastern countries whose democracies the CIA has meddled with over the years.[25] But what Russia has shown is that the internet, once seen as an engine and symbol of freedom, can be reverse-engineered to pump poison back into Western politics. Russian trolls appear to have been deployed in support of campaigns as different as Marine Le Pen's Front National in France, Scottish independence and Jeremy Corbyn's Labour Party in the UK.[26] Although it is probably easy to exaggerate the extent to which such interference has had real influence, the persistent theme of their interventions has been to support campaigns or candidates the Kremlin believes would do most to destabilise liberal democracy. And there is a wealth of evidence to suggest that democracy is more vulnerable than at any point since the end of the Cold War.

Harvard University's Yascha Mounk has dug deep into data from the World Values Survey to show that in democratic countries across the developed world—Australia, the Netherlands, New Zealand, Sweden, the UK and the US—the percentage of people, particularly young people, who think it is important to live in a democracy has plummeted.[27] His fear is that liberal democracy is collapsing into either 'undemocratic liberalism', where unelected technocratic bodies protect rights but give ordinary citizens little power, or 'illiberal democracy' with regimes elected by a majority proceeding to ride roughshod over minorities.

Illiberal democracy vs undemocratic liberalism

One of the standard bearers for illiberal democracy is Viktor Orbán, Hungary's right wing nationalist prime minister, who won his fourth term in office in April 2018 elections where he secured the super-majority required to change the constitution.

He had already scapegoated Muslims, immigrants and Jewish liberals like the Hungarian-born George Soros, undermined civil society and brought much of the media under the control of oligarchs close to his regime, even while attacking a European Union that he claims is frustrating the 'will of the people'.[28] Other examples of such illiberal democrats range from Orbán's ally in Poland, Jarosław Kaczynski,[29] Turkey's president, Recep Tayyip Erdoğan, as well as Vladimir Putin and Donald Trump himself.

But it also finds an echo in the rising rage against anything that might get in the way of the 'democratic will' expressed in Britain's referendum on Europe. The *Daily Mail* denounced high court judges as 'ENEMIES OF THE PEOPLE' because they had made a legal ruling on Brexit that, it said, had 'declared war on democracy.'[30] Conservative MPs opposed to leaving Europe have been compared to mutineers or traitors in the old media, while receiving messages saying they should be executed for their crimes on social media.[31]

A less extreme, but possibly equally dangerous version of illiberal democracy, may be the logical consequence of experiments with online voting and petitions enabled by digital technology. People have got used to the instant gratification of liking a post of Facebook, retweeting on Twitter, upvoting on Reddit or in some cases, trolling the powerful. Their votes count on *Strictly Come Dancing* or the *X Factor* and, in comparison, people find representative democracy unsatisfactory and unresponsive.

The Pew Research Centre has published a global survey of attitudes across thirty-eight Western countries that shows although 80 per cent of people still support democracy, 70 per cent want a system where 'citizens, not elected officials, vote directly on major national issues to decide what becomes law.'[32] Ben Rattray, the founder of the online petition site Change.org is among those excited by the possibility of making politicians more directly accountable. There is already technology that uses location services to show when people are waiting to vote and he says this is when he wants to remind voters about how particular politicians have responded to petitions. 'We will push messages to your phone as your walk to the polling station,' he says. 'We can send people stuff with all the information they need.' Although Rattray acknowledges that there is a danger in politicians being 'too responsive,' he adds, 'The biggest problem in politics now is not that citizens have too much power.'[33]

Michael Gove, one of the leaders of the Leave campaign, believes the direct democracy of the EU referendum 2016 served as a safety valve on pent-up popular resentment about immigration and 'burst the Ukip bubble.' He says: 'Attitudes to migration are less illiberal in the UK now that in any continental European country. It has been a release of pressure, a humbling of the elites.'[34] Gove's interview for this book came before the danger of politicians reacting too readily to pent-up resentments over immigration was underlined by revelations about the 'hostile environment' his government had created for immigrants—including those of the Windrush generation who came from the Caribbean as citizens of the United Kingdom and Colonies in the 1950s.[35] In fairness to Gove, he does a better job than most Brexiteers at making the prospect of leaving the EU sound both democratic and liberal. At the time of writing this, he is busy banning plastic bags and straws in his incarnation as an environmentalist secretary of state for environment. And he also has a justifiable point that those endangering democracy can also be spotted on the other side of the political divide: 'There is a danger in the response to Brexit that the anti-undemocratic spirit, the elitist spirit, could re-enter public debate. The real danger is not so much populism, although that of course is a particular form of danger, but technocrats who are not taking sufficient account of democratic pressures.'[36]

# # #

Andrew Sullivan, a liberal conservative thinker who helped pioneer the blogosphere, is among those who suggested that the 'passions of the mob' and 'untrammelled emotions' had too much influence on the 2016 presidential election. In an essay entitled, 'Democracies End When They Are Too Democratic', he argued a better 'elitist sorting mechanism' is needed to save us.[37]

And, in Britain, such sentiments were legion among public intellectuals at the time of the Brexit vote. Richard Dawkins declared that it was ridiculous to ask 'ignoramuses' to decide such questions in a referendum because most members of the public, including anyone like himself who lacked degrees in History and Economics, did not know enough about the 'highly complex' issues at stake.[38] The philosopher, A. C. Grayling, wrote an open letter to MPs saying they should not allow the UK to leave because a vote by 'crowd acclamation' had been too easily influenced by 'misinformation, distortion, and false promises,' no to mention 'tabloid urgings'.[39]

Thoughtful, liberal people who have dedicated much of their lives to democracy are now tempted to turn away. Matthew Parris, my former colleague at *The Times*, was typically honest as he wrote: 'The reason I am beginning to question democracy is that it is producing results I profoundly dislike.' He said that the system seemed more considered and wise when 'we weren't governed by the mob, real or virtual' and when 'there was no internet, no Facebook, no Twitter, no social media.'[40]

As Parris acknowledged, such language about 'crowds' and 'mobs' are a throw-back to the nineteenth century when educated opinion was pretty sure that giving votes to what Walter Bagehot called the 'ignorant multitude' was a very bad idea. Even before Brexit and Trump won, there was revived interest in the poisonous writing of Gustave Le Bon who, in late nineteenth-century France, had characterised 'the crowd' as an organism infected by popular hysteria, hate and conspiracy and resistant to reason just as bodies are infected by disease.[41] Others looked for inspiration to John Stuart Mill, the nineteenth-century liberal thinker who had advocated widening the franchise to give every male and female citizen a vote even as he worried they might do something stupid with it. Mill had wanted a system of voting that was weighted according to educational qualifications.

Jason Brennan, a politics professor at Georgetown, wrote a book in 2016 entitled *Against Democracy* advocating a system of epistocracy—government by the knowledgeable few on behalf of the many. It was well-timed: the media never stopped calling him and the book got translated into six languages. Brennan compares the blind faith in equal voting rights to the belief among the Fore tribe in Papua New Guinea that eating 'the rotting raw flesh' of their dead relatives was a way of showing respect for them.[42] His argument is that if democracy is not producing good outcomes, it is rational to find a better way of choosing governments. As Brennan puts it, 'asking everyone to vote is like asking everyone to litter.'[43]

There has been a lot of this stuff around since Brexit and Trump. Will Straw, who was the director of the Remain campaign in the 2016 referendum, is sick of hearing it from people on his side of the argument. He says: 'If only I had a pound for every snooty elitist metropolitan who said we should not give "these people" the vote—I mean, for fuck's sake—we're in danger of going back to the 1860s! This is no way to change people's minds.'[44]

In these circumstances, it is not entirely surprising that so many apparently decent liberal people are beginning to sound a bit like Walter Lippmann back in the 1920s. He had been an adviser to the US government at the end of the First World War, an experience that had left him horrified by the success of government censorship and propaganda. He feared that technological advances and new systems of information control made it impossible to have genuine public participation in government because modern society was far too complicated—and the possibility of people being manipulated through propaganda too great—to let the mob rule. Lippmann said that an expert elite was needed to tell people what they needed to know through the media and take all the important decisions.

But Lippmann was challenged by another radical American progressive, John Dewey, in a debate that has since become the stuff of legend. Dewey's case was that unless citizens were actively engaged through a functioning democracy, any decisions would inevitably be flawed. His argument back then, almost 100 years ago, is even more relevant now when so much of the anger directed at both the media and politics seems sourced in a sense that people have no voice in the media and no control over what politics decides. Dewey, particularly in his later writing, was not so naïve as to think it was enough simply to create democratic institutions; he recognized that mendacious and powerful forces needed to be resisted, but never at the expense of the liberal values he believed it was so vital to protect.[45]

Indeed, almost a century later, what has gone wrong in the new information age can be traced to a failure to engage people with the honesty, respect and radicalism that democracy needs if it is to survive.

'The worst form of government except for...'

Too many liberal democratic elitists have too often shown themselves to be poor liberals and even worse democrats over the last few decades. In the years to come, they cannot necessarily be trusted to remain either democratic or liberal; they can only really be trusted to remain elites.

Since the shocks of 2016 and 2017, progressives have become overly fond of blaming Russian trolls, fake news or dastardly Old Etonian data scrapers from Cambridge Analytica for their failings. But they cannot absolve themselves from responsibility for the polarisation of politics because this is a problem not just with the alt-left and the alt-right extremes but also with moderates—with what might be called 'the alt-centre'.

In my progressive well-to-do north London filter bubble, I hear people sneering at the Brexit-backing working class voters about whom they were once so sentimental. One Labour-voting friend tells me he hopes Sunderland car workers lose their jobs if Britain leaves the EU. Another talks of the need for a 'really big economic set-back' to shock voters in industrial towns out of their stupidity.

And in America too, there are plenty of people on the left who now want poor people who backed Trump to suffer. Markos Moulitas is one of the 'net-roots' liberal activists who worked so hard to create an inclusive digital democracy during the early days of the blogosphere. But on the blog that he writes from Berkeley, California, he had this to say in December 2016 about the loss of health insurance for coal miners in hardscrabble areas that had swung hard to Trump: 'Don't weep for these coal miners … They are getting exactly the government that they voted for. Democrats can no longer offer unrequited love and cover for them. And isn't this what democracy is all about? They won the election! This is what they wanted!'[46]

In the nineteen and twentieth centuries, elites in some nation states decided—reluctantly, truculently and spasmodically—to share some of their power with the wider populace. Sometimes, this was done out of genuine idealism and a humanist belief that all people are created equal. But it also coincided with a period when factory owners needed workers to pull levers and push buttons, governments needed soldiers to fight in wars, and elites generally became a bit worried that an angry mob might appear outside their gates if they did not extend to them some more democratic rights.

The most dystopian analyses of our own time warn that technology will set elites free of any lingering sense that they are required to support democracy at all. Automation and data analytics are already starting to replace human beings in many jobs without all that awkwardness of having to put up with trade unions, days, parental leave and pensions. Drones are replacing soldiers on the battlefield without the messy massacres, occasional mutinies or the coffins coming home. Improved digital surveillance should be able to protect the wealthy from the mob. And, as for those liberal humanist ideals about equality, genetic engineering should be able to fix that too by ensuring rich people can not only live longer but also produce nicer, prettier and more intelligent children who are, for the first time in history, genuinely 'a class above' the offspring of the poor.[47]

Even if none of this nightmare vision comes to pass, technology will certainly not stand still. The people who work in it are a new elite and even though they are overwhelmingly liberal, that is probably more through habit than a rational analysis of their economic self-interest. It would be a very risky bet to assume this will always be the case as technology makes further advances. Liberals might sometimes indulge in a pleasant fantasy to imagine how a benign enlightened technocrat like Bill Gates might be selected by a council of the elite to do a better job of running things. But once the small amount of political power people still have through democracy is handed over, there will be no going back; there would be nothing to stop Gates being succeeded perhaps by another billionaire who cares nothing for the poor, or even other members of the elite.

Winston Churchill's oft-quoted line about how 'democracy is the worst form of government except for all those other forms that have been tried' still holds true.[48] A liberal democracy sustained through honest and engaged debate with citizens remains the best way of taking decisions such as how resources should be distributed, when to go to war, who controls surveillance systems, what rules there should be for genetic engineering, or even the programming of driverless cars.

There are some who believe that digital technology is fundamentally incompatible with democracy. But, as we have seen, the current crisis has at least as much to do with the relationship media and politics have had with the new information age as with the technology itself.

Whatever the case, whether we like it or not, digital technology is here to stay. Any solutions we might find to today's problems, therefore, have to begin with both the media and politics adapting to the new information age a lot better than they have done before.

The media

The task of rebuilding a public sphere where people's voices can be heard in a debate informed by a shared set of facts, is not an easy one. And yet, even in the midst of this crisis of democracy, there are flashes of hope in the use of the very same technology that has helped create the problem in the first place.

#BlackLivesMatter and #MeToo went from being hashtags to become social movements precisely because people whose claims of police violence or sexual harassment had been ignored were able to connect with each other through social media. Similarly, as *The Guardian*'s editor, Katharine Viner, points out, it would be hard to imagine the police and *The Sun* being able to lie about what happened in the Hillsborough football disaster in 1989 if it happened today 'in front of 53,000 smart phones, with photographs and eyewitness accounts all posted to social media.'[49] At the BBC, its User-Generated Content Hub not only does extraordinary work sorting genuine content from fakery but also tries to teach its journalists how to spot information and trends they would never normally get from established sources.

There are endless examples of citizen journalism that perform much of the role of a traditional media in exposing the truth and holding the powerful to account. One of them is a formerly unemployed man from Leicester called Eliot Higgins who now runs the Bellingcat website.[50] He has helped reveal the use of chemical weapons by the Assad regime in Syria and the Kremlin's involvement in shooting down a Malaysia Airlines flight in Ukraine by meticulously sifting through vast amounts of data uploaded on sites such as YouTube, Twitter and Russian social media used by its soldiers.[51]

Upmarket newspapers in both Britain and America are beginning to believe they have found a technological solution to the advertising revenue crisis that had so disabled them in the early years of this century. By 2018, almost all of them had introduced digital paywalls, with the belated co-operation of Google and Facebook. It has meant their business model is once again being built around good journalism rather chasing viral stories for clicks. In the US, publications from the centre-left like

The Washington Post, *The New York Times*, *The Atlantic* and *The New Yorker* have experienced a significant 'Trump bump' in the number of subscriptions as liberal voters look to them for solace or perhaps protection. Even as the president appears to threaten his country's traditions of a free press with his attacks on the media he is succeeding in making many of America's great national newspapers profitable again.

There is a still a risk, that this will lead to them being sucked into a subscription-boosting partisan fight with the president, best illustrated not by the press in the US but broadcast. CNN, which has also enjoyed improved ratings from being in Trump's line of fire, seems a bit too keen on producing a viral internet sensation or studio shouting match with every item of news. Jeff Zucker, who made Trump a reality TV star by commissioning NBC's *The Apprentice*, is now head of CNN where he has said politics should be covered as if it is 'sport'.[52] In the deeply weird world of Trump's obsessive relationship with the media, the protagonists sometimes resemble each other.

Although Trump seems to have inspired a sustained revival in high quality journalism, *The Washington Post*—which has produced much of it and saw subscriptions double during 2017—has also benefitted from the technology wealth of Jeff Bezos, Amazon's chief executive. He invested heavily in *The Post*'s journalism and digital systems after buying the newspaper in 2013 for $250 million (a sum that is little more than pocket change for a man estimated by Forbes to be worth $133 billion.)[53] It has left a newspaper renowned across the world for its investigations of the powerful owned by the world's richest man. Trump likes to tweet that the 'Amazon Washington Post' is merely a lobbyist for an internet retailer that has caused job losses in other industries.[54] Such charges are vigorously denied by *The Post*'s editor, Marty Baron, who says Bezos has 'never suggested a story to anybody here, he's never critiqued a story, he's never suppressed a story.'[55]

The greater danger is that the excellence of journalism behind paywalls simply widens the divide between those willing to spend money on *The Times* or *The New Yorker* and those who are not. The difference between the so-called 'informed' and 'uninformed' voting publics was starkly apparent in both the EU referendum and the US presidential elections of 2016. Those unwilling to pay for news are not going without information, but are being fed via the internet what is, at best, the junk-food of click-bait—or, at worst, deeply misleading or false news, trolling, porn, libel and hate speech.

Facebook and Google still benefit from the 1996 US Telecommunications Act, passed before they even existed, that largely absolves them from responsibility for the content they host on their platforms. A similar system has been established in the UK and across Europe. Back then, the internet was seen merely as a tube through which information could travel like a telephone line, but algorithms now promote some forms of material and relegate others to keep people's attention, while Facebook deploys artificial intelligence to block any pictures of naked genitals, breasts and buttocks that might offend users. Among traditional journalists there is often disbelief that a site so good at spotting a stray nipple cannot take responsibility for the kind of false stories that see Hillary Clinton accused of running a paedophile ring from a Washington pizzeria.

But Facebook's nudity ban also shows the difficulty of trying to police billions of posts with imperfect algorithms which have blocked photos of breastfeeding mothers, Renaissance statues in Italy and the 1972 Pulitzer-winning photograph of a naked girl running in terror from napalm attacks during the Vietnam war.[56] Although these sites are now clearly more than neutral platforms for content, the prospect of Silicon Valley's algorithms or even teams of human editors taking full responsibility for deciding what is true—and what isn't—is no more appealing than 'fake news' itself. Zuckerberg was probably speaking from the heart when he said: 'I feel fundamentally uncomfortable sitting here in California in an office making content policy decisions for people around the world.'[57]

Both Google and Facebook, along with other tech companies, have tried to get better at removing the most extreme material, including fully 40,000 terrorist videos in 2017 alone.[58] They have also experimented with fact-checkers that can tag stories as false. But anyone hoping such measures can come to the rescue of reasoned debate may be waiting a while yet. An analysis of the fifty most shared items of false news in 2017 shows that despite fact checkers having produced comprehensive rebuttals for thirty-one of them, they received just a tiny fraction— 0.5 per cent—of the Facebook shares generated by the original claims.[59] In this regard, as in so many others, social media is replicating a trend established by the old media in the 1990s, when the likes of Boris Johnson were making up stories in Brussels. The European Commission office in London set up its own unit called to refute such claims but, by its own admission, often found it would get 'only the last paragraph' in newspaper stories. After twenty-five years of existence, the Commission's 'euro-myths' website was running at more than 700 items, the most successful of which had readership numbered in the tens of thousands.[60] By contrast, some of Johnson's stories, which have been recycled and repeated for years, will be known and believed by tens of millions.

There have even been suggestions that rebuttals may do more harm than good. Some studies detect a possible 'Backfire Effect' in which people who agree with a statement become more convinced than ever it is true if shown evidence that it is false.[61] After all, if you are already convinced the 'MSM' lies, being told by one of its 'fact-checking units' that your beliefs are stupid is unlikely to make you think otherwise.

What can be done better is verifying social media accounts to remove the cloak of anonymity behind which trolls or bots do their most abusive work. Facebook has admitted that as many as 270 million of its accounts may be fake or duplicate and insists it is trying to remove them [62] But the business model for social media companies is still based on making it as easy as possible to sign up and, unless they take decisive action themselves, calls will only get louder for legislation that might require users to provide proof of identity.

But whatever happens, false news, trolling, bots and extreme content are not going to be eradicated any time soon. Part of the answer, perhaps, is to educate people in how to read and watch news, how to tell the difference between a credible source and a Russian troll, how to spot a real story and one that is fake.

This means recognising that news is not merely a commodity or a business but a public good necessary to sustain democracy.

In Britain, such values are enshrined in the mission of the BBC to inform, educate and entertain, as well as its legal obligation to stay within the public sphere and help voters sort what is real from what is not. More than ever, the UK's regulated and impartial broadcasters, including ITV News, Channel 4 News and, yes, Murdoch's Sky News, need to be nurtured and protected as unique habitats where democratic debate can prosper. Their task is probably harder than at any time in British broadcasting history as they are attacked, not just by political parties and the *Daily Mail*, but also by legions of trolls mobilised by the alt-right and alt-left media. Funding cuts, so casually imposed on the BBC by David Cameron and George Osborne before they left office, do not help. Nor does the attitude of almost anyone in politics, including myself in the past, that the BBC is a punch bag on which to take out their frustrations with the world.

Andrew Marr, who has watched all this unfold over the past thirty years with a wary eye, says the shows he hosts on the BBC are designed to nurture the deliberative, consensual debate necessary for democracy. But he feels the shrillness of the new information age intruding.

He says: 'My biggest problem is the lack of civility but I suppose my job is to be the still small voice of calm in what is becoming a louder and louder environment. I want to keep the public square open so it is a space where people can disagree while still treating each other with respect; where you can have a civilised conversation on neutral ground without people shouting. Even what might be seen as the centre is now getting as angry as everyone else. We're getting quite close to the point where you cannot have that debate. But I know—I hope—there are still millions of people who want to hear a grown-up conversation.'[63]

When I go to meet Marr, he is sitting in a pub in Primrose Hill, London, nursing a ginger beer which he is only drinking, he explains quickly, because he has just had an operation on his teeth and was told to stay off alcohol. Conversation quickly turns to his complaints about how the old-fashioned pubs nearby have been bought and closed by property developers who care nothing for their local community. Even though Marr has spent his entire career in national media, he seems to light up when discussing local stories. At one point, he leaves the table and returns triumphantly waving a copy of the recently opened local newspaper. He wants to show me how, even in this wealthy part of London, it still covered stories of gang killings.

Marr is right to highlight local news because it goes to the heart of the decay in democracy. The channels that once enabled people to know what was going on in their area, to sort fact from rumour and, above all, to have their own stories heard, have dried up.

The big tech companies, which newspapers claim have swallowed much their advertising revenue, are trying to address the issue. Facebook has said it is moving local news publishers higher up in its news feed, while Google has said it will invest $300m in helping news organisations fight fake news and expand.[64] Google is also piloting a project called Bulletin, a crowdsourced form of citizen journalism that allows users to share stories, photos and videos of events in their communities on a smartphone app.[65] But local news sites are now heavily dependent on traffic from these tech giants and even the slightest change in algorithms can have unintended or outsized impacts. For instance, efforts by Facebook to combat false news by prioritising posts from friends and family appear to have inflicted further damage on local newspapers in the US.[66]

One idea that has been mooted is to impose a special levy on the tech companies to support reporting of local councils and courts.[67] A fund could be created and administered by a charity or an independent trust that would issue grants if conditions of professional standards and impartiality were met. There are already examples of websites that have helped fill the void left behind by the decline of local newspapers—and with much lower overheads. But the fragility of such new infrastructure has been shown by the closure of the *Port Talbot Magnet* or that of the award-winning Gothamist website in New York.[68]

# # #

Local news has helped to restore local democracy 60 miles north of New York in a small town called Garrison, overlooking the Hudson River. There, local people showed not only they could meet the challenges of the new information age, but tackle one of the biggest beasts of the old media at the same time.

It was 2007 when Roger Ailes, the monstrous and by-then paranoid chief executive of Fox News, bought himself a weekend retreat in Garrison. He swiftly fortified his hilltop home by buying up neighbouring properties, cutting down surrounding trees and installing an underground bunker that he filled with survival rations.[69]

The following year, he purchased the area's sleepily old-fashioned newspaper, *The Putnam County News & Recorder*, made his wife Elizabeth the publisher, and began transforming it into a print version of Fox News. It carried religiously-fired and moralising editorials, attacked local liberals who wanted laws to rein in new development and began campaigning for Republican candidates favoured—or even hand-picked—by Ailes across a wider district known as Philipstown. At one stage, all reference to Barack Obama winning a high school mock presidential election was cut from a report in the *News & Recorder*, while a later headline said Ailes had been 'hailed as an angel' for promising a charitable donation. When the editor of the *News & Recorder* began to get doubts, he found himself being followed by black SUVs with tinted windows that turned to be driven by News Corp security staff.[70]

Jacob Weisberg, the editor of *Slate*, who also has a home nearby, wrote about Ailes's apparent desire for siege and conflict, saying: 'He could have moved there to live and let live. Instead, in a way that seems to have been almost involuntary, he recapitulated the culture war he was already busily inciting at a national level. Within a short time of his arrival, town meetings turned ugly. Issues of patriotism, religion and political correctness overtook the normal debates about road paving and property taxes. Single-handedly and almost instantaneously, he injected a peaceable civic space with an aggression and unpleasantness that weren't there before.'[71]

Dave Merandy was among the local Democrats targeted by Ailes when he ran for office in Cold Spring, bordering Garrison and down the hill from Ailes's property. 'We're just a tiny village,' he tells me when I reach him by phone, 'but Roger Ailes threw everything he could at us. His candidates would get a lot of coverage in the paper, it would run their pictures and we would get nothing; he had complete control over the news.'[72] In 2010, Merandy joined up with a group of other locals— led by a Dar Williams, a folk singer, and Gordon Stewart, a former speechwriter for Jimmy Carter—to do something about what they called the 'Ailes problem'. Their solution was to set up a rival publication online called Philipstown.info run by Stewart and staffed with refugees from Ailes's newspaper. Stewart was determined it should be politically neutral and copiously fair.

Although Ailes was furious, it was enough to turn the tide. Along with other Democrats, Merandy got re-elected after boycotting *News & Recorder* sponsored debates. Ailes took legal action against Williams and four others, including Merandy's wife, Stephanie Hawkins, over Facebook posts. She describes getting 'cease and desist' letters at home and at work from Ailes's high-powered Manhattan lawyers. 'It cost me $6,000; he was trying to scare me; he was a bully,' says Hawkins.[73]

And then, all of a sudden, the battle was over. In 2016, Ailes was forced out at Fox News after being shamed as a serial sexual harasser. Hawkins says Ailes was 'never seen here again' and the following year he died in Florida. Philipstown.info, renamed the *Highlands Current*, is thriving and expanding with print editions in competition to what Hawkins describes as a 'de-fanged' *News & Recorder*.

As for Merandy, he has been elected mayor of Cold Spring and says the media coverage he gets is 'pretty fair'. He then grumbles that they 'have their moments when they give me a hard time'—which is, of course, exactly what the relationship between journalists and elected politicians, be they national or local, should be.

Politics

Much of this book has been about Britain and America because the fate of these two democracies has so often been intertwined. Tony Blair followed Bill Clinton's recipe for success in winning elections before he then followed George W. Bush into the wars in Afghanistan and Iraq. The global financial crisis began in New York and swiftly spread to the City of London. The victories of Brexit and Donald Trump happened within a few months of each other in 2016 when both appeared to be driven by similar surges of nationalism and populism.

And, as we have seen, the impact of technology designed in Silicon Valley has swept eastwards to have deep impacts on both Washington and Westminster as it disrupts the norms of democracy, just as it has disrupted the old newspaper industry and everything else.

But, in looking for solutions to the current crisis, the differences between the UK and US matter too. Compared to the glittering circus of billion-dollar presidential campaigns, British elections have usually been dowdy and even slightly dull affairs. American political consultants who fly into London to teach their British counterparts the secrets of their success often seem frustrated that their cutting-edge campaign techniques cannot be applied so effectively in the UK because lack of money or more stringent regulations get in the way.

The most noticeable contrast has been the absence in Britain of that toxic tide of negative TV attack adverts that has been washing over every American campaign since 1960. Some of the most noxious racially charged adverts were made by Roger Ailes—before he became a cable news executive—and Lee Atwater for the Republicans in the 1988 presidential campaign. One showed menacing prisoners going through a 'revolving door' as they were let out early from jail in a scheme supported by Michael Dukakis, the Democratic candidate. Others focused specifically on Willie Horton, a black prisoner who had escaped while on furlough and later raped a white woman.

Ever since Britain's first commercial channels were launched in the 1950s, all forms of political advertising have been illegal on radio and television except for party political broadcasts, which are strictly rationed according to support at previous elections.[74] For a long time, it meant that billboard poster advertising became the single biggest item of expenditure in elections. The Conservatives generally outspent Labour by a factor of more than two to one. In 1992, Tory attack posters appeared on 4,500 billboard sites compared to Labour's 2,200[75] while the advertising campaign designed by Steve Hilton that featured the 'New Labour, New Danger' slogan cost £13 million between 1996 and 1997.[76]

But this relatively stable system has been turned on its head. The old billboard posters have virtually disappeared from high streets, while ever increasing amounts of money are spent on social media advertising to put attack adverts straight into Facebook news feeds. In the EU referendum, the Leave campaign devoted fully 98 per cent of its advertising budget to social media. The proportion was lower in the 2017 General Election, when parties spent heavily on targeted direct mail[77] but the amount going on digital advertising still more than doubled compared to the contest between David Cameron and Ed Miliband two years earlier—which itself had seen unprecedented sums going to digital.[78] In the US, spending on social media increased by nearly 800 per cent compared to the previous presidential election as the big money began to migrate from TV to digital advertising.[79]

Democracy has always required rules to operate effectively but there is now almost universal consensus that these need to be updated. Facebook's founder Mark Zuckerberg has promised to prevent Russians or any other malevolent force buying adverts using fake accounts until their identity and affiliation have been authenticated. He has also indicated support for legislative proposals in America to require public disclosure of who is paying for adverts and a public register of different variations of political messages targeted at users.[80] In Britain, at the time of writing, the Information Commissioner was considering even tougher measures requiring digital companies to reveal how and why individuals' data is used to target them for political advertising.[81]

Whatever the fate of the many proposals washing around, there is good reason to doubt if any of them will be adequate. The speed with which technology changes and the murkiness of the world of political strategy and communications makes the task of those with oversight very difficult. Even if it is a stretch to blame Cambridge Analytica for the victories of Brexit and Trump, the potential for highly sophisticated analytics and targeted adverts determining the result of future elections will grow. Any campaign would be crazy not to use them but the advantage will usually be with the deepest pockets and lowest morals.

The heart of the problem is not Russian ads, the theft of data, or even the lack of transparency about the content or targeting of such messages. It is the existence of political advertising on the internet in the first place.

# # #

Although political campaigns have always tried to target their messages to different groups of voters, historically, they have been pretty poor at it for the same reason that the effectiveness of advertising was once so notoriously haphazard. As John Wanamaker, a US department store owner, once said: 'Half the money I spend on advertising is wasted; the trouble is, I don't know which half.'

In the 1990s when Derek Draper and Steve Hilton were involved in designing messages for their respective parties, the height of sophistication was to conduct a focus group of maybe twenty people in a marginal seat and test whether a new poster might make them switch their votes. But, as technology has improved, so has the effectiveness of advertising. In years to come, a combination of data analytics and psychometric social media advertising is likely to mean individual voters are targeted with obscure or even contradictory adverts that tap into their deepest fears or desires. Self-learning algorithms that fine-tune messages with millions of variations could put much of this even beyond the control of the campaigns themselves let alone an external regulator.

As Matthew Taylor, the chief executive of the RSA and a former head of the Downing Street policy unit, puts it: 'Politicians' desire to manipulate public opinion has not changed. What has changed is the weaponry available to them. We used to be armed with rifles; they now have nukes.'[82]

In Britain, the best solution would be to ban, or at least ration, political advertising on social media. It is how party political broadcasts have worked for almost a century, and there are very few politicians or voters who would want to change these rules to allow US-style adverts onto British television. Extending the ban would set a level playing field for everyone, preventing the result of elections being distorted by billionaires pushing their personal agenda, and giving political leaders less reason to humiliate themselves going cap-in-hand to rich donors for the cash needed to pay for such adverts.

If anyone worried that the absence of attack adverts would reduce engagement with democracy, Facebook and other digital platforms could easily allocate campaigns space on their feeds for untargeted adverts like the political broadcasts that already appear on TV. And there would still be nothing to stop a campaign posting a video on Facebook or YouTube that went viral because people liked it—but that would depend on the quality of a campaign's message, not the depth of its donors' pockets. If elections are meant to be fought on a level playing field, campaigns should not be able to buy more attention for their messages either directly through such advertising, or by purchasing 'likes' and hiring 'bots' to push content higher up in news feeds.

The last big change to Britain's electoral laws implemented Patrick Neill's Report on Standards in Public Life in 1998 that recommended disclosure of political donors' identities and the introduction of strict spending limits in election campaigns. But a long since forgotten recommendation of that ground-breaking report said that, because technology was likely to overtake existing legislation banning political advertising on TV, the law should 'be reviewed to ensure that its reach is sufficiently wide to block attempts at evasion by new modes of communication.'[83] The issue was kicked over to the new Electoral Commission, which eventually ruled that banning online political advertising might contravene the right to free speech.[84] Back then, there was some nervousness among ministers that the European Court of Human Rights could rule against the ban on television advertising.[85] But when it was given the chance to do just that in 2013, the court upheld the law prohibiting TV political adverts in the UK, albeit by only nine votes to eight, on the grounds that it protected 'the democratic debate and process from distortion by powerful financial groups with advantageous access to influential media.'[86] At the time, the court did not believe social media was a similar threat, but there is a good argument to make that circumstances have substantially altered since. Social media adverts are usually in the short video format that closely resembles negative attack ads on American TV. And the case for banning them altogether is even stronger than it is for broadcasting since individual voters can be targeted with tailor-made messages.

Gavin Millar QC, who specialises in media law, says: 'We have always taken the position that TV and radio advertising has to be controlled. The problem is that people have only just begun evaluating the impact of advertising on the internet. I believe it would be possible to ban political advertising, particularly if you were not prohibiting content on the internet, merely the purchase of ads which give one campaign or another an unfair advantage. That is a well-established principle.'[87]

Doubtless, there will be some who object to extending a ban on political advertising to Facebook and other sites, saying it would be the thin end of the wedge and open the possibility of banning billboards, direct mail or even the humble leaflet. But all of these have been part of the political system for years whereas digital advertising is a new phenomenon already having a huge impact on democracy. Another measure that should be considered would be to reduce spending limits for campaigns so they have less money to chuck around in the first place. In fact, targeted social media adverts aimed at key groups of voters in marginal seats are already making a mockery of local campaign spending limits since they are often claimed as national campaign expenditure.[88]

In America it would certainly be impossible to impose a ban on digital advertising, since courts there have interpreted the First Amendment guaranteeing rights of free speech to strike down even the mildest restrictions on advertising or existing laws on campaign finance.[89] What may yet be possible is to protect the other flank in this debate: the harvesting and use of people's data, and not only in political campaigns.

In May 2018, Europe's General Data Protection Regulation (GDPR) came into effect, placing new requirements on how companies like Facebook and Google collect and handle users' personal information, as well as strengthening peoples' rights over it. Zuckerberg said Facebook will offer its users all over the world similar, if not quite the same, privacy controls, even though his company then swiftly moved 1.5 billion users in Africa, Asia, Australia and Latin America outside Europe's jurisdiction.[90]

The British government has said GDPR will be maintained even after Brexit and political parties have been scrambling to re-think how they have been using data to avoid potentially debilitating fines from the authorities. Even existing lists of supporters' emails that have been built previously could become a potential liability if people have not explicitly opted-in to their data being used. The Tories collected emails and other data by offering people the chance to calculate how much their income tax might be cut. When I was working for the Party, Labour built lists of voters with a tool that calculated what number baby to have been born under the NHS one was. For instance, I am, apparently, baby number 12,279,106 welcomed into the world by our NHS and the price I have paid for knowing that is the surrender of my email address and age to my former colleagues at the party.[91]

It is not hard to find officials from any party who privately complain that the advent of GDPR is putting an unnecessary regulatory burden on them. But some also acknowledge the bigger issue is that any wrong-doing or intrusion into privacy is unlikely to emerge until after voting has taken place. Enforcement action such as fines will not change the result and, particularly in one-off contests like a referendum, the incentive to purchase data of dubious origins from brokers or scrape it off the internet will still be there. At the time of writing, it is still a bit of a mystery why Vote Leave decided to spend £2.7 million with AggregateIQ, an obscure digital adverts and data firm linked to Cambridge Analytica, based 4,800 miles away in Canada. Martin Moore, a senior fellow at King's College, London says the location of AggregateIQ will make it difficult ever to discover what happened. 'If you are outside the jurisdiction of the UK, you can gather data of all kinds in all kinds of ways not subject to UK data protection laws. Trying to track it back is virtually impossible.'[92]

Several ideas have been mooted to tackle this, including the idea that information regulators would be able to make unannounced audits of political campaigns, a bit like drugs tests in sport, to check that their data—and the way it is being used—complied with privacy laws.[93]

In the end, however, rule changes for the conduct of politics will be less relevant to the future of democracy than the extent to which campaigns learn to adapt to the digital world that they—and the voting public—now inhabit.

# # #

Bill Clinton and Tony Blair had won elections by developing a message that appealed to as many people as possible—particularly those on the centre ground—which they then pushed as hard as they could through the media.

But that formula began to lose its potency over the next quarter of a century. It became progressively more difficult to deliver messages to voters without it being filtered through, at best, the world-weary cynicism of the media—or more likely put through the mincing machine of its hostile contempt. As politicians sought to spin their way out of trouble, the more distrustful the media and the public became of politics in general. And hopes that the new information age might revitalise politics through the empowerment of voters, as it briefly did with Barack Obama in 2008, largely evaporated as campaigns became addicted to data and microtargeting or the grim world of social media attack adverts, further debasing democracy.

Instead, digital technology has helped populists and charlatans gain huge audiences or, in some cases, even to win elections. But too many mainstream politicians from the centre-left and centre-right seem to throw their hands up in despair at the prospect of ever competing with the extremism that flies so far and fast on social media.

There is no easy answer, not least because digital campaigning does favour emotional resonance and clarity rather nuance and moderation. But it is nonetheless worth looking at what works—and what doesn't.

Even though the trolls that patrol social media on Jeremy Corbyn's behalf do nothing for democracy, there is more to his digital operation than that. When he first ran for the Labour leadership in 2015, his campaign immediately spotted that their best hope of success lay in galvanising party members and signing-up new ones with messages on social media designed to inspire rather than depress. In contrast, blindsided mainstream candidates did little to sign up new members as they pitched their campaigns towards the traditional media. When it became clear that Corbyn was a genuine challenger, some of his rivals panicked and said new members should be prevented from taking part in the contest. Trying to take votes away from people has never been a good way of winning their support but, remarkably, when Labour MPs tried to oust Corbyn a year later in 2016, they made further procedural efforts to limit the franchise in the leadership election.[94]

Many of these MPs are my friends whose principles I share. But I could never understand why they seemed resigned to the notion they would never be able to recruit new members themselves, particularly at a time when so many Remain voters had been left distraught by Corbyn's tepid support for EU membership in the referendum. These were politicians who, presumably, went into their profession because they thought they had powerful skills of persuasion. But, they abandoned the battlefield to a far left fringe that had only just stumbled out of the woods.

In France, Emmanuel Macron proved that the new information age does not have to be the dominated by either the far left or the far right. Macron went about creating policies for a new party by sending volunteers out to conduct 25,000 fifteen-minute voter interviews, in a strategy modelled on Barack Obama's breakthrough campaign in 2008.[95] By the time he was running for president Macron claimed his new party, *En Marche*, already had as many members as the Socialist Party.[96] When he was confronted by angry workers outside a factory, Macron broadcast it live on Facebook.[97] And, when the Russian hackers came for him, like they had for Hillary Clinton—just days before his election as president— his digital team was ready, laying traps and false trails to frustrate them or waste their time.[98]

Macron is obviously a very different creature to Corbyn, but they share many of the characteristics needed to succeed in the digital world—or least one with a relatively level playing field. Both display a healthy insouciance for critics in the press, they are comfortable in their own skin, and their teams understand that what goes viral on the internet is very different to what might make a splash in *The Guardian* or *Le Monde*. Macron's water bottle flip on Twitter—'*Voilà*', with 2 million views, was to social media authenticity what looking presidential used to be to his analogue forebears.[99] He is also deeply aware of the dangers of these new forms of communication and, since he became French president, has promised new laws to strictly regulate the content of social media in future elections to limit the damage that can be inflicted by Russia or anyone else.[100] It remains to be seen what effect that will have but, at every stage, Macron has demonstrated a willingness to engage in this new political territory rather than retreat from it.

There is no innate reason why other politicians from the centre-left and centre-right cannot inspire and excite in what is, admittedly, a tougher environment. To do so, they should learn from the success of Corbyn, the Leave campaign and Trump so that they too can make an emotional connection with voters or even offer their own version of insurgency. They need to develop better arguments that allow people to locate their patriotic and cultural identity in the modern world rather than the never-never land of inward-looking atavistic nationalism. They can learn how to campaign with new technology so that they are popular without having to be populist.

Above all, however, they must address head-on the challenges of this age, which include the wealth and disruptive power of technology itself.

Technology

Jimmy Wales is sick and tired of Wikipedia being described as what the internet might have been if only more tech entrepreneurs had stuck to their early ideals—not least because the next sentence usually points out how he is a lot poorer than them.

And, indeed, Wikipedia's own entry on its founder estimates Wales's net worth at around $1 million. That is compared to the combined total of $388 billion for Amazon's Jeff Bezos, Microsoft's Bill Gates, Facebook's Mark Zuckerberg, and Google's Larry Page and Sergey Brin.

'Yeah, yeah, tell me about it,' says Wales when we meet in a café near his Marylebone home. He then explains how the absence of adverts and aggressive data harvesting—or anything which might make any money—was really an accident. Recalling how he set up Wikipedia, which went on to become the fifth most popular site in the world, he says: 'I just remember thinking, "wow, this is amazing, we can share knowledge and that seems like a good a use of the internet." In the early days, I thought maybe we would have ads one day but we didn't really need to worry about the business model; it was 2001 and we were in the dotcom boom. Then we had the dotcom crash and there was no more money, so a lot of the innovation came from that.'

Instead of paying salaries for teams of editors and managers to police Wikipedia entries, to which anyone can contribute material, the site relies on a community of volunteer administrators who try to stop trolls wrecking what they have built and to construct a system to prevent any one of them abusing their power. Wales compares it to a restaurant where, instead of putting diners in cages to prevent them stabbing each other with table knives, people co-exist in the shared assumption of good behaviour. 'Of course, occasionally, stabbings do happen in restaurants,' says Wales between mouthfuls of fried egg, 'but we generally sort that out together too.'

As its best, Wikipedia is a genuinely democratic space where reasoned, factual and open debate works its way towards a shared truth, then improves the knowledge of billions of people. In contrast, much of the social media sites run for—vast—profit consist either of Facebook's echo chambers where different groups reinforce their prejudices towards others, or what Wales describes as the 'bloodbath' of platforms like Twitter.

Even as successive waves of scandal crash over Silicon Valley, Wales resists any temptation to make a virtue of his relative poverty. Instead, he expresses sympathy for the tech firms and particularly for Zuckerberg who he describes as 'a good person'. He emphasises there is nothing wrong with selling ads—as he does himself with a separate for-profit company he has launched—or collecting data. 'It's just that a lot of things never occurred to them like the use of all that data for political shenanigans; it's just something no one ever really considered.'

He points out that Zuckerberg has maintained a 'fairly unprecedented degree of personal control' and he could yet announce 'he is changing the service in such a way it will reduce profits by half and stop being so aggressive because it's in the long-term interests of the company for the world not to hate it.'

But there is little history of industries self-regulating effectively, particularly powerful ones, and Wales recognises change is much more likely if there is regulatory pressure from government. It is a prospect that nonetheless fills him with dread. 'Politicians very rarely have a clue … too many MPs and Senators still get their secretaries to print off their emails to read,' he says. His fears that the regulators may be about to make matters worse deserve to be listened to, not least because he has a relatively small financial stake in it. 'They often propose solutions that won't work and they can be very short termist just because the public is a tizzy about something,' Wales adds, glancing at his phone and realising he is late for another meeting. 'I have to go,' he says, 'is it okay if I leave you to pay for breakfast?'

# # #

One politician who dared take the tech titans on—even before it was fashionable—is Margrethe Vestager, the European Commissioner for Competition. She has slapped fines totalling many billions of dollars on Apple, Google, Facebook and Amazon for failing to pay taxes or anti-competitive behaviour.

At a London tech festival, where she is later introduced on stage as 'the woman Silicon Valley fears most,' Vestager insists she is a 'tech-optimist' and says several times that 'Facebook is wonderful'. But she also acknowledges her concerns about technology go beyond the confines of her competition brief to include issues of data privacy and its effect on democracy. Vestager deletes her cookies 'more than once a week,' says she 'got scared after reading one paragraph' of Facebook's terms of service agreement and, although she has not gone so far as to put tape over her laptop's webcam to stop surveillance, adds that 'my husband keeps reminding me I should get it done.'

She goes on to list a series of fears about false news, political adverts on social media and microtargeting of voters leading to a 'kind of privatisation of public debate'. Such comments are seen by some of the tech firms as proof she has a 'political agenda'. That is, of course, exactly what politicians are meant to have and Vestager—who previously had been a liberal deputy prime minister of Denmark—says these issues are 'something of concern to any citizen who lives in a democracy—and I'm still a citizen.'

Democratic politicians and regulators, as well as citizens, have every right—even a duty—to engage with such issues. The laissez-faire era when technology was virtually free from all regulation is over and it is also the case that any such action is best done at a supranational level where institutions are strong enough to resist the power of these firms. The irony of Britain preparing to leave the EU just when it is needed most has not been lost on Vestager, who says '500 million citizens in Europe give me sufficient muscle.' I ask her whether Britain, on its own, will have the clout needed to get into the ring with the likes of Google and Facebook. 'That remains to be seen,' she replies with a thin smile, adding that British voters will have to decide on what sort of 'country they want to live in.'

Vestager was once criticised by Barack Obama who suggested her actions were the result of Europe's tech-envy because they 'can't compete' with Silicon Valley.[101] But, as the 'tech-lash' continued in the wake of election shocks and Facebook scandals, she has been more often cited as a role model for much bigger interventions.

Old instruments of political power are being dusted down in legislatures from Westminster to Washington and beyond. Some say that Google and Facebook should be broken up just as the Standard Oil was by anti-trust laws in America a century ago, because these tech giants operate an effective monopoly on data, the 'oil' of the digital economy.[102] Others have called for them to open up their 'black box' of algorithms and their data for others to use, just as AT&T was forced to with its patents, as a way of encouraging innovation.[103] Still more have argued the tech giants should be regulated like a utility for the public good or even nationalised.[104]

Some tech billionaires have themselves voiced support for new tax proposals that have more usually only been advocated by those on the left. Bill Gates has backed a 'robot tax' to pay for the retaining of displaced workers and to slow down the pace of automation.[105] Zuckerberg has joined the growing clamour for a Universal Basic Income, a regular payment to each citizen, irrespective of income or behaviour, to help people enjoy the enforced freedom of no longer having jobs. He even said: 'People like me should pay for it.'[106] Such rhetoric has not, however, generally been reflected in the tax revenues received from companies like Microsoft and Facebook, which have often been accused of jumping through whatever loopholes they can find.[107]

Despite tech firms saying repeatedly that they are not opposed to all regulation, it remains highly probable that anything they regard as too draconian will be met with fierce resistance. They are probably justified in being perturbed about laws on technology made by politicians who have scant understanding of it. And it is doubtful that solutions to fast-moving problems can be found entirely in tax-and-regulate measures that date back to the early years of the twentieth century, when democratic governments first tried to tackle corporate power.

# # #

The challenge the big tech firms present to democracy is not only to do with their size and destructive power but also to do with their core business model. Google and Facebook make their money largely through advertising, much of which is harmless or even beneficial if you are looking for a cheap flight or second-hand car: Facebook pays for a service that enables people to stay in touch with those they love by selling adverts, just as Google does when it guides people through the world's greatest library.

But there has long been a fear, ever since Vance Packard wrote *The Hidden Persuaders* in the 1950s, that advertising is also a form of manipulation that can use psychological and subliminal techniques. And if that was a problem back then, it is an even bigger one now as social media becomes ever-more addictive, adverts on Facebook break down the distinction between the personal and the public as they jostle for attention alongside photographs of children and the news, and all the while algorithms crunch through data to target users' minds with greater precision.

Jimmy Wales's Wikipedia has an entry[108] listing more than 100 cognitive flaws in human beings, including many of those like confirmation bias and in-group polarisation, that early chapters of this book have already discussed can affect what people believe. These cognitive flaws have always preyed upon by marketing, PR and spin. But the development of artificial intelligence will create further opportunity for manipulation—perhaps beyond the understanding of any human engineer—across not only not only the media and politics but all human interactions.

In these circumstances, any organisation feeding data into self-learning algorithms will face louder calls for greater scrutiny or regulation. Already, concerns about the effect of all forms of advertising—not just political—have seen critics of Facebook and Google suggesting their business model should be replaced by a flat-rate fee to use an ad-free service, even if that prices poorer people off them all together.[109]

As politicians and regulators begin to wake from a thirty-year slumber, there will inevitably be increased tension between technology and democracy—between Silicon Valley and Capitol Hill. But there is also a recognition among progressives in both tech and politics that they will yet need each other in facing down the challenge of populism at home and competition from alternative models abroad.

China has copied Western technology but has also created an entirely different internet that it is now extending into the comprehensive surveillance over its entire population. The regime intends to allocate resources such as housing according a 'citizen's score' based on the digital records of their political persuasions, comments, associations, and even consumer habits.[110] Although that may sound like an Orwellian nightmare, by many measures China is succeeding where the West is failing. Trust in institutions such as government and the media rose by 27 per cent in 2017 among Chinese citizens, even as for those of the United States it fell by 37 per cent.[111] At the same time China's home-grown technology, fuelled by huge state investment in Artificial Intelligence, is no longer just copying Silicon Valley but is estimated by *The Economist* to be ten to fifteen years away from catching up and maybe overtaking it.[112]

For all the flaws of Facebook and other technology firms, it is better to have northern Californians running the web than to cede it into the hands of autocrats. You do not see the chief executives of Tencent, Alibaba and Baidu, China's home-grown tech titans, publicly agonising about issues like truth, surveillance and democracy as Mark Zuckerberg now does on an almost daily basis.

Tim Berners-Lee, who created the world wide web back in 1989, says the solution is not to constrain, break-up or punish Western technology but to guide it in a different direction. He suggests putting tech firms under a legal obligation so they are required not to maximise profit but 'to maximise social good.'[113] A similar message is delivered by Mustafa Suleyman, who founded a company in London called DeepMind that he sold to Google for £400 million in 2014. A former left-wing activist, he is frustrated by the way the world's brightest minds have been used to invent new ways to 'order pizza on a phone when half a billion people don't have access to clean water' and has called for a fundamental 'reorientation of market incentives.'[114]

Whether it is crowd-sourcing news, improving health outcomes with big data, or using blockchain technology to control and earn money from our own information, there are vast possibilities for scientific and social progress to advance together.[115]

Western democracy must mend, rather than end, its thirty-year abusive relationship with the new information age. The rules by which news is produced and elections are conducted are in desperate need of reform. And tech firms need to understand that the benefits they get from a stable society, as well as the dynamism of free markets, and the creativity that comes with free speech, do not come free-of-charge. We need some of that idealistic spirit of '89 together with greater oversight, higher taxes and a legal duty to do more than make profits.

The introduction to this book described how the command, Ctrl+Alt+Del, had been designed to fix a computer that had crashed without the need to kick out the power supply at the mains. Holding all three keys down simultaneously meant the system could re-start with minimal damage—but pressing any one of them individually did nobody any good.

This book has shown how controlling information is unlikely to succeed outside totalitarian regimes, why populist alternatives have challenged progressive values, and that, even in our despair, we must avoid deleting democracy altogether.

Instead, the truly bold response to the current crisis is to harness technology to become more, and not less, democratic.

It's time for a 'soft re-boot' without disconnecting the power supply people have through democracy to speak out, to force change at the ballot box, and to rein in the world's most powerful corporations.
Here's to the three-fingered salute: Ctrl+Alt+Del.

Notes

INTRODUCTION

1. 'Hillary Clinton has got this. Probably. Very probably', *The Economist*, 8 November 2016. https://www.economist.com/blogs/graphicdetail/2016/11/election-forecasting-wars
2. https://www.youtube.com/watch?v=K_lg7w8gAXQ
3. Tom Warren, 'Bill Gates admits Control-Alt-Delete was a mistake, blames IBM', The Verge, 26 September 2103, https://www.theverge.com/2013/9/26/4772680/bill-gates-admits-ctrl-alt-del-was-a-mistake

1. HOW THE MEDIA CHALLENGED FOR CONTROL

1. Leon Aron, 'Everything You Think You Know About the Collapse of the Soviet Union Is Wrong', *Foreign Policy*, 20 June 2011, http://foreignpolicy.com/2011/06/20/everything-you-think-you-know-about-the-collapse-of-the-soviet-union-is-wrong/
2. Michael Binyon, 'Thatcher told Gorbachev Britain did not want German reunification', *The Times*, 11 September 2009, https://www.thetimes.co.uk/article/thatcher-told-gorbachev-britain-did-not-want-german-reunification-vwjg8nq375j
3. http://info.cern.ch/Proposal.html
4. Margaret Thatcher, Bruges speech, 20 September 1988.
5. Boris Johnson, *Daily Telegraph*, 15 September 2003.
6. *Daily Telegraph*, 31 May 1991.
7. Interview with author.
8. Boris Johnson, *Sunday Telegraph*, 3 May 1992, front page.
9. Boris Johnson, *Daily Telegraph*, 15 September 2003, https://www.telegraph.co.uk/news/uknews/1441470/Europe-my-part-in-its-downfall.html
10. Interview with author.
11. Interview with author.
12. Sonia Purnell, *Just Boris: The Irresistible Rise of a Political Celebrity*, London: Aurum, 2011, p. 123.

13. Interview with author.
14. BBC Radio 4, Desert Island Discs, 30 October 2005.
15. Interview with author.
16. Interview with author.
17. https://freedomhouse.org/reports
18. Bill Clinton, speech to the Seattle APEC Host Committee, 19 November 1993.
19. 'Talk Radio by the Numbers', Center for American Progress, 10 July 2007.
20. Zev Chafets, *Rush Limbaugh: An Army of One*, New York: Sentinel, 2010, p. 81.
21. Ibid., p. 80.
22. Rush Limbaugh, 'Everything I Say Here Has a Purpose', 18 August 2015, https://www.rushlimbaugh.com/daily/2015/08/18/everything_i_say_here_has_a_purpose/
23. Randy Bobbitt, *Us Against Them: The Political Culture of Talk Radio*, Lanham, MA: Lexington Books, 2010.
24. Fairness and Accuracy In Reporting, *The Way Things Aren't: Rush Limbaugh's Reign of Error*, New York: The New Press, 1 May 1995, p. 18.
25. Oliver Darcy, 'Rush Limbaugh evacuates Florida home after floating unfounded theories about Hurricane Irma', CNN, 8 September 2017, http://money.cnn.com/2017/09/08/media/rush-limbaugh-evacuates-hurricane-irma/index.html
26. Rush Limbaugh, 'I Never, Ever Said the Hurricane Was Fake News, Drive-Bys', 6 September 2017.
27. 'Rush Limbaugh's Original & Updated 35 "Undeniable Truths"', Lectric Law Library's Stacks, http://www.lectlaw.com/files/cur52.htm
28. Dana Milbank, 'The Bombastic Limbaugh Has Nothing to Say to Wanda Sykes', *Washington Post*, 12 May 2009, washingtonpost.com/wp-dyn/content/article/2009/05/11/AR2009051103385.html
29. 'Radio Host Charlie Sykes Says Conservative Media Will Give Cover To Trump', WFDD, 10 February 2017, http://www.wbur.org/hereandnow/2017/02/10/charlie-sykes
30. Zev Chafets, *Rush Limbaugh: An Army of One*, p. 85. See also Clarence Page, 'Rush Limbaugh Can Dish It Out, But He Sure Can't Take It', *Chicago Tribune*, 5 May 1993.
31. 'Tom Brokaw says "no thanks" to White House Correspondents' Dinner, Politico, 26 April 2013, https://www.politico.com/story/2013/04/tom-brokaw-white-house-correspondents-dinner-90427_Page2.html
32. James Fallows, *Breaking the News: How the Media Undermine American Democracy*, London: Vintage, 1997, pp. 10–14. Full disclosure: Fallows was my landlord when I worked in Washington between 2005 and 2009.
33. Ibid.
34. 'Trump Time Capsule #92: 'How the Media Undermine American Democracy', *The Atlantic*, 3 September 2016, https://www.theatlantic.com/notes/2016/09/trump-time-capsule-92-how-the-media-undermine-american-democracy/498461/
35. Kathleen Hall Jamieson and Paul Waldman, *The Press Effect: Politicians, Journalists, and the Stories That Shape the Political World*, Oxford: Oxford University Press, 2003, p. 167, and Joseph Cappella and Kathleen Hall Jamieson, *Spiral of Cynicism: The Press and the Public Good*, OUP, 1997.
36. Thomas E. Patterson, 'Doing Well and Doing Good', Kennedy School of Government,

Working Paper No. 01–001, Harvard University, December 2000, https://research.hks.harvard.edu/publications/getFile.aspx?Id=1

37. Richard Kreitner, 'Post-Truth and Its Consequences: What a 25-Year-Old Essay Tells Us About the Current Moment', *The Nation*, 30 November 2016.

38. Michael Brunson, *A Ringside Seat*, London: Hodder & Stoughton, 2000, p. 197.

39. Robert Harris, *Good and Faithful Servant: The Unauthorized Biography of Bernard Ingham*, London: Faber and Faber, 1990, p. 82.

40. See, for instance, Jackie Ashley, 'Profile—The Lobby', *New Statesman*, 18 October 1999, https://www.newstatesman.com/node/150017

41. *Sunday Telegraph*, 16 February 1997, p. 1.

42. The promise to sell off the Tote appeared in the Labour manifestos of 2001 and 2005 but the privatisation was only completed by the Conservative-led government in 2010.

43. Interview with author.

44. *The Sunday Telegraph*, 9 November 1997, front page.

45. Andrew Marr, *My Trade: A Short History of British Journalism*, London: Pan Macmillan, 2004, pp. 186–7.

46. Robin Cook, *The Guardian*, 7 January 2005, https://www.theguardian.com/politics/2005/jan/07/labour.uk

47. The James MacTaggart Memorial Lecture, Jeremy Paxman, 24 August 2007, http://www.bbc.co.uk/blogs/newsnight/2007/08/the_james_mactaggart_memorial_lecture.html

48. Martyn Lewis, 'Not my idea of good news', *The Independent*, 25 April 1993.

49. Izabella Kaminska, 'A lesson in fake news from the info-wars of ancient Rome', *Financial Times*, 17 January 2017, https://www.ft.com/content/aaf2bb08-dca2-11e6-86ac-f253db7791c6

50. Ken Auletta, 'Non-stop News', *The New Yorker*, 25 January 2010, https://www.newyorker.com/magazine/2010/01/25/non-stop-news

51. Hugh Cudlipp, quoted at length here: http://www.pressgazette.co.uk/sir-harold-evans-2013-hugh-cudlipp-lecture-full-written-version/

52. Harold Evans, *Good Times, Bad Times: The Explosive Inside Story of Rupert Murdoch*, London: Bedford Square Books, 2016, preface to the fifth edition.

53. Ibid.

54. Walter Cronkite, interviewed in Robert Greenwald's 2004 film, *Outfoxed*.

55. Chris Horrie and Peter Chippindale, *Stick It Up Your Punter! Rise and Fall of The Sun*, London: William Heinemann, 1990.

56. Dennis Potter, interviewed in LWT's *Without Walls*, 4 April 1994.

57. Leveson Inquiry, transcript 25 April 2012, National Archives, p. 54.

58. Chris Horrie and Peter Chippindale, *Stick it up Your Punter!*

59. Jerome Tuccille, *Rupert Murdoch: Creator of a Worldwide Media Empire*, Washington, DC.: Beard Books, 1989, pp. 28–29.

60. 'Harper Collins Apologises to Patten', BBC News, 6 March 1998, http://news.bbc.co.uk/1/hi/uk/62877.stm

61. Rupert Murdoch interview with William Shawcross, *Vanity Fair*, September 1999.

62. Jack Shafer, 'Murdoch Lies to the Financial Times', Slate, 24 March 2007, http://

www.slate.com/articles/news_and_politics/press_box/2007/05/murdoch_lies_to_
the_financial_times.html

63. The James MacTaggart Memorial Lecture, Rupert Murdoch, Edinburgh, 25 August 1989.

64. Gabriel Sherman, *The Loudest Voice in the Room: How the Brilliant, Bombastic Roger Ailes Built Fox News—And Divided a Country*, New York: Random House, 2014, p. xii

65. Rupert Murdoch, Federal News Service transcript of speech to National Press Club, 26 February 1996.

66. Scott Collins, *Crazy Like A Fox: The Inside Story of How Fox News Beat CNN*, New York: Penguin Portfolio, 2004, p. 130.

67. Jon Micklethwaite and Adrian Woolridge, *The Right Nation: Conservative Power in America*, New York: Penguin, p. 162.

68. 'Turner Lashes Out At Murdoch, Comparing Him To "Late Fuhrer"', Chicago Tribune, 27 September 1996, http://articles.chicagotribune.com/1996-09-27/news/9609280152_1_fox-news-channel-turner-broadcasting-system-time-warner

69. 'In Taking On Fox, Democrats See Reward in the Risk', *The New York Times*, 1 October 2006.

70. https://web.archive.org/web/20060506230321/http://pewresearch.org/assets/files/trends2005-media.pdf

71. Jay D. Hmielowski, Michael A. Beam, and Myiah J. Hutchens, 'Structural Changes in Media and Attitude Polarization: Examining the Contributions of TV News Before and After the Telecommunications Act of 1996', *International Journal of Public Opinion Research*, Volume 28, Issue 2, 2 July 2015, https://doi.org/10.1093/ijpor/edv012

72. 'Rosen's Trust Puzzler: What Explains Falling Confidence in the Press?', Press Think, 17 April 2012, http://pressthink.org/2012/04/rosens-trust-puzzler-what-explains-falling-confidence-in-the-press/

73. Gabriel Sherman, *The Loudest Voice in the Room*, p. 197.

74. See Christian Wolmar, *Fire and Steam: A New History of the Railways in Britain*, London: Atlantic Books, 2007.

75. Interview with author.

76. Quoted in Aeron Davis, *Public Relations Democracy: Politics, Public Relations and the Mass Media in Britain*, Manchester: Manchester University Press, 2002.

77. Interview with author.

78. Piers Robinson, *The CNN Effect: The Myth of News, Foreign Policy and Intervention*, Abingdon: Routledge, 2002.

79. 'Hurd hits out again at media', *Daily Telegraph*, 10 September 1993.

80. Ken Auletta, 'Non-stop News', *The New Yorker*, 25 January 2010, https://www.newyorker.com/magazine/2010/01/25/non-stop-news

81. Rupert Murdoch, The James MacTaggart Memorial Lecture, Edinburgh, 25 August 1989.

82. Ben Bagdikian, *The Media Monopoly*, Boston, MA: Beacon Press, 1983.

83. Ashley Lutz, 'These 6 Corporations Control 90% Of The Media In America', Business Insider, 14 June 2012, http://uk.businessinsider.com/these-6-corporations-control-90-of-the-media-in-america-2012-6

84. Peter DiCola and Kristin Thomson, 'Radio Deregulation: Has it Served Musicians and Citizens?', The Future of Music Coalition, 18 November 2002, https://www.futureofmusic.org/article/research/radio-deregulation-has-it-served-musicians-and-citizens

2. HOW POLITICS TRIED TO REGAIN CONTROL

1. Cornell Legal Information Institute, 47 U.S. Code § 230—Protection for private blocking and screening of offensive material.
2. Bill Clinton, signing ceremony at the Library of Congress, 8 February 1996.
3. Andy Greenberg, 'Its been 20 Years Since This Man Declared Cyberspace Independence', Wired, 8 February 2016, https://www.wired.com/2016/02/its-been-20-years-since-this-man-declared-cyberspace-independence/
4. John Perry Barlow, 'A Declaration of the Independence of Cyberspace', Electric Frontier Foundation, https://www.eff.org/cyberspace-independence
5. Reno vs ACLU, US 521 (1997).
6. Bill Clinton, speech to the Seattle APEC Host Committee, 19 November 1993.
7. Sandra Weber, *The Internet*, New York: Infobase Publishing, 2003, p. 71.
8. Mike Shields, 'An Oral History of The First Presidential Campaign Websites in 1996', *Wall Street Journal*, 18 February 2016, https://www.wsj.com/articles/an-oral-history-of-the-first-presidential-campaign-websites-in-1996-1455831487?ns=prod/accounts-wsj
9. John Schwartz, 'Looking for Dole on the Web? Dot's the Real Way Home', *Washington Post*, 8 October 1996, https://www.washingtonpost.com/archive/politics/1996/10/08/looking-for-dole-on-web-dots-the-real-way-home/467abab5-d9e2-421c-b9d9-71f1be4a75be/?utm_term=.0dcb7372e472.
10. Peter Mandelson, *The Third Man: Life at the Heart of New Labour*, London: Harper Press, 2010, p. 151.
11. Interview with author.
12. Tony Blair, Leader's speech, Blackpool, 1994.
13. Interview with author.
14. Leader's speech, Blackpool, 1996, http://www.britishpoliticalspeech.org/speech-archive.htm?speech=202
15. David Hill, 'Letter to the Editor', *The Independent*, 22 May 1996.
16. Interview with author.
17. Richard Stengel and Eric Pooley, 'Masters of the Message', *Time*, 6 November 1996, http://content.time.com/time/magazine/article/0,9171,985538,00.html
18. Alastair Campbell, *Diaries Vol. Two: Power and the People, 1997–1999*, London: Hutchinson, 2011, p. 99.
19. Philip Gould and Patricia Hewitt, *Tribune*, 8 January 1993.
20. Philip Gould, *Unfinished Revolution: How the Modernisers Saved the Labour Party*, London: Little, Brown 1998, p. 333.
21. Tony Blair, *A Journey*, London: Arrow, 2011, p. 660.
22. Interview with author.

23. Interview with author.

24. Interview with author.

25. Interview with author.

26. Interview with author.

27. *The Sun*, 21 April 1997.

28. Interview with author.

29. Andrew Marr, 'Cry "God for Tony Blair, England and *The Sun*"', *The Independent*, 22 April 1997, http://www.independent.co.uk/incoming/cry-god-for-tony-blair-england-and-the-sun-5570832.html

30. http://www.britishpoliticalspeech.org/speech-archive.htm?speech=200

31. Interview with author.

32. https://www.theguardian.com/politics/1996/aug/08/labour.uk

33. David Butler and Dennis Kavanagh, *The British General Election of 1997*, London: Palgrave Macmillan, pp. 36–38.

34. Vanessa Thorpe, 'Major's banned Faust ad revealed, *The Observer*, 24 October 1999, https://www.theguardian.com/politics/1999/oct/24/labour.labour 1997to99

35. Donald MacIntyre, *Mandelson and the Making of New Labour*, London: Harper Collins 2000, p. 360

36. Tom Baldwin, *The Sunday Telegraph*, 9 November 1997, p. 1.

37. Fran Abrams, 'Blair: "I think I'm a pretty straight sort of guy"', *The Independent*, 17 November 1997, https://www.independent.co.uk/news/blair-i-think-im-a-pretty-straight-sort-of-guy-1294593.html

38. Gregory Palast, *The Observer*, 5 July 1998, p. 1.

39. *Daily Mail*, 8 July 1998, p. 2.

40. Interview with author.

41. British Social Attitudes, p. 23, Table A4, Trust in Government, 1986–2013, http://www.bsa.natcen.ac.uk/media/38978/bsa32_politics.pdf

42. Pew Research, Trust in Government, 1958–2013, http://www.people-press.org/2015/11/23/1-trust-in-government-1958-2015/

43. Evan Davis, *Post Truth: Peak Bullshit—and What We Can Do About It*, London: Little Brown, 2017, pp. 8–11

44. John F. Freie, *The Making of the Postmodern Presidency: From Ronald Reagan to Barack Obama*, Abindon: Routledge, 2010, p. 90.

45. Jessica Mathews, 'Saving America', Thomas Jefferson Foundation Medal Lecture in Citizen Leadership, University of Virginia, 2012.

46. Moisés Naím, 'Power Has Become Easier to Get, Harder to Use and Easier to Lose', 25 March 2014, https://www.huffingtonpost.com/moises-naim/power-has-become-easier-t_b_4651869.html

47. Joseph S. Nye, Philip Zelikow and David C. King. *Why People Don't Trust Government*, Boston, MA: Harvard University Press, 2007, p. 242.

48. Susan Pharr and Robert Putman (eds), *Disaffected Democracies: What's Troubling the Trilateral Countries?*, Princeton, NJ: Princeton University Press, 2000, http://www.people.fas.harvard.edu/~spharr/Documents/disaffected.PDF

49. Hannah Arendt, *Men in Dark Times*, New York: Harvest Books, 1970, p. 83.

50. John Lloyd, *The Power and the Story: The Global Battle for Journalism*, Atlantic Books, 2017, pp. 213–239.

51. President Bill Clinton, 8 March 2000.

52. 'Meddling publishers draw journalists' fire', *Moscow Times*, 4 March 1998.

53. Daphne Skillen, *Freedom of Speech in Russia: Politics and Media from Gorbachev to Putin*, Abingdon: Routledge, 2017, p. 222.

54. Ibid., Chapter 7.

55. https://www.youtube.com/watch?v=eZJx9bgwdv0

56. Angus Roxburgh, *The Strongman: Vladimir Putin and the Struggle for Russia*, London: I. B. Tauris, 2011, p. 88.

57. Ibid., p. 90.

58. Skillen, *Freedom of Speech in Russia*, p. 284.

59. Masha Gessen, *The Man Without a Face: The Unlikely Rise of Vladimir Putin*, London: Granta, 2012.

60. David Hoffman, 'Russian Media Policy Likened to Soviet Era', *Washington Post*, 14 September 2000, https://www.washingtonpost.com/archive/politics/2000/09/14/russian-media-policy-likened-to-soviet-era/36a9e14d-5de7–4502–843b-ce82e3c8e740/?utm_term=.f9b770032fb6

61. https://www.rferl.org/a/1142270.html

62. https://cpj.org/killed/europe/russia/

63. Ibid., p. 265.

64. Peter Pomerantsev, *Nothing is True and Everything is Possible: Adventures in Modern Russia*, London: Faber and Faber, 2017, pp. 79–81

65. Dmitry Sudakov, 'It was US and UK that sank Russia's Kursk submarine', *Pravda*, 12 August 2016, http://www.pravdareport.com/society/stories/1208–2016/121163-kursk_submarine-0/

66. 'The Accidental President', *The Economist*, 14 December 2000, http://www.economist.com/node/451229; 'Hanging chads' refers to partially punched card ballots.

67. Morris Fiorina, Samuel Abrams and Jeremy Pope, 'The 2000 U.S. Presidential Election: Can Retrospective Voting be Saved?', *British Journal of Political Science*, April 2003, Vol. 33, Issue 2, pp. 163–187, http://www.uvm.edu/~dguber/POLS125/articles/fiorina.htm

68. https://www.snopes.com/quotes/internet.asp

69. David Frum, *The Right Man: The Surprise Presidency of George W. Bush*, New York: Random House, 2003.

70. George W. Bush, Concord, New Hampshire, 29 January 2000.

71. Frank Bruni, *Ambling into History: The Unlikely Odyssey of George W. Bush*, New York: Harper Collins, 2002, p. 25.

72. Ibid.

73. Matt Bai, 'Rove's Way', *The New York Times* Magazine, 20 October 2002, https://www.nytimes.com/2002/10/20/magazine/rove-s-way.html

74. Ken Auletta, 'Fortress Bush', *The New Yorker*, 19 January 2004, https://www.newyorker.com/magazine/2004/01/19/fortress-bush

75. Karl Rove, The Base Strategy 2004, PBS Frontline, https://www.pbs.org/wgbh/pages/frontline/shows/architect/rove/2004.html; see also John Cloud, 'How the Wedge Issues Cut', *Time*, 17 October 2004, http://content.time.com/time/magazine/article/0,9171,725075,00.html

76. Lawrence F. Kaplan and William Kristol, *The War Over Iraq: Saddam's Tyranny and America's Mission, New York:* Encounter Books, 2003, pp. 56–57. See also David Noon, 'Cold War Revival: Neoconservatives and Historical Memory in the War on Terror', *American Studies*, Volume 48, Number 3, Fall 2007.

77. Anatol Lieven, *America Right or Wrong: An Anatomy of American Nationalism*, Oxford: Oxford University Press, 2012.

78. Eric Alterman, *What Liberal Media? The Truth About Bias and The News*, New York: Basic Books, 2002, p. 35.

79. Jon Micklewait and Adrian Woolridge, *The Right Nation: Why America is Different*, London: Penguin, p. 163.

80. 'It Pays to be Right', *The Economist*, 5 December 2002, http://www.economist.com/node/1482250

81. Bob Woodward, *Bush at War*, London: Simon and Schuster, 2002.

82. John Kampfner, 'The truth about Jessica', *The Guardian*, 15 May 2003, https://www.theguardian.com/world/2003/may/15/iraq.usa2

83. Tom Ridge, *The Test of Our Times*, New York: St Martin's, 2009, p. 239.

84. Ron Suskind, *The New York Times* Magazine, 17 October 2004.

85. Stephen Colbert, AV/TV Club 25 January 2006.

86. 'The Times and Iraq', *The New York Times*, 26 May 2004, https://www.nytimes.com/2004/05/26/world/from-the-editors-the-times-and-iraq.html

87. Dana Milbank, 'Curtains Ordered for Media Coverage of Returning Coffins', *Washington Post*, 21 October 2003, https://www.washingtonpost.com/archive/politics/2003/10/21/curtains-ordered-for-media-coverage-of-returning-coffins/13375c81-187e-4f91-a565-2ce8f3bf3549/?utm_term=.1fbd00b920da

88. Tom Baldwin and Gerard Baker, 'President Bush regrets his legacy as man who wanted war', *The Times*, 11 June 2008, https://www.thetimes.co.uk/article/president-bush-regrets-his-legacy-as-man-who-wanted-war-8mq2b8zn68w

89. Interview with author.

90. Larissa MacFarquhar, 'The Populist', *The New Yorker*, 16 February 2004, https://www.newyorker.com/magazine/2004/02/16/the-populist

91. Philip Gould, *The Unfinished Revolution: How New Labour Changed British Politics Forever*, London: Abacus, 1998, p. 173.

92. Figures from Liberal Democrat Party reproduced in Andrew Marr, *My Trade: A Short History of British Journalism*, London: Pan Macmillan, 2004, p. 180.

93. Blair memo, July 2000, http://news.bbc.co.uk/1/hi/uk_politics/836822.stm

94. Interview with author.

95. Interview with author.

96. Interview with author.

97. BBC Radio 4 archive, Today programme.

98. https://www.youtube.com/watch?v=r4bAuSgr9oQ

99. http://www.alastaircampbell.org/blog.php

100. Interview with author.

101. Interview with author.

102. *Sunday Express* memo, reprinted in *The Guardian*, 4 July 2003.

103. David Hughes and Rebecca Paveley, 'Blair is asked: Did Leo go to France for separate jabs?', *Daily Mail*, http://www.dailymail.co.uk/health/article-104889/Blair-asked-Did-Leo-France-separate-jabs.html

104. Sarah Womack, 'Blair silent over Leo's MMR jab', *Daily Telegraph*, 20 December 2001, https://www.telegraph.co.uk/news/uknews/1365829/Blair-silent-over-Leos-MMR-jab.html

105. Peter Oborne, *The Rise of Political Lying*, London: Simon and Schuster, 2005, pp. 180–182.

106. Interview with author.

107. See Matthew d'Ancona, *Post Truth: The New War on Truth and How to Fight Back*, London: Ebury, 2017, pp. 70–75 for a good account of this. Also Tammy Boyce, *Health, Risk and News: The MMR Vaccine and the Media*, Oxford: Peter Lang, 2007, pp. 56–57.

108. Carmen Paun, 'Trump offers vindication to vaccine skeptic doctor', Politico, 9 February 2017, https://www.politico.eu/article/disgraced-doctor-who-questioned-vaccine-safety-looks-to-trump-with-hope/

109. Nicole Rojas, 'UK health officials fear Russian cyber units are "spreading false information" on flu and measles jabs', *International Business Times*, 27 November 2017, https://www.ibtimes.co.uk/uk-health-officials-fear-russian-cyber-units-are-spreading-false-information-flu-measles-jabs-1648981

110. BBC Radio 4 Archive, Today programme.

111. Rod Liddle, 'Invasion of privacy? Or just hiding the truth', *The Guardian*, 23 December 2001, https://www.theguardian.com/politics/2001/dec/23/politicalnews.jacquismith

112. Kevin Marsh, *Stumbling Over Truth: The Inside Story of the Sexed Up Dossier, Hutton and the BBC*, London: Biteback, 2012.

113. Ibid., p. 13.

114. Ibid., pp. 83–87.

115. Hansard, 28 January 2004, Column 338.

116. Interview with author.

117. Nick Cohen, 'Dinner at Luigi's', *The Observer*, 11 January 2004, https://www.theguardian.com/politics/2004/jan/11/davidkelly.conservatives

118. Katherine Viner, 'The ministry of truth', *The Guardian*, 9 August 1997, https://www.theguardian.com/politics/1997/aug/09/labour.mandelson

119. Roger Scruton, *Modern Philosophy: An Introduction and Survey*, London: Arrow, 1999, p. 470.

120. Oborne, *The Rise of Political Lying*, pp. 142–3.

121. See Freie, *The Making of the Postmodern Presidency*.

122. Interview with author.

123. The Report of the Iraq Inquiry Executive Summary, 6 July 2016.

124. R. Nickerson, 'Confirmation Bias: A Ubiquitous Phenomenon in Many Guises', *Review of General Psychology*, Vol. 2, No. 2, June 1998, pp. 175–220.

125. http://www.politifact.com/personalities/donald-trump/

126. Tony Blair, *A Journey*, p. 516.

127. Interview with author.

128. Tony Blair, speech to Reuters, 12 June 2007.

129. Jean Baudrillard, *The Implosion of Meaning in Media*, 1944.

3. HOW EVERYONE BEGAN TO LOSE CONTROL

1. 'Gorilla Tactics', *The Guardian*, 27 April 2005, https://www.theguardian.com/society/2005/apr/27/guardiansocietysupplement.politics

2. 3 May 2002. BBC News.

3. 'Gorilla Tactics', *The Guardian*.

4. http://mediajackals.org/

5. Nick Davies, *Flat Earth News: An Award-winning Reporter Exposes Falsehood, Distortion and Propaganda in the Global Media*, London: Vintage, 2009, p. 10.

6. C-SPAN, 2 December 2002, https://www.c-span.org/video/?174100-1/senator-thurmond-100th-birthday.

7. 'Big media meets the bloggers', Harvard University Kennedy School of Government, 2012, https://shorensteincenter.org/wp-content/uploads/2012/03/1731_0_scott.pdf?x78124

8. *The Stranger*, 10 January 2012, https://www.thestranger.com/slog/archives/2012/01/10/the-gay-guy-who-smeared-santorum

9. Josh Levin, 'Rather Suspicious', Slate, 10 September 2004, http://www.slate.com/articles/arts/tangled_web/2004/09/rather_suspicious.html

10. Kevin Gillan, Jenny Pickerill and Frank Webster, *Anti-War Activism: New Media and Protest in the Information Age*, London: Palgrave, 2008.

11. Kevin Gillan, Jenny Pickerill and Frank Webster, *Campaigning in a Changing Information Environment: The Anti-War and Peace Movement in Britain*, https://www.research.manchester.ac.uk/portal/files/33083463/FULL_TEXT.PDF

12. Amanda Little, 'Industry flacks learn how to snooker the public with their not-so-eco-friendly messages', Grist, 21 January 2004, http://www.grist.org/news/muck/2004/01/21/spin/index.html

13. Eli Pariser, *The Filter Bubble: What the Internet is Hiding From You*, London: Penguin, 2011, p. 5.

14. Joe Trippi, *The Revolution Will Not Be Televised: Democracy, the Internet, and the Overthrow of Everything*, Regan Books, 2004, pp. 77–79.

15. Zephyr Teachout and Thomas Streeter, *Mousepads, Shoe leather and Hope: Lessons from the Howard Dean Campaign for the Future of Internet Politics*, Abingdon: Routledge, 2008, pp. 15–16.

16. Center for Responsive Politics, 2004

17. Zephyr Teachout and Thomas Streeter, *Mousepads, Shoe leather and Hope*, p. 33.

18. Ian Katz, 'The last post', *The Guardian*, 21 October 2004, https://www.theguardian.com/world/2004/oct/21/uselections2004.usa4

19. Oliver Burkeman, 'My fellow non-Americans …', *The Guardian*, 13 October 2004, https://www.theguardian.com/world/2004/oct/13/uselections2004.usa11

20. Ian Katz, 'The last post'.

21. Ibid.

22. Interview with author.

23. Andy Bowers, '"Dear Limey Assholes…"', Slate, 8 November 2004, http://www.slate.com/articles/news_and_politics/politics/2004/11/dear_limey_assholes_.html

24. Elisabetta Povoledo, 'Irreverent protest movement unnerves Italian establishment', *The New York Times*, 12 September 2007, https://www.nytimes.com/2007/09/12/world/europe/12iht-italy.4.7483565.html

25. 'First Annual Blog Index', *Time*, http://content.time.com/time/specials/2007/article/0,28804,1725323_1725329_1725342,00.html

26. Simon Collister, 'Networked Journalism or pain in the RSS? An examination of political bloggers and media agenda-setting in the UK', Submission for Politics: Web 2.0: An International Conference, Royal Holloway, University of London, 17–18 April 2008, https://www.researchgate.net/publication/265306149_Networked_Journalism_or_pain_in_the_RSS_An_examination_of_political_bloggers_and_media_agenda-setting_in_the_UK

27. Andrew Ironside, 'O'Reilly defends comparison of Daily Kos to Nazis and KKK', Media Matters, 18 July 2007, https://www.mediamatters.org/research/2007/07/18/oreilly-defends-comparison-of-daily-kos-to-nazi/139360

28. Andy Beckett, 'Tim Montgomerie: pushing for a rightwing Tory party—with a heart', *The Guardian*, 23 October 2012, https://www.theguardian.com/politics/2012/oct/23/profile-tim-montgomerie-conservativehome

29. Iain Dale blog, 23 May 2006, http://iaindale.blogspot.co.uk/2006/05/cherie-hutton-report-its-up-to-blogs.html

30. Collister, 'Networked Journalism or pain in the RSS?'.

31. Gordon Rayner, 'Guido Fawkes: the colourful life of the man who brought down Damian McBride', *Daily Telegraph*, 17 April 2009, https://www.telegraph.co.uk/news/politics/5173475/Guido-Fawkes-the-colourful-life-of-the-man-who-brought-down-Damian-McBride.html

32. Collister, 'Networked Journalism or pain in the RSS?'.

33. Adam Sherwin, 'Paul Staines: "I pummel them until they beg for mercy"', *The Guardian*, 31 January 2011, https://www.theguardian.com/media/2011/jan/31/interview-paul-staines-guido-fawkes

34. Interview with author.

35. BBC Editors, 18 April 2007.

36. Kate Coyer, Tony Dowmunt and Alan Fountsin, *The Alternative Media Handbook*, Abingdon: Routledge, 2007, pp. 125–127.

36. Robert Lewis, 'David Kelly: An end to the conspiracy theories?', *The Guardian*, 4 July 2013, https://www.theguardian.com/books/2013/jul/04/david-kelly-man-secrets

38. Robert Lewis, *Dark Actors: The Life and Death of David Kelly*, London: Simon and Schuster, 2013.

39. Ibid.

40. Interview with author.

41. 'The dark side of Guardian comments', *The Guardian*, 12 April 2016, https://www.theguardian.com/technology/2016/apr/12/the-dark-side-of-guardian-comments

42. Interview with author.

43. Nic Newman, 'The rise of social media and its impact on mainstream journalism', Reuters Institute, September 2009, https://reutersinstitute.politics.ox.ac.uk/our-research/rise-social-media-and-its-impact-mainstream-journalism

44. Suzanne LaBarre, 'Why We're Shutting Off Our Comments', Popular Science, 24 September 2013, https://www.popsci.com/science/article/2013–09/why-were-shutting-our-comments

45. https://twitter.com/jessicavalenti/status/758347430765232128?lang=en

46. 'The dark side of Guardian comments', *The Guardian*, 12 April 2016, https://www.theguardian.com/technology/2016/apr/12/the-dark-side-of-guardian-comments

47. Interview with author.

48. *Time*, 25 December 2006, http://content.time.com/time/magazine/europe/0,9263,901061225,00.html

49. See John R. Suler, *Psychology of the Digital Age: Humans Become Electric*, Cambridge: Cambridge University Press, 2015.

50. *Oxford English Dictionary*, https://en.oxforddictionaries.com/definition/troll

51. http://www.4chan.org/advertise

52. Whitney Phillips, *This is Why We Can't Have Nice Things: Mapping the Relationship Between Online Trolling and Mainstream Culture*, Cambridge, MA: MIT Press, 2015, pp. 60–61.

53. Ibid., pp. 2–6.

54. Ibid., pp. 28–37.

55. Ibid., pp. 74–75

56. Caitlin Dewey, 'Absolutely everything you need to know to understand 4chan, the Internet's own bogeyman', *Washington Post*, 25 September 2014, https://www.washingtonpost.com/news/the-intersect/wp/2014/09/25/absolutely-everything-you-need-to-know-to-understand-4chan-the-internets-own-bogeyman/?utm_term=.75c99be3096c

57. See Michael Burleigh, *Blood and Rage: A Cultural History of Terrorism*, London: Harper, 2008.

58. Simon Cottee, 'The Pornography of Jihadism', *The Atlantic*, 12 September 2104, https://www.theatlantic.com/international/archive/2014/09/isis-jihadist-propaganda-videos-porn/380117/

59. Tony Blair, speech to Reuters, 12 June 2007, http://news.bbc.co.uk/1/hi/uk_politics/6744581.stm

60. Andrew Rawnsley, 'Tony Blair wants a good kicking', *The Observer*, 20 February 2005, https://www.theguardian.com/politics/2005/feb/20/media.media

4. DISABLEMENT AND DEPENDENCY IN THE MEDIA

1. Apple press release, 9 January 2007, https://www.apple.com/uk/newsroom/2007/01/09Apple-Reinvents-the-Phone-with-iPhone/

2. Niall McCarthy, 'Apple Has Sold 1.2 Billion iPhones Over the Past 10 Years, Forbes, 29 June 2017, https://www.forbes.com/sites/niallmccarthy/2017/06/29/apple-has-sold-1-2-billion-iphones-over-the-past-10-years-infographic/#2bc4d33d42f8

3. Thomas L. Friedman, *Thank you For Being Late: An Optimist's Guide to Thriving in the Age of Accelerations*, Penguin 2017, pp. 20–37.

4. 'The Changing Newsroom', Pew Research Center, 21 July 2008, http://www.journalism.org/2008/07/21/the-changing-newsroom-2/

5. Corey Hutchins, 'Virginian-Pilot editor resigns after a long career, staff cuts, and a crisis', *Columbia Journalism Review*, 14 March 2015, https://www.cjr.org/united_states_project/denis_finley_virginian_pilot_editor_resigns.php

6. Rupert Murdoch, Speech to the Worshipful Company of Stationers and Newspaper Makers, March 2006, https://www.thetimes.co.uk/article/murdoch-speech-at-stationers-hall-full-text-8908kbqdv7z

7. State of the News Media 2007, Pew Research Center, http://assets.pewresearch.org/wp-content/uploads/sites/13/2017/05/24141602/State-of-the-News-Media-Report-2007-FINAL.pdf

8. Figures from the Newspaper Association of America in evidence to House of Representatives Sub-Committee on Communications and Technology, 11 June 2014, https://www.gpo.gov/fdsys/pkg/CHRG-113hhrg91517/html/CHRG-113hhrg91517.htm

9. 'A Guy Named Craig', *New York Magazine*, 16 January 2006, http://nymag.com/nymetro/news/media/internet/15500/index2.html

10. Inc Magazine, September 2016, https://www.inc.com/magazine/201609/jon-fine/inc-interview-craigslist.html

11. 'A Guy Named Craig'.

12. Larry Page and Sergey Brin, 'The Anatomy of a Large-Scale Hypertextual Web Search Engine', April 1998, http://infolab.stanford.edu/~backrub/google.html

13. 'Google's revenue worldwide from 2002 to 2017', Statista, https://www.statista.com/statistics/266206/googles-annual-global-revenue/

14. 'Facebook advertising revenue worldwide from 2009 to 2017', Statista, https://www.statista.com/statistics/271258/facebooks-advertising-revenue-worldwide/

15. Nicholas Lemann, 'Paper Tigers', *The New Yorker*, 13 April 2009, https://www.newyorker.com/magazine/2009/04/13/paper-tigers

16. https://www.youtube.com/watch?v=LDy7vn7-LX4

17. Thomas L. Friedman, 'Dancing in a Hurricane', *The New York Times* Sunday Review, 19 November 2016, https://www.nytimes.com/2016/11/20/opinion/sunday/dancing-in-a-hurricane.html

18. David Carr, 'At Flagging Tribune, Tales of a Bankrupt Culture', *The New York Times*, 5 October 2010, http://www.nytimes.com/2010/10/06/business/media/06tribune.html

19. Ken Doctor, 'Newsonomics: The halving of America's daily newsrooms', Nieman Lab, 28 July 2015, http://www.niemanlab.org/2015/07/newsonomics-the-halving-of-americas-daily-newsrooms

20. François Nel, 'Laid Off: What do UK journalists do next?', University of Central

Lancashire and Journalism.co.uk, p. 10, https://www.journalism.co.uk/uploads/laid-offreport.pdf

21. James Harding, 'The Valley and the Hill: Technology, Democracy and the Future of Free Expression, The University of Navarra, Madrid, 1 February 2018, https://www.youtube.com/watch?v=uTEv2PvXSG8&t=4923s

22. Anup Kaphle, 'The foreign desk in transition', *Columbia Journalism Review*, April/May 2105, https://www.cjr.org/analysis/the_foreign_desk_in_transition.php

23. Tom Baldwin, 'America tunes in to see Paris sent back to jail, kicking and screaming', *The Times*, 9 June 2007, https://www.thetimes.co.uk/article/america-tunes-in-to-see-paris-sent-back-to-jail-kicking-and-screaming-9qfk3mj7fgt

24. Robert G. Kaiser, 'The Bad News About the News', Brookings, 16 October 2014, http://csweb.brookings.edu/content/research/essays/2014/bad-news.html

25. Lindsay Renick Mayer, 'Fannie Mae and Freddie Mac Invest in Democrats', Open Secrets, Center for Responsive Politics, 16 July 2008, http://www.opensecrets.org/news/2008/07/top-senate-recipients-of-fanni/

26. Dean Starkman, 'The Hamster Wheel', *Columbia Journalism Review*, September/October 2010, https://archives.cjr.org/cover_story/the_hamster_wheel.php

27. 'The Changing Newsroom', Pew Research Center, 21 July 2008, http://www.journalism.org/2008/07/21/the-changing-newsroom-2/

28. 'A Study of the News Ecosystem of One American City', Pew Research Centre, 11 January 2010, http://www.journalism.org/2010/01/11/how-news-happens/

29. Ken Auletta, 'Non-Stop News', *The New Yorker*, 25 January 2010, https://www.newyorker.com/magazine/2010/01/25/non-stop-news

30. Interview with author.

31. The Leveson Inquiry was a judicial public inquiry into the culture, practices and ethics of the British press, reporting in November 2012.

32. Michelle Stanistreet, Evidence to Leveson Inquiry, 16 July 2012, http://webarchive.nationalarchives.gov.uk/20140122193236/http://www.levesoninquiry.org.uk/wp-content/uploads/2012/07/Closing-Submission-from-the-NUJ.pdf

33. Ibid.

34. Gordon Brown, *My Life, Our Times*, London: Bodley Head, 2017, p. 290.

35. Michael Calderone, 'For producer rallied tea party protesters', Politico, 20 September 2009, https://www.politico.com/blogs/michaelcalderone/0909/Fox_producer_rallied_tea_party_protesters.html#site-content

36. Brendan Nyhan, 'Why the "Death Panel" Myth Wouldn't Die: Misinformation in the Health Care Reform', Debate, *The Forum*, Volume 8, Issue 1, University of Michigan, 2010, http://www.dartmouth.edu/~nyhan/health-care-misinformation.pdf

37. James Macintyre and Mehdi Hasan, *Ed: The Milibands and the Making of a Labour Leader*, London: Biteback, 2011.

38. Adam Sherwin and Oliver Wright, 'Rupert Murdoch berated *Sun* journalists for not doing enough to attack Ed Miliband and stop him winning the general election', *The Independent*, 20 April 2015, http://www.independent.co.uk/news/media/rupert-murdoch-berated-sun-journalists-for-not-doing-enough-to-attack-ed-miliband-10191005.html

39. Interview with author.
40. Evidence given by Tony Gallagher, editor of *The Sun* and Rebekah Brooks, chief executive of News UK to the Competition and Markets Authority's 21st Century Fox / Sky merger inquiry, 14 November 2017, https://www.gov.uk/cma-cases/twenty-first-century-fox-sky-merger-european-intervention-notice
41. Jonathan Paige, 'British public wrong about nearly everything, survey shows', *The Independent*, 9 July 2013, https://www.independent.co.uk/news/uk/home-news/british-public-wrong-about-nearly-everything-survey-shows-8697821.html
42. United Nations, 24 April 2015, http://www.ohchr.org/EN/NewsEvents/Pages/DisplayNews.aspx?NewsID=15885&LangID=E
43. 'Research on local advertising markets', report for Nesta prepared by Oliver and Ohlbaum Associates Ltd, May 2013, p. 28, https://www.nesta.org.uk/sites/default/files/research_on_local_advertising_markets.pdf
44. House of Lords Select Committee on Communications 1st Report of Session 2007–08, 'The ownership of the news', p. 46.
45. House of Lords Select Committee on Communications 1st Report of Session 2007–08, 'The ownership of the news', p. 79.
46. Oliver Luft, 'Ofcom head Ed Richards sounds death knell for ITV regional news', *The Guardian*, 28 April 2009, https://www.theguardian.com/media/2009/apr/28/ofcom-ed-richard-local-tv-news; Jeremy Hunt, speech to the Hospital Club, London, 9 June 2010, https://www.gov.uk/government/speeches/media-keynote-speech
47. House of Commons, Oral Evidence to DCMC Committee, 'Regulation of the Press', 21 May 2013, https://publications.parliament.uk/pa/cm201314/cmselect/cmc-umeds/uc143-i/uc14301.htm
48. Dominic Ponsford, '"Heartbroken" reporter Gareth Davies says Croydon Advertiser print edition now 'thrown together collection of clickbait', *Press Gazette*, 31 July 2016, http://www.pressgazette.co.uk/heartbroken-reporter-gareth-davies-says-croydon-advertser-print-edition-now-thrown-together-collection-of-clickbait/
49. Jasper Cox, 'New research: Some 198 UK local newspapers have closed since 2005', *Press Gazette*, 19 December 2016, http://www.pressgazette.co.uk/new-research-some-198-uk-local-newspapers-have-closed-since-2005/
50. Rachel Howells, 'Journey to the centre of a news black hole: examining the democratic deficit in a town with no newspaper', Cardiff School of Journalism, Media and Cultural Studies, June 2015, https://orca.cf.ac.uk/87313/1/2016howellsrphd.pdf
51. Ibid.
52. Ibid.
53. Interview with author.
54. Interview with author.
55. https://m.facebook.com/groups/276603459201045/
56. Interview with author.
57. interview with author.
58. Interview with author.
59. *The New York Times* Innovation report 2014, https://www.scribd.com/doc/224332847/NYT-Innovation-Report-2014

60. 'State of the News Media', Pew Research Center, http://www.pewresearch.org/top-ics/state-of-the-news-media/

61. Eli Pariser, *The Filter Bubble: What the Internet is Hiding From You*, London: Penguin, 2011, p. 49.

62. Franklin Foer, *World Without Mind: The Existential Threat of Big Tech*, London: Jonathan Cape, 2017, pp. 131–132.

63. Buzzfeed, 9 July 2014, https://www.buzzfeed.com/ariellecalderon/cats-who-failed-so-hard-they-won?utm_term=.vlYJjZnBY#.vsrDNKjzo

64. Nick Denton, 'How Things Work', Gawker, 22 August 2016, https://web.archive.org/web/20170402192138/http://gawker.com/how-things-work-1785604699

65. James Fallows, 'Learning to Love the (Shallow, Divisive, Unreliable) New Media', *The Atlantic*, April 2001, https://www.theatlantic.com/magazine/archive/2011/04/learning-to-love-the-shallow-divisive-unreliable-new-media/308415/

66. Eli Pariser, *The Filter Bubble*, p. 69.

67. Franklin Foer, *World Without Mind*, p. 155

68. Martha Waggoner, 'Click Goals: For journalists, the pressure is always there. But are they improving reporting?', News Guild, 16 January 2018, http://www.newsguild.org/mediaguild3/7670/

69. Ben Frampton, 'Clickbait: The changing face of online journalism', http://www.bbc.co.uk/news/uk-wales-34213693

70. David Weigel, 'If You Want Reporters to Check Stories Before They Publish, You're a Hater', Slate, 28 November 2016, http://www.slate.com/blogs/weigel/2013/12/03/buzzfeed_and_elan_gale_s_internet_hoax_too_good_to_check.html

71. Ravi Somaiya and Leslie Kaufman, 'If a Story Is Viral, Truth May Be Taking a Beating', *The New York Times*, 9 December 2013, http://www.nytimes.com/2013/12/10/business/media/if-a-story-is-viral-truth-may-be-taking-a-beating.html

72. Ibid.

73. Katharine Viner, 'A Mission for Journalism in a Time of Crisis', *The Guardian*, 16 November 2017, https://www.theguardian.com/news/2017/nov/16/a-mission-for-journalism-in-a-time-of-crisis

74. 'Breast Chancer, Did Jasmine Tridevil undergo cosmetic surgery to add a third breast?', Snopes, https://www.snopes.com/photos/bodymods/jasminetridevil.asp

75. Radhika Sanghani, '"I had a third breast implant so I can turn off men"', *The Daily Telegraph*, 22 September 2014, http://www.telegraph.co.uk/women/womens-life/11113452/Third-boob-woman-I-had-a-third-breast-implant-so-I-can-turn-off-men.html

76. Craig Silverman, 'Lies, Damn Lies and Viral Content, Tow Center for Digital Journalism', February 2015, Tow Center for Digital Journalism, http://towcenter.org/wp-content/uploads/2015/02/LiesDamnLies_Silverman_TowCenter.pdf

77. Peter Oborne, 'Why I have resigned from *The Telegraph*', Open Democracy, 17 February 2015, https://www.opendemocracy.net/ourkingdom/peter-oborne/why-i-have-resigned-from-telegraph

78. Interview with author.

79. Hugh Baxter, *Habermas: The Discourse Theory of Law and Democracy*, Stanford, CA: Stanford University Press, 2001, p. 1.

80. Jürgen Habermas, *The Structural Transformation of the Public Sphere: An Inquiry into a category of Bourgeois Society*, Cambridge: Polity, 1962 trans 1989.

81. Yochai Benkler, *The Wealth of Networks: How Social Production Transforms Markets and Freedom*, New Haven, CT: Yale University Press, 2006.

82. Jürgen Habermas, Speech to the International Communication Association, 'Does Democracy Still Enjoy Epistemic Dimension? The Impact of Normative Theory on Empirical Research', *Communication Theory*, 16, 4, 2006, pp. 411–426.

83. Howard Rheingold, 'Habermas blows off question about the internet and the public sphere', 5 November 2007, http://www.univie.ac.at/internetforschung/2008/02/habermas-blows-off-question-about-the-internet-and-the-public-sphere/

84. The phrase was invented by the technology specialist, Nicholas Negroponte, but later expanded upon by Cass Sunstein in *Republic.com 2.0*, Princeton, NJ: Princeton University Press, 2009.

85. See David Berreby, *Us and Them: The Science of Identity*, Chicago, IL: University of Chicago Press, p. 178.

86. Cass Sunstein, 'The rise of the Daily Me threatens democracy', *Financial Times*, 10 January 2008, https://www.ft.com/content/3e2ee254-bf96-11dc-8052-0000779fd2ac

87. Jürgen Habermas, How to save the quality press?', 16 May 2007, *Süddeutsche Zeitung* http://www.signandsight.com/features/1349.html

5. TYRANNY AND TEMPTATION IN POLITICS

1. Tom Geoghegan, 'The petition, the "prat" and a political ideal', BBC News Magazine, 13 February 2007, http://news.bbc.co.uk/1/hi/magazine/6354735.stm

2. Interview with author.

3. Gordon Brown, *My Life, Our Times*, London: Bodley Head, 2017, pp. 6–7.

4. Damian McBride, *Power Trip: A Decade of Policy, Plots and Spin*, London: Biteback, 2013.

5. Gaby Hinsliff and Mark Tran, 'McBride and Draper emails: "Gents, a few ideas"', *The Observer*, 12 April 2009, https://www.theguardian.com/politics/2009/apr/12/damian-mcbride-derek-draper-emails

6. Interview with author.

7. https://www.youtube.com/watch?v=6VaP1HB7Vew

8. https://www.youtube.com/watch?v=sBXj5l6ShpA

9. Simon Hoggart, 'Gordon Brown on YouTube: a certain smile—random, and a bit scary', *The Guardian*, 22 April 2009, https://www.theguardian.com/politics/2009/apr/22/hoggart-brown-expenses-video-smile

10. Interview with author.

11. Hansard, 22 March 2006, Col 306, https://publications.parliament.uk/pa/cm200506/cmhansrd/vo060322/debtext/60322-06.htm

12. Jon Slattery Blog, 2 November 2010, http://jonslattery.blogspot.co.uk/2010/11/steve-bell-why-i-put-cameron-in-condom.html

13. David Cameron, Speech at Google Zeitgeist conference in San Francisco, 12 October 2007, http://conservative-speeches.sayit.mysociety.org/speech/599768

14. Gavin Freeguard, Lucy Campbell, Aron Cheung, Alice Lilly, Charlotte Baker, 'Whitehall Monitor 2018: The General Election, Brexit and beyond', The Institute for Government, pp. 93–105, https://www.instituteforgovernment.org.uk/publication/whitehall-monitor-2018/communication-and-transparency

15. 'The life and strange death of the big society charity', The Third Sector, 28 January 2015, https://www.thirdsector.co.uk/life-strange-death-big-society-charity/article/1329775

16. Interview with author.

17. James Crabtree, 'David Cameron's battle to connect', Wired, 24 March 2010, http://www.wired.co.uk/article/david-camerons-battle-to-connect

18. Interview with author.

19. Interview with author.

20. Rachel Sylvester, 'Parties set sights on mothers in the mumsnet election', The Times, 3 April 2010, https://www.thetimes.co.uk/article/parties-set-sights-on-mothers-in-the-mumsnet-election-zjl8hz2q7bb

21. Interview with author.

22. Web 2.0 Summit '08, 5–7 November 2008, https://conferences.oreilly.com/web2008/

23. Web 2.0 Summit '08, 'The Web and Politics', 7 November 2008, https://www.youtube.com/watch?v=CBeePcCOBQM

24. Ibid.

25. Valentino Larcinesey and Luke Minerz, 'The Political Impact of the Internet in US Presidential Elections', London School of Economics and Political Science, June 2017, http://sticerd.lse.ac.uk/dps/eopp/eopp63.pdf

26. Jody C. Baumgartner and Jonathan S. Morris, 'Who wants to be my friend? Obama, youth. and social networks in the 2008 campaign', in John Hendricks and Robert Denton Jr (eds), Communicator-in-Chief: How Barack Obama Used New Media Technology to Win the White House, Lanham, MD: Lexington Books, 2010, pp. 58–61.

27. Interview with author.

28. Ibid.

29. Barack Obama's Caucus Speech, 3 January 2008, http://www.nytimes.com/2008/01/03/us/politics/03obama-transcript.html

30. Peter Dreier and Marshall Ganz, 'We Have Hope; Where's the Audacity?', Washington Post, 30 August 2009, http://www.washingtonpost.com/wp-dyn/content/article/2009/08/28/AR2009082801817.html?sid=ST2009090403398

31. Micah L. Sifry, 'Obama's Lost Army', The New Republic, 9 February 2017, https://newrepublic.com/article/140245/obamas-lost-army-inside-fall-grassroots-machine

32. Peter Wallsten, 'President Obama bristles when he is the target of activist tactics he once used', Washington Post, 10 June 2012, https://www.washingtonpost.com/politics/president-obama-bristles-when-he-is-the-target-of-activist-tactics-he-once-used/2012/06/09/gJQA0i7JRV_story.html?utm_term=.a7434aff56f5

33. Interview with author.

34. Tech President, 10 October 2007, http://techpresident.com/blog-entry/you-don%E2%80%99t-have-power

35. Steven Levy, 'The Final Days of Obama's Tech Surge', Wired, 18 January 2017, https://www.wired.com/2017/01/the-final-days-of-obamas-tech-surge/

36. Jane Mayer, 'Covert Operations', *The New Yorker*, 30 August 2010, https://www.newyorker.com/magazine/2010/08/30/covert-operations

37. Barack Obama, interviewed on NPR's Morning Edition, 19 December 2016, Barack Obama, interviewed on NPR's Morning Edition, 19 December 2016.

38. See, for instance, Sheldon Himelfarb, 'Social Media in the Middle East', United States Institute for Peace, 11 April 2011.

39. Techcrunch, 19 February 2011, https://techcrunch.com/2011/02/19/facebook-egypt-newborn/

40. Barack Obama, speaking at the US State Department, 19 May 2011.

41. Marc Lynch, 'Twitter Devolutions', *Foreign Policy*, 7 February 2013, http://foreignpolicy.com/2013/02/07/twitter-devolutions/

42. Bethany Allen-Ebrahimian, 'The Man Who Nailed Jello to the Wall', *Foreign Policy*, 29 June 2016, http://foreignpolicy.com/2016/06/29/the-man-who-nailed-jello-to-the-wall-lu-wei-china-internet-czar-learns-how-to-tame-the-web/

43. 'China employs two million microblog monitors state media say', BBC News, 4 October 2013, http://www.bbc.co.uk/news/world-asia-china-24396957

44. Ibid.

45. Lim Yan Liang, 'China continues to push for its vision of the Internet', *The Straits Times*, 3 December 2017, http://www.straitstimes.com/asia/east-asia/xi-jinping-says-china-will-not-close-door-to-global-internet-but-insists-on-cyber

46. Andrei Soldatov and Irina Borogan, *The Red Web: The Struggle Between Russia's Digital Dictators and the New Online Revolutionaries*, New York: Public Affairs, 2015, p. 140.

47. Ibid., p. 159

48. Lucan Kim, 'Banned From Election, Putin Foe Navalny Pursues Politics By Other Means', NPR, 8 February 2018, https://www.npr.org/sections/parallels/2018/02/08/584369719/banned-from-election-putin-foe-navalny-pursues-politics-by-other-means

49. Soldatov and Borogan, *The Red Web*, p. 125.

50. Evan Osnos, David Remnick and Joshua Yaffa, 'Trump, Putin and the New Cold War', *The New Yorker*, 6 March 2017, https://www.newyorker.com/magazine/2017/03/06/trump-putin-and-the-new-cold-war

51. Alec Ross, speaking at *The Guardian* Activate Summit, 22 June 2011, https://www.theguardian.com/media/2011/jun/22/hillary-clinton-adviser-alec-ross

52. Soldatov and Borogan, *The Red Web*, pp. 153–154.

53. Andrei Soldatov and Irina Borogan, 'Russia's Surveillance State', World Policy Institute, Autumn 2013, http://www.worldpolicy.org/journal/fall2013/Russia-surveillance

54. 'From the Streets To The Rada: Euromaidan Activists Enter Politics', Radio Free Europe, 23 October 2014, https://www.rferl.org/a/ukraine-euromaidan-activists-parliament-elections/26651905.html

55. Miriam Elder, 'Kremlin internet bill "signals growing repression of critics by Putin"', *The Guardian*, 10 July 2012, https://www.theguardian.com/world/2012/jul/10/kremlin-internet-bill-repression-putin

56. Interview with author.

57. Ibid.

58. Ibid.
59. Evan Osnos, David Remnick and Joshua Yaffa, 'Trump, Putin and the New Cold War'.
60. Nathan Hodge, 'Kremlin launches "school of bloggers"', Wired, 27 May 2009, https://www.wired.com/2009/05/kremlin-launches-school-of-bloggers/
61. Soldatov and Borogan, *The Red Web*, pp. 281–283.
62. Dmitry Volchek and Daisy Sindelar, 'One Professional Russian Troll Tells All', Radio Free Europe, 25 March 2015, https://www.rferl.org/a/how-to-guide-russian-trolling-trolls/26919999.html
63. Dominic Kennedy, 'Kremlin sows discord with new weapon at heart of UK', *The Times*, 30 July 2016, https://www.thetimes.co.uk/article/kremlin-sows-discord-with-new-weapon-at-heart-of-uk-q377tch6q
64. Martin Williams, 'The women who head up the new Edinburgh base of a Russia state-funded news agency', *Sunday Herald*, 11 August 2016, www.heraldscotland.com/news/14674468.
The_women_who_head_up_the_new_Edinburgh_base_of_a_Russia_state_funded_news_agency/
65. Interview with author.
66. Evan Osnos, David Remnick and Joshua Yaffa, 'Trump, Putin and the New Cold War'.
67. Ellen Nakashima, 'New details emerge about 2014 Russian hack of the State Department: It was "hand to hand combat"', *Washington Post*, 3 April 2017, https://www.washingtonpost.com/world/national-security/new-details-emerge-about-2014-russian-hack-of-the-state-department-it-was-hand-to-hand-combat/2017/04/03/d89168e0-124c-11e7-833c-503e1f6394c9_story.html?utm_term=.2820b0e0cdc7
68. Evan Osnos, David Remnick and Joshua Yaffa, 'Trump, Putin and the New Cold War'.
69. 'U.S. Intelligence Report Identifies Russians Who Gave DNC Emails to Wikileaks', Reuters, 6 January 2017, http://time.com/4625301/cia-russia-wikileaks-dnc-hacking/
70. Evan Osnos, David Remnick and Joshua Yaffa, 'Trump, Putin and the New Cold War'.
71. Interview with author.
72. Ari Berman, 'Jim Messina, Obama's Enforcer', *The Nation*, 30 March 2011, https://www.thenation.com/article/jim-messina-obamas-enforcer/
73. Zeynap Tufekci, 'Beware the Smart Campaign', *The New York Times*, 16 November 2012, https://www.nytimes.com/2012/11/17/opinion/beware-the-big-data-campaign.html
74. Ibid.
75. Sasha Issenberg, 'How Obama's Team Used Big Data to Rally Voters', *MIT Technology Review*, 19 December 2012, https://www.technologyreview.com/s/509026/how-obamas-team-used-big-data-to-rally-voters
76. Michael Scherer, 'Inside the Secret World of the Data Crunchers Who Helped Obama

Win', *Time*, 7 November 2012, http://swampland.time.com/2012/11/07/inside-the-secret-world-of-quants-and-data-crunchers-who-helped-obama-win/

77. See Michael Lewis, *Moneyball: The Art of Winning an Unfair Game*, New York: W. W. Norton, 2003.

78. Jim Messina interviewed at the Milken Institute, 23 May 2013, https://www.youtube.com/watch?v=mZmcyHpG31A

79. Scherer, 'Inside the Secret World of the Data Crunchers Who Helped Obama Win'.

80. Issenberg, 'How Obama's Team Used Big Data to Rally Voters'.

81. Ed Pilkington and Amanda Michel, 'Obama, Facebook and the power of friendship: the 2012 data election', *The Guardian*, 17 February 2012, https://www.theguardian.com/world/2012/feb/17/obama-digital-data-machine-facebook-election

82. Elisabeth Dwoskin and Tony Romm, 'Facebook's rules for accessing user data lured more than just Cambridge Analytica', *The Washington Post*, 19 March 2018, https://www.washingtonpost.com/business/economy/facebooks-rules-for-accessing-user-data-lured-more-than-just-cambridge-analytica/2018/03/19/31f6979c-658e-43d6-a71f-afdd8bf1308b_story.html?utm_term=.c8d5a7148b92

83. Jim Messina interviewed at the Milken Institute, 23 May 2013, https://www.youtube.com/watch?v=mZmcyHpG31A

84. NASSCOM Big Data and Analytics Summit 2015, https://www.slideshare.net/nasscom/nasscom-big-data-and-analytics-summit-2015session-xthe-secret-sauce-for-the-obama-campaign-learning-for-the-enterprises

85. *Financial Times*, 8 October 2014, https://www.ft.com/content/8a9b65d8-4d68-11e4-bf60-00144feab7de

86. John Dickerson, 'How To Run a Killer Campaign', Slate, 15 November 2012, http://www.slate.com/articles/news_and_politics/politics/2012/11/jim_messina_offers_his_tips_on_how_barack_obama_s_campaign_team_beat_mitt.html

87. Ryan Lizza, 'The Final Push', *The New Yorker*, 29 October 2012, https://www.newyorker.com/magazine/2012/10/29/the-final-push

88. See, for instance, Messina's profile at the Harry Walker Speakers' Agency, http://www.harrywalker.com/speakers/jim-messina-karl-rove

89. Interview with author.

90. Interview with author.

91. Interview with author.

92. Jim Waterson, 'How The Tories Spent £1.2 Million On Facebook Adverts In Run-Up To Election', BuzzFeed, 20 January 2016, https://www.buzzfeed.com/jimwaterson/how-the-tories-spent-ps12-million-on-facebook-adverts-in-run?utm_term=.abO9a-Joj6#.cwpZElxVz

93. Interview with author.

94. Interview with author.

95. Interview with author.

96. Ed Miliband, speech to the Royal Institute of British Architects, 25 July 2014.

97. Interview with author.

98. James Chapman and John Stevens, 'Labour in chaos over sacking of snob MP: War breaks out in party as desperate Miliband claims he respects White Van Man', *Daily*

Mail, 21 November 2014, http://www.dailymail.co.uk/news/article-2844749/ Labour-chaos-sacking-snob-MP-War-breaks-party-desperate-Miliband-claims-respects-White-Van-Man.html#ixzz57ITwDT9n

99. Information supplied to author.

100. Sarah Vine, 'Why their kitchen tells you all you need to know about the mirthless Milibands… and why there's nothing to suggest that Ed and Justine are not, in fact, aliens', *Daily Mail*, 12 March 2015, http://www.dailymail.co.uk/news/article-2990810/Why-kitchen-tells-need-know-mirthless-Milibands-s-suggest-Ed-Justine-not-fact-aliens.html#ixzz57YITz2OY

101. Ben Riley-Smith, 'Ed "Two Kitchens" Miliband under fire in bizarre row', *Daily Telegraph*, 12 March 2015, http://www.telegraph.co.uk/news/politics/ed-miliband/11468704/Ed-Two-Kitchens-Miliband-under-fire-in-bizarre-row.html

102. Interview with author.

103. Ed Miliband, speech to the IPPR at the Royal Festival Hall, 22 June 2012, http://www.politics.co.uk/comment-analysis/2012/06/22/ed-miliband-s-immigration-speech-in-full

104. Interview with author.

105. Ibid.

106. Jonathan Portes, 'Immigration and Wages: Getting the Numbers Right', National Institute of Economic and Social Research, 11 June 2016, https://www.niesr.ac.uk/blog/immigration-and-wages-getting-numbers-right

107. Interview with author.

108. Adam Pasick and Tim Fernholz, 'The stealthy, Eric Schmidt-backed startup that's working to put Hillary Clinton in the White House', Quartz, 9 October 2015, https://qz.com/520652/groundwork-eric-schmidt-startup-working-for-hillary-clinton-campaign/

109. Sebastian Payne, Jim Messina interview: how the pollsters got it wrong and why Labour lost, *The Spectator*, 12 May 2015, https://blogs.spectator.co.uk/2015/05/jim-messina-interview-how-the-pollsters-got-it-wrong-and-why-labour-lost/

6. THREE SHOCKS TO 'THE SYSTEM'

1. Craig Oliver, *Unleashing Demons: The Inside Story of Brexit*, London: Hodder, 2016, pp. 2–3.

2. Jonathan Allen and Amie Parnes, *Shattered: Inside Hillary Clinton's Doomed Campaign*, London: Crown, pp. 371–387.

3. Nate Silver, 'Election Update: Why Our Model Is More Bullish Than Others On Trump', FiveThirtyEight, 24 October 2016, http://fivethirtyeight.com/features/election-update-why-our-model-is-more-bullish-than-others-on-trump/

4. Nick Cafardo, 'John Henry says Red Sox will rely less on analytics', *Boston Globe*, 24 February 2016, https://www.bostonglobe.com/sports/2016/02/24/john-henry-says-red-sox-will-rely-less-analytics/95uy1OmoQw0ojxr7SRcOWO/story.html

5. Interview with author.

6. Private information.

7. Interview with author.

8. Interview with author.

9. Allen and Parnes, *Shattered*, pp. 367–368.

10. Interview with author.

11. John Wagner, 'Clinton's data-driven campaign relied heavily on an algorithm named Ada. What didn't she see?', *The Washington Post*, 9 November 2016, https://www.washingtonpost.com/news/post-politics/wp/2016/11/09/clintons-data-driven-campaign-relied-heavily-on-an-algorithm-named-ada-what-didnt-she-see/?utm_term=.953b069d5c39

12. Edward-Isaac Dovere, 'How Clinton lost Michigan—and blew the election', Politico, 14 December 2016, https://www.politico.com/story/2016/12/michigan-hillary-clinton-trump-232547

13. Tim Shipman, *Fall Out: A Year of Political Mayhem*, London: William Collins, 2017, p. 241.

14. Jim Waterson, 'The Conservatives' Social Media Game Is Absolutely Terrible', BuzzFeed, 4 October 2017, https://www.buzzfeed.com/jimwaterson/the-conservatives-social-media-game-is-absolutely-terrible?utm_term=.og7PzVj5N#.pd1j8zBY7

15. Interview with author.

16. Shipman, *Fall Out*, p. 376.

17. Gareth Baines, 'Gareth Baines: How good Tory candidates in Wales were betrayed by a dire central campaign', ConservativeHome, 16 June 2017, https://www.conservativehome.com/platform/2017/06/gareth-baines-what-fighting-a-welsh-marginal-taught-me-about-the-conservative-campaign.html

18. Shipman, *Fall Out*, pp. 407–8.

19. Nick Timothy, 'Nick Timothy: Where we went wrong', *The Spectator*, 17 June 2017, https://www.spectator.co.uk/2017/06/nick-timothy-where-we-went-wrong/

20. Nick Timothy, 'Nick Timothy: Why I have resigned as the Prime Minister's adviser', ConservativeHome, 10 June 2017, https://www.conservativehome.com/platform/2017/06/nick-timothy-why-i-have-resigned-as-the-prime-ministers-adviser.html

21. Greg Heffer, 'Farage's final rallying call: "It's us versus the Establishment—go and vote for Britain"', *Daily Express*, 22 June 2016, https://www.express.co.uk/news/politics/682304/EU-referendum-Ukip-Nigel-Farage-final-rally-tell-Britons-vote-for-your-country-Brexit

22. Donald Trump, Facebook page, 25 January 2016, https://www.facebook.com/DonaldTrump/videos/10156563265515725/

23. 'Jeremy Corbyn first speech of the 2017 General Election campaign', 20 April 2017, https://labour.org.uk/press/jeremy-corbyn-first-speech-of-the-2017-general/

24. Philip Tetlock, *Expert Political Judgment: How Good Is It? How Can We Know?*, Princeton, NJ: Princeton University Press, 2005, pp. 25–66.

25. Ibid., 2017 edition, pp. xviii and xliii.

26. Dominic Cummings blog, 29 October 2016, https://dominiccummings.com/tag/ppe/

27. Ibid.

28. Jason Farrell and Paul Goldsmith, *How To Lose A Referendum: The Definitive Story of Why The UK Voted for Brexit*, London: Biteback, 2017, Chapter 18.

29. Interview with author.

30. Robert Peston, *WTF*, London: Hodder & Stoughton, 2017, pp. 89–90.

31. Carole Cadwalladr, 'The great British Brexit robbery: how our democracy was hijacked', *The Observer*, 7 May 2017, https://www.theguardian.com/technology/2017/may/07/the-great-british-brexit-robbery-hijacked-democracy

32. Dominic Cummings blog, 29 October 2016, https://dominiccummings.com/tag/ppe/

33. Electoral Commission, http://www.electoralcommission.org.uk/__data/assets/pdf_file/0019/213139/Pre-poll-4-Summary-Document.pdf

34. Dominic Cummings blog, 29 October 2016, https://dominiccummings.com/tag/ppe/

35. 'Cambridge Analytica: Will data scandal firm return from the dead?', BBC News, 3 May 2018, http://www.bbc.co.uk/news/technology-43989046

36. Alexander Nix, HC 363, 27 February 2018, http://data.parliament.uk/writtenevidence/committeeevidence.svc/evidencedocument/digital-culture-media-and-sport-committee/fake-news/oral/79388.html

37. Kate Brannelly, 'Trump Campaign Pays Millions to Overseas Big Data Firm', NBC News, 4 November 2016, https://www.nbcnews.com/storyline/2016-election-day/trump-campaign-pays-millions-overseas-big-data-firm-n677321

38. Cambridge Analytica, 8 August 2017, https://ca-commercial.com/news/don-drapers-dead-alexander-nix-meets-ogilvys-rory-sutherland

39. Concordia Annual Summit in New York, 27 September 2016, https://www.youtube.com/watch?v=n8Dd5aVXLCc

40. Michal Kosinski, David Stillwell and Thore Graepel, 'Private traits and attributes are predictable from digital records of human behaviour', PNAS, 9 April 2013, http://www.pnas.org/content/110/15/5802

41. Jane Mayer, 'The Reclusive Hedge Fund Tycoon Behind the Trump Presidency', *The New Yorker*, 27 March 2017, https://www.newyorker.com/magazine/2017/03/27/the-reclusive-hedge-fund-tycoon-behind-the-trump-presidency

42. Mike Schroepfer, Chief Technology Officer, Facebook, Written submission to DCMS Select Committee—Fake news inquiry, 26 April 2018, https://www.parliament.uk/documents/commons-committees/culture-media-and-sport/Written-evidence-Facebook.pdf

43. Nicholas Confessore and Danny Hakim, 'Data Firm Says "Secret Sauce" Aided Trump', *The New York Times*, 6 March 2017, https://www.nytimes.com/2017/03/06/us/politics/cambridge-analytica.html

44. Joanna Walters, 'Steve Bannon on Cambridge Analytica: "Facebook data is for sale all over the world"', *The Guardian*, 22 March 2018, https://www.theguardian.com/us-news/2018/mar/22/steve-bannon-on-cambridge-analytica-facebook-data-is-for-sale-all-over-the-world

45. Brad Pascale, 'Secret Weapon', CBS 60 Minutes, 8 October 2017, https://www.cbsnews.com/video/secret-weapon/

46. Ibid.

47. *Sarah Frier*, 'Trump's Campaign Said It Was Better at Facebook. Facebook Agrees',

Bloomberg, 3 April 2018, https://www.bloomberg.com/news/articles/2018-04-03/
trump-s-campaign-said-it-was-better-at-facebook-facebook-agrees

48. Joshua Green and Sarah Issenberg, 'Inside the Trump Bunker, With Days to Go', Bloomberg,
27 October 2016, https://www.bloomberg.com/news/articles/2016-10-27/inside-
the-trump-bunker-with-12-days-to-go

49. Ibid.

50. The Computational Propaganda Project, University of Oxford, 18 November 2016,
http://comprop.oii.ox.ac.uk/research/public-scholarship/resource-
for-understanding-political-bots/

51. Sad Bot True, http://sadbottrue.com/article/24/

52. https://www.twitteraudit.com/realdonaldtrump

53. Donnie O'Sullivan and Dylan Byers, 'Exclusive: Fake black activist accounts linked
to Russian government', CNN 28 September 2017, http://money.cnn.com/2017/
09/28/media/blacktivist-russia-facebook-twitter/index.html

54. Leslie Shapiro, 'Anatomy of a Russian Facebook ad', The Washington Post, 1 November
2017, https://www.washingtonpost.com/graphics/2017/business/russian-ads-face-
book-anatomy/?utm_term=.fdef45d56e7f

55. Anthonio Garcia Martinez, 'How Trump Conquered Facebook—Without Russian
Ads', Wired, 23 February 2018, https://www.wired.com/story/how-trump-conquered-
facebookwithout-russian-ads/

56. Ibid.

57. Ibid.

58. CIPR Influence, 13 July 2017, https://influenceonline.co.uk/2017/07/13/inside-
corbyn-campaign-team-guest-blog-steve-howell/

59. Amol Rajan, 'Five election lessons for the media', BBC News, 13 June 2017, http://
www.bbc.co.uk/news/entertainment-arts-40255428

60. Helena Horton, Jeremy Corbyn's campaign group directs activists away from key marginal seats of his most vocal critics', Daily Telegraph, 15 May 2017, https://www.tele-
graph.co.uk/news/2017/05/15/jeremy-corbyns-campaign-group-directs-activists-away-key-
marginal/

61. Private information.

62. Hillary Rodham Clinton, What Happened?, London: Simon & Schuster, 2017, p. 75.

63. www.facebook.com/tom.steinberg.503/posts/10157028566365237?pnref=story

64. David Goodhart, The Road to Somewhere: The Populist Revolt and the Future of Politics,
London: Hurst, 2017.

65. 'Open owns the future', Global Future, 28 February 2018, http://ourglobalfuture.
com/reports/open-owns-future/

66. Rebecca Roache, 'If you're a Conservative, I'm not your friend', Practical Ethics,
8 May 2015, http://blog.practicalethics.ox.ac.uk/2015/05/if-youre-a-conservative-
im-not-your-friend/

67. Jenna Amatulli, 'FriendsWhoLikeTrump.com Will Make You Want To Delete Your
Facebook', Huffington Post, 9 December 2015, https://www.huffingtonpost.com/
entry/friends-who-like-trump-facebook_us_566873efe4b009377b235791

68. The Public Religion Research Institute, 19 December 2016, https://www.prri.org/
research/poll-post-election-holiday-war-christmas/

69. Ivana Kottasova, 'Trump's win smashes social media records', CNN, 9 November 2016, http://money.cnn.com/2016/11/09/technology/election-trump-social-media-records/

70. 'Blue Feed, Red Feed', *The Wall Street Journal*, http://graphics.wsj.com/blue-feed-red-feed/

71. Simon Hattenstone, 'Brian Eno: "We've been in decline for 40 years—Trump is a chance to rethink"', *The Guardian*, 23 January 2017, https://www.theguardian.com/music/2017/jan/23/brian-eno-not-interested-in-talking-about-me-reflection

72. 'As David Letterman's first Netflix guest, Barack Obama warns against the "bubble" of social media', 260Blog, 13 January 2018, https://260blog.com/technology/as-david-lettermans-first-netflix-guest-barack-obama-warns-against-the-bubble-of-social-media/

73. Jessi Hempel, 'Eli Pariser Predicted the Future, Now He Can't Escape It.', Wired, 24 May 2017, https://www.wired.com/2017/05/eli-pariser-predicted-the-future-now-he-cant-escape-it/

74. John Samples, 'The Case for Government Control of Internet Speech Grows Weaker: Filter Bubble Edition', The Cato Institute, 8 March 2018, https://www.cato.org/blog/case-government-control-internet-speech-grows-weaker-filter-bubble-edition. See also Cristian Vaccari, 'How Prevalent are Filter Bubbles and Echo Chambers on Social Media? Not as Much as Conventional Wisdom Has It', 13 February 2018, https://cristianvaccari.com/2018/02/13/how-prevalent-are-filter-bubbles-and-echo-chambers-on-social-media-not-as-much-as-president-obama-thinks/?blogsub=confirming#subscribe-blog

75. Jack Nicas, 'How YouTube Drives People to the Internet's Darkest Corners', *The Wall Street Journal*, 7 February 2018, https://www.wsj.com/articles/how-youtube-drives-viewers-to-the-internets-darkest-corners-1518020478

77. Andrew Guess, Brendan Nyhan, Jason Reifler, 'Selective Exposure to Misinformation: Evidence from the consumption of fake news during the 2016 U.S. presidential campaign', European Research Council, 9 January 2018, http://www.dartmouth.edu/~nyhan/fake-news-2016.pdf

78. Nazi Pepe controversy, Know Your Meme, http://knowyourmeme.com/memes/events/nazi-pepe-controversy

79. https://www.youtube.com/watch?v=aN8w7lUMc1o

80. https://www.kickstarter.com/projects/566429325/tropes-vs-women-in-video-games

81. https://twitter.com/femfreq/status/504718160902492160

82. Zoe Quinn, *Crash Override: How Gamergate (Nearly) Destroyed My Life, and How We Can Win the Fight Against Online Hate*, New York: Public Affairs, 2017, p. 20.

83. Ibid., p. 235.

84. Joel Stein, 'How Trolls Are Ruining the Internet', *Time*, 18 August 2016, http://time.com/4457110/internet-trolls/

85. Jeremy W. Peters, 'Milo Yiannopoulos Resigns From Breitbart News After Pedophilia Comments', *The New York Times*, 21 February 2017, https://www.nytimes.com/2017/02/21/business/milo-yiannopoulos-resigns-from-breitbart-news-after-pedophilia-comments.html

85. Wil S. Hylton, 'Down the Breitbart Hole', *The New York Times*, 16 August 2017, https://www.nytimes.com/2017/08/16/magazine/breitbart-alt-right-steve-bannon.html

87. 'Partisanship, Propaganda, and Disinformation: Online Media and the 2016 U.S. Presidential Election', The Berkman Klein Center for Internet & Society, 16 August 2017, https://cyber.harvard.edu/publications/2017/08/mediacloud

88. http://wilkins.law.harvard.edu/projects/2017-08_mediacloud/Graphics/Fig8_13.pdf

89. 'Partisan Right-Wing Websites Shaped Mainstream Press Coverage Before 2016 Election, Berkman Klein Study Finds', The Berkman Klein Center for Internet & Society, 16 August 2017, https://cyber.harvard.edu/node/99982

90. Ibid.

91. Wil S. Hylton, 'Down the Breitbart Hole'.

92. Andrew Guess, Brendan Nyhan, Jason Reifler, 'Selective Exposure to Misinformation'.

93. John Herrman, 'Inside Facebook's (Totally Insane, Unintentionally Gigantic, Hyperpartisan) Political-Media Machine', *The New York Times*, 24 August 2016, https://www.nytimes.com/2016/08/28/magazine/inside-facebooks-totally-insane-unintentionally-gigantic-hyperpartisan-political-media-machine.html

94. PPP polling, 9 August 2016, https://www.publicpolicypolling.com/wp-content/uploads/2017/09/PPP_Release_NC_80916.pdf

95. https://www.facebook.com/groups/WeSupportJeremyCorbyn/permalink/985349431626931/

96. Ibid.

97. https://www.youtube.com/watch?v=Edt3d0xjEdU

98. Another Angry Voice, 9 June 2017, http://anotherangryvoice.blogspot.co.uk/2017/06/how-three-tiny-facebook-pages-took-on.html

99. Ibid.

100. Jim Waterson, 'The Rise Of The Alt-Left British Media', BuzzFeed, 6 May 2017, https://www.buzzfeed.com/jimwaterson/the-rise-of-the-alt-left?utm_term=.ccJNL6ly3#.wqgqZ8JdR

101. Interview with author.

102. Jim Waterson, 'This Was The Election Where The Newspapers Lost Their Monopoly On The Political News Agenda', BuzzFeed, 18 June 2017, https://www.buzzfeed.com/jimwaterson/how-newspapers-lost-their-monopoly-on-the-political-agenda?utm_term=.qe7pJWNEa#.xwK2o5nmz

103. https://www.thecanary.co/topics/laura-kuenssberg/

104. Jasper Jackson, 'Laura Kuenssberg petition taken down over sexist abuse', *The Guardian*, 10 May 2016, https://www.theguardian.com/media/2016/may/10/laura-kuenssberg-petition-sexist-abuse-38-degrees-bbc

105. Freddy Mayhew, 'Impress rules Canary breached standards code over Laura Kuenssberg article', *Press Gazette*, 20 December 2017, http://www.pressgazette.co.uk/impress-rules-canary-broke-standards-code-over-laura-kuenssberg-article/

106. Jane Martinson, 'BBC Trust says Laura Kuenssberg report on Corbyn was inaccurate', *The Guardian*, 18 January 2017, https://www.theguardian.com/media/2017/

jan/18/bbc-trust-says-laura-kuenssberg-report-on-jeremy-corbyn-was-inaccurate-labour

107. Lucy Fisher, 'BBC political editor Laura Kuenssberg gets bodyguards', *The Times*, 25 September 2017, https://www.thetimes.co.uk/article/bbc-political-editor-laura-kuenssberg-gets-bodyguards-kz3dd7n3s

108. Interview with author.

109. Ibid.

110. Ibid.

111. Jessica Elgot, 'Labour suspends party members in "anti-Semitic" Facebook group', *The Guardian*, 8 March 2018, https://www.theguardian.com/politics/2018/mar/08/labour-suspends-party-members-in-antisemitic-facebook-group

112. Gabriel Pogrund, Jon Ungoed-Thomas and Richard Kerbaj, 'Vitriol and threats of violence: the ugly face of Jeremy Corbyn's cabal', *Sunday Times*, 1 April 2018, https://www.thetimes.co.uk/article/vitriol-and-threats-of-violence-the-ugly-face-of-jeremy-corbyns-cabal-gxdk69m8f

113. Hansard, 17 April 2018, Vol. 639.

114. Janice Turner, 'Labour has been lost to fools and crackpots', *The Times*, 31 March 2018, https://www.thetimes.co.uk/article/labour-has-been-lost-to-fools-and-crackpots-hlv783z7j

115. Skwawkbox, 11 August 2017, https://skwawkbox.org/2017/08/11one-of-labours-new-rising-stars-talks-class-westminster-and-the-enemy/

116. https://twitter.com/eddygraham39/status/970052291159101442

117. YouGov/BBC Radio 4 Today Programme survey results, http://d25d2506sfb94s.cloudfront.net/cumulus_uploads/document/x4iynd1mn7/TodayResults_160614_EUReferendum_W.pdf

118. https://www.youtube.com/watch?v=GGgiGtJk7MA

119. Interview with author.

120. Dominic Cummings blog, 29 October 2016, https://dominiccummings.com/tag/ppe/

121. Frances Perraudin, 'Iain Duncan Smith backtracks on leave side's £350m NHS claim', *The Guardian*, 26 June 2016, https://www.theguardian.com/politics/2016/jun/26/eu-referendum-brexit-vote-leave-iain-duncan-smith-nhs

122. Ibid.

123. Rowena Mason, 'Gove: EU immigrant influx will make NHS unsustainable by 2030', *The Guardian*, 20 May 2016, https://www.theguardian.com/politics/2016/may/20/eu-immigrant-influx-michael-gove-nhs-unsustainable

124. 'Turkey EU accession poses security risk—Michael Gove', BBC News, 8 June 2016, http://www.bbc.co.uk/news/uk-politics-eu-referendum-36479259

125. Interview with author.

126. Question Time, 26 May 2016, https://www.youtube.com/watch?v=gZNoogkhnzw

127. Channel 4 News, 27 May 2016, https://www.youtube.com/watch?v=NgO3a0HFBYw

128. Interview with author.

129. Luke Harding, 'Offshore secrets of Brexit backer Arron Banks revealed in Panama Papers', *The Observer*, 16 October 2016, https://www.theguardian.com/world/2016/oct/15/panama-papers-reveal-offshore-secrets-arron-banks-brexit-backer

130. Robert Booth, Alan Travis and Amelia Gentleman, 'Leave donor plans new party to replace Ukip—possibly without Farage in charge', *The Guardian*, 29 June 2016, https://www.theguardian.com/politics/2016/jun/29/leave-donor-plans-new-party-to-replace-ukip-without-farage

131. Kate Reilly, 'Donald Trump Says He "Could Shoot Somebody" and Not Lose Voters', *Time*, 23 January 2016, http://time.com/4191598/donald-trump-says-he-could-shoot-somebody-and-not-lose-voters/

132. Politifact scorecard, http://www.politifact.com/personalities/donald-trump/

133. Michael Wolff, *Fire and Fury: Inside the Trump White House*, London: Little Brown, pp. 9–19.

134. Scott Nell Hughes, speaking on The Diane Rehm Show, 30 November 2016, https://dianerehm.org/audio/#/shows/2016-11-30/how-journalists-are-rethinking-their-role-under-a-trump-presidency/114095/@14:40

135. Hillary Rodham Clinton, *What Happened?*, London: Simon & Schuster, 2017, p76.

136. Craig Silverman, 'This Analysis Shows How Viral Fake Election News Stories Outperformed Real News On Facebook', BuzzFeed, 16 November 2016, https://www.buzzfeed.com/craigsilverman/viral-fake-election-news-outperformed-real-news-on-facebook?utm_term=.rn9GzYO0x#.ms99X7BRm

137. Jim Waterson, 'Britain Has No Fake News Industry Because Our Partisan Newspapers Already Do That Job', BuzzFeed, 24 January 2017, https://www.buzzfeed.com/jim-waterson/fake-news-sites-cant-compete-with-britains-partisan-newspape?utm_term=.lh61eA9DX#.uaRm2ZXyq

138. David Maddox, 'Major leak from Brussels reveals NHS will be "KILLED OFF" if Britain remains in the EU', *Sunday Express*, 3 May 2016, https://www.express.co.uk/news/uk/666454/NHS-EU-killed-off-Brexit-Remain-Leave-referendum-Brussels-European-Union

139. Duncan J. Watts and David M. Rothschild, 'Don't blame the election on fake news. Blame it on the media.', *Columbia Journalism Review*, 5 December 2007, https://www.cjr.org/analysis/fake-news-media-election-trump.php

140. James Hohmann, 'The Daily 202: At acrimonious post-election conference, Trump and Clinton strategists agree only on anger at the media. Even then, not really.', *The Washington Post*, 2 December 2016, https://www.washingtonpost.com/news/power-post/paloma/daily-202/2016/12/02/daily-202-at-acrimonious-post-election-conference-trump-and-clinton-strategists-agree-only-on-anger-at-the-media-even-then-not-really/5840423ce9b69b7e58e45f24/?utm_term=.28142aa1ae7f

141. Paul Bond, 'Leslie Moonves on Donald Trump: "It May Not Be Good for America, but It's Damn Good for CBS"', *Hollywood Reporter*, 29 February 2016, https://www.hollywoodreporter.com/news/leslie-moonves-donald-trump-may-not-871464

142. Raffi Khatchadourian, 'Julian Assange, A Man Without a Country', *The New Yorker*, 21 August 2017, https://www.newyorker.com/magazine/2017/08/21/julian-assange-a-man-without-a-country

143. Ibid.

144. Email exchange with author.

145. Maggie Haberman, Glenn Thrush and Peter Baker, 'Inside Trump's Hour-by-hour Battle for Self-Preservation', *The New York Times*, 9 December 2017, https://www.nytimes.com/2017/12/09/us/politics/donald-trump-president.html

146. https://twitter.com/wikileaks/status/855378158379573248?lang=en

147. 'Donald Trump made vulgar comments about women during taping of Access Hollywood episode in 2005', ABC News, 8 October 2016, http://www.abc.net.au/news/2016–10–08/
donald-trump-access-hollywood-vulgar-comments-women/7915146

148. Sonia Purnell, 'Boris Johnson peddled lies, half-truths and evasions. Now he's paid the price', *The Guardian*, 1 July 2016, https://www.theguardian.com/commentis-free/2016/jul/01/boris-johnson-lies-no-10

149. Michael Cockerell, BBC 2, 25 March 2013, https://www.youtube.com/watch?v=yZgP45gh-_Y

150. Rachel Sylvester and Alice Thomson, 'Lynton Crosby: the Wizard of Oz who knew scarecrow had brains to win', *The Times*, 7 May 2012, https://www.thetimes.co.uk/article/
lynton-crosby-the-wizard-of-oz-who-knew-scarecrow-had-brains-to-win-s95c0tfrxg0

151. 'Jeremy Corbyn asked five times to condemn IRA violence', BBC News, 8 August 2015, https://www.bbc.co.uk/programmes/p02z3x45

152. Freddy Mayhew, 'How daily newspaper readers voted by title in the 2017 general election',*PressGazette*,14June2017,http://www.pressgazette.co.uk/how-daily-newspaper-readers-voted-by-title-in-the-2017-general-election/

7. CRASHING DEMOCRACY

1. YouTube, 15 June 2017, https://www.youtube.com/watch?v=qcJPlkqOYX0

2. http://soundsfromthepark.on-the-record.org.uk/people/ishmail-blagrove/

3. Dominic Ponsford, '1,500 complain to IPSO over Mail Online story naming Grenfell Tower resident "whose fridge exploded"', *Press Gazette*, 19 June 2017, http://www.press-gazette.co.uk/1500-complain-to-ipso-over-mail-online-story-naming-grenfell-tower-resident-whose-fridge-exploded/

4. Interview with author.

5. 'Over half of the country's top journalists went to private school', Sutton Trust, 5 July 2017, https://www.suttontrust.com/newsarchive/half-countrys-top-journalists-went-private-schools/

6. Jon Snow, MacTaggart Lecture at Edinburgh TV Festival, 23 August 2017, https://www.channel4.com/news/by/jon-snow/blogs/mactaggart-lecture-edinburgh-2017

7. *Financial Times*, 21 August 2107, https://www.ft.com/content/194f270a-84df-11e7-bf50-e1c239b45787

8. Gemma Newby, 'Why no-one heard the Grenfell blogger's warnings', BBC News, 24 November 2017, http://www.bbc.co.uk/news/stories-42072477

9. Grenfell Action Group, 20 November 2016, https://grenfellactiongroup.wordpress.com/2016/11/20/kctmo-playing-with-fire/

10. Dominic Ponsford, 'Journalists and Grenfell Tower: "You aren't the guys getting the call at 2.30 in the morning when a survivor wants to cut their wrists"', *Press Gazette*, 29 November 2017, http://www.pressgazette.co.uk/journalists-and-grenfell-tower-you-arent-the-guys-getting-the-call-at-2–30am-in-the-morning-when-a-survivor-wants-to-cut-their-wrists/

11. Peter Preston, 'A functioning local press matters. Grenfell Tower showed us why', *The Observer*, 2 July 2017, https://www.theguardian.com/media/2017/jul/02/grenfell-tower-local-newspapers-authority-journalism

12. Skwawkbox, 16 June 2017, https://skwawkbox.org/2017/06/16/video-govt-puts-d-notice-gag-on-real-grenfell-death-toll-nationalsecurity/

13. Gordon Rayner and Christopher Hope, 'Corbyn supporters "spread fake news" about Grenfell Tower death toll', *Daily Telegraph*, 16 June 2017, https://www.telegraph.co.uk/news/2017/06/16/corbyn-supporters-spread-fake-news-grenfell-house-death-toll/

14. Rachel Sylvester, 'I'm sure Theresa will be really sad that she doesn't have children'. *The Times*, 9 July 2016, https://www.thetimes.co.uk/article/i-m-sure-theresa-will-be-really-sad-that-she-doesn-t-have-children-t77dswngp

15. Peter Preston, 'Trust in the media is the first casualty of a post-factual war', *The Observer*, 25 September 2016, https://www.theguardian.com/media/2016/sep/24/trust-in-media-first-casualty-post-factual-war-corbyn-trump

16. http://downloads.bbc.co.uk/aboutthebbc/insidethebbc/howwework/reports/pdf/bbc_report_trust_and_impartiality_nov_2017.pdf

17. Interview with author.

18. 'MP Ben Bradley apologises for Corbyn tweet', BBC News, 25 February 2018, http://www.bbc.co.uk/news/uk-43183344

19. Interview with author.

20. Interview with author.

21. Interview with author.

22. Edelman Trust Barometer, 2018, https://www.edelman.com/trust-barometer

23. Jack Shafer and Tucker Doherty, 'The Media Bubble Is Worse Than You Think', Politico, May/June 2017, https://www.politico.com/magazine/story/2017/04/25/media-bubble-real-journalism-jobs-east-coast-215048

24. Michael Wolff, 'Ringside With Steve Bannon at Trump Tower as the President-Elect's Strategist Plots "An Entirely New Political Movement" (Exclusive)', *Hollywood Reporter*, 18 November 2016, https://www.hollywoodreporter.com/news/steve-bannon-trump-tower-interview-trumps-strategist-plots-new-political-movement-948747?utm_source=twitter

25. Jack Shafer and Tucker Doherty, 'The Media Bubble Is Worse Than You Think'.

26. Jennifer Wadsworth, 'Bay Area News Group Hammered by More Layoffs, Resignations', San Jose Inside, 9 February 2018, http://www.sanjoseinside.com/2018/02/09/bay-area-news-group-hammered-by-more-layoffs-resignations/

27. Yemile Bucay, Vittoria Elliott, Jennie Kamin, Andrea Park, 'America's growing news deserts', *Columbia Journalism Review*, Spring 2017, https://www.cjr.org/local_news/american-news-deserts-donuts-local.php; see also Ken Doctor, 'The news media and

Trump', Politico, 10 November 2016, https://www.politico.com/media/story/2016/11/the-news-media-and-trump-004850

28. Steven Waldman and Charles Sennott, 'The crisis in local journalism has become a crisis of democracy', *The Washington Post*, 11 April 2018, https://www.washington-post.com/opinions/the-crisis-in-journalism-has-become-a-crisis-of-democ-racy/2018/04/11/a908d5fc-2d64-11e8–8688-e053ba58f1e4_story.html?utm_term=.eb70b20f7460

29. Snopes, https://www.snopes.com/fact-check/burqa39s-law/#oukPQTTcl3QUt Fwa.99; Ken Doctor, 'The news media and Trump'.

30. 'Americans' Trust in Mass Media Sinks to New Low', Gallup, 4 September 2016, http://news.gallup.com/poll/195542/americans-trust-mass-media-sinks-new-low.aspx

31. Chris Ariens, 'Who Do Americans Believe Is the Most Objective News Source?', Adweek, 28 January 2018, http://www.adweek.com/tvnewser/who-do-americans-believe-is-the-most-objective-news-source/355232

32. James Harding, Cudlipp Lecture, 21 March 2018.

33. YouTube, 11 February 2016, https://www.youtube.com/watch?v=Y3ttxGMQOrY

34. Julia Hahn, 'Video: 1,400 American Workers Outraged as Company Informs Them It's Sending Their Jobs to Mexico', Breitbart News, 12 February 2016, http://www.breitbart.com/big-government/2016/02/12/video-1400-american-workers-outraged-as-company-informs-them-its-sending-their-jobs-to-mexico/

35. Bernie Sanders campaign website, http://feelthebern.org/bernie-sanders-on-trade/

36. Linda Qiu, 'Donald Trump's largely accurate about Clinton's past support for NAFTA, TPP', Politifact, 21 July 2017, http://www.politifact.com/truth-o-meter/state-ments/2016/jul/21/donald-trump/donald-trumps-largely-accurate-about-clintons-past/

37. Bryan Gruley and Rick Clough, 'Remember When Trump Said He Saved 1,100 Jobs at a Carrier Plant?', Bloomberg, 29 March 2017, https://www.bloomberg.com/news/features/2017–03–29/remember-when-trump-said-he-saved-1-100-jobs-at-a-carrier-plant

38. Chris Isidore, 'Carrier to ultimately cut some of jobs Trump saved', CNN Money, 9 December 2016, http://money.cnn.com/2016/12/08/news/companies/carrier-jobs-automation/index.html

39. John Tuohy, 'Carrier plant to lay off 215 workers on Thursday', *Indy Star*, 10 January 2018, https://www.indystar.com/story/news/local/2018/01/10/carrier-plant-lay-off-215-workers-thursday/1021745001/

40. Charles Bethea, 'What the Layoffs Look Like at the Carrier Plant Trump Said He'd Save', *The New Yorker*, 21 July 2017, https://www.newyorker.com/news/news-desk/what-its-like-to-get-laid-off-at-the-carrier-plant-trump-said-hed-save

41. Michael J. Hicks and Srikant Devaraj, 'The Myth and Reality of Manufacturing in America', Ball State University, June 2015, https://projects.cberdata.org/reports/MfgReality.pdf

42. Carl Benedikt Frey, Thor Berger, Chinchih Chen, 'Political Machinery: Did Robots Swing the 2016 U.S. Presidential Election?' University of Oxford, 13 October 2017, https://www.oxfordmartin.ox.ac.uk/downloads/academic/Political%20 Machinery_171008_CF5.pdf

43. Kate Taylor, 'Fast-food CEO says he's investing in machines because the government is making it difficult to afford employees', Business Insider, 16 March 2016, http:// uk.businessinsider.com/carls-jr-wants-open-automated- location-2016–3?r=US&IR=T

44. Carl Benedikt Frey and Michael A. Osborne, 'The Future of Employment: how sus- ceptible are jobs to computerization?', University of Oxford, 17 September 2013, https://www.oxfordmartin.ox.ac.uk/downloads/academic/The_Future_of_Employ- ment.pdf

45. UK Economic Outlook, Price Waterhouse Coopers, 24 March 2017, https://www. pwc.co.uk/services/economics-policy/insights/uk-economic-outlook.html

46. 'Automation, skills use and training' OECD, 8 March 2018, https://www.oecd-ili- brary.org/docserver/2e2f4eeaen.pdf?expires=1522667544&id=id&accname=guest &checksum=1E7D7FB6BE6D1C171F1A585CD72B93D4

47. Carl Benedikt Frey and Michael A. Osborne, 'Technology at Work v2.0: The Future Is Not What It Used to Be', University of Oxford, January 2016, https://www.oxford- martin.ox.ac.uk/downloads/reports/Citi_GPS_Technology_Work_2.pdf

48. Andrew Keen, *The Internet is Not the Answer*, London: Atlantic Books, 2015, pp. 100– 118.

49. See, for instance: Jerry Kaplan, *Humans Need Not Apply: A Guide to Wealth and Work in the Age of Artificial Intelligence*, New Haven, CT: Yale University Press, 2013; Martin Ford, *The Rise of the Robots: Technology and the Threat of Mass Unemployment*, London: Oneworld, 2015; Jaron Lanier, *Who Owns the Future?*, London: Penguin, 2013; Astra Taylor, *The People's Platform: Taking Back Power and Culture in the Digital Age*, London: Fourth Estate, 2014; Erik Brynjolfsson and Andrew McAfee, *The Second Machine Age: Work, Progress, and Prosperity in a Time of Brilliant Technologies*, W. W. Norton, 2014.

50. Richard Susskind and Daniel Susskind, *The Future of Professions: How Technology Will Transform the Work of Human Experts*, Oxford: Oxford University Press, 2015.

51. Quoctrung Bui, 'Map: The Most Common* Job In Every State', NPR, 5 February 2015, https://www.npr.org/sections/money/2015/02/05/382664837/map-the-most- common-job-in-every-state

52. Larry Elliott, 'Robots will not lead to fewer jobs—but the hollowing out of the mid- dle class', *The Guardian*, 20 August 2017, https://www.theguardian.com/busi- ness/2017/aug/20/robots-are-not-destroying-jobs-but-they-are-hollow-out-the-middle- class

53. The Labour Share in G20 Economies. OECD, February 2015, https://www.oecd. org/g20/topics/employment-and-social-policy/The-Labour-Share-in-G20-Econo- mies.pdf

54. Paul Mantoux, *The Industrial Revolution in the Eighteenth Century*, New York: Harcourt, Brace & Co., 1928.

55. Jaron Lanier, *Who Owns the Future?*, p. 16.

56. Trump supporters were more likely to come from the four highest income brackets while people on the lowest incomes voted for Clinton. See, for instance, Nicholas Carnes and Noam Lupu, 'It's time to bust the myth: Most Trump voters were not working class', *The Washington Post*, 5 June 2017, https://www.washingtonpost.com/news/monkey-cage/wp/2017/06/05/its-time-to-bust-the-myth-most-trump-voters-were-not-working-class/?utm_term=.0620885d0e0a; in the UK referendum, Labour voters backed Remain over Leave by 65 per cent to 35 per cent: 'How Britain Voted', YouGov, 27 June 2016, https://yougov.co.uk/news/2016/06/27/how-britain-voted/

57. CNN exit polls, 23 November 2016, https://edition.cnn.com/election/2016/results/exit-polls; Kirby Swales, 'Understanding the Leave vote', http://natcen.ac.uk/media/1319222/natcen_brexplanations-report-final-web2.pdf

58. See Yascha Mounk, *The People vs Democracy*, Boston, MA: Harvard University Press, 2018, pp. 232–233.

59. Nicole Goodkind, 'Trump tax plan give jobs away to robots', *Newsweek*, 19 November 2017, http://www.newsweek.com/tax-plan-robots-jobs-senate-republicans-712930

60. 'Brexit: Official forecasts suggest economies throughout UK will be hit', BBC News, 8 February 2018, http://www.bbc.co.uk/news/uk-politics-42977967

61. Ipsos MORI, 9 June 2016, https://www.ipsos.com/sites/default/files/migrations/en-uk/files/Assets/Docs/Polls/16–029926–01%20EU%20Perils%20of%20Perception_weighted_FINAL%20for%20website.pdf

62. Interview with author.

63. Private information.

64. Isabel Hardman, 'New figures show Cameron's net migration target in tatters', *The Spectator*, 26 February 2015, https://blogs.spectator.co.uk/2015/02/new-figures-show-camerons-net-migration-target-in-tatters/

65. Rachel Sylvester, '"We all made a terrible mistake on migration"', *The Times*, 21 November 2016, https://www.thetimes.co.uk/article/we-all-made-a-terrible-mistake-on-migration-hr7qknsx8

66. Tony Blair, foreword, *Technology for the Many*, 11 November 2017, https://institute.global/insight/renewing-centre/tony-blair-foreword-technology-ma

67. Ed Miliband, speech to Google Big Tent, 22 May 2013, http://www.politics.co.uk/comment-analysis/2013/05/22/ed-miliband-s-google-speech-in-full

68. Labour Party Manifesto 2015, https://action.labour.org.uk/page/-/A4%20BIG%20_PRINT_ENG_LABOUR%20MANIFESTO_TEXT%20LAYOUT.pdf

69. *Financial Times*, 23 January 2016, https://www.ft.com/content/c8a11c10-c1c5-11e5-808f-8231cd71622e

70. 'Spotlight on train companies', http://hub.companycheck.co.uk/community/spotlight-train-operating-companies/

71. Christopher Williams, 'Google has better access to No 10 than I do, says minister', *Daily Telegraph*, 26 September 2013, https://www.telegraph.co.uk/technology/google/10335645/Google-has-better-access-to-No-10-than-I-do-says-minister.html

72. *Financial Times*, 27 March 2017, https://www.ft.com/content/3c5ebc20-1300-11e7-80f4-13e067d5072c; see also Guy Adams, 'Cameron, Osborne, their glamorous chum and the great Uber stitch-up', *Daily Mail*, 24 March 2017, http://www.dailymail.co.uk/news/article-4347676/David-Cameron-s-chum-ocracy-links-Uber-bosses.html

73. 'London cabbies start Uber tax campaign', BBC News, 11 June 2015, http://www.bbc.co.uk/news/technology-33093678

74. David Dayen, 'The Android Administration', The Intercept, 22 April 2016, https://theintercept.com/2016/04/22/googles-remarkably-close-relationship-with-the-obama-white-house-in-two-charts/

75. Open Secrets, The Center for Responsive Politics, http://www.opensecrets.org/lobby/top.php?showYear=2014&indexType=s

76. Barack Obama, *The Audacity of Hope: Thoughts on Reclaiming the American Dream*, Edinburgh: Canongate, 2006, pp. 140–141.

77. World Development Report, 2016, Digital Dividends, World Bank, http://documents.worldbank.org/curated/en/896971468194972881/pdf/102725-PUB-Replacement-PUBLIC.pdf

78. Claire Cain Miller, 'A Darker Theme in Obama's Farewell: Automation Can Divide Us', *The New York Times*, 12 January 2017, https://www.nytimes.com/2017/01/12/upshot/in-obamas-farewell-a-warning-on-automations-perils.html

79. Hillary Clinton, 'Internet Freedom', *Foreign Policy*, 21 January 2010, http://foreignpolicy.com/2010/01/21/internet-freedom/

80. Quoted by Edward Luce in *The Retreat of Western Liberalism*, London: Little, Brown, 2017, p. 67.

81. Nicold Goodkind, 'Robots are not our friends says Hillary Clinton', *Newsweek*, 23 November 2017, http://www.newsweek.com/hillary-clinton-robots-automation-720925

82. Interview with author.

83. Interview with author.

84. Interview with author.

85. Gaby Hinsliff, 'The robots are coming—and Labour is right to tax them', *The Guardian*, 29 September 2017, https://www.theguardian.com/commentisfree/2017/sep/29/robots-labour-tax-jobs

86. See, for instance, Nicholas Thompson and Fred Vogelstein, 'Inside two years that shook Facebook—and the world', *Wired*, 12 February 2018, https://www.wired.com/story/inside-facebook-mark-zuckerberg-2-years-of-hell/

87. Michael Nunez, 'Mark Zuckerberg Asks Racist Facebook Employees to Stop Crossing Out Black Lives Matter Slogans', Gizmodo, 16 February 2016, https://gizmodo.com/mark-zuckerberg-asks-racist-facebook-employees-to-stop-1761272768

88. Nicholas Thompson and Fred Vogelstein, 'Inside two years that shook Facebook—and the world'.

89. Mark Zuckerberg, speaking at the Techonomy conference, 10 November 2016, https://www.facebook.com/zuck/videos/10103248351713921/

90. Facebook, 4 January 2018, https://www.facebook.com/zuck/posts/10104380170714571

91. Deepa Seetharaman, 'Facebook's Profit Rises, but Users Spend Less Time on Network', *Wall Street Journal*, 16 February 2018, https://www.wsj.com/articles/facebook-posts-61-rise-in-operating-profit-in-the-fourth-quarter-1517434065?ns=prod/accounts-wsj

92. Mike Allen, 'Sean Parker unloads on Facebook: "God only knows what it's doing to our children's brains"', Axios, 9 November 2017, https://www.axios.com/sean-parker-unloads-on-facebook-god-only-knows-what-its-doing-to-our-childrens-brains-1513306792-f855e7b4–4e99–4d60–8d51–2775559c2671.html

93. Chamath Palihapitiya, Stanford Graduate School of Business, 13 November 2017, https://www.youtube.com/watch?v=PMotykw0SIk&feature=youtube

94. Jonathan Albright, 'Itemized Posts and Historical Engagement—6 Now-Closed FB', 5 October 2017, Pages, https://public.tableau.com/profile/d1gi#!/vizhome/FB4/TotalReachbyPage

95. Sam Levin, 'Facebook told advertisers it can identify teens feeling "insecure" and "worthless"', The Guardian, 1 May 2017, https://www.theguardian.com/technology/2017/may/01/facebook-advertising-data-insecure-teens

96. https://www.facebook.com/business/success/conservative-party#u_0_2

97. https://www.facebook.com/business/success/snp

98. Interview with author.

99. Jose Antonio Vargas, 'The Face of Facebook', The New Yorker, 20 September 2010, https://www.newyorker.com/magazine/2010/09/20/the-face-of-facebook

100. Alex Hern, 'Why have we given up our privacy to Facebook and other sites so willingly?', The Guardian, 21 March 2018, https://www.theguardian.com/uk-news/2018/mar/21/
why-have-we-given-up-our-privacy-to-facebook-and-other-sites-so-willingly

101. Caitlin Dewey, '98 personal data points that Facebook uses to target ads to you', The Washington Post, 19 August 2016, https://www.washingtonpost.com/news/the-intersect/wp/2016/08/19/98-personal-data-points-that-facebook-uses-to-target-ads-to-you/?utm_term=.24a29f9f8e2b

102. Kashmir Hill, 'How Facebook Figures Out Everyone You've Ever Met', Gizmodo, 7 November 2017, https://gizmodo.com/how-facebook-figures-out-everyone-youve-ever-met-1819822691

103. Shoshana Zuboff, The Age of Surveillance Capitalism: The Fight for a Human Future at the New Frontier of Power, London: Hachette, 2015.

104. Ben Tarnoff, 'Silicon Valley siphons our data like oil. But the deepest drilling has just begun', The Guardian, 23 August 2017, https://www.theguardian.com/world/2017/aug/23/silicon-valley-big-data-extraction-amazon-whole-foods-facebook

105. Private information.

106. Michael Winnick, 'Putting a Finger on Our Phone Obsession', Dscout, 16 June 2016, https://blog.dscout.com/mobile-touches

107. Claire Cain Miller, 'Google Unveils Tool to Speed Up Searches', The New York Times, 8 September 2010, https://www.nytimes.com/2010/09/09/technology/tech-special/09google.html?dbk&_r=0

108. Nick Saint, 'Eric Schmidt: Google's Policy Is To "Get Right Up To The Creepy Line And Not Cross It"', Business Insider, 1 October 2010, http://www.businessinsider.com/eric-schmidt-googles-policy-is-to-get-right-up-to-the-creepy-line-and-not-cross-it-2010–10?IR=T

109. Interview with author.

110. Ibid.

111. Ibid.

112. Ibid.

113. *Cate Cadell and Pei Li*, 'Tea and Tiananmen: Inside China's new censorship machine', Reuters, 29 September 2017, https://www.reuters.com/article/china-congress-censorship/tea-and-tiananmen-inside-chinas-new-censorship-machine-idUSL4N1LW25C

115. *Financial Times*, 5 January 2018, https://www.ft.com/content/19d7ca34-f1fd-11e7-b220-857e26d1aca4

116. Frank Pasquale, 'From territorial to functional sovereignty: the case of Amazon', *Open Democracy*, 5 January 2018, https://www.opendemocracy.net/digitaliberties/frank-pasquale/from-territorial-to-functional-sovereignty-case-of-amazon; Lina M. Khan, 'Amazon's Antitrust Paradox', *Yale Law Journal*, January 2017, https://www.yalelaw-journal.org/note/amazons-antitrust-paradox

117. Richard Susskind and Daniel Susskind, *The Future of Professions: How Technology Will Transform the Work of Human Experts*, Oxford: Oxford University Press, 2015, pp. 66–70 and 47–55.

118. Farai Chideya, 'Nearly All Of Silicon Valley's Political Dollars Are Going To Hillary Clinton', FiveThirtyEight, 26 October 2016, https://fivethirtyeight.com/features/nearly-all-of-silicon-valleys-political-dollars-are-going-to-hillary-clinton/

119. See Eric Schmidt and Jared Cohen, *The New Digital Age: Reshaping the Future of People, Nations and Business*, New York: Knopf, 2013, p. 50.

120. Private information.

121. Interview with author.

122. Interview with author.

123. Jaqueline Lee, 'Palo Alto: Mark Zuckerberg "compound" raises red flags for city board', *Mercury News*, 15 September 2016, https://www.mercurynews.com/2016/09/15/palo-alto-mark-zuckerberg-compound-raises-red-flags-for-city-board/

124. Madeline Stone, *'Silicon Valley CEOs Just Want a Little Privacy. $100 million and 750 Acres of It'*, Slate, 18 May 2015, http://www.slate.com/blogs/business_insider/2015/05/18/tech_billionaires_and_privacy_why_facebook_s_mark_zuckerberg_is_spending.html

125. Gary Richards, 'Roadshow: My BART train resembles a homeless encampment', *Mercury News*, 14 June 2017, https://www.mercurynews.com/2017/06/14/roadshow-homeless-on-bart-draw-concern/

126. Steven Levy, 'One More Thing: Inside Apple's Insanely Great (or Just Insane) New Mothership', *Wired*, 16 May 2017, https://www.wired.com/2017/05/apple-park-new-silicon-valley-campus/

127. YouTube, 7 June 2011, https://www.youtube.com/watch?v=gtuz5OmOh_M

128. Open Democracy, 5 January 2018, https://www.opendemocracy.net/digitaliberties/frank-pasquale/from-territorial-to-functional-sovereignty-case-of-amazon

129. Adrian Weckler and Michael Cogley, '"No one did anything wrong here and Ireland is being picked on… It is total political crap"—Apple chief Tim Cook', *Irish Independent*, 1 September 2016, https://www.independent.ie/business/irish/no-one-

did-anything-wrong-here-and-ireland-is-being-picked-on-it-is-total-political-crap-apple-chief-tim-cook-35012145.html

130. Astra Taylor, *The People's Platform: Taking Back Power and Culture in the Digital Age*, London: Fourth Estate, 2014, pp. 11–39; also Nicholas Carr, 'Sharecropping the long tail', Rough Type Blog, 19 December 2006, http://www.roughtype.com/?p=634

131. List of countries by projected GDP 2018, Statistics Times, http://statisticstimes.com/economy/countries-by-projected-gdp.php

132. See, for instance, Devi Sridhar, 'Misfinancing Global Health: a case for transparency in disbursements and decision making', *The Lancet*, 2008; also, Jeremy Youde, 'The Rockefeller and Gates Foundations in Global Health Governance', *Global Society*, 26 February 2013, https://www.tandfonline.com/doi/abs/10.1080/13600826.2012.762341

133. Dan Alexander, 'Warren Buffett Toasts The World's Two Greatest Philanthropists, Bill And Melinda Gates', *Forbes*, 4 June 2015, https://www.forbes.com/sites/danalexander/2015/06/04/warren-buffett-toasts-the-worlds-two-greatest-philanthropists-bill-and-melinda-gates/#33455af84e01

134. Ross Douthat, 'Obama the Theologian', *The New York Times*, 7 February 2015, https://www.nytimes.com/2015/02/08/opinion/sunday/ross-douthat-obama-the-theologian.html

135. Reinhold Niebuhr, *Moral Man and Immoral Society*, New York: Continuum, 1932, pp. 5–6; see also Marc Stears, *Demanding Democracy: American Radicals in Search of a New Politics*, Princeton, NJ: Princeton University Press, 2010, pp. 71–75.

8. CAN DEMOCRACY BE REBOOTED?

1. Nellie Bowles, 'Silicon Valley Now Has Its Own Populist Pundit', *The New York Times*, 12 August 2017, https://www.nytimes.com/2017/08/12/style/steve-hilton-fox-news-silicon-valley-populist-pundit.html

2. Joe Garofoli, 'Could this San Francisco tech CEO's show pull Fox to the middle?', *San Francisco Chronicle*, 31 May 2017, https://www.sfchronicle.com/politics/article/Could-this-San-Francisco-tech-CEO-s-show-pull-11186597.php

3. Steve Hilton, 'Hey Gov. Jerry Brown, why won't you talk to me about illegal immigration?', Fox News Opinion, 10 March 2018, http://www.foxnews.com/opinion/2018/03/10/hey-gov-jerry-brown-why-won-t-talk-to-me-about-illegal-immigration.html

4. Interview with author.

5. Steve Hilton, with Scott Bade and Jason Bade, *More Human: Designing a World Where People Come First*, New York: Public Affairs, 2015.

6. Martin Gilens and Benjamin I. Page 'Testing Theories of American Politics: Elites, Interest Groups, and Average Citizens', *Perspectives on Politics*, 2014, https://scholar.princeton.edu/sites/default/files/mgilens/files/gilens_and_page_2014_-testing_theories_of_american_politics.doc.pdf

7. Dylan Matthews, 'Remember that study saying America is an oligarchy? 3 rebuttals say it's wrong', Vox, 9 May 2016, https://www.vox.com/2016/5/9/11502464/gilens-page-oligarchy-study

8. Steve Hilton, *More Human*.

9. *The Daily Show*, 30 April 2014, http://www.cc.com/video-clips/kj9zai/the-daily-show-with-jon-stewart-martin-gilens—benjamin-page

10. Stephen Pinker, *Enlightenment Now: The Case for Reason, Science, Humanism, and Progress*, London: Allen Lane, 2018.

11. Margaret Thatcher, Bruges speech, 20 September 1988, https://www.margaretthatcher.org/document/107332

12. Francis Fukuyama, 'The End of History?', *The National Interest*, 1989, https://www.worldcat.org/title/national-interest/oclc/805051249

13. Ishaan Tharoor, 'The man who declared the "end of history" fears for democracy's future', *The Washington Post*, 9 February 2017, https://www.washingtonpost.com/news/worldviews/wp/2017/02/09/the-man-who-declared-the-end-of-history-fears-for-democracys-future/?utm_term=.15ccb7bd8648

14. Steve Levitsky and Daniel Ziblatt, *How Democracies Die: What History Reveals About Our Future*, London: Viking, 2018.

15. David Nakamura, 'Trump again blames "both sides" in Charlottesville, says some counterprotesters were "very, very violent"', *The Washington Post*, 15 August 2017, https://www.washingtonpost.com/news/post-politics/wp/2017/08/15/trump-again-blames-both-sides-in-charlottesville-says-some-counterprotesters-were-very-very-violent/?utm_term=.0e9d3a02e299

16. Elisabeth O'Leary, 'Britons ever more deeply divided over Brexit, research finds', Reuters, 31 January 2018, https://uk.reuters.com/article/uk-britain-eu-attitudes/britons-ever-more-deeply-divided-over-brexit-research-finds-idUKKBN1FK02L

17. 'The Clenched Fist of Truth', https://www.youtube.com/watch?v=tOfLjGg5gP0

18. https://www.youtube.com/watch?v=43wKT9NzPdA

19. Interview with author.

20. Tom Miles, 'U.N. investigators cite Facebook role in Myanmar crisis', Reuters, 12 March 2018, https://uk.reuters.com/article/us-myanmar-rohingya-facebook/u-n-investigators-cite-facebook-role-in-myanmar-crisis-idUKKCN1GO2PN

21. Freedom in the World 2018, Democracy in Crisis, Freedom House, https://freedomhouse.org/report/freedom-world/freedom-world-2018

22. Tom Miles, 'U.N. investigators cite Facebook role in Myanmar crisis'.

23. Sean Williams, 'Rodrigo Duterte's Army of Online Trolls', *The New Republic*, 4 January 2017, https://newrepublic.com/article/138952/rodrigo-dutertes-army-online-trolls

24. Imran Awan, 'Cyber-Extremism: Isis and the Power of Social Media', *Society*, April 2017, Volume 54, Issue 2, pp. 138–149, https://link.springer.com/article/10.1007/s12115-017-0114-0

25. Channel 4 News FactCheck, 23 November 2017, https://www.channel4.com/news/factcheck/americas-long-history-of-meddling-in-other-countries-elections

26. 'Exposed: Russian Twitter bots tried to swing general election for Jeremy Corbyn', *The Sunday Times*, 29 April 2018, https://www.thetimes.co.uk/edition/news/exposed-russian-twitter-bots-tried-to-swing-general-election-for-jeremy-corbyn-zffv8652x

27. Yascha Mounk and Roberto Stefan Foa, 'Yes, people really are turning away from democracy', *The Washington Post*, 8 December 2016; see also Yascha Mounk, *The People*

vs Democracy: Why Our Freedom Is in Danger and How to Save It, Boston, MA: Harvard, 2018, p. 99–131.

28. 'The Rise of "Illiberal Democracy"', Freedom House, 2018, https://freedomhouse. org/report/modern-authoritarianism-illiberal-democracies; see also Jan-Werner Müller, 'Democracy Still Matters', *The New York Times*, 5 April 2018, https://www. nytimes.com/2018/04/05/opinion/hungary-viktor-orban-populism.html

29. Anne Applebaum, 'Illiberal democracy comes to Poland', *The Washington Post*, 22 December 2016, https://www.washingtonpost.com/news/global-opinions/wp/2016/12/22/illiberal-democracy-comes-to-poland/?utm_term=.193a761a5d21

30. James Slack, 'Enemies of the people: Fury over "out of touch" judges who have "declared war on democracy" by defying 17.4m Brexit voters and who could trigger constitutional crisis', *Daily Mail*, 3 November 2016, http://www.dailymail.co.uk/news/article-3903436/Enemies-people-Fury-touch-judges-defied-17–4m-Brexit-voters-trigger-constitutional-crisis.html

31. Peter Walker, 'Anna Soubry receives messages calling for her to be hanged as a traitor', *The Guardian*, 15 December 2017, https://www.theguardian.com/politics/2017/dec/15/anna-soubry-receives-messages-calling-for-her-to-be-hanged-as-a-traitor-brexit

32. Richard Wike, Katie Simmons, Bruce Stokes and Janell Fetterolf, 'Globally, Broad Support for Representative and Direct Democracy', Pew Research Centre, October 2017, http://www.pewglobal.org/2017/10/16/globally-broad-support-for-representative-and-direct-democracy/; see also Janan Ganesh, *Financial Times*, 30 October 2017, https://www.ft.com/content/73349dae-bd5b-11e7-9836-b25f8adaa111

33. Interview with author.

34. Interview with author. The figures he referred are from an Ipsos MORI survey showing the UK is more tolerant than eight other EU countries although the other nineteen are not included, https://www.ipsos.com/sites/default/files/ct/news/documents/2017–09/ipsos-global-advisor-immigration-refugee-crisis-slides_0.pdf; Europe's own polling suggest Britain still lags behind some EU countries, https://ec.europa.eu/home-affairs/news/results-special-eurobarometer-integration-immigrants-european-union_en

35. Amelia Gentleman exposed this story with a series of articles for *The Guardian* in 2018, 'Amelia Gentleman on Windrush: "I've felt like an immigration case worker"', https://www.theguardian.com/membership/2018/apr/20/amelia-gentleman-windrush-immigration

36. Interview with author.

37. Andrew Sullivan, Democracies end when they are too democratic', *New York Magazine*, 1 May 2016, http://nymag.com/daily/intelligencer/2016/04/america-tyranny-donald-trump.html

38. Richard Dawkins, 'Ignoramuses should have no say on our EU membership—and that includes me', *Prospect*, 9 June 2016, https://www.prospectmagazine.co.uk/magazine/eu-referendum-richard-dawkins-brexit-23rd-june-ignoramuses

39. Adele Hampton, 'Professor A C Grayling's letter to all 650 MPs urging Parliament not to support a motion to trigger Article 50 of the Lisbon Treaty', New College of

the Humanities, 1 July 2016, https://www.nchlondon.ac.uk/2016/07/01/professor-c-graylings-letter-650-mps-urging-parliament-not-support-motion-trigger-article-50-lisbon-treaty-1-july-2016/

40. Matthew Parris, 'After Trump, I'm losing faith in democracy', *The Spectator*, 12 November 2016, https://www.spectator.co.uk/2016/11/after-trump-im-losing-faith-in-democracy/

41. Robert Zaretsky, 'Donald Trump and the Myth of Mobocracy', *The Atlantic*, 26 July 2016, https://www.theatlantic.com/international/archive/2016/07/trump-le-bon-mob/493118/

42. Jason Brennan, *Against Democracy*, Princeton, NJ: Princeton University Press, 2016, pp. 130–131.

43. Ibid., preface to 2017 edition.

44. Interview with author.

45. Inevitably, I am not doing full justice to the many twists and turns this debate took. If you want to read a proper account of this debate, see Marc Stears, *Demanding Democracy: American Radicals in Search of a New Politics*, Princeton, NJ: Princeton University Press, 2010, pp. 85–104.

46. 'Be happy for coal miners losing their health insurance. They're getting exactly what they voted for', Daily Kos, 12 December 2016, https://www.dailykos.com/stories/2016/12/12/1610198/-Be-happy-for-coal-miners-losing-their-health-insurance-They-re-getting-exactly-what-they-voted-for

47. For a good account of this, see Yuval Noah Harari, *Homo Deus: A Brief History of Tomorrow*, New York: Harvill Secker, 2016, pp. 307–350.

48. Winston Churchill, House of Commons, 11 November 1947.

49. Katharine Viner, 'How technology disrupted the truth', *The Guardian*, 12 July 2016, https://www.theguardian.com/media/2016/jul/12/how-technology-disrupted-the-truth

50. https://www.bellingcat.com/

51. Ian Burrell, 'With Isis, Assad and Putin exposed, who's next on citizen journalist Eliot Higgins' list?', *The Independent*, 15 January 2015, https://www.independent.co.uk/news/people/profiles/with-isis-assad-and-putin-exposed-whos-next-on-citizen-journalist-eliot-higgins-list-9983831.html

52. Jonathan Mahler, 'CNN Had a Problem. Donald Trump Solved It', *The New York Times*, 4 April 2017, https://www.nytimes.com/2017/04/04/magazine/cnn-had-a-problem-donald-trump-solved-it.html

53. Luisa Kroll and Kerry Dolan, 'Meet The Members Of The Three-Comma Club', *Forbes*, 6 March 2018, https://www.forbes.com/billionaires/#1a786658251c

54. https://twitter.com/realDonaldTrump/status/897763049226084352

55. Sydney Ember, 'To Trump, It's the "Amazon Washington Post." To Its Editor, That's Baloney', *The New York Times*, 2 April 2018, https://www.nytimes.com/2018/04/02/business/media/to-trump-its-the-amazon-washington-post-to-its-editor-thats-baloney.html

56. Alice Ross and Julia Carrie Wong, 'Facebook deletes Norwegian PM's post as "napalm girl" row escalates', *The Guardian*, 9 September 2016, https://www.theguardian.com/technology/2016/sep/09/facebook-deletes-norway-pms-post-napalm-girl-post-row

57. Kurt Wagner, 'Mark Zuckerberg says he's "fundamentally uncomfortable" making content decisions for Facebook', Recode, 22 March 2018, https://www.recode.net/2018/3/22/17150772/mark-zuckerberg-facebook-content-policy-guidelines-hate-free-speech

58. Jeremy Kahn, 'Tech Companies Identify, Remove 40,000 Terrorist Videos, Images', Bloomberg, 4 December 2017, https://www.bloomberg.com/news/articles/2017-12-04/tech-companies-identify-remove-40-000-terrorist-videos-images

59. Craig Silverman, Jane Lytvynenko and Scott Pham, 'These Are 50 Of The Biggest Fake News Hits On Facebook In 2017', BuzzFeed, 28 December 2017, https://www.buzzfeed.com/craigsilverman/these-are-50-of-the-biggest-fake-news-hits-on-face-book-in?utm_term=.eiRqvNDjK#.gpJ5WanV7; see also Chris J. Vargo, Lei Guo, Michelle A. Amazeen, 'The agenda-setting power of fake news: A big data analysis of the online media landscape from 2014 to 2016', *New Media and Society*, Volume 20, Issue 5, pp. 2028–2049, 15 June 2017, http://journals.sagepub.com/doi/10.1177/1461444817712086

60. 'Euro-myths blog', European Commission, https://blogs.ec.europa.eu/ECintheUK/euromyths-a-z-index/

61. Brendan Nyhan and Jason Reifler, 'When Corrections Fail: The persistence of political misperceptions', *Political Behaviour*, 2010, https://www.dartmouth.edu/~nyhan/nyhan-reifler.pdf

62. Alex Heath, 'Facebook quietly updated two key numbers about its user base', Business Insider, 1 November 2017, http://uk.businessinsider.com/facebook-raises-duplicate-fake-account-estimates-q3-earnings-2017-11?r=US&IR=T

63. Interview with author.

64. https://newsroom.fb.com/news/2018/01/news-feed-fyi-local-news/

65. https://posts.google.com/bulletin/share

66. Laura Hazard Owen, 'Facebook's News Feed changes appear to be hurting—not helping—local news', Nieman Lab, 19 April 2018, http://www.niemanlab.org/2018/04/facebooks-news-feed-changes-appear-to-be-hurting-not-helping-local-news/

67. Among those who have backed this idea are John Whittingdale, the former Culture Secretary, who raised it at a meeting of the Society of Editors in January 2018, https://www.telegraph.co.uk/news/2018/01/18/google-facebook-should-help-fund-local-journalism-former-culture/

68. Laura Wamsley, 'Billionaire Owner Shuts Down DNAinfo, Gothamist Sites A Week After Workers Unionize', NPR, 3 November 2017, https://www.npr.org/sections/thetwo-way/2017/11/03/561830256/billionaire-owner-shuts-down-dnainfo-gothamist-sites-a-week-after-workers-unioni

69. Gabriel Sherman, *The Loudest Voice in the Room: How the Brilliant, Bombastic Roger Ailes Built Fox News—and Divided a Country*, New York: Random House, 2014, pp. 345–395.

70. Ibid.

71. Jacob Weisberg, 'Networker', *The New York Times*, 12 January 2014, https://www.nytimes.com/2014/01/19/books/review/gabriel-shermans-loudest-voice-in-the-room.html

72. Interview with author.

73. Interview with author.

74. The ban was originally implemented as part of the general ban on the BBC carrying any advertising. The Television Act 1954, extended the ban to the newly created independent television in the 1950s. Party Political Broadcasts began on radio in 1924 and were formalised in 1947 when a Committee on Political Broadcasting was set up between the BBC and the political parties. http://www.bbc.co.uk/historyofthebbc/elections/ppb

75. David Butler and Denis Kavanagh, *The British General Election of 1997*, London: Palgrave MacMillan, 1997, p. 116.

76. David Beetham and Stuart Weir, *Political Power and Democratic Control in Britain*, Abingdon: Routledge, 1999, p. 85.

77. Electoral Commission, Expenditure in 2017 General Election, http://search.electoralcommission.org.uk/Search/Spending?currentPage=1&rows=20&sort=TotalExpenditure&order=desc&tab=1&et=pp&includeOutsideSection75=true&evt=ukparliament&ev=3568&optCols=ExpenseCategoryName&optCols=AmountInEngland&optCols=AmountInScotland&optCols=AmountInWales&optCols=AmountInNorthernIreland&optCols=DatePaid

78. Joey D'Urso, 'Who spent what on Facebook during 2017 election campaign?', BBC News, 31 March 2018, http://www.bbc.co.uk/news/uk-politics-43487301

79. Patrick Kulp, 'Record amount spent on political ads despite Donald Trump', Mashable, 4 January 2017, https://mashable.com/2017/01/03/record-high-spent-on-political-ads-despite-donald-trump/#FZneJRFb9qqV

80. Mark Zuckerberg, Facebook, 6 April 2018, https://www.facebook.com/zuck/posts/10104784125525891; see also Ali Breland, 'Zuckerberg announces support for regulating political ads on social media', The Hill, 6 April 2018, http://thehill.com/policy/technology/381990-zuckerberg-announces-support-for-regulating-political-ads-on-social-media

81. Elizabeth Denham, Information Commission blog, May 2017, https://iconewsblog.org.uk/2017/05/17/information-commissioner-elizabeth-denham-opens-a-formal-investigation-into-the-use-of-data-analytics-for-political-purposes; see also 'Political finance regulation at the June 2017 UK general election', Electoral Commission, November 2017, https://www.electoralcommission.org.uk/__data/assets/pdf_file/0004/237550/Political-finance-regulation-at-the-June-2017-UK-general-election-PDF.pdf

82. Interview with author.

83. Fifth Report of Committee on Standards in Public Life, October 1998, p. 176, https://assets.publishing.service.gov.uk/government/uploads/system/uploads/attachment_data/file/336870/5thInquiry_FullReport.pdf

84. 'Electoral Commission report on political advertising', June 2004, https://www.electoralcommission.org.uk/__data/assets/pdf_file/0007/213784/Political-Advertising-report-and-recommendations-June-2004.pdf

85. The UK government said in 2017 that Britain will remain a signatory to the European Declaration on Human rights for at least the lifetime of the next parliament.

86. European Court of Human Rights, ADI v United Kingdom, (Application no. 48876/08), Strasbourg, 22 April 2013, https://hudoc.echr.coe.int/eng#{"itemid":["001-119244"]}

87. Interview with author.

88. Jim Waterson, 'These Are The Anti-Corbyn Adverts The Tories Are Paying To Promote On Facebook', BuzzFeed, 1 June 2017, https://www.buzzfeed.com/jim-waterson/conservative-election-adverts?utm_term=.lbP7AzdOJ#.ufKxgNrDK

89. See, for instance, Citizens United v. Federal Election Commission, US Supreme Court, 21 January 2010, http://www.scotusblog.com/case-files/cases/citizens-united-v-federal-election-commission/

90. Sarah Jeong, 'Zuckerberg says Facebook will extend European data protections worldwide—kind of', The Verge, 11 April 2018, https://www.theverge.com/2018/4/11/17224492/zuckerberg-facebook-congress-gdpr-data-protection See also, 'Facebook to exclude billions from European privacy laws', BBC News, 19 April 2018, http://www.bbc.co.uk/news/technology-43822184

91. https://action.labour.org.uk/page/content/nhs-birthday/

92. Interview with author.

93. Matthew McGregor, 'The Sophisticated Use Of Our Data Has Gone In A Dark Direction—So What Now?', The Huffington Post, 23 March 2018, https://www.huffingtonpost.co.uk/entry/cambridge-analytica_uk_5ab4af16e4b008c9e5f5ff82

94. 'Brexit changed everything—Corbyn's opponents are relying on an outdated plan, writes Ed M's former media chief', Labourlist, 5 July 2016, https://labourlist.org/2016/07/brexit-changed-everything-corbyns-opponents-are-relying-on-an-outdated-plan-writes-ed-ms-former-media-chief/

95. Emily Schultheis, 'Can a French Political Upstart Ride Obama's Strategy to Victory', The Atlantic, 21 April 2017, https://www.theatlantic.com/international/archive/2017/04/france-election-macron-obama/523872/

96. Marie-Pierre Haddad, 'Présidentielle 2017: pourquoi Macron court-circuite l'agenda de Hollande', RTL, 14 October 2016, http://www.rtl.fr/actu/politique/presidentielle-2017-macron-decidera-d-une-candidature-probablement-en-decembre-7785284071

97. https://www.facebook.com/EmmanuelMacron/videos/1954327514799825/

98. Adam Nossiter, David E. Sanger and Nicole Perlroth, 'Hackers Came, but the French Were Prepared', The New York Times, 9 May 2017, https://www.nytimes.com/2017/05/09/world/europe/hackers-came-but-the-french-were-prepared.html

99. https://twitter.com/emmanuelmacron/status/855033309495046144?lang=en

100. 'Emmanuel Macron: French president announces "fake news" law', BBC News, 3 January 2018, http://www.bbc.co.uk/news/world-europe-42560688

101. Financial Times, 16 February 2015.

102. Greg Ip, 'The Antitrust Case Against Facebook, Google and Amazon', The Wall Street Journal, 30 April 2018, https://www.wsj.com/articles/the-antitrust-case-against-facebook-google-amazon-and-apple-1516121561

103. See, for instance, Jonathan Taplin, 'Is It Time to Break Up Google?', The New York Times, 22 April 2017, https://www.nytimes.com/2017/04/22/opinion/sunday/is-it-time-to-break-up-google.html

104. Paul Mason, 'Choice: Break up Facebook—or Take It Into Public Ownership? I Am

Not Kidding', Novara Media, 19 March 2018, http://novaramedia.com/2018/03/19/choice-break-up-facebook-or-take-it-into-public-ownership-i-am-not-kidding/

105. *Financial Times*, 19 February 2017, https://www.ft.com/content/d04a89c2-f6c8-11e6-9516-2d969e0d3b65

106. Mark Zuckerberg, Commencement Speech at Harvard, 23 May 2017, https://news.harvard.edu/gazette/story/2017/05/mark-zuckerbergs-speech-as-written-for-harvards-class-of-2017/

107. See, for instance, Max Ehrenfreund, 'How Microsoft avoided billions in taxes, and what the GOP says it will do about it', *The Washington Post*, 2 February 2017, https://www.washingtonpost.com/news/wonk/wp/2017/02/10/how-microsoft-avoided-billions-in-taxes-and-what-the-gop-says-theyll-do-about-it/?utm_term=.8693b47f6a9a; also 'Facebook UK pays just £5.1m in corporation tax despite jump in profit', *The Guardian*, 4 October 2017, https://www.theguardian.com/technology/2017/oct/04/facebook-uk-corporation-tax-profit

108. https://en.wikipedia.org/wiki/List_of_cognitive_biases

109. For instance, see Geoffrey A. Fowler, 'What if we paid for Facebook—instead of letting it spy on us for free?', *The Washington Post*, 5 April 2018, https://www.washingtonpost.com/news/the-switch/wp/2018/04/05/what-if-we-paid-for-facebook-instead-of-letting-it-spy-on-us-for-free/?utm_term=.550f6c1bf173

110. Anna Mitchell and Larry Diamond, 'China's Surveillance State Should Scare Everyone', *The Atlantic*, 2 February 2018, https://www.theatlantic.com/international/archive/2018/02/china-surveillance/552203/

111. 2018 Edelman Trust Barometer, https://www.edelman.com/trust-barometer

112. Schumpeter, 'Silicon Valley may not hold onto its global superiority for much longer', *The Economist*, 15 February 2018, https://www.economist.com/news/business/21737075-silicon-valley-may-not-hold-its-global-superiority-much-longer-how-does-chinese-tech

113. Open letter, World Wide Web Foundation, 12 March 2018, https://webfoundation.org/2018/03/web-birthday-29/

114. Mustafa Suleyman, 'RSA President's Lecture: The Techologist's Dilemma', 14 November 2017, https://www.thersa.org/events/2017/11/rsa-presidents-lecture-the-technologists-dilemma

115. Julia Apostle, *Financial Times*, 21 March 2018, https://www.ft.com/content/43bc6d18-2b6f-11e8-97ec-4bd3494d5f14 See also Nathaniel Popper, 'Tech Thinks It Has a Fix for the Problems It Created: Blockchain', *The New York Times*, 1 April 2018, https://www.nytimes.com/2018/04/01/technology/blockchain-uses.html

Index

INDEX

INDEX

and comments sections, 98
and Corbyn, 204
Cox murder, 264
and data, 177–8, 179, 180–82, 185–8
divisiveness, 265
and echo chambers, 195–7
and economic opportunity, 196, 235
and experts, 209
and Facebook, 187, 188, 210, 246
and fake news, 214, 274
and false balance, 38
and freedom of movement, 235–6
and illiberal democracy, 267
and immigration, 177, 210, 211, 236–7, 268
and Johnson, 13, 181, 210, 217
Leave.EU, 187–8, 213
and mobility, 196
and NHS, 210, 214
and Port Talbot, 125–6
'Project Fear', 211
Remain campaign, 177, 180–82, 211, 236, 270
and social class, 196
'Take Back Control', 218, 235
Vote Leave, 185–7, 210, 285
Brighton, East Sussex, 171
Brin, Sergey, 110, 250, 288
Britain First, 204, 264
Britain Stronger in Europe, 180–81
British Broadcasting Corporation (BBC), 13, 25, 47
and Alt-Left, 205–6
Asian tsunami (2004), 91
and Blagrove, 222
5 Live, 36
Harding, 229
Have Your Say, 94–5
and Internet Research Centre, 157

Iraq dossier story (2003), 72, 73, 77
Kuenssberg–Labour relations, 3, 206–7
Major 'bastards' scandal (1993), 21–2
mission, 276–7
and MMR scare (2002), 71
News from Number 10 (2000), 68
News, 36, 114
Newsnight, 27
and Sky News, 36
Today, 27, 67–8, 71, 72
trust in, 225
User Generated Content, 91, 273
World Service, 32
Brokaw, Thomas, 19
Brookes, Peter, 169
Brooks, Rebekah, 119
Brown, Gordon, 107, 117, 139–41, 145–6, 170, 261
and authenticity, 141, 225
Duffy affair (2010), 145, 172
G20 summit (2009), 140
general election (2010), 145
and Guido Fawkes, 93
and Internet, 140–41
and Mumsnet, 145
Prime Minister, succession as (2007), 107, 139
and *Sun*, 117
and Tote privatisation, 24
Brunson, Michael, 21, 22
BSkyB, 119
Buffett, Warren, 185, 258
Bulletin, 277
Bullingdon Club, 217
Burkhard, Marat, 157
Burma Road, 22
Bush, George Herbert Walker, 54
Bush, George Walker, 60–66, 74, 78, 83, 85–9, 280

INDEX

INDEX

Dark Ages, 29
dark posts, 191
Davidsen, Carol, 161
Davies, Gareth, 121
Davis, Nick, 116
Dawkins, Richard, 87, 269
'dead tree' press, 35
Dean, Howard, 85–6, 90, 146, 147, 149
Dearborn, Michigan, 229
'death panels', 118, 151
'Declaration of the Independence of Cyberspace' (Barlow), 44
Deep State, 263
DeepMind, 293
Delors, Jacques, 11
'Democracies End When They Are Too Democratic' (Sullivan), 268
Democratic Party
  Carter administration (1977–81), 75, 279
  Clinton administration (1993–2001), see under Clinton, William
  House of Representatives election (1994), 14, 15
  midterm elections (2010), 118, 149
  Obama administration (2009–17), see under Obama, Barack
  presidential election (1992), 14, 160, 170
  presidential election (1996), 45, 47, 86, 160
  presidential election (2000), 60, 86, 87, 90
  presidential election (2004), 85–9, 146, 147, 149
  presidential election (2008), 107, 127, 145, 146–8, 159, 170, 198, 286
  presidential election (2012), 159–63, 170, 180, 182, 190

  presidential election (2016), see under presidential election, US
  and protectionism, 236
  and trust in media, 229
  TV attack adverts, 280
Deng Xiaoping, 55
Denmark, 11, 290
Denton, Nicholas, 129
deregulation, 40, 41
Derrida, Jacques, 75
design-thinking workshops, 143
Desmond, Richard, 69
Desperate Housewives, 188
Dewey, John, 270
Diana, Princess of Wales, 128
Diller, Barry, 129
Dirksen Senate Office Building, Washington, 80
disinhibition effect, 99
Disney, 40
Distributed Denial of Service (DDoS), 156
Dittoheads, 17
DMGT, 120, 121
Doctrine of Information Security, 58
Dodd, Christopher, 114
Dogs in the News (Lewis), 27
Dole, Robert 'Bob', 45, 80
Don't Trust the B—in Apt. 23, 161
Doncaster, South Yorkshire, 167, 171–2
Dorenko, Sergei, 58
Dowler, Milly, 116
doxxing, 101
Draper, Derek, 52, 66, 140–41, 261–3, 282
Driscoll, Matthew, 116
driverless vehicles, 233
drones, 272
Drudge Report, The, 34, 91
Drummond, Stuart, 79

349

INDEX

INDEX

INDEX

INDEX

Sullivan, Andrew, 81, 268
Sulzberger, Arthur Ochs, 109
Summers, Larry, 239
Sun, The, 29, 30–32, 34, 35, 41, 49–50, 252
   and Alt-Left, 206
   Blair, support for, 49–50
   and Brexit, 125–6, 225
   Brooks resignation (2011), 119
   Brown, criticism of, 117
   and Corbyn, 225
   Euroscepticism, 12, 50
   general election (1992), 31–2, 49
   general election (2017), 218
   and Harty, 31
   Hillsborough disaster (1989), 8, 30–31, 273
   and immigration, 120
   Kavanagh, power of, 25
   Major 'bastards' scandal (1993), 21
   St George's Day story (1997), 50
   Thatcher, support for, 29
   and Zephaniah, 31
Sun on Sunday, The, 120
Sunday Express, 69, 214
Sunday Telegraph, 1, 23–7, 72
Sunday Times, 29, 208
Sunderland, Tyne & Wear, 271
Sunstein, Cass, 135–6
Super Girl, 102–3
Surkov, Vladislav, 59, 156
surveillance capitalism, 249
Swansea, Wales, 122
swatting, 101
Sweden, 54, 266
Swift Boat Veterans, 86
Sykes, Charlie, 18
Sylvester, Rachel, 224
Syria, 64, 151, 152, 273
Syriza, 178

Take Back Control, 218, 235
Talk Radio, 15, 18, 118
Talking Points Memo, 81
TaskRabbit, 234
tax avoidance, 235, 238, 257, 289, 291
Taylor, Matthew, 282
Tea Party, 118, 148, 151
Teachout, Zephyr, 149
Technorati, 90
Telecommunications Act (1996), 39, 43–4, 252, 275
Tencent, 152, 292
terrorism, 55, 87, 90, 210, 229, 235, 266, 275
   beheading videos, 101, 102
   Charlottesville attack (2017), 264, 265
   Cox murder (2016), 264
   ISIS, 101, 229, 266
   September 11 attacks (2001), 7, 54, 61, 62, 63, 65, 208
   and social media, 235, 266, 275
Tesich, Stojan Steve, 20–21
Tetlock, Philip, 185–6
Thailand, 91, 153
Thalidomide, 29
Thank You for Being Late (Friedman), 108
Thatcher, Margaret, 8, 9, 29, 31, 49, 264
TheyWorkForYou, 196
Thiel, Peter, 253
'Things Everyone Does but Doesn't Talk About', 169
38 Degrees, 206
Thornberry, Emily, 168
Thurmond, Strom, 80–81
Tiananmen Square massacre (1989), 8–9, 55
Tibet, 32

INDEX